THE EASTERN CHURCH

LECTURES

ON THE HISTORY

OF

THE EASTERN CHURCH

WITH AN INTRODUCTION
ON THE STUDY OF ECCLESIASTICAL HISTORY

BY ARTHUR PENRHYN STANLEY, D. D.

REGIUS PROFESSOR OF ECCLESIASTICAL HISTORY IN THE UNIVERSITY OF
OXFORD, AND CANON OF CHRIST CHURCH

FROM THE SECOND LONDON EDITION, REVISED

NEW YORK
CHARLES SCRIBNER, 124 GRAND STREET
1862

[*Published by arrangement with the Author*]

177269

RIVERSIDE, CAMBRIDGE
STEREOTYPED AND PRINTED BY H. O. HOUGHTON

PREFACE

TO

THE AMERICAN EDITION.

IT is with pleasure that I commend this work, Christendom of the East, to the furthermost outposts of Christendom in the West. In so doing, I am but repaying a debt which on this very subject I owe to our brethren of the United States. For it was through the intelligent kindness of the good Americans at Athens so well known to every English traveller in Greece, that my attention was first awakened to the interest of the Greek Church. May Dr. Hill and his excellent wife accept this token of gratitude for an acquaintance formed in the winter of 1840, and resumed with undiminished pleasure in the autumn of 1861.

ARTHUR P. STANLEY.

Feb. 10, 1862.

PREFACE

TO

THE SECOND EDITION.

___

THE present edition has been carefully revised; and a few corrections or confirmations have been supplied by a visit to Constantinople and Mount Athos, in the summer of the past year.

Christ Church, Oxford:
January 29, 1862.

PREFACE

TO

THE FIRST EDITION.

THE Introduction to this volume consists of three
Lectures delivered in the spring of 1857, when I
entered upon my duties as Professor of Ecclesiastical
History. They are reprinted, partly for the sake of
presenting them in a more correct form than that
in which they first appeared, partly for the sake of
exhibiting the general plan under which will be
comprised any special Lectures like those which form
the bulk of the present volume.

It is my hope, if I may look so far forward into
the future, to fill up two of the departments indicated in the sketch of the first Introductory Lecture. I have already devoted a large share of each
Academical year to Lectures on the History of the
Jewish Church, which I trust at no very distant
period to publish; and it is my intention to appropriate at least a portion of my remaining time to
the History of the Church of England.

Meanwhile, it seemed to me that a course of instruction in the History of the Eastern Church would

not be unfitting. The general reasons for this selection are given in the Lectures themselves. The subject is one in which I had long felt an interest, and which may, perhaps, gain from being approached through a point of view more general than that usually taken in the learned works that have been devoted to its consideration.

In the choice and the treatment of the epochs of Eastern History which appear in the following pages, I have been guided by the necessities of the case, as well as by the wish to exemplify some of the principles laid down in my Introductory Lectures. The form of Lectures[1] lent itself to this mode of handling the subject; and, if the result should bear the appearance of a didactic rather than of a historical work, I have endeavored to rectify this defect by the references to authorities which begin, and by the chronological tables which end, the volume.

It so happens that one of these epochs (the Council of Nicæa), though receiving much attention from French and German writers, has never been thoroughly described by any English historian. In this instance, therefore, I have gone into every detail. I take this opportunity of mentioning some of the subordinate topics to which allusions have been made throughout the Lectures, and which might well

---

[1] Most of the Lectures are printed (with necessary corrections and abbreviations) as they were delivered. The First and Eighth are condensed from two courses of Lectures.

be followed up, in a supplemental volume on the Church of Constantinople and Greece, properly so called. The Councils of Ephesus and Chalcedon have never, as far as I know, been described with all the details which could be given. The life of Chrysostom has never been fully told. The Iconoclastic controversy is full of interest for the history both of art and religion. A full account has yet to be given of the rupture between the Greek and Latin Churches, and of the attempted reconciliation in the Council of Florence. The rise of the monastic community of Athos, and of the dispute on the Light of Tabor, forms a separate episode. The revival of the national Church of Greece contains many germs of hope for the future. A continuous history of Greek theology, from its peculiarities in the Eastern Fathers of the third and fourth centuries, through the schools of Constantinople, down to its last great effort in the revival of letters in the West, and its influence on the Cambridge Platonic divines, of the Church of England, and, through them, on John Wesley, in the eighteenth century, is still, I believe, a desideratum.

In regard to the relation of Christianity to the other religions of the East, which must be considered as one of the most important branches of the subject in connection with the fortunes of Eastern Christendom, I have been restrained, by my personal ignorance of the languages and customs of most of those countries, from offering more than a few general remarks on the one most directly connected with

2

the Christian Church and the Eastern branch of it, namely, Mahometanism. But, if I may be permitted to refer to the labors of the eminent scholar who has already done so much for elucidating in this country the nature of Oriental religions, it is to be hoped that Professor Max Müller may be induced to give us the benefit of his genius and learning in drawing forth the mutual relations of the religions of Asia and the Christian faith to each other, in their past history and in their future prospects.

The Lectures on the Russian Church are intended as an introduction to a sphere of history which probably will, in each succeeding generation, grow in importance. If this volume should fall into the hands of any of those Russians whose hospitality I enjoyed during my stay at Moscow in 1857, I trust that they will pardon, not only the inaccuracies in detail which a stranger can hardly escape, but the divergence of the general point of view from which a Western European must regard the Church and State of Russia. There is an expressive proverb written over the house of Archbishop Plato in the forests of the Troitzda Convent, " Let not him who " comes in here carry out the dirt that he finds " within." If this precept is not altogether practicable for an impartial traveller, I can yet truly say that my chief impressions are those of gratitude for the intelligence and courtesy with which I was received, both among laymen and ecclesiastics. It is a pleasure to me to hope that those kind friends at Moscow, to whom I would especially commend this part of my volume, may receive it as a token of sincere hope and good-will for their country in this great crisis of its social existence, and in its entrance on the thousandth anniversary of the foundation of their Empire.

Christ Church, Oxford:
March 6, 1861.

TABLE OF CONTENTS.

INTRODUCTION.

I.

THE PROVINCE OF ECCLESIASTICAL HISTORY.

II.

THE STUDY OF ECCLESIASTICAL HISTORY.

III.

THE ADVANTAGES OF ECCLESIASTICAL HISTORY.

LECTURE I.

THE EASTERN CHURCH.

LECTURE II.

THE COUNCIL OF NICÆA, A. D. 325.

LECTURE III.

THE MEETING OF THE COUNCIL.

3

LECTURE IV.

THE OPENING OF THE COUNCIL.

LECTURE V.

THE CONCLUSION OF THE COUNCIL.

LECTURE VI.

THE EMPEROR CONSTANTINE. A. D. 312–338.

LECTURE VII.

ATHANASIUS, A. D. 312–372.

LECTURE VIII.

MAHOMETANISM IN ITS RELATIONS TO THE EASTERN CHURCH.

LECTURE IX.

THE RUSSIAN CHURCH.

LECTURE X.

THE RUSSIAN CHURCH IN THE MIDDLE AGES.

LECTURE XI.

THE PATRIARCH NICON.

LECTURE XII.

PETER THE GREAT AND THE MODERN CHURCH OF RUSSIA.

AT END OF VOLUME.

Plan of the Patriarchal Cathedral of Moscow.
Map of the Eastern Churches.

INTRODUCTION

TO THE

STUDY OF ECCLESIASTICAL HISTORY.

IN THREE INAUGURAL LECTURES

DELIVERED IN THE LENT TERM OF 1857.

4

INTRODUCTION.

I.

THE PROVINCE OF ECCLESIASTICAL HISTORY.

WHEN Christian the Pilgrim, in his progress towards the Celestial City, halted by the highway-side at the Palace of which the name was Beautiful, he was told, that " he should " not depart till they had shown him the rarities of that place. " And first they had him into the study, where they showed " him records of the greatest antiquity : " in which was " the " pedigree of the Lord of the hill, the Son of the Ancient of " Days. . . . Here also were more fully recorded the acts that " he had done, and the names of many hundreds that he had " taken into his service ; and how he had placed them in such " habitations, that could neither by length of days nor decays of " nature be dissolved. Then they read to him some of the wor- " thy acts that some of his servants had done ; as how they had " subdued kingdoms, wrought righteousness, obtained promises, " stopped the mouths of lions, quenched the violence of fire, " escaped the edge of the sword, out of weakness were made " strong, waxed valiant in fight, and turned to flight the armies " of the aliens. Then they read again in another part of the " records of the house, how willing their Lord was to receive in " his favor any, even any, though they in time past had offered " great affronts to his person and proceedings. Here also were " several other histories of other famous things, of all which " Christian had a view ; as of things both ancient and modern, " together with prophecies and predictions of things that have " their certain accomplishment, both to the dread and amazement " of enemies, and the comfort and solace of pilgrims."

These simple sentences from the familiar story of our childhood contain a true description of the subjects, method, and advantages of the study of Ecclesiastical History, which I now propose to unfold in preparation for the duties which I have been called to discharge. And with this object, it will be my endeavor in this opening Lecture to reduce to order the treasures which were shown to solace and cheer the Pilgrim on his way, by defining the limits of the province on which we are about to enter.

I. First, then, where does Ecclesiastical History commence? Beginning of Ecclesiastical History. Shall we begin with the Reformation — with the framework of religion with which we ourselves are specially concerned? Or with the new birth of Christendom, properly so called, in the foundation of modern Europe? Or with the close of the first century — with the age of those to whom we accord the name of our "Fathers" in the Christian faith? In a certain sense, each of these periods may be taken, and by different classes of men always will be taken, respectively, as the boundaries of the history of the Church. But, if we are fixing, not merely the accidental limits of convenience, but the true limits involved in the nature of the subject; if Ecclesiastical History means the History of the Church of God; if that history is one united whole; if it cannot be understood without embracing within its range the history of the events, of the persons, of the ideas which have had the most lasting, the most powerful effect on every stage of its course; we must ascend far higher in the stream of time than the sixteenth, or the fifth, or the second century, — beyond the Reformers, beyond the Popes, beyond the Fathers.

. . . . Far in the dim distance of primeval ages, is discerned Call of Abraham. the first figure in the long succession which has never since been broken, — in Ur of the Chaldees, the Patriarchal chief, followed by his train of slaves and retainers, surrounded by his herds of camels and asses, moving westward and southward he knew not whither, — the first Father of the universal Church, — Abraham, the Founder of the Chosen People, the Father of the faithful, whose seed was to be as the sand upon the sea-shore, as the stars for multitude.

Earlier manifestations doubtless there had been of faith and hope ; in other countries also than Mesopotamia or Palestine there were yearnings after a higher world. But the call of Abraham is the first beginning of a continuous growth ; in his character, in his migration, in his faith was bound up, as the Christian Apostle well describes, all that has since formed the substance and fibre of the history of the Church.

From this point, then, we start, and from this shall be prepared to enter on the history of the people of Israel, as the true beginning and prototype of the Christian Church. So in old times it was ever held ; to the Apostolic age it could not be otherwise ; even Eusebius, writing for a special purpose, is constrained to commence his work by going back (almost in the words with which I opened this Lecture) to " records of the greatest antiquity, showing the " pedigree of the Son of the Ancient of Days," both divine and human ; and, in spite of the ever-increasing materials of later times, the elder dispensation has been included, actually or by implication, in some of the greatest works on Ecclesiastical History. So it must be in the nature of the case, however much, for the sake of convenience or perspicuity, we may divide and subdivide what is in itself one whole. Speaking religiously, the history of the Christian Church can never be separated from the life of its Divine Founder, and that life cannot be separated from the previous history, of which it was the culmination, the explanation, the fulfilment. Speaking philosophically, the history of the religious thoughts and feelings of Europe cannot be understood without a full appreciation of the thoughts and feelings of that Semitic race which found their highest expression in the history of the Jewish nation.

The History of Israel, the first period of Ecclesiastical History.

Nor is it only for the sake of a mere formal completeness that we must thus combine the old and the new in our historical studies. Consider well what that history is, — what a field it opens, what light it receives, what light it gives, by the mere fact of being so regarded. So far from being exempt from the laws of gradual progress and development to which the history of other nations is subject, it is the most remarkable exemplification of those laws. In no people does the history move forward in so regular a course, through beginning, middle, and end, as in the people of Israel. In none are the be-

Its peculiar interest.

ginning, middle, and end so clearly distinguished, each from each. In none has the beginning so natural and so impressive a preparation as that formed by the age of the Patriarchs. In none do the various stages of the history so visibly lead the way to the consummation, which, however truly it may be regarded as the opening of a new order, is yet no less truly the end of the old. And nowhere does the final consummation more touchingly linger in the close, more solemnly break away into new forms and new life, than in the last traces of the effects of the Jewish race on the Apostolic age.

The form, too, of the sacred books of the Old Testament is one of all others most attractive to the historical student. Out of a great variety of documents, sometimes contemporaneous, sometimes posthumous, sometimes regular narratives, sometimes isolated fragments, is to be constructed the picture of events, persons, manners most diverse. The style and language, of primitive abruptness, pregnant with meaning, are eminently suggestive. The historical annals are combined with rich and constant illustration, from what in secular literature would be called the poets and orators of the nation. There is everything to stimulate research, even did these remains contain no more than the merely human interest which attaches to the records of any great and ancient people.

But the sons of Israel, as we all know, are much more than this. They are, literally, our spiritual ances-
Its religious importance in connection with Christian History. tors: their imagery, their poetry, their very names have descended to us; their hopes, their prayers, their psalms are ours. In their religious life we see the analogy of ours; in the gradual, painful, yet sure unfolding of divine truth to them, we see the likeness of the same light dawning slowly on the Christian Church. They are truly "our ensamples." Through the reverses, the imperfections, the sins of His ancient Church, we see how "God "at sundry times and in divers manners spake in time past to " our fathers," bringing out of manifold infirmity the highest of all blessings, as we trust that He may still, through like vicissitudes, to the Church of the present and to the Church of the future.

Political principles, we are told, are best studied in the

history of classical antiquity, because they are there discussed and illustrated with a perfect abstraction from those particular associations which bias our judgment in modern and domestic instances. And so, in a still higher degree, in the history of the Jewish Church, we find the principles of all religious and ecclesiastical parties developed, not amidst names and events which are themselves the subjects of vehement controversy, but in a narrative of acknowledged authority, free from all the bitterness of modern watchwords, and yet with a completeness and variety such as within the same compass could be found in no modern church or nation.

Reproduce this history with all the detail of which it is capable. Recall Abraham resting under the oak of Mamre; Joseph amidst the Egyptian monuments; Moses under the cliffs of Horeb; Joshua brandishing his outstretched spear; Samuel amidst his youthful scholars; David surrounded by his court and camp; Solomon in his Eastern state; the wild, romantic, solitary figure of the great Elijah; " the goodly fel- " lowship" of gifted seers, lifting up their strains of joy or sorrow, as they have been well described, like some great tragic chorus, as kingdom after kingdom falls to ruin, as hope after hope dies and is revived again. Represent in all their distinctness the several stages of the history, in its steady onward advance from Egypt to Sinai, from Sinai to the Jordan, from the Jordan to Jerusalem, from the law to the Judges, from the Judges to the Monarchy, from the Monarchy to the Prophets, from the Prophets to the great event to which, not the Prophets only, but the yearnings of the whole nation had for ages borne witness.

Let us not fear lest our reverence should be diminished by finding these sacred names and high aspirations under the garb of Bedouin chiefs and Egyptian slaves and Oriental kings and Syrian patriots. The contrast of the ancient inward spirit with the present degraded condition of the same outward forms is the best indication of the source whence that spirit came. Let us not fear lest we should, by the surpassing interest of the story of the elder Church, be tempted to forget the end to which it leads us. The more we study the Jewish history, the more shall we feel that it is but the prelude of a vaster and loftier history, without which it would be itself unmeaning. The voice of the old dispensation is pitched in too loud a key for the ears of one small people.[1] The place of the Jewish nation is too strait for the abode of thoughts which want a wider room in which to dwell. The drama, as it rolls on through its successive stages, is too majestic to end in anything short of a divine catastrophe.

This is a brief but necessary sketch of the first part of our subject. This is the ancient period of Ecclesiastical History. Its full treasures must be unfolded hereafter. Its accessories belong to other departments of study. The critical interpretation of the sacred books in which the history is contained falls under the province of General Theology and Exegesis ; the explanation of the languages in which they are written I gladly leave to the Professor of Hebrew and the Professor of Greek. But the history itself of the chosen people, from Abraham to the Apostles, belongs to this Chair by right ;[2] and, if health and strength are spared to me, shall also belong to it in fact.

II. The fortunes, however, of the seed of Abraham after the flesh form but a small portion of the fortunes of his descendants after the spirit : they are, as I have said, but the introduction to the history which rises on their ruin. With the close of the Apostolic age the direct influence of the chosen people expires ; neither in religious nor in historical language can the Jewish race from this time forward be said to be charged with any divine message for the welfare of mankind. Individual instances of long endurance, of great genius, of lofty character, have indeed arisen amongst them in later times ; but, since the days when the Galilean Apostle, S. John, slept his last sleep under the walls of Ephesus, no son of Israel has ever exercised any wide-spread or lasting control over the general condition of mankind.

End of Ancient Ecclesiastical History.

[1] I am indebted for this expression to a striking sermon of Professor Archer Butler (vol. i. p. 210).

[2] I believe that I am correct in stating that in all other European universities, where a Chair of Ecclesiastical History exists, the Jewish history falls within its province.

We stand, therefore, at the close of the first century, like travellers on a mountain ridge, when the river which they have followed through the hills is about to burst forth into the wide plain. It is the very likeness of that world-famous view from the range of the Lebanon over the forest and city of Damascus. The stream has hitherto flowed in its narrow channel, its course marked by the contrast which its green strip of vegetation presents to the desert mountains through which it descends. The further we advance the more remarkable does the contrast become; the mountains more bare, the river-bed more rich and green. At last its channel is contracted to the utmost limits; the cliffs on each side almost close it in; it breaks through and over a wide extent, far as the eye can reach, it scatters a flood of vegetation and life, in the midst of which rise the towers and domes of the great city, the earliest and the latest type of human grandeur and civilization.

Beginning of Christian Ecclesiastical History.

Such is the view, backwards and forwards, and beneath our feet, which Ecclesiastical History presents to us, as we rest on the grave of the last Apostle and look over the coming ages of our course. The Church of God is no longer confined within the limits of a single nation. The life and the truth, concentrated up to this point within the narrow and unbending character of the Semitic race, have been enlarged into the broad, fluctuating, boundless destinies of the sons of Japheth. The thin stream expands and loses itself more and more in the vast field of the history of the world. The Christian Church is merely another name for Christendom; and Christendom soon becomes merely another name for the most civilized, the most powerful, the most important nations of the modern habitable world.

What, then, it may be asked, is the difference henceforward between Civil and Ecclesiastical History? How far are the duties of this professorship separable from those of the Chair of Modern History?

Relations of Civil and Ecclesiastical History.

To a great extent the two are inseparable; they cannot be torn asunder without infinite loss to both. It is indeed true that, in common parlance, Ecclesiastical History is often confined within limits so restricted as to render such a distinc-

tion only too easy. Of the numerous theological terms, of
which the original sense has been defaced, marred, and clipped
by the base currency of the world, few have suffered so much,
in few has "the gold become so dim, the most fine gold so
"changed," as in the word "ecclesiastical." The substantive
from which it is derived has fallen far below its ancient
Apostolical meaning, but the adjective "ecclesiastical" has
fallen lower still. It has come to signify, not the religious,
not the moral, not even the social or political interests of the
Christian community, but often the very opposite of these, —
its merely accidental, outward, ceremonial machinery. We
call a contest for the retention or the abolition of vestments
"ecclesiastical," not a contest for the retention or the abolition of the slave-trade. We include in "ecclesiastical history" the life of the most insignificant bishop or the most
wicked of Popes, not the life of the wisest of philosophers or
the most Christian of kings. But such a limitation is as
untenable in fact as it is untrue in theory. The very stones
of the spiritual temple cry out against such a profanation of
the rock from which they were hewn. If the Christian religion be a matter, not of mint, anise, and cummin, but of
justice, mercy, and truth ; if the Christian Church be not a
priestly caste, or a monastic order, or a little sect, or a handful of opinions, but "the whole congregation of faithful men,
"dispersed throughout the world ; " if the very word which
of old represented the chosen "people" (λαὸς) is now to be
found in the "laity ; " if the Biblical usage of the phrase
"Ecclesia" literally justifies Tertullian's definition, *Ubi tres
sunt laici, ibi est ecclesia ;* then the range of the history of the
Church is as wide as the range of the world which it was
designed to penetrate, as the whole body which its name
includes.

By a violent effort, no doubt, the two spheres can be kept
apart ; by a compromise, tacit or understood, the student of
each may avoid looking the other in the face ; under special
circumstances, the intimate relation between the course of
Christian society and the course of human affairs may be
forgotten or set aside. Josephus the priest may pass over in
absolute silence the new sect which arises in Galilee to dis-

turb the Jewish hierarchy. Tacitus the philosopher may give nothing more than a momentary glance at the miserable superstition of the fanatics who called themselves Christians. Napoleon the conqueror, when asked on the coast of Syria to visit the holy city, may make his haughty reply, — "Jeru- "salem does not enter into the line of my operations." But this is not the natural nor the usual course of the greatest examples both in ancient and modern times. Observe the description of the Jewish Church by the sacred historians. Consider the immense difference for all future ages, if the lives of Joshua, David, Solomon, and Elijah had been omitted, as unworthy of insertion, because they did not belong to the priestly tribe; if the Pentateuch had been confined to the Book of Leviticus; if the Books of Kings and Chronicles had limited themselves to the sayings and doings of Zadok and Abiathar, or even of Nathan and Gad. Remember also the early chroniclers of Europe; almost all of them at once the sole historians of their age, yet, even by purpose and profession, historians only of the Church. Take but one instance, the Venerable Bede. His "Ecclesiastical History of England" begins, not with the arrival of Augustine, but with the first dawn of British civilization at the landing of Cæsar; and, for the period over which it extends, it is the sufficient and almost the only authority for the fortunes of the Anglo-Saxon commonwealth.

In later times, since history has become a distinct science, the same testimony is still borne by the highest works of genius and research in this wide field. Gibbon's "Decline and Fall of the Roman Empire" is, in great part, however reluctantly or unconsciously, the history of "the rise and progress of the Christian Church." His true conception of the grandeur of his subject extorted from him that just concession which his own natural prejudice would have refused; and it was remarked not many years ago, by Dr. Newman, that up to that time England had produced no other Ecclesiastical History worthy of the name. This reproach has since been removed by the great work of Dean Milman; but it is the distinguishing excellence of that very history that it embraces within its vast circumference the whole story of mediæval Europe. Even in that earlier period when the world and the Church were of necessity distinct and antagonistic, Arnold rightly perceived, and all subsequent labors in this field tend to the same result, that each will be best understood when blended in the common history of the Empire which exercised so powerful an influence over the development of the Christian society within its bosom, whilst by that society it was itself undermined and superseded. And the two chief historians of France and England in recent times — Guizot in his Lectures on French Civilization, Macaulay in his English History — have both strongly brought out, as necessary parts of their dissertations or narratives, the religious influences which by inferior writers of one class have been neglected, or by those of another class been rent from their natural context.

Never let us think that we can understand the history of the Church apart from the history of the world, any more than that we can separate the interests of the clergy from the interests of the laity, which are the interests of the Church at large.

How to adjust the relations of the two spheres to each other
Points of contact between Civil and Ecclesiastical History.
is almost as indefinite a task in history as it is in practice and in philosophy. In no age are they precisely the same. Sometimes, as in the period of the Roman Empire, the influence of one on the other is more by contagion, by atmosphere, even by contrast, than by direct intercourse. Sometimes the main interest of religious history hangs on an institution, like Episcopacy; on a war, like the Crusades; on a person, like Luther. In some periods, as in the Middle Ages, the combination of the secular and religious elements will be effected by the political or the intellectual influence of the clergy. The lives of the Archbishops of Canterbury and the lives of the Prime-Ministers of England are for five hundred years almost indivisible. The course of European revolution for nearly a thousand years moves round the throne of the Papacy. Or again, the rise of a new power or character will, even in these very ages, suddenly transfer the spiritual guidance of men to some high-minded ruler or gifted writer, who is for the time the true arbiter or interpreter of the interests and the feelings of Christendom. In the close of the thirteenth century, it is not

a priest or a Pope, but a king and an opponent of Popes, who
stands forward as the acknowledged representative of the
Christian Church in Europe; S. Louis in France, not Gregory IX. at Rome.   In the fourteenth century it is not a
schoolman or a bishop that we summon before us as the best
exponent of mediæval Christianity; it is not the "seraphic"
or the "angelic doctor," but the divine poet Dante, who
reveals to us the feelings and thoughts of the whole age respecting this world and the next.   And if we pass to our own
country, he must be a blind guide who would take us through
the English Reformation without seeing on every stage of it
the impress of the iron will and broad aims of Henry VIII.;
or who would portray the English Church without recogniz-
ing the comprehensive policy of Elizabeth.   Or yet again, of
all our brilliant English divines of the seventeenth century,
there is not one who can be fairly said to have exercised as
much influence over the popular theology of this nation, as
has been undoubtedly exercised by a half-heretic half-Puritan
layman, the author of "Paradise Lost."

These instances indicate with sufficient precision the devious
yet obvious path which, without losing sight of the wide horizon on the one hand, or without undue contraction of his view
on the other, the student of Ecclesiastical History may safely
follow.   If we may for a moment return to our for-   Points of
mer position, and imagine ourselves overlooking the divergence
broad expanse into which the stream bursts forth from between
Civil and
the mountains of its earlier stages, our purpose hence- Ecclesiasti-
forth will be, not so much to describe the products of cal History.
the forest or the buildings of the city which have grown up
on the banks of the river, but to track the river itself through
its various channels, under its overhanging thickets, through the
populous streets and gardens to which it gives life; to see what
are its main, what its tributary streams; what the nature of its
waters; how far impregnated with new qualities, how far colored,
by the various soils, vegetations, uses, through which they pass;
to trace their secret flow, as they go softly through the regions
which they fertilize; not finding them where they do not exist,
not denying their power where they do exist; to welcome their
sound in courses however tortuous; to acknowledge their value

however stained in their downward and onward passage. Difficult as it may often be to find the stream, yet when it is found it will guide us to the green pastures of this world's wilderness, and lead us beside the still waters.

Three landmarks, at least, may be mentioned, by which this course of Ecclesiastical History may be distinguished from that of history generally.

First, there are institutions, characters, ideas, words, which can be traced to the religious, especially to the Christian, principle in man, and to nothing besides. There are virtues and truths now in the world, which can only be ascribed to the influence of Christian society: and there are corruptions of those virtues and of those truths, which have produced crimes and errors to be ascribed also, though remotely and indirectly, to the same source. There are events in the common course of history — revolutions, wars, divisions of races and nations — which in themselves can hardly be called religious, but which have at least one aspect distinctly religious. There are also institutions, customs, ceremonies, even vestures and forms of ritual, in which, though originally pagan or secular, Christian ideas have now become fixed so as to be inseparable from them. All these it is the task of Ecclesiastical History to adjust and discriminate.

Secondly, in every age, even the worst, there have been beneath the surface latent elements of religious life and of active goodness, which it will be our duty to bring to light, as the true signs of a better world beyond, and of the Divine Presence abiding with us even here, — a Church, as it were, within a Church; a "remnant," to use the language of the older covenant.

Thirdly, the whole history of the Church, though usually flowing in the tracks marked out for it by the great national and geographical boundaries of the world, yet has a course, not always, and therefore not of necessity, identical with the channel of human civilization. In the history of the Church as in that of the world, in the history of the Christian Church as in that of the Jewish, there is a distinct unity of parts, an onward progress from scene to scene, from act to act, towards an end yet distant and invisible; a unity and a progress such as give consistency and point to what would else be a mere collection of isolated and disjointed facts.

Let us then, before we conclude, briefly notice the successive stages through which, eventually, our course of study must lead us, and the interest especially attaching to each. *Stages of the History of the Church.*

The first period is that which contains the great question, almost the greatest which Ecclesiastical History has to answer, — How was the transition effected from the age of the Apostles to the age of the Fathers, from Christianity as we see it in the New Testament, to Christianity as we see it in the next century, and as, to a certain extent, we have seen it ever since? *1. The transition from the Church of the Apostles to the Church of the Fathers.*

No other change equally momentous has ever since affected its fortunes, yet none has ever been so silent and secret. The stream, in that most critical moment of its passage from the everlasting hills to the plain below, is lost to our view at the very point where we are most anxious to watch it; we may hear its struggles under the overarching rocks; we may catch its spray on the boughs that overlap its course; but the torrent itself we see not, or see only by imperfect glimpses. It is not so much a period for Ecclesiastical History as for ecclesiastical controversy and conjecture. A fragment here, an allegory there; romances of unknown authorship; a handful of letters of which the genuineness of every portion is contested inch by inch; the summary examination of a Roman magistrate; the pleadings of two or three Christian apologists; customs and opinions in the very act of change; last, but not least, the faded paintings, the broken sculptures, the rude epitaphs in the darkness of the catacombs, — these are the scanty, though attractive, materials out of which the likeness of the early Church must be reproduced, as it was working its way, in the literal sense of the word, " under ground," under camp and palace, under senate and forum, — " as unknown, yet well known; as dying, " and behold it lives."

This chasm once cleared, we find ourselves approaching the point where the story of the Church once more becomes

history — becomes once more the history, not of an iso-
The African lated community, or of isolated individuals, but of
Churches. an organized society incorporated with the political systems of the world. Already, in the close of the
second and beginning of the third century, the Churches of
Africa, now seen for a few generations before their final dis-
appearance, exhibit distinct characters on the scene. They
are the stepping-stones by which we cross from the obscure
to the clear, from chaos to order. Of these the Church of
Carthage illustrates the rise of Christianity in the West, the
Church of Egypt that of Christianity in the East.

But the first great outward event of the actual history of
the Church is its conversion of the Empire; and,
2. The
conversion in close connection with this, its first wide sphere
of the Em- in the face of mankind, is the Oriental world out of
pire; and
the Eastern which it sprang, and in which the external forms of
Church.
its early organization can still be most clearly studied.
In the usages of the ancient systems which have grown up
on that soil — Coptic, Greek, Asiatic — we may still trace
the relics, the fossilized relics, of the old Imperial Church.[1]
In the period of the first Councils, and in some passages of
the Byzantine Empire, the fortunes of the Eastern Church
are identified with the fortunes of Christendom.[2] Its connection with the general course of Ecclesiastical History in subsequent times depends chiefly on two developments of religious life of a very different kind from each other, the rise of
Mahometanism,[3] and the rise of the Church and Empire of
Russia.[4]

With the exception of these three periods or stages, and
viewed as part of the continuous history of the Church,
Eastern Christianity must be considered but as the temporary halting-place of the great spiritual migration which,
from the day that Abraham turned his face away from the
rising of the sun, has been stepping steadily westward.

Another and a wider sphere was in store for the progress
3. The   of the Church than its own native regions; another
Latin
Church.   and a nobler conquest than that of its old worn-out

---

[1] Lecture I.   [2] Lect. II. — VII.
[3] Lect. VIII.   [4] Lect. IX. — XII.

enemy on the tottering throne of the Cæsars. The Gothic tribes descended on the ancient world; the fabric of civilized society was dissolved in the mighty crisis; the Fathers of modern Europe were to be moulded, subdued, educated. By whom was this great work effected? Not by the Empire — it had fled to the Bosphorus; not by the Eastern Church — its permanent conquests were in another direction. In the Western, Latin, Roman clergy, in the missionaries who went forth to Gaul, to Britain, and to Germany, the barbarians found their first masters; in the work of controlling and resisting the fierce soldiers of the Teutonic tribes lay the main work, the real foundation, the chief temptation of the Papacy. From the day when Leo III. placed the crown of the new Holy Roman German Empire on the head of Charlemagne, the stream of human progress and the stream of Christian life, with whatever interruptions, eddies, countercurrents, flowed during the next seven centuries in the same channel. As the history of the earlier stages revolved round the characters of the Fathers or of the Emperors, so the history of the Middle Ages, with all their crimes and virtues, revolved (it is at once the confession of their weakness and their strength) round the character and policy of the Popes. What good they did, and what good they failed to do, by what means they rose, and by what they fell, during that long period of their power, form the main questions by which their claims must be tested.

And now a new revolution was at hand, almost as terrible in its appearance and as trying in its results as any 4. The Reformation. that had gone before. The fountains of the great deep were again broken up. New wants and old evils had met together. The failure of the Crusades had shaken men's belief in holy places. Long abuses had shaken their belief in Popes, bishops, monasteries, sacraments, and saints. The revival of ancient learning had revealed truth under new forms. The invention of printing had raised up a new order of scribes, expounders, readers, writers, clergy. Institutions which had guided the world for a thousand years, now decayed and out of joint, gave way at the moment when they were most needed. Was it possible that the Christian Church should

meet these trials as it had met those which had gone before?
It had lived through the fall of Jerusalem; it had lived through
the ten Persecutions; it had lived through its amalgamation
with the Empire; it had lived through the invasion of the
barbarians: but could it live through the struggles of internal
dissolution? could it live through the shipwreck of the whole
outward fabric of its existence? could the planks of the vessel,
scattered on the face of the raging flood, be so put together
again as to form any shelter from the storm, any home on
the waters? Did the history of the Church come to an end,
as many thought it would, when its ancient organization came
to an end, in the great change of the Reformation?

We know that it still lived on. That it survived at all is
Protes-   the best proof which it has yet presented of its inherent
tantism.   vitality; that it survived, in a purified form, is the
best pledge of its future success. To Ancient Christianity, to
Byzantine Christianity, to Roman Christianity, was now added
the fourth and equally unmistakable form of Protestant Christianity: like the others, clothed in an outward shape of its own,
and confining itself specially to distinct branches of the European family, yet also penetrating with its spirit institutions
and nations outwardly most repugnant to it. Amidst many
conflicts, therefore, Ecclesiastical History still continues in the
general tracks that were opened for it in the sixteenth century. Whatever political troubles have agitated the world
since that time, and whatever changes may be fermenting in
the inner heart and mind of the Church, none have since
altered its outward aspect and divisions. In one respect a
wide difference exists between the history of Christendom as
it was before, and as it has been since, the Reformation.
Henceforward we cannot follow its course as a whole: each
country must have its own ecclesiastical as well as its own
civil history. Italy, Spain, Sweden, Holland, Geneva, Scotland, — the very names have each, in theological language, a
peculiar pathos and significance imparted by the Reformation.
In each that great event awakened a different note as it traversed their several chords. Still there are three countries in
which, beyond all others, the religious history of Europe has
been specially carried on.

It is in France that the fortunes of Christianity during the last three centuries have been most visibly represent- The French ed in the brightest and in the darkest colors. The Church and the French Gallican Church, in the seventeenth century the most Revolution. brilliant in Europe, brilliant alike in its works of active mercy and in its almost Augustan age of great divines — Vincent of Paul, Bossuet, Fenelon, Pascal, — became in the eighteenth century the miserable parent, and then the victim, of the great convulsion which, whilst it shook the belief of the whole of Europe, in France for eleven years suppressed it altogether. The French Revolution must always be considered as an epoch in the religious history of man. Not only was its hostility to the Christian faith the most direct that the world has seen since the days of Julian; not only did it spring, in great measure, out of the corrupt state of the French clergy, the Church of Dubois and of Talleyrand; but it possessed in itself that frightful energy which, as has been truly observed by its latest exponent,[1] can only be likened to the propagation of a new religion — the wild fanaticism, the proselytism, the self-devotion, the crimes, as though of a Western Mahometanism, — of what its own disciples have often called it, an imitation, a parody, a new, distorted edition of the Gospel. Not only is its history instructive as a moral warning to all existing Churches, and as an interpreter of the great religious storms of former ages, but it changed the whole external constitution of the Church on the Continent generally; and, in the inward sifting and trial of the religious thoughts of men, its effects can still now be felt, even in countries the furthest removed from its immediate influence.

Germany, the seat of the original movement of the Refor-mation, has never lost the hold which it then first The German acquired on the reason and imagination of mankind. Church. Its collective power as a Church has been too impalpable to attach itself to any definite course of outward events. But its individual divines have, more than any others, taken the place occupied by the schoolmen of the Middle Ages. No others, within the last hundred years, have exercised so powerful an

---

[1] Tocqueville : L'Ancien Régime et la Révolution, c. iii.   Compare Burke's " Thoughts on French Affairs," vol. iv. p. 10.   (Bohn's Ed.)

influence over the rest of Europe, as the philosophical and critical theologians of the German universities.

And this leads us finally to the third great ecclesiastical The Church system which stands alone and apart, yet with its own of England. peculiar mission, in the general fortunes of the Western Church. At least for Englishmen, no Ecclesiastical History since the Reformation can be so instructive as that of our own Church of England. To see how, out of that wide shipwreck the fragments of our vessel were again pieced together; how far it has realized the essential condition of the ark on the stormy waters; how far it has contained within itself the necessary, though heterogeneous, elements of our national faith and character; how far it may still hope to do so; what is its connection with the past, what its hold upon the future; — this is the last and most important task of the English ecclesiastical historian. The peculiar constitution of our State has borne the brunt and survived the shock of the French Revolution : it is the hope of the peculiar constitution of our Church that it should in like manner meet, overcome, and absorb the shock of the new thoughts and feelings to which, directly or indirectly, that last of European movements has given birth.

I have been induced thus, at the outset, to dwell on this Conclusion. broad extent of prospect, first, because it is only by a just appreciation of the whole that any part can be properly understood; and, secondly, because I wish to impress on my hearers the many points of contact which Ecclesiastical History presents to the various studies of this place. If at times it is impossible not to be oppressed with the load which has to be taken from the stores of the Pilgrim's Palace, it is a satisfaction to remember that there are many travellers passing along the same road who will, almost of necessity, lighten the burden and cheer the journey by their common interest in the treasures borne away.

One such has been before me in this path, my lamented pred- The late ecessor. Personally he was almost unknown to me. Professor Hussey. In our mode of dealing with the subject before us we might have widely differed. But I cannot enter on this office without bearing my humble testimony to the conscientious industry with which, as I have heard from those who attended his Lectures, he guided them over the rugged way which he had chosen for them ; without expressing my grateful sense of the characteristic forethought and munificence with which he bequeathed to this Chair the valuable endowment of his library. Still more, I should be doing wrong both to him and to the University, were I not to dwell for a moment on what I have always understood was the chief ground of the respect which he commanded in this place.   He was emphatically a "just man; " he possessed in an eminent degree that rare gift of public integrity and fairness too rare in the world, too rare in the Church, too rare in Ecclesiastical History, too rare even in great seats of learning, not to be noticed when it comes before us, especially when, as in the present case, it passes away with the marked approbation and regret of all who witnessed it.   In times of much angry controversy, he never turned aside from his straightforward course to excite needless alarms.   He never stooped[1] to win theological favor by attacking unpopular names.   He never allowed any religious sentiment or fancy to interfere with his manly and severe sense of truth and duty.   He showed that it was possible to be impartial without weakness, and orthodox without bitterness. May the University long remember that such was the character which she delighted to honor !   May his successors in this Chair be encouraged and enabled to act and to speak, in this most important respect, according to his example !

For the sake of convenience I subjoin the leading chronological divisions, which to some extent cross the historical and geographical divisions laid down in the foregoing Lecture.

I. The rise of the Christian Church.   A. D. 30–312.
    1. The Apostolic age.   30–70.
    2. The transition from the Apostolic age.   70–160.
    3. The age of Persecution.   160–312.

[1] As one instance, it may suffice to record the remarkable Ordination sermon on " The Atonement," preached by Professor Hussey in December, 1855, in which he defended the doctrine of an eminent theologian, at that time the object of much vehement obloquy, and showed in guarded but decisive terms its substantial identity with that of the ancient Fathers.

II. The Church of the Empire.

The Western Church.	*The Eastern Church.*
1. The beginning of the Roman Church and of Latin theology. 312–476.	1. The age of the Eastern Councils. 312–781.
	2. The rise of the Greek Empire and Church. 330–1453.
	3. The rise of Mahometanism. 622–732.
	4. The rise of the Russian Church. 988–1700.

III. The Church of the Middle Ages. 476–1517.
 1. Conversion of the Barbarians. 450–800.
 2. The Papacy and the Crusades. 800–1300.
 3. The Western Councils and preludes of the Reformation. 1300–1517.

IV. The Churches of the Reformation. 1517–1789.
 1. The crisis of the Reformation. 1517–1550.
 2. The wars of the Reformation. 1550–1660.
 3. The rise of Latitudinarianism, of Methodism, of Gallicanism, and of German theology. 1660–1789.

V. The French Revolution. 1789–1815.

II.

THE STUDY OF ECCLESIASTICAL HISTORY.

It is sometimes said, that of all historical studies that of Ecclesiastical History is the most repulsive.   We seem to be set down in the valley of the Prophet's vision, — strewn with bones, and behold they are " very many," and " very dry ; " skeletons of creeds, of churches, of institutions ; trodden and traversed by the feet of travellers again and again ; the scape-goat of one age lying lifeless by the scape-goat of the next ; craters of extinct volcanoes, which once filled the world with their noise, and are now dead and cold ; the salt shores of a barren sea, which throws up again dead and withered the branches which the river of life had cast into it full of beauty and verdure, — the very reverse of that green prospect which I set before you in my opening Lecture; the more dreary, it may be said, from the wide extent into which it spreads. " How are we to give interest to such a task ; how shall the " healing streams penetrate into those dead waters ; how shall " those dry bones live ? "

There may be many answers to this question, but I shall content myself with the most obvious.   *Remember, that of all these things there is a history.*   These relics, these institutions, these characters (take them at their worst), had each a part to play amongst mankind ; they were men of flesh and blood like ourselves, or they dwelt with men of flesh and blood like ourselves ; they were living human spirits, or they were the instruments of living human spirits ; however decayed, however antiquated they may be, yet in their very age they have an interest which no novelty can give.   We cannot, it is true, enter on Ecclesiastical History, whether in its wider or its narrower sense, with the feeling of fresh enthusiasm which inspires the discoverers of unexplored regions, whether of

Dryness of Ecclesiastical History.

Remedy to be found in a Historical view of the Church.

science or history, " the first who ever burst into the silent
" sea," or secluded ruins, which no eye of man has seen before.
But we can enter upon it with the yet deeper delight which
fills our minds, as we feel rising beneath our feet the ground
of the Seven Hills ; or as we gaze, knowing that hundreds
of thousands have gazed before us, on the everlasting outline
of the Pyramids. So view the history of the Church, even
in its most lifeless and withered forms ; so view it as part of a
whole, as once having lived, as living still in ourselves, as destined to live on in future generations ; so prophesy over its dry
bones as they lie scattered and disjointed over the surface of the
world, — and we shall soon hear " a noise and a shaking," and
" the bones will come together," each to each, and " the breath
" will come into them, and they will live, and stand up upon their
" feet, an exceeding great army."

Let me point out how this remedy is involved in the very na-
I. History ture of the case. Take, for example, the history of
of Doc-
trines. doctrines and opinions. Many ecclesiastical histories
contain little else ; half of theology is taken up in stating them.
How immensely do they gain in liveliness, in power, in the capacity of being understood and appreciated, if we view them
through the medium of the lives, characters, and circumstances
of those who received and taught them ! Trace the actual course
of any opinion or dogma ; see the influences by which it was
colored ; compare the relative importance attached to it at one
period and another ; ask how far the words in which it has been
expressed convey the same or a different meaning to us or to our
fathers ; discover, if possible, its fountain-head in the time, the
country, or the person in which it first originated. Look at Au-
gustinianism as it arose in the mind of Augustine ; at Lutheranism
as it was conceived by Luther ; at Wesleyanism as it was set
forth by Wesley. It will cease to be a phantom, it will speak
to us as a man : if it is an enemy, we shall slay it more easily ;
if a friend, we shall embrace it more warmly.

Still more is this the case with the kindred subject of Con-
II. History fessions and Articles of Faith. If we regard them
of Creeds
and Arti- merely in their cut and dried results, they may in-
cles. deed serve many useful ends ; they supply stakes to
make hedges against intruders, planks to cross our enemy's

trenches, fagots to burn heretics. But go to the soil from which they sprang. Watch them in their wild, native, luxuriant growth. Observe the moss which has grown over their stems, the bough rent away there and grafted in here, the branches inextricably intertwined with adjacent thickets. So regarded, they will not be less, but more, of a shelter; we shall not value them the less for understanding them better. Figure to yourselves, as you read any creeds or confessions, the lips by which they were first uttered, the hands by which they were first written. Hear the Apostles' Creed, as it summed up in its few simple sentences the belief of the Roman martyrs. Watch the Nicene Bishops meeting each other, and their opponents, and the Emperor Constantine, for the first time, on the shores of the Bithynian lake. Listen to the triumphs of Clovis and Recared over the Arians of France and Spain, the rising storms between East and West, and you will more clearly catch the true meaning of their echo in the old Latin hymn, *Quicunque vult*, then first welcomed into the worship of Western Europe. Read the Articles of the English Church in their successive mutilations, excrescences, variations. Go to that most precious of collegiate libraries in the sister University, where the venerable autograph which contains them may still be seen: look at the signatures of those whose names are affixed: conceive the persons whom those names represent: imagine them, as any one who has ever taken part in any council, or commission, or committee, or conclave of any kind whatever, can and must imagine them; one sacrificing, another insisting on, a favorite expression; a new turn given to one sentence, a charitable color thrown over another; the edge of a sharp exclusion blunted by one party, the sting of a bitter sarcasm drawn by another. Start from this view, as certain as it can be made by the facts of human nature and by the facts of history, both universal and particular. Regard confessions of faith in this their only true historical light, and in that light many a new glimpse will be obtained of their practical justice and moderation; many a harsh expression will be explained, many a superfluous scruple of honest minds will vanish away, many a foolish controversy will be extinguished forever.

But the proper material for Ecclesiastical History is, after all,

7

not institutions or opinions, but events and persons. Leviticus and the Proverbs have their own special value,
but they are not reckoned amongst the "historical
books" of the Jewish Church. Bingham's learned
work, however useful as an auxiliary, contains "the antiquities,"
not the history, of the Christian Church. It is on its special
incidents and characters that the vitality of any history depends. How can we best make ourselves acquainted with
these?

III. History of events and persons.

In this, as in so many other branches of knowledge, the
question can only be fully answered in each particular
case. Whatever way will best enable each man, in
his own peculiar situation, character, and opportunities, to
remember, and understand, and profit, that is to him the best,
and can be taught only by consulting his own experience.

General study.

For general readers, the best general counsel which can be
given is that which I have already indicated. Study the history of the Church in connection with the collateral subjects
with which it is bound up; let us keep our eyes and ears open
to the religious aspects of history, and they will break in upon
us, we know not whence, or how.

Let us read also, whatever we do read, as elsewhere, so here,
in the works of eminent historians rather than in those of writers
without a name and without a character; and yet more, read,
if possible, works which describe what they describe at length
and in detail, and which therefore leave a lasting impression on
the memory and imagination, rather than in the crowded pages
of meagre abstracts, which are forgotten as soon as read. Great
works and full works, not small works and short works, are in
the end the best economy of time as well as of everything
else.

But this leads me to what is, on the whole, the most instructive, though (it may be) not the only practicable,
course to be followed by those who wish, in the true
sense of the word, to be "students" of Ecclesiastical
History. We cannot attempt to describe or to study every event
in detail, for time and labor would fail; we need not do it com-
pendiously, for this has been done to our hands again and again,
and of late years with such candor and research as to render

Detailed study of great events.

any further work of the kind superfluous.   One method remains
to us, at once the most obvious and the most interesting.   Lay
aside the lesser events, or read them only so far as to preserve a
continuous knowledge of the general thread of the history: it
is for this purpose that the briefer narratives, when clearly and
ably written, are of substantial use.   But study the greater
events, scenes, places, and revolutions, in all the detail in which
they can be represented to us.

Take, for example, the General Councils of the Church.
They are the pitched battles of Ecclesiastical History. The
Ask yourselves the same questions as you would about Councils.
the battles of military history.   Ask when, and where, and why
they were fought.   Put before your minds all the influences of
the age which there were confronted and concentrated from different quarters as in one common focus.   See why they were
summoned to Nicæa, to Constance, to Trent: the locality often
contains here, as in actual battles, the key of their position, and
easily connects the Ecclesiastical History of the age with its
general history and geography.   Look at the long procession as
it enters the scene of assembly; see who was present and who
was absent.[1]   Let us make ourselves acquainted with the several
characters there brought together, so that we may recognize
them as old friends if we meet them again elsewhere.   Study
their decrees,[2] as expositions of the prevailing sentiments of
the time; study them, as Mr. Froude has advised us to study
the statutes of our own ancient Parliaments; see what evils are
most condemned, and what evils are left uncondemned; observe
how far their injunctions are still obeyed, or how far set at
nought, and ask in each case the reason why.   Read them, as
I have just now noticed, with the knowledge given to us by our
own experience of all synods of all kinds; read them with the
knowledge which each gives of every other.   Do this for any
one Council, and you will have made a deep hole into Ecclesiastical History.

And still more let this same rule be followed with regard to
persons.   Take any one character.   It may be we shall Detailed
be attracted towards him by some accidental con- study of
nection; it may, and should rather, be on account of his pre- great men.

---

[1] See Lecture III.   [2] See Lecture V.

eminent greatness. Do not let him leave you till you have, at
any rate, retained some one distinctive feature by which you will
know him again in the multitudes amongst which he will else be
lost; some feature of mind or person which he has, and which
others have not.[1]

Many of us must have read, in part at least, Neander's
Neander and his History of the Church. "History of the Christian Church," and will have
admired, as every one must admire, the depth, the
tenderness, the delicacy of Christian sentiment which
pervades the whole of his vast work, and fulfils his own beautiful motto, "It is the heart which makes the theologian," —
Pectus theologum facit. Yet, without disparaging the value
of such a mirror of Christian history in such a character, we
cannot help feeling that it is often rather the theologian than
the historian whose works we read; that it is often rather the
thoughts, than the actual persons and deeds, of men, that he is
describing to us. They are the ghosts of Ossian, rather than
the heroes of Homer; they are refined, they are spiritualized, to
that degree, that their personality almost vanishes; the stars of
heaven shine through them: but we have no hold on their
earthly frames; we can trace no human lineaments in their
features, as they pass before us. Let us endeavor to fill up
this outline; however much of deeper interest it may have for
the more philosophical mind, it will hardly lay hold on the
memory or the affections of the more ordinary student, unless it
is brought closer to our grasp. How differently we learn to estimate even Neander himself, according as we merely regard him
as a thinker of holy thoughts, the writer of a good book, or as
we see the venerable historian in his own proper person, — his
black, shaggy, overhanging eyebrows and his strong Jewish
physiognomy revealing the nation and religion to which he
first belonged, — working at his history night and day with
insatiable ardor, to show to his unconverted countrymen what
Christianity really was; abstracted from all thought of worldly
cares, of food, and dress, and money, and time; living, dying,
buried in the affections, in the arms, of his devoted pupils!
What by proximity of time we are enabled to do for the historian, true research usually enables us to do for those whom he

[1] See Lectures VI. VII. XI. XII.

describes. Watch their first appearance, their education, their conflicts, their death-beds. Observe their relative position to each other; see what one did which another would not have done, what one thought or said which to another would have been heretical or superstitious; or, lastly, what all did, and said, and thought in common.

If I were to name one especial excellence amongst the many which render Mr. Grote's great achievement so im- Representation of the distinction of characters. portant an addition, not merely to Grecian history, but to all historical study, of whatever kind, it would be the keen discrimination with which he presents, not merely distinct characters, but distinct types of character in the lineage of the Grecian mind, whom before we had been accustomed to regard much as we usually regard the fixed stars — their distance from each other being lost in comparison with the distance from ourselves. In these contrasts and combinations of character we find exactly what is most needed in the history of the Church. Here, even more than in common history, we are apt to blend together the different persons of the story under one common class. Yet here, even more than in common history, we ought to keep each separate from each, if we would learn the lessons they have to teach to the world. Of ordinary readers, how few there are to whom the Fathers, the Schoolmen, nay, even the Reformers, although divided as classes, are not confounded as individuals! How few there are who can trace the descent, step by step, as the genealogy (so to speak) of the Church is unrolled before us! From Ignatius to Cyprian, from Origen to Athanasius, from Athanasius to Augustine, from Augustine to Bernard, from Bernard to Aquinas, to Tauler, to Luther, how wide are the gaps, how necessary the connection, how startling the difference! Or, again, in the more outward history, how various are the trains of association awakened by the successive representatives of the Empire and of the Papacy, in Constantine, in Clovis, in Charlemagne, in Barbarossa, in Charles V.; or, on the other hand, in Gregory I., in Gregory VII., in Innocent III., in Leo X., in Sixtus V.! Each has his own message to deliver; each has his own work to perform; each is a link in that manifold chain which conveys the electric spark from the first to the nineteenth century. It was a happy thought of Eusebius, that he would trace the history of the various ancient churches through the succession of Bishops, who in those early times were literally the personifications of their flocks. It is a yet happier arrangement, whenever the interest of the history of the whole Church can be concentrated in the still grander succession of those who have stood forth as the overseers and guides of Christendom, whether by good or bad eminence, — not only from generation to generation, but from century to century, and from age to age.

It is not without reason that I have thus recommended for Uses of this your study the selection of the detailed representation method. of some one event, person, or institution of commanding interest. Not only will it furnish us with the best mode of giving life to what is often a barren labor, but it will also be the best safeguard against many of the evils with which the student of Ecclesiastical History is beset.

First, it is always useful to be reminded of the various de- I. Grada- grees of importance in the different events and insti- tion of im- tutions of the Church. There is no more common portance in ecclesiastical error of theological students than to regard every- subjects. thing connected with religion as of equal significance. They will allow of no light or shade, no difference between things essential and things unessential, no proportion between means and ends, between things moral and things ceremonial, between things doubtful and things certain. Against this *levelling* tendency of ecclesiastical study, History lifts up a warning which may be heeded when all else fails. Believe that Athanasius and Augustine are worthier objects of interest than Flavian or Optatus, and you will have made one step towards believing that there is a gradation of importance in the several controversies in which the Church has been engaged. Believe that the invasion and conversion of the barbarians was the great crisis and work of mediæval religion, and you will have made a step towards believing that the Church of Christ has higher aims than the disputes respecting the observance of Easter, or the shape of the clerical tonsure.

Secondly, this combination of study round one main object solves, in part, the difficulty which I noticed in my first Lecture, respecting the relations of Civil and Ecclesiastical History. The subordinate persons and events of each may be easily divided from one another. But the greater characters of necessity combine both elements; they are the meeting-points of the two spheres of human life; they rise above the point of divergence; they show that in the most important moments of social and individual action all the influences of life, physical, intellectual, political, moral, come together : in these cases, whatever we may do elsewhere, we cannot disentangle the web without breaking it. Those divisions of history which we sometimes see under the heads of "civil and military," "political" and "religious," though convenient for common wars or common controversies, yet utterly fail when they touch an age like the Reformation, though possible in the cases of Melanchthon or Jeremy Taylor, break down entirely when applied to Luther or Oliver Cromwell. The unity of purpose which is the main characteristic of any great mind, the close connection of leading ideas which is the main interest of any great age, is grievously marred when we have to seek the disjointed fragments from different quarters, and take up over and over again the thread of the same interrupted story.

II. Combination of Civil and Ecclesiastical History.

Thirdly, this same method will be a protection against the prevailing sin of ecclesiastical historians — exclusiveness and partiality.

III. Caution against partiality.

It is well known that Eusebius openly avows his intention of relating only those incidents in the lives of the martyrs of Palestine which would reflect credit on the Church, and that Milner constructs his whole history on the principle that he will omit all mention of ecclesiastical wickedness, and record only the specimens of ecclesiastical virtue. Such a process, however edifying and useful for certain purposes, yet is never wholly safe, and happily is rendered almost impossible as soon as we wish to consider the full character and bearings of any person or institution on which we are engaged. If once we are inspired with a genuine desire of seeing the man as he really was, if he was worth being seen at all, we shall not be satisfied unless we see him altogether. Here, as in so many other respects, the sacred history of the Jewish Church is our best example. We there see, not the half, but the whole of David. We are told not only of his goodness, but of his sins; and we can there judge how wonderfully the history of the Church has gained by such a frank disclosure: how thin, how pale in comparison, would that biography have been, had the darker side been suppressed and the bright side only exhibited. Such a completeness of view we are almost driven to take, when we explore, not one, but all the sources whence our knowledge can be drawn.[1] We may still lament that the story of the lion is so often told only by the man, that the lives and opinions of heretics can be traced only in the writings of the orthodox, that the clergy have been so often the sole historians of the crimes of the laity. But we shall have learned at least to know that there is another side, even when that side has been torn away or lost. We shall often find some ancient fragment or forgotten parchment, like that which vindicates Edwy and Elgiva from the almost unanimous calumny of their monastic enemies. We shall see that in the original biographies of Becket, partial though they be, enough escapes to reveal that he is not the faultless hero represented to us in modern martyrology.

The mere perusal of the indiscriminate praise and abuse lavished on the same person by two opposite historians is instructive, even for our guidance in the present. The mere collection of the cross-fire of vituperation from modern partisans is useful as teaching us distrust in any one-sided view of the past. Selden, who knew well the danger and falsehood of extremes, confines his advice on "ecclesiastical story" to this single point — to study the exaggerated statements of Baronius on the one side, and of the Magdeburg Centuriators on the other, "and be our own judges." Nor let any one suppose that this conflict of evidence renders the attainment of certainty impossible. Doubtless there are many points both in sacred and in common history, both in civil and ecclesiastical records, where we must be content to remain in suspense. History will have left half its work undone, if it does not teach us humility and caution. But essential truth can almost always be found, truth of all kinds can with due research be usually found: she lies, no doubt, in a well; but

_____
[1] See Lecture II.

we may be sure that she is there if we dig deep enough. In this labor teachers and students must all work together. What one cannot discover, many at work on the same point can often prove beyond doubt. Like Napoleon and his comrades, when lost in the quicksands of the Red Sea, let each ride out a different way, and the first that comes to firm ground bid the others halt and follow him.

Fourthly, this method of study will enable us all from time to time to set our foot on that firmest of all ground, IV. Reference to which every student of history ought to touch once original in his life, original authorities. We cannot do it al- authorities. ways, but by the mere necessity of exploring any one subject to the bottom we must do it at times. It will be a constant charm of the history of the Chosen People that there we shall rarely be absent from, at any rate, the nearest approaches which can now be made to the events described. But it will be a charm also in the minute investigation of any point in the later history, that, however well told by modern compilers, there is almost sure to be something in the original records which we should else have overlooked. How inestimable are the fragments of Hegesippus and the Epistle of the Church of Lyons embedded in the rhetoric of Eusebius! How lifelike, in the dead partisanship of Strype, are the letters, injunctions, and narratives of the actors whose words and deeds he so feebly undertakes to represent!

And original records are not confined merely to contemporaneous histories, nor even to contemporaneous literature, sermons, poems, laws, decrees. Study the actual statues and portraits of the men, the sculptures and pictures of the events: if they do not give us the precise image of the persons and things themselves, they give us at least the image left on those who came nearest to them. Study their monuments, their gravestones, their epitaphs, on the spots where they lie. Study, if possible, the scenes of the events, their aspect, their architecture, their geography; the tradition which has survived the history, the legend which has survived the tradition; the mountain, the stream, the shapeless stone, which has survived even history, and tradition, and legend.

Take two examples instead of a hundred. There are few

more interesting episodes in modern Ecclesiastical History than
Graves of that of the Scottish Covenanters. But the school
the Cove-
nanters. in which that episode must be studied is Scotland
itself. The caves, and moors, and moss-hags of the Western
Lowlands; the tales, which linger still, of the black charger
of Claverhouse, of the strange encounters with the Evil one,
of the cry of the plover and pewit round the encampments
on the hill-side, are more instructive than many books. The
rude gravestones which mark the spots where those were laid
who bore testimony to "the covenanted work of reformation,
"and Christ's kingly government of His house," bring before
us in the most lively, because in the most condensed, authentic, original form, the excited feeling of the time, and the
most peculiar traits of the religion of the Scottish people.
Their independence, their fervor, their fierceness, may have
belonged to the age. But hardly out of Scotland could be
found their stubborn endurance, their thirst for vengeance,
their investment of the narrowest questions of discipline and
ceremony with the sacredness of universal principles. We
almost fancy that we see the survivors of the dead spelling
and scooping out their savage rhymes on the simple monuments, each catching from each the epithets, the texts, the
names, almost Homeric in the simplicity and the sameness
with which they are repeated on those lonely tombstones from
shore to shore of the Scottish kingdom.

Or turn to a similar instance of kindred but wider interest.
The Cata- What insight into the familiar feelings and thoughts
combs. of the primitive ages of the Church can be compared to that afforded by the Roman catacombs! Hardly
noticed by Gibbon or Mosheim, they yet give us a likeness
of the life of those early times beyond that derived from any
of the written authorities on which Gibbon and Mosheim repose. Their very structure is significant; their vast extent,
their labyrinthine darkness, their stifling atmosphere, are a
standing proof both of the rapid spread of the Christian conversions, and of the active fury of the heathen persecutions.
The subjects of the sculptures and paintings place before us
the exact ideas with which the first Christians were familiar;
they remind us, by what they do not contain, of the ideas

with which the first Christians were not familiar. We see
with our own eyes the very stories from the Old and the
New Testament which sustained the courage of the early
martyrs, and the innocent festivities of the early feasts of
Christian love. The barbarous style of the sculptures, the
bad spelling, the coarse engraving of the epitaphs, impresses
upon us more clearly than any sermon the truth that God
chose the weak, and base, and despised things of the world
to bring to nought the things which are mighty. He who is
thoroughly steeped in the imagery of the catacombs will be
nearer to the thoughts of the early Church than he who has
learned by heart the most elaborate treatise even of Tertullian or of Origen.

And now, having set before you the method of the study
which, for all who enter upon it seriously, and in its Opportunities for this
general features even for all who enter upon it super- study.
ficially, is the most desirable, let me briefly notice some of the
special opportunities which we ourselves possess for following up
the study of all.

First, if there ever was a Church in which Ecclesiastical
History might be expected to flourish, it is the English. I. In the
Church of
Unlike almost all the other Churches of Europe, alone England.
in its constitution, in its origin, in its formularies, it touches all the
religious elements which have divided or united Christendom.
He may be a true son of the Church of England who is able to
throw himself into the study of the first Four Councils to which
the statutes of our constitution refer, or of the mediæval times
in which our cathedrals and parishes were born and nurtured.
He also may be a true son of the same who is able to hail as
fellow-workers the great Reformers of Wittenberg, of Geneva,
and of Zurich, whence flowed so strong an influence over at least
half of our present formularies. But he is the truest son of all
who, in the spirit of this union, feels himself free to sympathize
with the several elements and principles of good which the
Church of England has thus combined, who knows that the
strength of a national Church, especially of the Church of a
nation like ours, lies in the fact that it has never been
surrendered exclusively to any one theological influence, and
that the Christian faith which it has inherited from all

is greater than the differences which it has inherited from each.

The Prayer-book as it stands is a long gallery of Ecclesiastical History, which, to be understood and enjoyed thoroughly, absolutely compels a knowledge of the greatest events and names of all periods of the Christian Church. To Ambrose we owe the present form of our *Te Deum;* Charlemagne breaks the silence of our ordination prayers by the *Veni Creator Spiritus*.[1] The Persecutions have given us one creed, and the Empire another. The name of the first great Patriarch of the Byzantine Church closes our daily service; the Litany is the bequest of the first great Patriarch of the Latin Church, amidst the terrors of the Roman pestilence. Our collects are the joint productions of the Fathers, the Popes, and the Reformers. Our communion service bears the traces of every fluctuation of the Reformation, through the two extremes of the reign of Edward to the conciliating policy of Elizabeth, and the reactionary zeal of the Restoration. The more comprehensive, the more free, the more impartial is our study of any or every branch of Ecclesiastical History, the more will it be in accordance with the spirit and the letter of the Church of England.

Secondly, I cannot forbear to notice the special advantages vouchsafed to all of us in this place, as members of this great University. Its libraries enable us to pursue our cross-examination of ancient witnesses, our reproduction of ancient scenes and events through all the appliances of antiquarian and artistic knowledge. Its peculiar mixture of various characters and callings, students and studies, invites us to that fusion of lay and clerical, of modern and ancient, of common and sacred, which is so vital to a full understanding of our subject, yet which would be so easily lost in institutions more purely theological, more strictly professional. But, besides all this, the very place itself is teeming with history, if not of the more universal Church, yet of the Church of our own country, to which, sooner or later, our studies must be turned.

II. In the University of Oxford.

In those studies I trust that we shall find that " Alfred the " Great, our first Founder," did well to plant his seat of learning beside the venerable shrine of S. Frideswide. We shall be the better able to comprehend Duns Scotus and the schoolmen

[1] Daniel's Thesaurus Hymnologicus, i. 213, 290.

as we stand in the ancient quadrangle of Merton, or listen to the dim traditions of Brasenose. Mediæval theology and practice will stand out clearly in the quaint customs of Queen's, and the romantic origin of All Souls. The founders of Exeter and of New College will give us a true likeness of mediæval prelates, — architects, warriors, statesmen, and bishops, all in one. Wycliffe will assume a more distinct shape and form to those who trace his local habitation as Master of Balliol. Erasmus will not soon die out of our recollection when we remember the little college of Corpus, which he hoped would be to Great Britain what the Mausoleum was to Caria, and what the Pyramids were to Egypt. The unfinished splendor of Christ Church is the enduring monument of the magnificence and of the fall of Wolsey. The Reformation will not be unaptly represented to us in the day when the quadrangles were knee-deep in the torn leaves of the scholastic divines, or when Ridley and Latimer suffered for their faith beside the gate-way of Bocardo. Its successive retirements and advances have left their traces in the foundation of Wadham, Trinity, and Jesus. From St. John's began the counter-reformation of Laud. Magdalen and University are the two memorials of resistance and subservience to James II. From Lincoln and Pembroke sprang the great religious movement of Wesley and Whitfield, and Oriel will not allow us to forget that we too have witnessed a like movement in our own day, of various forms and various results, already become historical, which will at least help us to appreciate such events in former times, and to remember that we too are parts of the Ecclesiastical History of our country.

Finally, this leads us to the reflection that there will be probably many amongst my hearers who are looking for-III. In active clerical ward to an active life in the various ministrations, life. near and distant, of the English Church. They too will have in their different localities, in those from which they came hither, in those to which they will go hence, the same atmosphere of ancient times surrounding them, wherever their lot be cast. Our Ecclesiastical History is not confined to Oxford or to any one sacred city. Everywhere we shall find something to keep alive in our recollections the growth and spread of the Christianity of this great country. Almost every church and church-yard has its own antiquities. Almost every parish and every sect has its own strange spiritual experiences, past or present. In almost every county and province we may study those august trophies of Ecclesiastical History, instructive beyond those of almost any other country, our cathedrals. I need name but one, the most striking and the most obvious instance, the cradle of English Christianity, the seat of the English Primacy, my own proud cathedral, the Metropolitical Church of Canterbury.

But, beyond any mere antiquarian interest, there must also be many occasions, in the work of every English clergyman, when the history of the Church may yield lessons of a practical and substantial value in his manifold duties and labors. What those lessons are I shall trust in some measure to represent in my next Lecture. Meanwhile, let me express the hope and the stimulus which ought to be given by the thought that I shall be addressing myself, not merely to students, but to those who will have to turn their study into practice; not merely to the confined atmosphere of a lecture-room, but to a spirit blowing out from us and in upon us, to and from the four winds of heaven. There has been doubtless a tendency in past times (perhaps there will be in all times) which recent measures have wisely endeavored to counteract, a tendency to absorb the general functions of the University into the special departments of ecclesiastical thought and education. But we must not forget that there is also an academical narrowness, and dryness, and stiffness; and that there is, on the other hand, an ecclesiastical breadth, and freedom, and warmth, which is for that evil, if not the highest, at least to many of us the nearest, remedy. To think that any words here spoken, any books here studied, may enliven discourses and ministrations far away in the dark corners of London alleys, in the free air of heaths and downs in north or south, on western mountains or in eastern fens; that records of noble deeds achieved, and of wise sayings uttered, long ago, may lend a point to practical precepts, or soften needless differences, or raise dull souls heavenward, or give a firmer grasp on truth; — this will of itself cheer many an hour of labor here. In that labor and with that hope it is for all of us to join. By constant communication of mutual knowledge, by contribution of the results of the several researches and gifts of all, students and learners will really be to their Professor not only (according to the well-known and now almost worn-out saying of Niebuhr) his wings, but also his feet, and his hands, and his eyes. By bearing in mind the large practical field in which our work may be afterwards used, we shall all bring to the very driest bones of our study sinews, and flesh, and blood, and breath, and spirit, and life.

III.

THE ADVANTAGES OF ECCLESIASTICAL HISTORY.

In my first Lecture, when defining the province of Ecclesiastical History, I was led to describe it in its widest extent; in my second, when stating the method by which life could be given to the study, I was led to dwell upon its narrower limits. And we must endeavor, in our future course, never, whilst studying the parts, to forget the whole; nor ever so to lose ourselves in the whole, as to neglect the study of one or more of the parts. Breadth without accuracy, accuracy without breadth, are almost equal evils.

In the present Lecture I propose to consider some of the chief practical advantages of the study.

Whatever may be the uncertainties of History, whatever its antiquarian prejudices, whatever its imaginative temptations, there is at least one sobering and enlarging effect always to be expected from it — that it brings us down from speculations and fancies to what at least profess to be facts, and that those facts transport us some little distance from the interests and the illusions of the present. This is especially true of History in connection with Theology. As it is one of the main characteristics of Christianity itself, that alone of all religions it claims to be founded on historical fact; that its doctrines and precepts, in great measure, have been conveyed to us in the form of History; and that this form has given them a substance, a vitality, a variety, which could, humanly speaking, have been attained in no other way; so we need not fear to confess that the same connection has existed through all the subsequent stages of the propagation of the religion. " The " disciple is not above his Master: " Theology is not above Christianity : the Christian Church is in many respects the best practical exposition of the Christian Religion. Facts are still the

I. Importance of facts in theological study.

most powerful, the most solid, the most stubborn guides in the mazes of speculation and casuistry ; they cut through difficulties which arguments cannot overturn ; they overturn theories which will surrender to nothing else. Ecclesiastical History is thus, as it were, the backbone of Theology. It keeps the mind of the theological student in an upright state. Often as facts are per-verted, and twisted, and bent to meet a purpose, yet they offer a sterner resistance than anything else short of the primary in-stincts of humanity.

They offer, too, not only the most convincing, but the least irritating modes of persuasion, an advantage in theological mat-ters of no mean importance. The wrath which is kindled by an anathema, by an opinion, by an argument, is often turned away by a homely fact. It is like suddenly meeting an enemy face to face, of whom we have known only by report ; he is different from what we expected ; we cannot resist the pressure of his hand and the glance of his eye ; he has ceased to be an abstraction, he has become a person. How many elaborate arguments respect-ing terms of salvation and terms of communion are shivered to pieces, yet without offence, almost without resistance, as they are " walked through " (if I may use the expression) by such hea-thens as Socrates, such Nonconformists as Howard, such Quak-ers as Elizabeth Fry.

This applies more and more strongly as our range of facts is enlarged. The more numerous and the more varied are the objects which we embrace within our range of vision, the less likely are we to place our trust in what Bacon well calls " the " idols of the cave," in which our own individual lot is cast.

It will be vain to argue, on abstract grounds, for the absolute and indefeasible necessity of some practice or ceremony, of which we have learned from history that there is no instance for one, two, three, or four hundred years, in the most honored ages of the Church. It will be vain to denounce as subversive of Chris-tianity, doctrines which we have known from biography to have been held by the very saints, martyrs, and reformers whom else we are constantly applauding. Opinions and views which, in a familiar and modified form, waken in us no shock of surprise, or even command our warm admiration, will often for the first time be truly apprehended when we see them in the ritual or the

9

creed of some rival, or remote, or barbarous Church, which is
but the caricature and exaggeration of that which we ourselves
hold.   Practices which we insist on retaining or repudiating, as
if they involved the very essence of the Catholic faith or of the
Reformation, will appear less precious or less dangerous, as the
case may be, in the eyes of the respective disputants, if history
shows us clearly that we thereby make ourselves, on the one
hand, more papal than the Pope, more Roman than Rome ; on
the other hand, more Lutheran than Luther, more Genevan than
Calvin.

If this be the effect of the study of even isolated facts of
II. Impor- Christian history, much more will it result from the
tance of a study of the general phenomena which mark its course.
general
view of There may be a tendency in special subjects of ecclesi-
Ecclesi-
astical astical study to cramp and narrow the mind, but there
History. is none such in the more general view, which embraces
its relations to the world at large, and which compels us to
view the lay as well as the clerical element of the Church, the
broad secular framework in which the whole Church itself is
set.

It is always useful to see, as must be seen in any extensive
survey, how large a portion of our ecclesiastical diversities is to
be traced, not to religious causes, but to the more innocent, and
in one sense irresistible, influences of nation, of climate, of race,
of the general course of human affairs.   The bitterness of English partisanship will be greatly diminished in proportion as we
recognize the fact, that the divergence between the Church of
England and Nonconformists springs from differences not so
much of theological principle or opinion, as of social and hereditary position.   The greater divisions of Christendom can be
regarded " calmly and kindly," in proportion as we are able to
take in, as from a summit, the whole view of which they form
the intersecting lines.   What seemed, near at hand, to be mere
deformities, from a more distant point are lost in the sense of the
vast prospect to which each feature contributes its peculiar part.
The most cursory view of the various sects and Churches of
the world will make us suspect that we are not all truth and
goodness, nor they all error and vice.   The very names of the
chiefest among them, Greek and Latin, Gallican, Anglican,

will show us how much of the distinction between them must be traced simply to national and geographical influences.

Nor let it be supposed that a philosophical or a general view of Ecclesiastical History is of necessity a cold or contemptuous view. There is, it is true, a melancholy feeling suggested by any wide contemplation of Christendom. We think of the contrast between the story as it might have been and the story as it is. We ask what ought to have been " more noble or " more beautiful than the gradual progress of the Spirit of light " and love, dispelling the darkness of folly, and subduing into " one divine harmony all the jarring elements of evil; " and we have in its place (if I may use words the more touching from the keenness of regret with which they were uttered), " no " steady, unwavering advance of heavenly spirits, but one con- " tinually interrupted, checked, diverted from its course, driven " backward ; as of men possessed by some bewildering spell, " wasting their strength upon imaginary obstacles, hindering " each other's progress and their own, by stopping to analyze " and dispute about the nature of the sun's light till all were " blinded by it, instead of thankfully using its aid to show them " the right path onward." [1]

Most true, — yet even in its very sadness containing grounds of hope and consolation.

For, first, though the course of Ecclesiastical History be thus dark, there is always a bright side to be found in Ecclesiastical Biography.

Study the lives, study the thoughts, and hymns, and prayers, study the death-beds of good men. They are the salt, III. Use of not only of the world, but of the Church. In them the biography of we see, close at hand, what on the public stage of his- good men. tory we see through every kind of distorted medium and decep- tive refraction. In them we can trace the history, if not of " the Catholic Church," at least of " the Communion of Saints." The *Acta Sanctorum* were literally, as a great French historian has observed, the only light, moral and intellectual, of the cen- turies, from the seventh to the ninth, which may without exag- geration be called " the dark ages." [2]   " Their glories," it has

1 Arnold's Miscellaneous Works, p. 286.
2 Guizot's Lectures on the Civilization of France, c. xvii.

been well said, " shine far beyond the limits of their daily walk
" in life; their odors are wafted across the boundaries of un-
" friendly societies ; their spiritual seed is borne away, and takes
" root and bears manifold in fields far distant from the gardens
" of the Lord where they were planted." [1] We have to be on
our guard against the proverbial exaggerations of biographers;
we have to disentangle fable and legend from truth and fact.
But the profit is worth the risk; the work will be its own
reward. It is well known that, amidst the trials which beset
Henry Martyn the missionary, on his voyage to India, the study
in which he found his chief pleasure and profit was in the kindly
notices of ancient saints which form the redeeming points of
Milner's " History of the Church." " I love " (so he writes
in his diary) " to converse, as it were, with those holy bishops
" and martyrs, with whom I hope, through grace, to spend a
" happy eternity. . . . The example of the Christian saints in
" the early ages has been a source of sweet reflection to me. . . .
" The holy love and devout meditations of Augustine and Am-
" brose I delight to think of. . . . No uninspired sentence ever
" affected me so much as that of the historian, that to believe,
" to suffer, and to love, was the primitive taste." [2] What he
so felt and expressed may be, and has been, felt by many
others. Such biographies are the common, perhaps the only
common, literature alike of rich and poor. Hearts, to whom
even the Bible speaks in vain, have by such works been roused
to a sense of duty and holiness. However cold the response
of mankind has been to other portions of ecclesiastical story,
this has always commanded a reverential, even an excessive
attention.

Let us also remember, that what there is of instruction here
is exactly of the kind which we ought to expect. Christianity
affects the springs of action, rather than the actions themselves;
from its very beginning it has been seen in the lowly rather than
the lofty places of the world; in the manger of Bethlehem, in
the peasants of Galilee, in the caves and dens of the earth: we
may therefore fairly look for its chief influences out of the beaten
track of history; when we cannot trace it on the great highway

[1] Wilson's Bampton Lectures, p. 275.
[2] Memoir of Henry Martyn, pp. 127, 130, 136.

of the world, we may fairly conclude that its effects will be found in the corners and pathways of life : —

> " Sprinkled along the waste of years,
> Full many a soft green isle appears :
> Pause where we may along the desert road,
> Some shelter is in sight, some sacred, safe abode."

On the other hand, if we turn from the case of individual Christians to the case of the great masses of individuals which form the main bulk of the Church, they too have a lesson to teach, less palpable, but by no means to be despised, though it has been sometimes pushed to exaggeration.

IV. Use of the general authority of the Church.

We know the old saying of Vincentius, " Quod semper, quod " ubique, quod ab omnibus," " Believe what has been believed " always, everywhere, and by everybody." It is needless to repeat the arguments by which it can be shown that, in a literal sense, this axiom is always either untrue or inapplicable. The solitary protest[1] is always to be honored — the lonely martyr is avenged at last. Churches and nations, and whole generations, often seem to lose their reason. Baronius himself confesses that in the Church of the tenth century there was no pilot to guide the helm, no captain to command the crew, at the moment of its greatest need.

But still the maxim of Vincentius contains a certain element of truth, which the facts of history entirely confirm. There is a common sense in the Church, as there is a common sense in the world, which cannot be neglected with impunity ; and there is an eccentricity in individuals and in sects which always tends to lead us, if not into dangerous, at least into crooked paths. The error which is held by great, ancient, and national communities, often loses its mischief, and entirely changes its meaning, when it becomes part of the general established belief. The truth which is held by a narrow sect often becomes error, from the mere fact of the isolation and want of proportion in which it is held.[2] The strange folly of Christians persecuting

1 See Lecture VII.

2 In the able essay by M. Renan, " On the Future of Religion " (Revue des Deux Mondes, Oct. 15, 1860), where he considers the prospects of the

Christians was first introduced on a large scale, not by the Orthodox, but by the heretics, of the fourth and fifth centuries. The fancies of Millenarians, however innocent and natural, and however widely diffused among small circles, have always been resisted by the robust sense of the universal Church. It is not, as a general rule, the larger, but the lesser congregations of Christendom, that have imposed the most minute and petty restrictions on opinion and practice. Whilst the Imperial, venerable, Orthodox Church of the whole East is content to repose on the short Creed of the first Councils, the little Church and State of Brunswick, under the auspices of Duke Julius, requires, or did require till recently, from its ministers a stringent subscription, not only to the three Creeds, the Augsburg Confession, the Apology for the Confession, and the Smalcaldic Articles, but to all that is contained in all the works of Luther, in all the works of Melanchthon, in all the works of Chemnitz. The "Nine Articles" of "the Evangelical Alliance" impose a yoke on the freedom of thought and conscience far heavier than that of the Thirty-nine Articles of the Church of England.

In fact, the higher and wider is the sweep of vision, the more difficult is it to stumble at trifles, and make mountains out of mole-hills. Power, no doubt, is often frightfully abused, whether in the hands of ecclesiastics or of laymen ; but to both, if there be any nobleness of character on which to work, it brings far more moderation and largeness of heart than is attainable by even better men in inferior stations. It was the charity and the wisdom of the Popes which protected the Jews in the Middle Ages against the fanatical attacks of individual zealots. The royal heart of the young King Edward was softer than the mercies even of a gentle prelate. Oliver Cromwell, when he came to wield the power of Church and State, of universities and of armies alike, was tolerant to a degree which his humbler followers were incapable of imitating or understanding.

It is difficult to express the deference due to these considera-

Catholic, the National, and the sectarian principle, I venture to think that the gifted writer, in the preference which he awards to the third of these principles, has overlooked the historical proofs of its inferiority to either of the two former, in all that regards true toleration and comprehensiveness, whatever may have been its services in other respects.

tions, without placing them below or above their just estimate.
But they form too obvious, too important, I may add too con-
soling, an inference from the course of ecclesiastical events, to
be omitted altogether.　Let us receive the fact both as an encouragement and as a caution.　Whatever other charges may be
brought against the history of Christendom, and however much
it may have embraced within or alongside of itself sallies of wild
sectarianism, yet it cannot fairly be called the history of Fanaticism, or even of Enthusiasm.　Gray hairs and high station
and long experience, whether of individuals or of communities,
have their own peculiar claims to respect.　The movement of
the Church to perfection has in it an element of solidity, of permanence, and of prudence, as well as of fluctuation and progress
and zeal.

But yet further, even when we consider more deeply the
darker points in our general view, a sense of unity v. Better
emerges from the midst of disunion, a sense of suc- understanding of
cess from the midst of failure.　Errors and truths differences
and of
which we are apt to ascribe to special sects, Churches, unity.
individuals, will often be seen to belong really to characters and
principles which underlie and countersect the artificial distinctions on the surface of controversy.　The ingenious essays in
which Archbishop Whately traces " the errors of Romanism "
to the general fallacies latent in every creed and every Church,
might be extended to all kinds of theological division.　The
celebrated treatise of Bossuet on " the Variations of Protes-
" tantism " might be overlaid by an instructive work on a larger
basis, in a more generous spirit, and with a nobler object, " the
" Variations of the Catholic Church," showing how wide a range
of diversities even the most ancient and exclusive communities
have embraced ; how many opposing principles, practices, and
feelings, like the creeks or valleys of some narrow territory, overlap, traverse, infold, and run parallel with each other into the
very heart of the intervening country, where we should least expect to find them.　Reformers, before the Reformation ; Popes,
in chairs not of S. Peter ; " new presbyter but old priest writ
" large ; " " old foes with new faces ; " heresy under the garb
of orthodoxy, orthodoxy under the garb of heresy ; they who
hold, according to the ancient saying, τὰ αἱρετικὰ καθολικῶς, and

they also who hold τὰ καθολικὰ αἱρετικῶς ; — strange companions will be thus brought together from the east and from the west, from the north and from the south. Pelagius lurks under the mitre of Chrysostom or the cowl of Jerome ; Loyola will find himself by the side of Wesley ; John Knox will recognize a fellow-worker in Hildebrand ; the austerities of Benedict, the intolerance of Dominic, will find their counterpart at Geneva and in Massachusetts ; the missionary zeal of the Arian Ulfilas, of the Jesuit Xavier, and of the Protestant Schwarz will be seen to flow from the same source. The judgment of history will thus far be able to anticipate the judgment of Heaven, and to supersede with no doubtful hand the superficial concords and the superficial discords which belong to things temporal, by the true separation and the true union which belong to things eternal.

But it is not only as a matter of wisdom and charity, but as a
VI. Evidence rendered to the truth of Christianity.
ground of Christian evidence, that a large view of ecclesiastical differences is specially useful. In the diversity of the Church will be found a more powerful argument for the divine origin of Christianity itself, than in the most perfect unity. It is not, humanly speaking, surprising that a religion should sustain itself from age to age in the same race and country. We argue truly that such a restriction was needed as a support, not for the strength, but for the infirmities of Judaism ; we argue truly against the universal truth of Mahometanism, that it has never been able permanently to establish itself in any but an Eastern climate. But the distinguishing characteristic of the Christian Church has been, that it has assumed different forms, and yet not perished in the process ; that the gulf, however wide, which separates Greek from Latin, and both from Protestant, has yet not been wide enough to swallow up the common Christianity which has been transmitted from one to the other. And, in like manner, to recognize the influence of races, institutions, and political convulsions on the history of the Church is assuredly, not to diminish, but to exalt its importance to men and to nations ; not to underrate its mission, but to represent it in its full grandeur. Nothing less than one of the prime agencies of the world could be so interwoven with the progress of great events, or in its different manifestations fall in so readily

with the broad lines of demarcation which Nature herself has drawn between the various branches of the human family.

And, yet further, the very imperfections and failings of the Church may tend to give us both a more sober and a more hopeful view of its ultimate prospects. The alarms, the dangers, the persecutions, the corruptions through which it has safely passed, are so many guarantees that it is itself indestructible. The fact that these obstructions to Christian truth and goodness are found, not in one Church only, but in all, instead of causing restlessness and impatience, ought to dispose us to make the best of our lot, whatever it be. We learn that every Church partakes of the faults, as well as of the excellences, of its own age and country ; that each is fallible as human nature itself ; that each is useful as a means, none perfect as an end. To find Christ *or* Antichrist exclusively in any one community is against charity and against humility, but, above all, against the plain facts of history. Let us hold this truth firmly, and we shall have then secured ourselves against two of the worst evils which infest the well-being of religious communities, the love of controversy and the love of proselytizing. *VII. Lessons from the failings of the Church.*

Every such reflection forces us back on a consideration which is both a chief safeguard and a chief advantage of Ecclesiastical History, the comparison which it suggests between what the Church is, and what in the Scriptures it was intended to be ; between what it has been, and what from the same source we trust that it may be. *VIII. Advantages of a comparison of Ecclesiastical History with the Scriptures.*

It is hard to say whether, by such a comparison, the study of the Bible or the study of Ecclesiastical History is most the gainer.

What is the history of the Church[1] but a long commentary on the sacred records of its first beginnings ? It is a fulfilment of prophecy in the truest and widest sense of that word ; a fulfilment, not merely of predictions of future events, but of that higher and deeper spirit of prophecy which " makes mani-

---

[1] " The fulness of the stream is the glory of the fountain ; and it is because the Ganges is not lost among its native hills, but deepens and widens until it reaches the ocean, that so many pilgrimages are made to its springs." — *Bishop Thirlwall's Charge,* 1857, p. 81.

"fest the secrets of the heart." The thoughts and deeds of good
Christians are still, as in the Apostolic times, a living Bible;
an Epistle, a Gospel, "written on the hearts of men, known
"and read of all men." The various fortunes of the Church
are the best explanation, as they are the best illustration, of the
parables which unfold the course of the kingdom of heaven.
The failures of the Church are but the fulfilments of the mournful, almost pensive, anticipations of its history (how unlike the
triumphant exultations of so many human founders of human
sects!), — "not peace, but a sword;" "a fire kindled on the
"earth;" "a savor of death unto death."

The actual effects, the manifold applications, in history, of
the words of Scripture, give them a new instruction, and afford
a new proof of their endless vigor and vitality. Look through
any famous passage of the Old, or yet more of the New, Testament: there is hardly one that has not borne fruit in the conversion of some great saint, or in the turn it has given to some
great event. At a single precept of the Gospels, Antony went
his way and sold all that he had; at a single warning of the
Epistles, Augustine's hard heart was melted beneath the fig-tree
at Milan; a single chapter of Isaiah made a penitent believer of
the profligate Rochester. A word to S. Peter has become the
stronghold of the Papacy; a word from S. Paul has become
the stronghold of Luther. The Psalter alone, by its manifold
applications and uses in after times, is a vast palimpsest, written
over and over again, illuminated, illustrated, by every conceiv-
able incident and emotion of men and of nations; battles, wanderings, dangers, escapes, death-beds, obsequies, of many ages
and countries, rise, or may rise, to our view, as we read it.

Nor is it only in special passages that the history of the
Church sets before us the greatness of its origin. It is on looking back upon a mountain range which we have left, that we
often for the first time understand its true character. The
peaks, which in a nearer view were all confused, now stand out
distinct; the line of heights is drawn out in its full length; the
openings and passes disentangle themselves from the surrounding
valleys; the nearer and lesser objects now sink to their proper
level, as they are seen backed and overtopped by the lofty range
behind and above them. Even so do we, at the distance of

eighteen hundred years, see in many respects the truths of Scripture with a clearer vision than they who lived even amidst their recesses or at their very foot. We who have traversed the long levels of Ecclesiastical History can see what they of old time could not see, the elevation of those divine words and acts, as compared with any that followed. We can see, as they could not see, the wide circumference of objects which those words and acts overlooked, embraced, comprehended. We can distinguish, as they could not distinguish, the relative importance, the due proportions, the general outline, of the various heights, and can sketch our picture and direct our steps accordingly.

The very extent of our departure from the original truth; the very violence which in successive ages has been put upon the sacred words; the attempts to warp them by false interpretation or by false teaching, or to overlay them by theories or forgeries of a later date, only bring us in a more lively and instructive form what was the point from which we started, what is the difference of the point to which we have now arrived. In that coarse but instructive tale in which Dean Swift described the development of Ecclesiastical History, when the father's will is at last brought to light by the three contending brothers, nothing could more clearly impress upon them the sense of its true meaning than the recollection of the artifices by which they had been induced to discover in it the sanction of their own deviations from it. "If not *totidem sententiis*, then *totidem verbis*; "if not *totidem verbis*, then *totidem literis*." So, with hardly an exaggeration, has Scripture been often handled. The next best clue to reading an oracle straightforwardly and honestly, is to be aware that we have been reading it backwards. The allegorical interpretations given by the early Fathers are virtual confessions that they have not attempted to expound the original meaning of the sacred authors. The variations of reading or rendering, which copyists or translators of later times have introduced into the text of the Scriptures, are positive proofs that they found the actual words insufficient to express the altered views of their own age. The attention paid to passages manifestly of secondary importance, and the neglect of passages manifestly of the very highest importance, may serve as gauges both of what we have hitherto lost and of what we may still hope to gain, in the application of the Scriptures to the wants of Ecclesiastical History.

This peculiar relation of the Bible to the history of the Church IX. Future invites one concluding train of thought. When, six-prospects of teen years ago, a revered teacher stood in this place, Ecclesiasti-cal History. and, after a survey of the field of Modern History, asked whether there were in the existing resources of the nations of mankind any materials for a new epoch, distinct from those which have gone before, you may remember how he answered that there were none. What if the same question be asked with regard to the prospects of Ecclesiastical History? We have seen that four great phases have passed over the fortunes of the Church: is there likely to be another? We are told that the resources of nation and race are exhausted for the outer world in which our history moves: are there any stores of spiritual strength yet unexplored in the forces of the Christian Church? With all reverence and with all caution, may not the reflections which we have just made encourage us to hope that such a mine does exist, a virgin mine, in the original records of Christianity? We need not speculate on the probable destinies of any Christian system or community now existing in the world; we need not determine whether, as our own Protestant historian has declared, the Papacy may still be standing ages hence,[1] after England shall have passed away; or whether, with the chiefs of Italian liberalism, we are to believe that it is steadily advancing year by year to the grave already dug to receive it. Still less need we compose volumes of future Ecclesiastical History out of fancied interpretations of the Apocalypse, in defiance alike of all human experience, all divine warnings. But a serious comparison of the actual contents of the Scriptures with the actual course of ecclesiastical events almost inevitably brings us to the conclusion that the existing materials, principles, and doctrines of the Christian Religion are far greater than have ever yet been employed; that the Christian Church, if it ever be permitted or enabled to use them, has a long lease of new life, and new hope before it, such as has never yet been enjoyed. Look at the Bible on the one hand, and History on the other; see what

[1] Macaulay's Essays, vol. iv. p. 301.

are the points on which the Scriptures lay most emphatic stress; think how much of the sap and life of Christendom has run to leaf, and not to fruit; remember how constant is the protest of Scripture, and, we may add, of the best spirits of the universal Church, against preferring any cause of opinion or ceremony to justice, holiness, truth, and love; observe how constantly and steadily all these same intimations point to One Divine Object, and One only, as the centre and essence of Christianity : — we cannot, with these experiences, hesitate to say, that, if the Christian Church be drawing to its end, or if it continue to its end with no other objects than those which it has hitherto sought, it will end with its acknowledged resources confessedly undeveloped, its finest hopes of usefulness almost untried and unattempted. It will have been like an ungenial spring cut short in full view of the summer, a stately vessel wrecked within the very sight of the shore.

It may be that the age for creating new forms of the Christian faith is past and gone, that no new ecclesiasti- Indications cal boundaries will henceforth be laid down amongst in History. men. It is certain that in the use of the old forms is our best chance for the present. Use them to the utmost; use them threadbare, if you will : long experience, the course of their history, their age and dignity, have made them far more elastic, far more available, than any that we can invent for ourselves. But do not give up the study of the history of the Church, either in disgust at what has been, or in despair at what may be. The history of the Christian Church, no less than of the Jewish, bears witness to its own incompleteness. The words which describe its thoughts constantly betray their deflection from the original ideas which they were meant to express; " Church, Gospel, Catholic, Evangelical," the very word " Ecclesiastical," as I noticed in first speaking of it, are now too often the mere shadows, sometimes even the exact opposites, of their ancient, orthodox, scriptural meaning. We need only trace the steps of their gradual descent to their present signification, in order to see how far they, and we with them, have to ascend again before we can reach the point from which they started, the point to which we have still to attain. Read, too, the expressions of the best and

wisest Christians in their best and wisest moments. Take
them, not in the passion of youth, not in the heat of controversy, not in the idleness of speculation, but in the presence
of some great calamity, or in the calmness of age, or in the
approach of death. Take that admirable summary of mature
Christian experience, which ought to be in the hands of every
student of Ecclesiastical History, — one might well add, of
every student of theology, of every English minister of religion,
— which is contained in Baxter's review of his own narrative
of his life and times.[1] See how he there corrects the narrowness, the sectarianism, the dogmatism of his youth, by the
comprehensive wisdom acquired in long years of persecution,
of labor, and devotion. Let us hope that what he has expressed as the result of his individual experience, we may find
and appropriate in the collective experience of the old age of
the Church.

Then turn and observe how with this best witness of Chris-
Indications tendom, the best witness of Christianity, as set forth
in Scripture. in the Scriptures, entirely agrees. Take any of the
chapters of the Old or New Testament, to which Prophets
and Apostles appeal as containing, in their judgment, the sum
and substance of their message ; take, above all, the summary
of all Evangelical and Apostolical truth in the Four Gospels.
Read them parallel with the so-called religious wars and controversies of former ages. Read them parallel with the so-
called enlightenment, and the so-called religious sects and
parties and journals, of our own age. Read, and fear, and
hope, and profit, by the extent of the contrast.

Doubtless there is much in the study of the Scriptures that
is uncertain and difficult. But this is nothing in comparison
with the light they have still to give, both in checking our
judgment of the past, in guiding our judgment of the present
and future. We may in former times have gone too much
by their letter and too little by their spirit ; but it has been
far oftener our fault that we have gone neither by letter nor
by spirit ; it has far oftener happened that, however much the
spirit .may be above the letter, yet the letter is far beyond

1 The whole passage may be conveniently read in Wordsworth's Ecclesiastical Biography, vol. v. pp. 559–597.

the spirit in which we have often been accustomed to deal with it. Each age of the Church has, as it were, turned over a new leaf in the Bible, and found a response to its own wants. We have a leaf still to turn, a leaf not the less new because it is so old, not the less full of consequences because it is so simple.

Of all the advantages which Ecclesiastical History can yield, this stimulus to a study of the Scriptures is the most important. That study, except to a limited extent, does not fall within our sphere ; the province of History, as such, will be sufficient to employ us ; and it will indeed be an ample reward, if I can be enabled, in any way, to give a new charm or a firmer basis to this great subject. But it would be a reward and an object far higher, if I could, in however slight a measure, make it point to the grandeur and the truth of that which is beyond itself ; if the study of the history of the Church should, by way of contrast, or illustration, or comparison, rouse any one to a deeper faith in the power and the design of the Bible, a stronger belief in what it has already done, a higher hope and clearer understanding of what its words may yet effect for us,[1] in the chapters of living history in which we or the coming generations may bear a part.

I ventured to commence this Introductory Course with the description of the treasures which were shown to the Pilgrim in the palace by the highway-side ; I will close it with the prospect which he beheld thence on the far-distant horizon, described in words too sacred, in part, perhaps, for us to use, but not too sacred for the truth and the hope which I have humbly, but in all seriousness, endeavored to set before you as the conclusion of the whole matter : —

" Then I saw in my dream, that on the morrow he got up " to go forwards, but they desired him to stay till the next " day also : and then, said they, we will, . . . if the day be " clear, . . . show you the Delectable Mountains : which, " said they, would further add to his comfort, . . . because " they were nearer to the desired haven than where at pres-

---

[1] For same thoughts, powerfully expressed, I cannot forbear to refer to the Essays of Dr. Temple and Professor Jowett (pp. 44 – 48, 404 – 418).

" ent he was. . . . So he consented and staid. When the
" morning was up, they had him to the top of the house, and
" bid him look south. So he did, and behold, . . . at a great
" distance, . . . he saw a most pleasant mountainous country
" — beautified with woods, vineyards, fruits of all sorts, flowers
" also, with springs and fountains, very delectable to behold.
" Then he asked the name of the country. They said it was
" ' Immanuel's Land ; ' . . . ' and it is as common,' said they,
" ' as this hill is to and for all the pilgrims. And when thou
" comest there, . . . from thence thou mayest see to the gate
" of the Celestial City, . . . as the shepherds that live there
" will make appear.' "

LECTURES ON THE HISTORY

OF

THE EASTERN CHURCH.

WORKS FOR REFERENCE, ON THE HISTORY OF THE EASTERN CHURCH.

THE following are the chief works which may be consulted with advantage on the general condition of the Eastern Church:

1. *Oriens Christianus.* By Michael le Quien. (French Dominican.) 1661–1732. An account of the Eastern dioceses, their extent, and the occupants of their sees from their foundation to 1732. 3 vols. folio.

2. *Bibliotheca Orientalis.* By Joseph Simon Assemanni. (Maronite Archbishop, Librarian of the Vatican.) 1687–1768. An account of the writers and manuscripts of Syria, Arabia, Egypt, and Æthiopia.

3. *Liturgiarum Orientalium Collectio.* By Eusebius Renaudot. (French Jesuit.) 1646–1720. 2 vols. 4to.

4. *Nomocanon.* (Collection of the Ecclesiastical Laws of the Greek Church, by Photius.) Edited at Paris, 1615.

5. *Euchologium* (sive *Rituale Græcum*). Jacob Goar. 1647.

6. *Codex Liturgicus Ecclesiæ Orientalis.* H. A. Daniel. Leipsic, 1853.

7. *Libri Symbolici Ecclesiæ Orientalis.* (Collection of modern Confessions of the Eastern Church.) Kimmel, at Jena, 1843.

8. Lives of the Eastern Saints are contained in the *Menologium Græcum*, or in the Latin translations of Symeon Metaphrastes, in the *Vitæ Sanctorum* of Laurence Surius. 1587.

9. Account of the eminent Writers of the Greek Church in Fabricius, *Bibliotheca Græca*, vols. vii.–xii.

10. *De Græcæ Ecclesiæ hodierno Statu.* By Thomas Smith. 1698.

11. *State of the Greek Church.* By J. Covell, D. D. 1722.

12. *Rites and Ceremonies of the Greek Church.* By John King, Chaplain at St. Petersburg. 1787.

13. *History of the Holy Eastern Church.* By John Mason Neale, M. A., Warden of Sackville College. Of this laborious and learned work two portions only have yet appeared:

    1. *The Patriarchate of Alexandria.* (See infra.)

    2. *The General Introduction.* 2 vols. 8vo. 1850.

To this, rather than to more recondite sources, I have usually referred the reader for the constitution and customs of the Oriental Church. I may also mention an excellent essay on *The Eastern Church,* which appeared as a review of Mr. Neale's work, in the Edinb. Rev. vol. cvii. p. 322.

For the general sentiment of the Eastern Churches a few works out of many are selected:

    1. *Dissertations on the Orthodox, or Eastern, Communion.* By William Palmer, M. A., late Fellow of Magdalen College, Oxford, and Deacon. 1853.

    2. *Question Religieuse de l'Orient et de l'Occident.* Moscow, 1856. *Lettres à un Ami sur l'Office Divin.* St. Petersburg, 1850. By Andrew Nicolaivitch Mouravieff.

    3. *Quelques Mots par un Chrétien Orthodoxe.* Paris, 1853; Leipsic, 1855, 1858. (See Lecture XII.)

    4. *Introduction to Orthodox Theology.* By Macarius, Rector of the Ecclesiastical Academy at St. Petersburg. Translated into French. 1857.

On more special subjects:

I. CHALDÆANS AND NESTORIANS.

    1. *Bibliotheca Orientalis,* vol. iv. (Assemanni.)

    2. *The Nestorians and their Rituals.* By the Rev. G. P. Badger. 1852.

II. ARMENIA.

    1. *Hist. d'Arménie et d'Ethiopie et des Indes.* By Mathurin de La Croze. (French merchant and scholar.) 1661–1739.

    2. Haxthausen's *Trans-Caucasia.* Translated into English. 1854.

    3. *Histoire, Dogmes, Traditions, et Liturgie de l'Eglise Arméniane.* By E. Dulaurier. Paris, 1859.

III. SYRIA.

    1. *Bibliotheca Orient.* vol. ii. (Assemanni.)

    2. *The Syrian Churches.* By J. W. Etheridge. 1846.

IV. EGYPT.

1. *Annales Patriarcharum Alexandrinorum.* By Eutychius. (See p. 145.)

2. Renaudot's *Historia Patriarcharum Jacobitarum.* 1713.

3. Lane's *Modern Egyptians.* (Supplement.) 1833.

4. Sharpe's *Egypt.* (From the earliest times to the Arab conquest.) 1846.

5. Neale's *Patriarchate of Alexandria.* 2 vols. 8vo. 1847.

V. ABYSSINIA.

1. La Croze (ut supra).

2. *Hist. Æthiopiæ.* By Job Ludolf. (German lawyer.) 1624–1714.

3. Harris's *Highlands of Ethiopia.* 1844.

VI. GEOROIA.

1. *Mosheim. Instit. Hist. Eccles.* p. 632.

2. *Chardin's Travels.* Vol. i. p. 171–174.

3. *A Russian History of Georgia,* (by M. Jossilian,) is highly spoken of.

VII. CONSTANTINOPLE AND THE GREEK CHURCH.

1. *The Byzantine Historians.* Edited by Niebuhr.

2. Dufresne's *Glossarium Med. et Infim. Græcitatis.*

3. *History of the Byzantine Empire.* By G. Finlay. 1853.

4. *History of Greece,* from 1453 to 1843. By G. Finlay. 1861.

5. *De Græcis Illustribus* (the Greek scholars of the fifteenth century). By Humphrey Hody, D. D. 1742.

VIII. RUSSIA.

See Prefaces to Lectures IX. X. XI. XII.

For a summary history of the Eastern Church, see —

Gibbon, cc. 17, 20, 21, 23, 26–28, 32, 40, 47–49, 51, 54, 55, 60, 61, 66–68.

Gieseler's Ecclesiastical History (under the chapters, on " the Oriental Churches ").

LECTURES

ON

THE EASTERN CHURCH.

LECTURE I.

THE EASTERN CHURCH.

THE Eastern Church occupies a vast field of Ecclesiastical History. But it is a field rather of space than of time. It is marked out rather by tracts of land and races of men than by successive epochs in the progress of events, of ideas, or of characters. Hence has arisen the frequent remark that, properly speaking, the Eastern Church has no history. The nations which it embraces have been, for the most part, so stationary, and their life so monotonous, that they furnish few subjects of continuous narration. The influence which it has exercised on the onward course of religious opinion has been so slight, that by tacit consent it has almost dropped out of the notice of ecclesiastical historians. The languages in which its records and its literature are composed are such as to repel even the learned classes of the West; even the Greek dialect of the East after the sixth century becomes almost intolerable to the eye and the ear of the classical student. Its system has produced hardly any permanent works of practical Christian benevolence. With very few exceptions, its celebrated names are invested with no stirring associations. It seems to open a field of interest to travellers and antiquarians, not to philosophers or historians.

Is there anything in such a subject to repay the labor or even the attention of a theological student? Had we not better pass on at once to more fertile and more genial regions? Can any Englishman, can any Protestant, nay, can any European, be fairly asked to look backwards on a field which the course of civilization seems to have left far behind?

All this and much more may be said. Yet, on these very grounds, I feel that the Professor of Ecclesiastical History is bound, if possible, once for all, to cast that one backward glance before he moves onward. Once plunged in the turmoil of the West, he will have no leisure to turn to the repose of the East. And further, although few may enter into the details of its history or constitution, there are some general points of view under which the Eastern Church may be profitably considered. Out of the blank which the larger part of its annals presents, emerge some salient scenes and epochs which beyond question touch the universal destinies of mankind. There are some peculiar reasons why the study even of the near West may always gain by the study of the distant East.

This general view of the Oriental Church, — these leading divisions in its history, — these reasons for devoting a short space to its study, — it will be my endeavor to set forth in the present Lecture.

I. I have said that the field of Eastern Christendom is a comparatively untrodden field. It is out of sight, and therefore out of mind. But there is a wise German proverb which tells us that it is good, from time to time, to be reminded that "Behind the mountains there are people to be found." "Hinter dem Berge sind auch Leute." This, true of all large

General divisions of the Eastern Church.

bodies of the human family from whom we are separated by natural or intellectual divisions, is eminently true of the whole branch of the Christian family that lies in the far East. Behind the mountains of our knowledge, of our civilization, of our activity, — behind the mountains, let us also say, of our ignorance, of our prejudice, of our contempt, is to be found nearly a third part of Christendom — one hundred millions of souls professing the Christian faith. Even if we enter no further into their history, it is important to remember that they are there. No theory of the Christian Church can be complete which does not take some account of their existence. The proper distances, the lights and shades, of the foreground which we ourselves occupy, of the prospect which we ourselves overlook, cannot be rightly represented without bearing in mind the enormous, dark, perhaps unintelligible, masses which form the background that closes the retrospect of our view.

But the Oriental Church has claims to be considered over and above its magnitude and its obscurity. By whatever name we call it — "Eastern," "Greek," or "Orthodox" — it carries us back, more than any other existing Christian institution, to the earliest scenes and times of the Christian religion. Even though the annals of the Oriental Patriarchates are, for the most part, as regards the personal history of their occupants, a series of unmeaning names, the recollections awakened by the seats of their power are of the most august kind. Jerusalem, Antioch, Alexandria, are centres of local interest which none can see or study without emotion. And the Churches which have sprung up in those regions retain the ancient customs of the East, and of the primitive age of Christianity, long after they have died out everywhere else. Look for a moment

12

at the countries included within the range of the Oriental Churches. What they lose in historical they gain in geographical grandeur. Their barbarism and their degradation have bound them to the local peculiarities from which the more progressive Church of the West has shaken itself free. It is a Church, in fact, not of cities and villages, but of mountains, and rivers, and caves, and dens of the earth. The eye passes from height to height, and rests on the successive sanctuaries in which the religion of the East has intrenched itself, as within huge natural fortresses, against its oppressors — Athos in Turkey, Sinai in Arabia, Ararat in Armenia, the Cedars of Lebanon, the catacombs of Kieff, the cavern of Megaspelion, the cliffs of Meteora. Or we see it advancing up and down the streams, or clinging to the banks of the mighty rivers which form the highways and arteries of the wide plains of the East. The Nile still holds its sacred place in the liturgies of Egypt. The Jordan, from Constantine downwards, has been the goal of every Eastern pilgrim. Up the broad stream of the Dnieper sail the first apostles of Russia. Along the Volga and the Don cluster the mysterious settlements of Russian nonconformity.

In this natural framework,— with that strong identity of religion and race so familiar to the East, so difficult to be understood in the West,— may be traced three main groups of Churches, which we will proceed to distinguish.

1. The first group contains those isolated fragments of an earlier Christendom, which emerge here and there from the midst of Mahometanism and heathenism in Africa and Further Asia. In the strict language of ancient theology they must (with one exception) be called heretical sects. But they are in fact the National Churches of their respective

The NATIONAL or HERETICAL CHURCHES of the remote East.

countries, protesting against the supposed innovations [1] of the see of Constantinople, and holding with a desperate fidelity to forms and doctrines of earlier date. Easternmost of all the Eastern Churches, easternmost in thought and custom always, and usually easternmost in situation also, they supply, in the wild and romantic interest of their position and of their habits, their almost total want of theological literature or historical events. The characteristic fable of Prester John — the invisible Apostle of Asia — the imperial priestly potentate in the remote East, or the remote South,[2] fills up in their traditions the vacant space which in Europe was occupied by the Pope of Rome and the Emperor of Constantinople.

a) The "Chaldean Christians,"[3] called by their opponents "Nestorians," are the most remote of these old separatists. Only the two first councils, those of Nicæa and Constantinople, have weight with them. The third — of Ephesus — already presents the stumblingblock of the decree which condemned Nestorius. Living in the secluded fastnesses of Kurdistan, they represent the persecuted remnant of the ancient Church of Central Asia. They trace their descent to the earliest of all Christian missions — the mission of

The "Chaldean" or Nestorian Churches.

---

[1] It must be remarked that a confusion runs through all these Churches from a tripartite division, growing out of their relations with the Churches from which they have parted, or which have parted from them : 1. The National or so-called heretical Church of each country. 2. The Orthodox branch of each Church, in communion with the see of Constantinople. 3. The "United" or "Catholic" branch, consisting of converts to the Roman Catholic Church. As a usual rule, most writers of the Greek or Orthodox Church, as well as of our own, in speaking of these Churches, mean only the second of these two divisions ; most writers of the Roman Catholic Church only the third. For the sake of perspicuity, I confine myself in each case to the first or national division in each of the groups of which I speak. A masterly sketch of these heretical communions, with the main authorities on each, is found in Gibbon, c. xlvii. One exception to this classification will be noticed further on. The Georgian Church is both National and Orthodox.

[2] See Neale's Introduction, i. 114.

[3] See Neale, i. 145 ; Layard's Nineveh, i. 240.

Thaddæus to Abgarus. Their sacred city of Edessa is
identical with the cradle of all ecclesiastical history —
the traditional birthplace of Abraham.   In their present
seclusion they have been confounded, perhaps[1] have confounded themselves, with the lost tribes of Israel.   In
their earlier days they sent forth missions on a scale
exceeding those of any Western Church except the see
of Rome in the sixth and sixteenth centuries, and for
the time redeeming the Eastern Church from the usual
reproach of its negligence in propagating the Gospel.
Their chief assumed the splendid title of " Patriarch of
Babylon," and their missionaries traversed the whole of
Asia, as far eastward as China, as far southward as Cey-
lon.   One colony alone remains of this ancient dominion,
in extent even greater than the Papacy.   The Chris-
Christians   tians of S. Thomas, as they are called, are still
of S.
Thomas.   clustered round the tomb of S. Thomas, whether
the Apostle, or the Nestorian merchant of the same name
who restored if he did not found the settlement.   In the
ninth century they attracted the notice of Alfred, and, in
the sixteenth century, of the Portuguese, and it was in
reaction from the missionaries of Portugal that they
finally exchanged their Nestorianism for the Monophysitism of Egypt and Syria.[2]

   b) The Armenians[3] are by far the most powerful, and
The Ar-   the most widely diffused, in the group of purely
menian
Churches.   Oriental Churches of which we are now speaking, and as such exercise a general influence over all of
them.   Their home is the mountain tract that encircles

---

1 Asahel Grant's Nestorians, 109.
   2 See Neale, i. 145 ; Buchanan's Christian Researches, 76 ; Swanston's
Memoirs in Journal of Asiatic Researches, i. 129, ii. 235, iv. 235, 248.
   3 Neale, i. 65, 104. " The Armenian nation is widespread and numerous
as the waves of the sea. It is said to number fifteen millions of souls. This
may be an exaggeration ; but the existence of more than eight millions we
assert with confidence." — *Haxthausen's Transcaucasia,* 298, 325.

Ararat.[1] But, though distinct from all surrounding nations, they yet are scattered far and wide through the whole Levant, extending their episcopate, and carrying on at the same time the chief trade of Asia. A race, a church of merchant princes, they are in quietness, in wealth, in steadiness, the "Quakers" of the East, the "Jews," if one may so call them, of the Oriental Church. They were converted by Gregory the Illuminator in the fourth century, whose dead hand is still used for continuing the succession of the patriarchs. The seat of the patriarchate is Etchmiazin, their sacred city.[2] Their canonical scriptures include two books in the Old and two in the New Testament acknowledged by no other Church; the history of Joseph and Asenath, the Testament of the Twelve Patriarchs, the Epistle of the Corinthians to S. Paul, and the third Epistle of S. Paul to the Corinthians.[3] Of the extreme Oriental Churches, they furnish, by their wide dispersion, the closest links with the West. The boundary of Russia runs across Mount Ararat. The Protestant and the Papal missionaries have won from them the most numerous converts. They call themselves orthodox. They are divided from the Constantinopolitan Church by an almost imperceptible difference, arising, it is said, out of the accidental absence of the Armenian bishops from the Council of Chalcedon, whose decrees were therefore never understood, and therefore never received.

c) The Church of Syria is the oldest of all the Gentile Churches.[4] In its capital, Antioch, the name of "Christians" first arose: in the age

The Syrian Churches.

---

[1] For the appearance and traditions of Ararat, see Haxthausen's Transcaucasia, 190, 323.

[2] Haxthausen, 283, 289, 304.

[3] Curzon's Armenia, 225.

[4] The Church of Palestine can hardly be reckoned among the Churches of the East which I am here considering. It is a mere colony of the Greek

of persecution, it produced Ignatius, and, in the age of
the Empire, Chrysostom and John of Damascus. In
the claim of Antioch to be founded by S. Peter, the
Eastern Church[1] has often regarded itself as possessing whatever privileges can be claimed by the see
of Rome on the ground of descent from the first
Apostle. The city itself became "the city of God."
To the chief pastor of Antioch alone in the world
by right belongs the title of "Patriarch."[2] The
purely national Church of Syria is represented by
two very different communions. The first is the
The Jacobite[3] or Monophysite Church, of which
Jacobites. the patriarch resides at Diarbekir. It has one
peculiar custom, the transmission of the same name
from prelate to prelate. The patriarch, doubtless
after the first illustrious Bishop of Antioch, is always
called Ignatius. The other communion of Syria is,
in like manner, the representative both of a sect
The Mar- and a nation. The Maronites,[4] so called from
onites. their founder Maro in the fifth century, com-
prise at once the only relics of the old Monothelite
heretics, and the whole Christian population of Mount
Lebanon, where the cedar grove and its neighboring
convent of Kanobin form their chief sanctuary. But
their main peculiarity is this, that, alone of all the
Eastern Churches, they have retained the close com-

Church, and its Patriarch, with the Greek Patriarchs of Antioch and Alexandria, resides at Constantinople. Neale, i. 159.

[1] Travels of Macarius, 222, 224. (For this work see Lecture XI.)

[2] Neale, i. 126.

[3] Ibid. 152, 153. In the doubtful derivation of their name from James the
Apostle, or James the heresiarch of the sixth century, there is the same ambiguity as in the Christians of S. Thomas.

[4] Ibid. 153. An interesting account of the Maronites, highly illustrative
of their connection with the French, as representatives of the Latin Church,
is given in the Journal of the Comte de Paris. (Damas et le Liban, p.
75–78.)

munion with the Latin Church which they adopted in the twelfth century through the Crusaders. Their allegiance is given to the see of Rome, and their learning has borne fruit in the West, through the labors of the two Assemans. They have lately acquired a more tragical claim on our interest through the atrocities perpetrated on their villages by their ancient hereditary enemies the Druses, provoked, it may be, but certainly not excused, by Maronite aggression, or Latin intrigues.

d) In the times of the early councils the Churches of Syria and Egypt were usually opposed: now they are united under the common theological name of Monophysite.   Both alike take their stand, not on the four, but on the three first Councils, and reject the decrees of Chalcedon, and protest against the heterodoxy, not only of the whole West, but of the whole East beside themselves. But the Church of Egypt is much more than the relic of an ancient sect. It is the most remarkable monument of Christian antiquity. It is the only living representative of the most venerable nation of all antiquity. Within its narrow limits have now shrunk the learning and the lineage of ancient Egypt. The language of the Coptic services, understood neither by people nor priests, is the language, although debased, of the Pharaohs. The Copts are still, even in their degraded state, the most civilized of the natives : the intelligence of Egypt still lingers in the Coptic scribes, who are, on this account, used as clerks in the offices of their conquerors, or as registrars of the water-marks of the Nile.

They also represent the proud Church of old Alexandria. Their heresy is an exaggeration of the orthodoxy of Athanasius and Cyril. For this they denied

the "human nature of Christ;" for this they broke off
from the Byzantine empire, and ultimately surrendered
to the Saracens. The Patriarch of Alexandria now resides at Cairo.[1] There is still, as in the first ages, a
wide distinction between the bishops and their head.
He alone has the power of ordination : they, if they
ordain at all, act only as his vicars. The Coptic Church
alone confers ordination, not by imposition of hands,
but by the act of breathing. Alone also it has succeeded in preventing the translation of bishops,[2] and
preserves, in the most rigid form, the *nolo episcopari* of
the patriarch.[3]

In the universal kiss, interchanged throughout the
whole of a Coptic congregation; in the prominent part
taken by the children, who act as deacons; in the union
of social intercourse with worship; in the turbaned
heads and unshod feet of the worshippers, the Coptic
service breathes an atmosphere of Oriental and of primitive times found in none of the more northern Churches,
even of the East.

But there is a daughter of the Coptic Church, yet
The Abys- farther south, which is the extremest type of
sinian
Church.   what may be called Oriental ultramontanism.
The Church of Abyssinia, founded in the fourth century
by the Church of Alexandria, furnishes the one example
of a nation savage yet Christian; showing us, on the
one hand, the force of the Christian faith in maintaining
its superiority at all against such immense disadvantages, and, on the other hand, the utmost amount of

---

[1] The ancient titles of Pope and Œcumenical Judge seem now to belong,
not to the Coptic, but to the Greek Patriarch of Alexandria. For the title
"Pope" see Lecture III. The title of Œcumenical Judge is derived (1)
from the right of the Alexandrian Church to fix the period of Easter (see
Lecture V.), or (2) from Cyril's presidency in the Council of Ephesus.

[2] Neale's Introd. i. 112, 119 ; Church of Alexandria, ii. 99–102.

[3] See Lecture VII.

superstition with which a Christian Church can be overlaid without perishing altogether. One lengthened
communication it has hitherto received from the West
— the mission of the Jesuits. With this exception it
has been left almost entirely to itself. Whatever there
is of Jewish or of old Egyptian ritual preserved in the
Coptic Church, is carried to excess in the Abyssinian.
The likeness of the sacred ark,[1] called the ark of Zion,
is the centre of Abyssinian devotion. To it gifts and
prayers are offered. On it the sanctity of the whole
Church depends. Circumcision is not only practised, as
in the Coptic Church, but is regarded as of equal necessity with baptism. There alone the Jewish Sabbath is
still observed as well as the Christian Sunday:[2] they
(with the exception of a small sect of "the Seventh-
day" Baptists) are the only true "Sabbatarians" of
Christendom. The "sinew that shrank," no less than
the flesh of swine, hare, and aquatic fowl, is still forbidden to be eaten. Dancing still forms part of their
ritual, as it did in the Jewish temple. The wild shriek
which goes up at Abyssinian funerals is the exact counterpart of that which Herodotus heard in ancient Egypt.
The polygamy of the Jewish Church lingers here after
having been banished from the rest of the Christian
world.

Whatever, it may be added, of extravagant ritualism, of excessive dogmatism, of the fatal division between religion and morality, disfigures to so large an
extent the rest of Oriental Christianity, is seen in its
most striking form in the usages of Abyssinia. The
endless controversies respecting the natures of Christ,
which have expired elsewhere, still rage in that bar-

[1] Harris's Ethiopia, iii. 132, 135, 137, 150, 156, 154–167.
[2] See Gobat's Abyssinia.

13

barous country.[1] The belief in the efficacy of external
rites to wash away sins is carried there to a pitch without a parallel. The greatest festival of all the year is
the vast lustration, almost amounting to an annual baptism of the whole nation,[2] on the feast of Epiphany.
One saint, elsewhere unrecognized, appears in the Ethi-
opian calendar; Pilate is canonized, because he washed
his hands and said, "I am innocent of the blood of this
just man."[3] The moral creed of Abyssinia is said to
be thus summed up : —

" That the Alexandrian faith is the only true belief.

" That faith, together with baptism, is sufficient for justification ; but that God demands alms and fasting as amends for sin
committed prior to the performance of the baptismal rite.

" That unchristened children are not saved.

" That the baptism of water is the true regeneration.

" That invocation ought to be made to the saints, because sin-
ning mortals are unworthy to appear in the presence of God,
and because, if the saints be well loved, they will listen to all
prayer.

" That every sin is forgiven from the moment that the kiss of
the pilgrim is imprinted on the stones of Jerusalem ; and that
kissing the hand of a priest purifies the body in like manner.

" That sins must be confessed to the priest, saints invoked, and
full faith reposed in charms and amulets, more especially if written in an unknown tongue.

" That prayers for the dead are necessary, and absolution indispensable ; but that the souls of the departed do not immediately enter upon a state of happiness, the period being in exact
accordance with the alms and prayers that are expended upon
earth."

This may have been colored in passing through the
mind of the European traveller. But his consciousness
of the wretched state of the Church which he describes,

---

[1] Harris, iii. 190.   [2] Ibid. iii. 202.   [3] Neale, i. 806.

gives more weight to the words of hope with which he concludes[1] his account : —

"Abyssinia, as she now is, presents the most singular compound of vanity, meekness, and ferocity; of devotion, superstition, and ignorance. But, compared with other nations of Africa, she unquestionably holds a high station. She is superior in arts and in agriculture, in laws, religion, and social condition, to all the benighted children of the sun. The small portion of good which does exist may justly be ascribed to the remains of the wreck of Christianity, which, although stranded on a rocky shore, and buffeted by the storms of ages, is not yet wholly overwhelmed; and from the present degradation of a people avowing its tenets, may be inferred the lesson of the total inefficacy of its forms and profession, if unsupported by enough of mental culture to enable its spirit and its truth to take root in the heart, and bear fruits in the character of the barbarian. There is, perhaps, no portion of the whole continent to which European civilization might be applied with better ultimate results; and although now dwindled into an ordinary kingdom, Hábesh, under proper government and proper influence, might promote the amelioration of all the surrounding people, whilst she resumed her original position as the first of African monarchies."

e) There is one of these remote Eastern Churches, which still maintains its original connection with the Orthodoxy of Constantinople, — the Church and kingdom, called by the ancients " Iberia," by the moderns, "Gruzia" or "Georgia."[2] The conversion of their king, through the example or the miracles of Nina, a Christian captive, was nearly simultaneous with that of Constantine. Originally dependent on Antioch, its allegiance was transferred to Constantinople. The nation bore a considerable part in the Crusades, and memorials of its princes long remained in the convents both of

---

[1] Harris, iii. 186.   [2] See Neale, i. 61–65.

Palestine and of Athos. At the beginning of this century Georgia was annexed to Russia.[1]

2. We are thus brought to the next group in Eastern Christendom, the Orthodox Imperial Church, which sometimes gives its name to the whole. It is "the Great Church" (as it is technically called) from which those which we have hitherto described have broken off, and those which we shall proceed to describe have been derived.

The
GREEK
CHURCH.

The "Greek Church," properly so called, includes the wide-spread race which speaks the Greek language, from its southernmost outpost in the desert of Mount Sinai, through all the islands and coasts of the Levant and the Archipelago; having its centre in Greece and in Constantinople.[2] It represents to us, in however corrupt and degraded a form, the old, glorious, world-inspiring people of Athens, Thebes, and Sparta. It is the means by which that people has been kept alive through four centuries of servitude. It was no Philhellenic enthusiast, but the gray-headed Germanus, Archbishop of Patras, who raised the standard of Greek independence: the first champion of that cause of Grecian liberty, in behalf of which in our own country the past generation was so zealous, and the present generation is so indifferent. The sanctuary of the Greek race, which is in a great degree the sanctuary and refuge of the whole Eastern Church, is Athos — "the Holy Mountain."[3]

The repre-
sentative of
ancient
Greece.

The old Greek mythology which made the peak of Samothrace the seat of the Pelasgic worship, and the many-headed range of Olympus the seat of the Hellenic

---

[1] See Neale, i. 26–31.   [2] Ibid. i. 26–31.

[3] See Urquhart's Spirit of the East, 157, 169, and an excellent description in the Christian Remembrancer, xxi. 288.

gods, left the beautiful peninsula and noble pyramid of Athos to receive the twenty monasteries which shelter the vast communities of Greek, Ionian, Bulgarian, Servian, and Russian monks.

The Greek Church reminds us of the time when the tongue, not of Rome, but of Greece, was the sacred language of Christendom. It was a striking remark of the Emperor Napoleon, that the introduction of Christianity itself was, in a certain sense, the triumph of Greece over Rome ; the last and most signal instance of the maxim of Horace, " Græcia capta ferum victorem cepit." [1] The early Roman Church was but a colony of Greek Christians, or Grecized Jews. The earliest Fathers of the Western Church, Clemens, Irenæus, Hermas, Hippolytus, wrote in Greek. The early Popes were not Italians but Greeks. The name of "Pope" is not Latin but Greek — the common and now despised name of every pastor in the Eastern Church. It is true that this Grecian color was in part an accidental consequence of the wide diffusion of the Greek language by Alexander's conquests through the East, and was thus a sign not so much of the Hellenic, as of the Hebrew and Oriental character of the early Christian communities. But the advantage thus given to the Byzantine Church has never been lost or forgotten. It is a perpetual witness that she is the mother and Rome the daughter. It is her privilege to claim a direct continuity of speech with the earliest times, to boast of reading the whole code of Scripture, old as well as new, in the language in which it was read and spoken by the Apostles. The humblest peasant who reads his Septuagint or Greek

Of the early Greek Christianity.

[1] Bertrand's Memoirs of Napoleon, i. 206. Compare Dean Milman's Latin Christianity, i. 54.

Testament in his own mother tongue, on the hills of
Bœotia, may proudly feel that he has an access to the
original oracles of divine truth, which Pope and Cardinal
reach by a barbarous and imperfect translation; that he
has a key of knowledge, which in the West is only to
be found in the hands of the learned classes.

The Greek Church is thus the only living representative of the Hellenic race, and speaks in the
only living voice which has come down to us
from the Apostolic age. But its main characteristic is its lineal descent from the first Christian Empire.
"Romaic," not "Hellenic," is the name by which, from
its long connection with the Roman Empire of Byzantium, the language of Greece is now known. "Roman"
('Ρωμαῖος), not "Greek," is the name by which (till quite
recently) a Greek would have distinguished himself
from the Mussulman population around him. Not
Athens, not Alexandria, not even Jerusalem, but Constantinople, is the sacred city to which the eyes of the
Greek race and of the Eastern Church are turned at
this day. We can hardly doubt that it was the point
to which the eyes of the whole Christian world were
turned, when at the opening of the fourth century it
rose as the first Christian city, at the command of the
first Christian Emperor, on a site which, by its unequalled advantages, was naturally marked out as the
capital of a new world, as the inauguration of a new
era.[1] The subsequent rise of the Papal city on the
ruins of the old Pagan metropolis must not blind us to
the fact that there was a period in which the Eastern
and not the Western Rome was the true centre of
Christendom. The modern grandeur of S. Peter's must
not be permitted to obscure the effect which was pro-

*Represent-
ative of the
Byzantine
Empire.*

---

[1] See Lecture VI.

duced on the taste and the feelings of the sixth century by the erection of S. Sophia. The learning of the Greek Church, which even down to the eleventh century excelled that of the Latin, in the fifteenth century directly contributed more than any other single cause to the revival of letters and the German Reformation. In Asia and in Constantinople it has long sunk under the barbarism of its conquerors. But in the little The Church of Greece. kingdom of independent Greece, the Greek clergy is still, within narrow limits, an enlightened body. In it, if in any portion of Eastern Christendom, lives the liberal, democratic spirit of ancient Hellas. Athens, with all the drawbacks of an ill-adjusted union between new and old ways of thought, is now the centre of education and enlightenment to the Greek clergy throughout the Levant.

3. The third group of the Eastern Church consists of those barbarian tribes of the north, whose The NORTH-ERN TRIBES. conversion by the Byzantine Church corresponds to the conversion of the Teutonic tribes by the Latin Church.

a) The first division embraces the tribes on the banks of the Lower Danube; the Sclavonic Bulgaria The Danu-bian Prov-inces. and Servia on the south; the Latin or Romanic Wallachia and Moldavia on the north.[1] Bulga- Bulgaria. ria, which was the first to receive Christianity from the preaching of Cyril and Methodius in the ninth century, communicated it to the three others.[2] Servia Servia. has since become independent of Constantinople, under a metropolitan or patriarch of its own, and in the reign of Stephen Dushan, in the twelfth century, presented a

---

[1] Neale, i. 45, 47, 69.

[2] The relations of the Bulgarian to the Byzantine Church are well stated, though from a one-sided point of view, in a Greek pamphlet published at Constantinople by Gregory, Chief Secretary of the Synod.

miniature of an Eastern Christian Empire. The Church
Wallachia of Wallachia and Moldavia is remarkable as
and Mol-
davia.   being of Latin origin, yet Greek in doctrine and
ritual; a counterpoise to the two Churches of Bohemia
and Poland, which, being Sclavonic by race, are Latin
by religion. To these national communities should be
added the extensive colony of Greek Christians who,
The "Rait- under the name of "Raitzen," occupy large dis-
zen," of
Hungary.   tricts in Hungary, and form the extreme westernmost outposts of the Eastern Church. The ecclesiastical as well as the political importance of these several
religious bodies has almost entirely turned on the position which they occupy on the frontier land of the West
and East. This is an importance which will doubtless
increase with each succeeding generation. But in their
past ecclesiastical history, the only epochs fruitful of
instruction will probably be found in the more stirring
moments of Servian history,[1] and in the conversion[2] of
Bulgaria.

The Church   b) There remains the far wider field of the
of Russia. Church of Russia.

If Oriental Christendom is bound to the past by its
Asiatic and its Greek traditions, there can be no doubt
that its bond of union with the present and the future
is through the greatest of Sclavonic nations, whose dominion has now spread over the whole East of Europe,
over the whole North of Asia, over a large tract of
Western America. If Constantinople be the local centre of the Eastern Church, its personal head is, and
has been for four centuries, the great potentate who,
under the successive names of Grand-Prince, Czar, and
Emperor, has reigned at Moscow and St. Petersburg
Not merely by its proximity of geographical situation,

<hr>

[1] See Ranke's Hist. of Servia.   [2] See Lecture IX.

but by the singular gift of imitation with which the
Sclavonic race has been endowed, is the Russian Church
the present representative of the old Imperial Church
of Constantine.   The Sclavonic alphabet is Greek.
The Russian names of emperor, saint, and peasant are
Greek.   Sacred buildings, which in their actual sites in
the East have been altered by modern innovations, are
preserved for our study in the exact models made from
them in earlier days by Russian pilgrims.[1]   And in like
manner, customs and feelings which have perished in
Greece and Syria, may still be traced in the churches
and monasteries of the North.   When Napoleon called
Alexander I., in bitter scorn, a Greek of the Lower
Empire, it was a representation of the Czar's position
in a fuller sense than Napoleon intended or would have
admitted.   For good or for evil, as a check on its development or as a spur to its ambition, the Church and
Empire of Russia have inherited the religion and the
policy of the New Rome of the Bosphorus far more
fully than any Western nation, even under Charlemagne himself, inherited the spirit or the forms of the
Old Rome beside the Tiber.[2]

II. These are the geographical landmarks of the
Eastern Church.   What are its historical landmarks ?
From the dead level of obscure names which HISTORICAL
these vast limits enclose, what leading epochs EPOCHS of the
or series of events can be selected of universal EASTERN CHURCH.
and enduring importance ?

1. The first great display of the forces of the Oriental
Church was in the period of the early Councils. 1. Period of
The first seven General Councils, with all their the Councils.
leading characters, were as truly Eastern Councils, as
truly the pride of the Eastern Church, as those of Constance and Trent are of the Western.   Almost all were

---

[1] See Lecture XI.   [2] See Lecture IX.

14

held within the neighborhood, most under the walls of Byzantium. All were swayed by the language, by the motives, by the feelings, of the Eastern world.

Yet these Oriental Councils were "general," were "Œcumenical" in a sense which fairly belonged to none besides. No Western Council has so fully expressed the voice of Christendom, no assembly, civil or ecclesiastical, can claim to have issued laws which have been so long in force in so large a portion of the civilized world, as those which emanated from these ancient parliaments of the Byzantine Empire. And if many of their decrees have now become virtually obsolete, yet those of the first and most characteristic of the seven are still cherished throughout the East, and through a large portion of the West. If with Armenia and Egypt we stumble at the decrees of Chalcedon, if with the Chaldæan and Lutheran churches we are startled by the language of the fathers of Ephesus, if with the Latins we alter the creed of Constantinople, yet Christendom, with but few exceptions, receives the confes-

The Council of Nicæa. sion of the first Council of Nicæa as the earliest, the most solemn, and the most universal expression of Christian theology. In that assembly the Church and Empire first met in peaceful conference : the confessors of the Diocletian persecution came into contact with the first prelates of an established church : the father of dogmatical theology, and the father of ecclesiastical history met for the first time in the persons of Athanasius and Eusebius. The General Council of Nicæa may be considered both as the most significant of all the seven, and also as the most striking scene, the most enduring monument of the Oriental Church at large.[1]

2. It is characteristic of Eastern history, that we can-

1 See Lectures II. III. IV. V.

not lay it out, as in the West, by regular chronological periods. The second epoch of universal 2. The rise importance in Eastern Christendom is the birth of Mahometanism. tanism. and growth of Mahometanism. All great religious movements which run parallel, even though counter, to Christianity, form a necessary part of ecclesiastical history. But the religion of Mahomet is essentially interwoven with the Eastern Church. Even without considering the directly Christian influences to which the Arabian teacher was subjected, no one can doubt that there are points which his system, in common with that of the Eastern Church, owes to its Oriental origin. In other points it is a rebound and reaction against that Church. The history of the Greek and Sclavonic races can only be understood by bearing in mind their constant conflict with the Arabs, the Tartars, and the Turks.[1]

3. The conversion and establishment of the Russian Church, and through the Russian Church, of 3. The history of the the Russian Empire, forms the third and most Russian fertile epoch of the history of Oriental Chris- Church. tendom.

It is enough to indicate the successive stages in the growth of the Empire, the rise and fall of the Patriarchate, the tragical struggle of Alexis and Nicon, the singular development of Russian dissent, the career and character of Peter the Great, hardly less remarkable in its religious than in its civil aspect. Every one of these events teems with dramatic, some with European interest, and every one of them is bound up with the history of the national Church, and therefore with the history of Eastern Christianity.[2]

III. These, then, are the principal divisions of the history, properly so called. But before considering

[1] See Lecture VIII.   [2] See Lectures IX. X. XI. XII.

any single period apart from the rest, it is important General to observe the characteristics which, more or character- istics of the less, are common to all the parts alike, and Eastern Church. which distinguish them all from the portion of Christendom to which we ourselves belong, whether we give to it the narrower name of the Latin, or the truer and more comprehensive title of the Western Church. In considering these differences it is not my intention to speak of the special points which led, in the twelfth century, to the actual external separation between the Roman and Byzantine communions. The true differences between the East and the West existed long before their formal disruption, and would exist, in all probability, long after any formal reunion. The disruption itself was rather a consequence than a cause of their estrangement. The theological pretexts, such as the doctrine of the Double Procession, the usage of leavened[1] and unleavened bread, the excommunications of Photius, and Michael Cerularius, and the failure of the last attempt at reconciliation in the Council of Florence, were themselves aggravated by more general grievances.[2] The jealousy of the two capitals of Rome and Constantinople; the rival claims of the Eastern and Western crusaders; the outrage of the Fourth Crusade; the antagonism of Russia in earlier times to Poland, in later times to France, have all contributed to the same result. But the internal differences lie deeper than any of these external manifestations, whether theological or political.

1. The distinction which has been most frequently remarked is that of the speculative tendency of the

[1] See " Historia Concertationum de Pane Azymo et Fermentato," 1737, by J. G. Hermann, pastor of Pegau in Saxony. Jenkins' Life of Cardinal Julian, 302.

[2] For the enumeration of dates and events in connection with these periods of history see the tabular statement at the end of this volume.

Oriental, and the practical tendency of the Western Church. This distinction is deep seated in the contrast long ago described by Aristotle between the savage energy and freedom of Europe, and the intellectual repose and apathy of Asia.[1] It naturally finds its point and expression in the theology of the two Churches. Whilst the Western prides itself on the title of the "Catholic," the Eastern claims the title of "Orthodox."[2] "The East," says Dean Milman, "enacted creeds, the West discipline." The first decree of an Eastern Council was to determine the relations of the Godhead. The first decree of the Pope[3] of Rome was to interdict the marriage of the clergy. All the first founders of theology were Easterns. Till the time of Augustine, no eminent divine had arisen in the West; till the time of Gregory the Great, none had filled the papal chair. The doctrine of Athanasius was received, not originated, by Rome. The great Italian Council of Ariminum lapsed into Arianism by an oversight. The Latin language was inadequate to express the minute shades of meaning for which the Greek is admirably fitted. Of the two creeds peculiar to the Latin Church, the earlier, that called "the Apostles'," is characterized by its simplicity and its freedom from dogmatic assertions; the later, that called the Athanasian, as its name confesses, is an endeavor to imitate the Greek theology,

Speculative tendency of Eastern Theology.

[1] Arist. Pol. vii. 7.

[2] The Eastern Church has a special celebration of "orthodoxy." On "Orthodox Sunday," at the beginning of Lent, the anathemas against heresy take the place of the curses on crimes and sins which mark the more practical services of our Ash-Wednesday. For example : " To Jacobus Zanzalus the Armenian, Dioscorus Patriarch of Alexandria, to Severus the Impious, to Paul and Pyrrhus of the same mind with Sergius the disciple of Lycopetrus — Anathema, anathema, anathema." And on the other hand, "For the orthodox Greek Emperors — Everlasting remembrance, everlasting remembrance, everlasting remembrance." Neale, ii. 874.

[3] The Decretal of Siricius A. D. 385. (Milman's Latin Christianity, i. 119.)

and by the evident strain of its sentences reveals the
ineffectual labor of the Latin phrases, "persona" and
"substantia," to represent the correlative but hardly
corresponding words by which the Greeks, with a natural facility, expressed "the hypostatic union." And
still more, when we touch the period at which the
divergence between the two Empires threw the two
Churches farther apart, the tide of Grecian and Egyptian controversy hardly arrived at the shores of Italy,
now high and dry above their reach.

"Latin Christianity," says Dean Milman, "contemplated with almost equal indifference, Nestorianism and
all its prolific race, Eutychianism, Monophysitism, Mo-
nothelitism. While in this contest the two great patriarchates of the East, Constantinople and Alexandria,
brought to issue, or strove to bring to issue, their rival
claims to ascendency; while council after council pro-
mulgated, reversed, reënacted their conflicting decrees;
while separate and hostile communities were formed in
every region of the East, and the fear of persecuted
Nestorianism, stronger than religious zeal, penetrated
for refuge remote countries, into which Christianity had
not yet found its way : in the West there was no Nestorian or Eutychian sect."[1]

Probably no Latin Christian has ever felt himself
agitated even in the least degree by any one of the
seventy opinions on the union of the two natures which
are said to perplex the Church of Abyssinia. Probably
the last and only question of this kind on which the
Latin Church has spontaneously entered, is that of the
Double Procession of the Spirit. The very word
"theology" ($\theta\epsilon o\lambda o\gamma\iota a$) arose from the peculiar questions
agitated in the East. The Athanasian controversy of
Constantinople and Alexandria is, strictly speaking,

1 Latin Christianity, i. 200.

*theo*logical; unlike the Pelagian or the Lutheran controversies, it relates not to man, but to God.

This fundamental contrast naturally widened into
other cognate differences.   The Western the- Rhetorical
ology is essentially logical in form, and based as opposed
to logical.
on law.[1]   The Eastern is rhetorical in form and based
on philosophy.   The Latin divine succeeded to the Roman advocate.   The Oriental divine succeeded to the
Grecian sophist.   Out of the logical and legal Philosophi-
elements in the West have grown up all that is cal as opposed to
most peculiar in the scholastic theology of the legal.
Middle Ages, the Calvinistic theology of the Reformation.   To one or both of these causes of difference may
be reduced many of the divergencies which the theological student will trace in regard to dogmatic statements,
or to interpretations[2] of Scripture, between Tertullian
and Origen, between Prosper and Cassian, between Augustine and Chrysostom, between Thomas Aquinas and
John Damascenus.

The abstract doctrines of the Godhead in the Alexandrian creed took the place, in the minds of theological
students, which, in the schools of philosophy, had been
occupied by the abstract ideas of the Platonic system.
The subtleties of Roman law as applied to the relations
of God and man, which appear faintly in Augustine, more
distinctly in Aquinas, more decisively still in Calvin and
Luther, and, though from a somewhat larger point of
view, in Grotius, are almost unknown to the East.   " Fo-
rensic justification," " merit," " demerit," " satisfaction,"
" imputed righteousness," " decrees," represent ideas
which in the Eastern theology have no predominant

---

1 This is well put by Professor Maine (Ancient Law, 354–364.)   Compare
Hampden's Bampton Lectures, 25.

2 On this point I am anxious to acknowledge my obligations to the learning
of the Rev. F. C. Cook.

influence, hardly any words to represent them. The few exceptions that occur may be traced directly to accidental gusts of Western influence.[1]

Hence arises the apparent contradiction, that, whenever the Eastern theologians enter on topics which touch not the abstract questions of the Divine essence, but the human questions of grace and predestination, there is a more directly moral and practical tone than often in corresponding treatises of the Protestant West. Chrysostom's transcendent genius and goodness would doubtless have lifted him above the trammels of any local influence; but the admiration felt in the East for his thoroughly practical homilies, which in the West have often incurred the suspicion of Pelagianism, is a proof of the general tendency of the Church which he so powerfully represents.

A single instance illustrates the Eastern tendency to a high theological view of the doctrine of the Trinity, combined with an absence of any precision of statement in regard to mediation or redemption. In the Western liturgies direct addresses to Christ are exceptions. In the East they are the rule. In the West, even in Unitarian liturgies, it is deemed almost essential that every prayer should be closed "through Jesus Christ." In the East, such a close is rarely, if ever, found.[2]

The speculative tendency of Eastern monastic life. 2. The contrast between the speculative tendency of the Eastern Church and the practical life of the Western appears, not only in the

[1] A curious exception occurs in the catechism of the Russian Church, drawn up by the present Metropolitan of Moscow, where the beatitude "Blessed are they that hunger and thirst after righteousness," is interpreted of "imputed righteousness." (Doctrine of the Russian Church, p. 112, translated by the Rev. W. Blackmore.) But I am assured by the learned translator that this is an unaccountable and almost solitary instance of this mode of interpretation in the East. Another specimen of this exceptional theology is perhaps to be found in the account of Peter's death-bed. See Lecture XII.

[2] Freeman, Principles of Divine Service, i. 373.

theological, but in the ecclesiastical, and especially in the monastic, system of Oriental Christendom.

No doubt monasticism was embraced by the Roman Church, even as early as the fifth century, with an energy which seemed to reproduce in a Christian form the dying genius of stoical philosophy. Still the East holds the chief place in the monastic world. The words which describe the state are not Latin but Greek or Syriac — *Hermit, monk, anchoret, monastery, cœnobite, ascetic, abbot, abbey.* It was not in the Apennines or on the Alps, but in the stony arms with which the Libyan and Arabian deserts enclose the valley of the Nile that the first monasteries were founded. Anthony the Coptic hermit, from his retreat by the Red Sea, is the spiritual father of that vast community which has now overrun the world. His disciple, Athanasius, was its first sponsor in the West. And not only was monasticism born in the Eastern Church; it has also thriven there with an unrivalled intensity. Indeed the earliest source of monastic life is removed even further than the Thebaid deserts, in the Manichean repugnance of the distant East towards the material world, as it is exhibited under its simplest form in the Indian Yogi or the Mussulman Fakir. It is this Oriental seclusion which, whether from character, or climate, or contagion, has to the Christian world been far more forcibly represented in the Oriental than in the Latin Church. The solitary and contemplative devotion of the Eastern monks, whether in Egypt or Greece, though broken by the manual labor necessary for their subsistence, has been very slightly modified either by literary or agricultural activity. There have, indeed, been occasional examples of splendid benevolence in Oriental monachism. The Egyptian monk, Telemachus, by the sacrifice of himself, extinguished the gladiatorial games

15

at Rome.   Russian hermits opposed the securest bulwark against the savage despotism of Ivan.[1]   But these
are isolated instances.   As a general rule, there has
arisen in the East no society like the Benedictines,
held in honor wherever literature or civilization has
spread; no charitable orders, like the Sisters of Mercy,
which carry light and peace into the darkest haunts of
suffering humanity.   Active life is, on the strict Eastern
theory, an abuse of the system.

Nor is it only in the monastic life that the severity
of Eastern asceticism excels that of the West.   Whilst
the fasts of the Latin Church are mostly confined to
Lent, liable, increasingly liable, to wide dispensations,
exercised for the most part by abstinence, not from all
food, but only from particular kinds of food, the fasts of
the Eastern Church, especially of its most remarkable
branch, the Coptic, extend through large periods of the
year, are regarded as all but indispensable — and, for
the time, repudiate all sustenance, though with strange
inconsistency they admit of drinking, even to the gross-
est intoxication.   And, finally, the wildest individual
excesses of a Bruno or a Dunstan seem poor beside the
authorized, national, we may almost say imperial, adora-
tion of the Pillar-saints of the East.   Amidst all the
controversies of the fifth century, on one religious subject the conflicting East maintained its unity, in the
reverence of the Hermit on the Pillar.   The West has
never had a Simeon Stylites.

3. Another important difference between the two
The Eastern Churches was one which, though in substance
Church
stationary. the same, may be expressed in various forms.
The Eastern Church was, like the East, stationary and
immutable; the Western, like the West, progressive

---

[1] See Lecture X.   Compare Montalembert's Monks of the West, i. 38–
133.

and flexible. This distinction is the more remarkable,
because, at certain periods of their course, there can be
no doubt that the civilization of the Eastern Church
was far higher than that of the Western. No one can
read the account of the capture of Constantinople by
the Crusaders of the thirteenth century, without perceiving that it is the occupation of a refined and civilized capital by a horde of comparative barbarians. The
arrival of the Greek scholars in Europe in the fifteenth
century was the signal for the most progressive step
that Western theology has ever made. And in earlier
ages, whilst it might still be thought that Rome, not
Constantinople, was the natural refuge of the arts of
the ancient classical world, the literature of the Church
was almost entirely confined to the Byzantine hemi-
sphere. Whilst Constantinople was ringing with the
fame of preachers, of whom Chrysostom was the chief
but not the only example, the Roman bishops and
clergy, till the time of Leo the Great, never publicly
addressed their flocks from the pulpit. But, notwithstanding this occasional superiority, the Oriental Church,
as a whole, almost from the time that it assumed a distinct existence, has given tokens of that singular immobility which is in great part to be traced to its Eastern
origin — its origin in those strange regions which still
retain, not only the climate and vegetation, but the
manners, the dress, the speech of the days of the Patriarchs and the Pharaohs. Its peculiar corruptions have
been such as are consequent, not on development, but
on stagnation ; its peculiar excellencies have been such
as belong to the simplicity of barbarism, not to the freedom of civilization.

The straws of custom show which way the spirit of
an institution blows. The primitive posture of standing
in prayer still retains its ground in the East, whilst

in the West it is only preserved in the extreme Protestant communities by way of antagonism to Rome.
Organs and musical instruments are as odious to a
Greek or Russian, as to a Scottish Presbyterian.
Jewish ordinances still keep their hold on Abyssinia. Even the schism[1] which convulsed the Russian
Church nearly at the same time that Latin Christendom was rent by the German Reformation, was
not a forward but a retrograde movement—a protest,
not against abuses, but against innovation. The calendars of the Churches show the eagerness with which,
whilst the one, at least till a recent period, placed herself at the head of European civilization, the other still
studiously lags behind it. The "new style," which the
world owes to the enlightened activity of Pope Gregory
XIII., after having with difficulty overcome the Protestant scruples of Germany, Denmark, and Switzerland,
and last of all (with shame be it said) of England and
Sweden, has never been able to penetrate into the wide
dominions of the old Byzantine and the modern Russian Empires, which still hold to the Greek Calendar,
eleven days behind the rest of the civilized world.

These contrasts might be indefinitely multiplied,
sometimes to the advantage of one Church, sometimes
to the advantage of the other. The case of the Sacraments and their accompaniments will suffice as final
examples.

The Latin doctrine on this subject is by Protestants
The Sacra-   so frequently regarded as the highest pitch of
ments.   superstition — by Roman Catholics as the highest pitch of reverence of which the subject is capable
— that it may be instructive to both to see the contrast
between the freedom and reasonableness of the sacramental doctrine as held by the highest Roman doctors,

[1] See Lectures XI. and XII.

compared with the stiff, the magical, the antiquarian
character of the same doctrine as represented in the
East. We are accustomed to place the essence of superstition in a devotion to the outward forms and elements
as distinct from the inward spirit which they represent,
convey, or express. Let us, for a moment, see which
has in this respect most tenaciously clung to the form,
which to the spirit, of the two great ordinances of
Christian worship.

There can be no question that the original form of
baptism — the very meaning of the word — Immersion
was complete immersion in the deep baptis- tism.
mal waters; and that, for at least four centuries, any
other form was either unknown, or regarded, unless in
the case of dangerous illness, as an exceptional, almost
a monstrous case. To this form the Eastern Church
still rigidly adheres; and the most illustrious and
venerable portion of it, that of the Byzantine Empire, absolutely repudiates and ignores any other mode
of administration as essentially invalid. The Latin
Church, on the other hand, doubtless in deference to
the requirements of a northern climate, to the change
of manners, to the convenience of custom, has wholly
altered the mode, preferring, as it would fairly say,
mercy to sacrifice; and (with the two exceptions of the
cathedral of Milan, and the sect of the Baptists) a few
drops of water are now the Western substitute for the
threefold plunge into the rushing rivers, or the wide
baptisteries of the East.

And when we descend from the administration itself
of the sacramental elements to their concomi- Confirma-
tant circumstances, still the same contrast ap- tion.
pears. In the first age of the Church it was customary
for the apostles to lay their hands on the heads of the
newly baptized converts, that they might receive the

"gifts of the Spirit." The "gifts" vanished, but the custom of laying on of hands remained. It remained, and was continued, and so in the Greek Church is still continued, at the baptism of children as of adults. Confirmation is, with them, simultaneous with the act of the baptismal immersion. But the Latin Church, whilst it adopted or retained the practice of admitting infants to baptism, soon set itself to remedy the obvious defect arising from their unconscious age, by separating and postponing, and giving a new life and meaning to the rite of confirmation. The two ceremonies, which in the Eastern Church are indissolubly confounded, are now, throughout Western Christendom, by a salutary innovation, each made to minister to the edification of the individual, and completion of the whole baptismal ordinance.

In like manner the East retained, and still retains, Extreme unction. the apostolical practice mentioned by S. James — for the sick to call in the elders of the Church, to anoint him with oil, and pray over him, that he may recover. "The elders," that is, a body of priests (for they still make a point of the plural number), are called in at moments of dangerous illness, and the prayer is offered. But the Latin Church, seeing that the special object for which the ceremony was first instituted, the recovery of the sick, had long ceased to be effected, determined to change its form, that it still might be preserved as an instructive symbol. And thus the "anointing with oil" of the first century, and of the Oriental Church has become with the Latins merely the last, "the extreme unction," of the dying man.

Yet once again it became a practice in the Church, Infant Communion. early — we know not how early — for infants to communicate in the Lord's supper. A literal application to the Eucharist of the text respecting the bread of life, in the sixth chapter of S. John, naturally followed on a literal application to baptism of the text respecting the second birth in the third chapter; and the actual participation in the elements of both sacraments came to be regarded as equally necessary for the salvation of every human being. Here again the peculiar genius of each of the two Churches displayed itself. The Oriental Churches, in conformity with ancient usage, still administer the Eucharist to infants. In the Coptic Church it may even happen that an infant is the only recipient. The Latin Church, on the other hand, in deference to modern feeling, has not only abandoned but actually forbidden a practice which, as far as antiquity is concerned, might insist on unconditional retention.

4. There is yet another more general subject on which the widest difference, involving the same principle, exists between the two communions, ^{Absence of religious art.} namely, the whole relation of art to religious worship. Let any one enter an Oriental church, and he will at once be struck by the contrast which the architecture, the paintings, the very aspect of the ceremonial, present to the churches of the West. Often, indeed, this may arise from the poverty or oppression under which most Christian communities labor whose lot has been cast in the Ottoman Empire; but often the altars may blaze with gold — the dresses of the priests stiffen with the richest silks of Brousa — yet the contrast remains. The difference lies in the fact that Art, as such, has no place in the worship or in the edifice. There is no aiming at effect, no dim religious light, no beauty of form or color, beyond what is produced by the mere display of gorgeous and barbaric pomp. Yet it would be a great mistake to infer from this absence of art — indeed no one who has ever seen it could infer — that this in-

volves a more decided absence of form and of ceremonial. The mystical gestures, the awe which sur-
rounds the sacerdotal functions, the long repetitions,
the severance of the sound from the sense, of the
mind from the act, both in priests and people, are not
less, but more, remarkable than in the churches of the
West. The traveller who finds himself in the interior
of the Roman Catholic cathedral of Malta, after having
been accustomed for a few weeks or months to the
ritual of the convents and churches of the Levant, experiences almost the same emotion as when he passes
again from the services of the Latin to those of the Reformed Churches. This union of barbaric rudeness and
elaborate ceremonialism is, however, no contradiction;
it is an exemplification of an important law in the
human mind. There is no more curious chapter in
the history of the relation of the two Churches than
that of the Iconoclastic controversy of the ninth century. It is true that the immediate effects of this
controversy were transient — the sudden ebullition, not
of a national or popular feeling, but almost, as it would
seem, of a Puritan, or even a Mahometan, fanaticism in
the breast of a single Emperor — "a mere negative
doctrine," "which robbed the senses of their habitual
and cherished objects of devotion without awakening
an inner life of piety." The onslaught on the image-
worship of the Church passed away almost as rapidly as
it had begun; and the fanaticism which the Emperor
Leo had provoked, the Empress Irene, through the second Council of Nicæa, effectually proscribed. But in
the Eastern Church the spirit of Leo has so far revived
that, although pictures are still retained and adored with
even more veneration than the corresponding objects
of devotion in the West, statues are rigidly excluded;
and the same Greek monk, who would ridicule the fig-

ures, or even bas-reliefs, of a Roman Catholic Church, will fling his incense and perform his genuflexions with the most undoubting faith before the same saint as seen in the paintings of his own convent chapel.

The result is well given by Dean Milman : —

" The ruder the art the more intense the superstition. The perfection of the fine arts tends rather to diminish than to promote such superstition. Not merely does the cultivation of mind required for their higher exe- cution, as well as the admiration of them, imply an advanced state, but the idealism, which is their crown- ing excellence, in some degree unrealizes them, and creates a different and more exalted feeling. There is more direct idolatry paid to the rough and ill-shapen image, or the flat unrelieved and staring picture — the former actually clothed in gaudy and tinsel ornaments, the latter with the crown of gold-leaf on the head, and real or artificial flowers in the hand — than to the noblest ideal statue, or the Holy Family with all the magic of light and shade. They are not the fine paint- ings which work miracles, but the coarse and smoke- darkened boards, on which the dim outline of form is hardly to be traced. Thus it may be said that it was the superstition which required the images, rather than the images which formed the superstition. The Chris- tian mind would have found some other fetiche to which it would have attributed miraculous powers. Relics would have been more fervently worshipped, and en- dowed with more transcendent powers, without the adventitious good, the familiarizing the mind with the historic truths of Scripture, or even the legends of Christian martyrs, which at least allayed the evil of the actual idolatry. Iconoclasm left the worship of relics, and other dubious memorials of the saints, in all their vigor, while it struck at that which, after all, was a

16

higher kind of idolatry. It aspired not to elevate the general mind above superstition, but proscribed only one, and that not the most debasing form." [1]

5. Another difference presents itself, arising partly from the same causes, in the mode of dealing which the Eastern Church adopts towards independent or hostile forms of religion.

Eastern Church not missionary.

In regard to missions, the inaction of the Eastern Churches is well known. Whilst the Latin Church has sent out missionaries for the conversion of England and Germany in the Middle Ages, of South America, of India, and of China, down to our own time; whilst many Protestants pour the whole of their religious energy exclusively into missionary enterprise, the Eastern Churches, as a general rule, have remained content with the maintenance of their own faith. The preaching of Ulfilas to the Goths, of the Nestorian missions in Asia, and, in modern times, of Russia in Siberia and the Aleutian Islands, are but striking exceptions. The conversion of the Russian nation was effected, not by the preaching of the Byzantine clergy, but by the marriage of a Byzantine princess. In the midst of the Mahometan East the Greek populations remain like islands in the barren sea, and the Bedouin tribes have wandered for twelve centuries round the Greek convent of Mount Sinai probably without one instance of conversion to the creed of men whom they yet acknowledge with almost religious veneration as beings from a higher world.

Yet, if Eastern Christians have abdicated the glory of missionaries, they are exempt from the curse of proselytism; and they have (with some mournful [2] exam-

---

[1] Latin Christianity, ii. 303–304.

[2] The difficulty of arriving at the truth of the alleged Russian persecution of the Roman Catholics in Poland renders any positive statement on this sub-

ples to the contrary) been free from the still darker curse of persecution. A respectful reverence But not for every manifestation of religious feeling ing. has withheld them from violent attacks on the rights of conscience, and led them to extend a kindly patronage to forms of faith most removed from their own. The gentle spirit of the Greek Fathers has granted to the heroes and sages of heathen antiquity a place in the Divine favor, which was long denied in the West. Along the porticos of Eastern churches[1] are to be seen portrayed on the walls the figures of Homer, Solon, Thucydides, Pythagoras, and Plato, as pioneers preparing the way for Christianity. In the vast painting of the Last Judgment, which covers the west end of the chief cathedral of Moscow, Paradise is represented as divided and subdivided into many departments or chambers, thus keeping before the minds, even of the humblest, the great doctrine of the Gospel — which has often been tacitly dropped out of Western religion — "In my Father's house are many mansions." No Inquisition, no S. Bartholomew's massacre, no Titus Oates, has darkened the history of any of the nobler portions of Eastern Christendom. In Armenia, Henry Martyn's funeral at Tokat is said to have received all the honors of an Armenian archbishop. In Russia, where the power and the will to persecute exist more strongly, though proselytism is forbidden, yet the worship, not only of their own dissenters, but of Latins and Protestants, is protected as sacred. In the fair of Nijni-Novgorod, on the confluence of the Volga and the Oka, the Mahometan mosque and the Armenian church stand side by side with the orthodox cathedral.

ject next to impossible. In earlier times the worst persecution perhaps was that of the Paulicians by Theodora A. D. 835. (Gibbon, c. liv.)

[1] They may be seen in several of the Moscow churches, and in the Iberian monastery in Mount Athos.

6. In like manner the theology of the East has under-

gone no systematizing process. Its doctrines
remain in the same rigid yet undefined state
as that in which they were left by Constantine
and Justinian. The resistance to the insertion of the
words "filioque," was the natural protest of the un-
changing Church of the early Councils against the
growth, whether by development or by corruption,
of the West. Even in points where the Protestant
Churches have gone back, as they believe, to a yet
earlier simplicity of faith, the Eastern Church still presents her doctrines in a form far less repugnant to such a
simplicity than is the case with the corresponding statements in the Latin Church. Prayers for the dead exist,
but no elaborate hierarchical system has been built upon
their performance. A general expectation prevails that
by some unknown process the souls of the sinful will be
purified before they pass into the Divine presence; but
this has never been consolidated into a doctrine of pur-
gatory. The Mother of our Lord is regarded with a
veneration which, in elevation of sentiment, equals any
of the devotions addressed to her in the West; but it
is too abstract and indefinite to allot to her in the
scheme of salvation, or the protection of the Church,
the powerful place which is so precisely ascribed to her
by Latin divines. The reverence for her sanctity has
never crystallized into the modern dogma of the Immaculate Conception. Her death, encompassed as it is
by legend, is yet "the sleep" (κοίμησις) of the Virgin, not
her "assumption." The boundary between the rhetorical, poetical addresses to the saints, in the Eastern worship, and the actual invocation of their aid, has never
been laid down with precision. "Transubstantiation,"
if used at all as a theological term, is merely one
amongst many to express the reverential awe with

which the Eucharist is approached. It is not in the
exact repetition of the words of the original institution
(as in the Churches of Rome, of Luther, and of England), but in the more general and more directly spiritual form of the invocation of the Spirit, that the Eastern Church places the moment of the consecration of
the elements.

7. A similar turn is given to the institution of the
Eastern clergy, by the absence of the organiz- The East-
ing, centralizing tendency which prevailed in ern hie-
rarchy not
the West. It is not that their spirit is less hie- organized.
rarchical than that of the Latin clergy. In some respects it is more so, in proportion as it more nearly
resembles the Jewish type, of which the extreme likeness, as we have seen, is preserved in Abyssinia. The
Greek priest concealed within the veil of the sanctuary
is far more entirely shut out from the congregation than
the Latin priest standing before the altar, in the presence
of the assembled multitude, who can at least follow with
their eyes his every gesture. For centuries in the Church
of Alexandria, and still in the Church of Armenia, the
dead hand of the first bishop has been employed as the
instrument of consecration in each succeeding generation. This is a more carnal and literal representation
of a priestly succession than is to be found in any Western ordinations. But the moment we enter into practical life, and even into the groundwork of the theory
of the two Churches, the powers and pretensions of the
Greek hierarchy shrink into nothing before those of the
Latin.

The authorized descriptions of the office at once be-
speak a marked difference. The lofty terms introduced
into the Latin Church in the thirteenth century, and
still retained in our own, — " Receive the Holy Ghost
. . . . whose sins thou dost retain they are retained," —

fill the place which in the Eastern Church is occupied
by a simple prayer for the Divine blessing. The priestly
expression of absolution, which in the Western Church
was in the same thirteenth century changed into the
positive form "I absolve thee," in the Eastern Church
is still as it always was, "May the Lord absolve thee."
The independent position conferred on the Western
clergy by tithes is, at least in one portion[1] of the
Eastern Church, almost unknown. However sacred
the office whilst it is held, and however difficult and
discreditable it may be to lay it aside, yet it is not, as
in the Latin Church, indelible. An Eastern priest can
divest himself of his orders and become a layman. Although confession to a priest is deemed necessary for
all, yet it never has descended into those details of
casuistry which have in the Latin Church made it so
formidable an engine both for good and evil. The
scandals, the influence, the terrors, of the confessional
are alike unknown in the East.

The laity, on the other hand, have a part assigned
Indepen-   to them in the Eastern Church, which even in
dence of
the laity.   the Protestant churches of the West has been
with difficulty recognized. The monastic orders, although
including many clergy, are yet in the East, to a great
extent, as they are never in the West, but as they were
entirely in early times, lay and not clerical institutions.
The vast community of Athos is, practically, a lay
corporation assisted by a small body of chaplains.
The independent manly assertion of religion which pervades the Mahometan world[2] has not been lost in the
Christian East. One special rite — that of the sacred
unction of Confirmation, which, as we have seen, is conferred simultaneously with baptism, has been explained
with a force and eloquence which, on such a subject,

[1] See Lecture IX.   [2] See Lecture VIII.

rings with the tone of a Tyndale or a Luther, as symbolizing the royal priesthood of every Christian. "It destroys the wall of separation that Rome has raised between the ecclesiastic and the layman, for we are all priests of the Most High — priests though not pastors[1] — in different degrees." This explanation of the ceremony may be doubtful; but that it should be put forth at all in connection with one of the most peculiar and significant of the Oriental ecclesiastical rites, is an indication of their general spirit.

In the study of the Scriptures, and the use of the liturgy in the vernacular languages of the several nations that have adopted Eastern Christianity, we have other traces, though less direct, of the same tendency. It is true that in most Oriental Churches these languages have, by the lapse of years, become antiquated, or even dead, in the mouths of those who use them; and the clergy have been too timid or too apathetic to meet the changing exigencies of time. But the principle is maintained, that the language[2] of each separate nation, not a sacred language peculiar to the clergy, is the proper vehicle for worship and religious life. And the study of the Bible, though neglected from the barbarism of the present state of Oriental Christendom, is nowhere discouraged. The Arabic translation of the Scriptures, even in the Coptic Church, is listened to with the utmost attention, and is taught in Coptic schools. In Russia, the efforts of the Bible Society were welcomed by Alexander I.; and in Greece (until the breaking out of the War of Independence) by the collective hierarchy of Constantinople.

Study of Scriptures and use of the vernacular tongue.

"God be praised," was the expression of a devout Russian layman, in speaking of the scandals occasioned

---

[1] Quelques Mots, par un Chrétien Orthodoxe, (1853) p. 53.
[2] See Lecture IX.

by the ignorance of the Russian priesthood; "the Eastern Church has never ruled that religious light and instruction are confined to the clergy. It is still in our
own power to redeem the future."

This aspect of the institution of the Oriental hierarchy is still further brought out by two general
points of contrast with the position of the clergy of
the West.

The centralization of the West, as displayed in the
Absence of Papacy, is unknown to the East. The institu-
a Papacy.   tion of the Patriarchates is entirely Oriental.
The very name carries us back to the primitive East.
The office,[1] though first recognized at the Council of
Chalcedon, has struck deep roots in the East, never in
the West. The august brotherhood of the "All Holy,"
"the Most Blessed," Patriarchs of Constantinople, Alexandria, Antioch, and Jerusalem, amidst the degradation which has beset their little courts, still remains
as a bond to the scattered Churches of the Levant.
In the West, the very name has been lost, and amongst
all the titles of the Pope, that of "Patriarch" is not one.
This contrast between the aristocratical and monarchical
principles of the two Churches, partly the result of the
general tendencies just mentioned has been encouraged by the difference of the political circumstances of
the respective Churches. What Imperial Rome lost by
the transfer of the seat of government to the East, the
Byzantine Empire gained. What Papal Rome gained
by the removal of a rival power and splendor, that the
Patriarch of Constantinople lost. As the Pope filled the
place of the absent Emperors at Rome, inheriting their
power, their prestige, the titles which they had themselves derived from the days of their paganism, so the
Emperors controlled, guided, personified, the Church at

[1] See Gregory's Vindication.

Constantinople. No one can read Eusebius's description of the Council of Nicæa without feeling that, amongst all who were then assembled in the hall, none occupied the same preëminence as the Emperor[1] Constantine. Justinian and Theodora, great as they were in legislating for the empire, exercised a hardly less important influence in their determination, not only of the discipline but of the doctrines of the Church; and what Constantine and Justinian began has been continued by the great potentates who have ever since swayed the destinies of the Oriental hierarchy. In Constantinople itself the Sultan still exercises the right which he inherited from the last of the Cæsars; and the virtual appointment and deposition of the patriarchs[2] still places in his hands the government of the Byzantine Church—a power, no doubt, more scandalous and more pernicious in the hands of the Mussulman than it was in the hands of the Christian despot, but not more decided and absolute. And how high a place is occupied by the Emperor of Russia[3] will be seen in treating of the Russian Church especially.

Along with this difference in the position of the Papacy and the Patriarchate, was another which affected the whole position of the hierarchy itself. The *Married Clergy.* Eastern Church at its outset basked in the sunshine of Imperial favor—a regular institution, forming part of the framework of civilized society, secure from the convulsion which shook the rest of the world in the invasion of the northern barbarians. The Latin Church, entering on her career, amidst the crash of a falling Empire, and with successive hordes of wild barbarians to control, instruct, and guide, was in a far more trying position. Amongst the various steps for the organiza-

[1] See Lecture IV.
[2] The Patriarch is elected by a Synod of Bishops. But the Porte is always consulted.
[3] See Lecture X.

tion of her clergy in this struggle the chief was the enforcement of celibacy. This principle has not only never been adopted in the East, but has been repudiated even more positively than by Protestants. However fervent the Oriental Church may have been at all times in its assertion of the ascetic and monastic system, yet for the clerical body marriage is not only permitted and frequent, but compulsory, and all but universal. It is a startling sight to the traveller, after long wanderings in the south of Europe, to find himself, amongst the mountains of Greece or Asia Minor, once more under the roof of a married pastor, and see the table of the parish priest furnished, as it might be in Protestant England or Switzerland, by the hands of an acknowledged wife. The bishops, indeed, being selected from the monasteries, are single. But the parochial clergy, — that is, the whole body of the clergy as such, — though they cannot marry after their ordination, must always be married before they enter on their office.[1] In one instance, that of the Chaldæan or Nestorian Christians, the patriarch is allowed to marry.

IV. These distinctions, which might be pursued to any Advantages of a study of the Eastern Church. extent, and illustrated in every particular, will suffice to show that the differences between the two divisions of Christendom, although in some points superficial, are yet in principle more radical than those which separate the other branches of the Christian Church from each other.

It is this inward moral divergence, more than any outward theological distinction or any local distance, which occasions our ignorance and our indifference to

---

[1] This has been so long an established custom, that, like the celibacy of the Latin clergy, though not part of the doctrine, it is part of the discipline of the Church. An exception, however, has occurred in the Russian Church within the past year. A theological professor has been ordained, although unmarried.

the Eastern Church. But it is from this very divergence that accrue the chief advantages of the study of the Eastern Church.

1. The ecclesiastical history of the West is full of our own passions, our own preconceived ideas and prejudices. We run round and round in the ruts of our own controversies; every object that we see has been long familiar to us; every step that we take is in footmarks of our own making. Every name is colored with some theological sympathy or antipathy; every sect and church is our personal enemy or ally.

This living interest the history of the Eastern Church can never acquire. Yet it is refreshing to turn for a time to a region where the incidents and the characters awaken no feelings except those which are purely historical; where the principles which agitate the Church at large can be traced without the disturbing force of personal and national animosities. The names of Hildebrand, Loyola, Luther, Calvin, carry with them each a tempest of its own, which scatters commotion and excitement around its whole circumference. But no one will be able to work himself into a frenzy in defending even Chrysostom or Basil; no one will lose his temper or his charity in deciding the claims of the false or the true Demetrius, or in defending the cause of Stephen Yavorski of Riazan against Theophanes Procopovitch of Pshkoff.

Isolation of the Eastern Church from Western controversy.

And what is true of individual events or persons, is true of the whole institution. It is not only unknown and therefore fresh to us, but it is compounded in such proportions, and of such materials, as to turn the force and blunt the edge of the implements of controversy with which in the West we are always destroying one another. Many a keen assailant of Popery or of Protestantism will find himself at fault in the presence of a

Church, which is Protestant and Catholic at once, sometimes in points where we least expect to find the respective elements of discord or concord. It cuts across
the grain of our most cherished prejudices. Our well-
ordered phrases are thrown into confusion by encoun-
tering a vast communion which, in some respects, goes
so far ahead of us, in others falls so far behind us. From
such an experience we may be taught that there is a
region above and beyond our own agitations. We may
learn to be less positive in pushing theological premises
to their extreme conclusions. We may find that there
is a stubborn mass of fact against which the favorite argument of driving our adversaries into believing all or
nothing is broken to pieces. It is useful to find that
churches and sects are not exactly squared according to
our notions of what our own logic or rhetoric would
lead us to expect. The discovery of the Syrian Christians of S. Thomas on the shores of India was a fruitful
source of perplexity to both sections of European Christendom. "Their separation from the Western world,"
says Gibbon, "had left them in ignorance of the im-
provements or corruptions of a thousand years; and
their conformity with the faith and practice of the fifth
century would equally disappoint the prejudices of a
Papist or a Protestant." Such two-edged disappointments are amongst the best lessons of ecclesiastical history; and such are the disappointments which not only
the small community on the coast of Malabar, but the
whole Eastern Church impresses on the inquirers of the
West, from whatever quarter they come.

2. Again, a knowledge of the existence and claims
of the Eastern Church keeps up the equipoise
of Christendom. The weight of authority, of
numbers, of antiquity, has various attractions
for different minds. Some characters are self-poised and

*Its compe-
tition with
the Latin
Church.*

independent. Loneliness and singularity in the present, the hopes of a remote and ideal future, are to them the notes of a true Church. But there are many who are in danger of being thrown off their balance by the magnetic power of those associations which appeal to the imaginative, the social, the devotional parts of our nature.

The body with which we are most familiar as producing this effect, is the ancient and energetic community whose seat is at Rome. In it we usually see the chief impersonation of high ecclesiastical pretensions, of an elaborate ritual, of outward devotion, of wide dominion, of venerable tradition. It is close at hand; and, therefore, whether we attack or admire, it fills the whole of our view. But this effect is considerably modified by the apparition of the Eastern Church. Turn from the Tiber to the Bosphorus: we shall see that there are *two* kings in the field, *two* suns in the heavens. That figure which seemed so imposing when it was the only one which met our view, changes all its proportions when we see that it is overtopped by a vaster, loftier, darker figure behind. If we are bent on having dogmatical belief and conservative tradition to its fullest extent, we must go not to the Church which calls itself Catholic, but to the Church which calls itself Orthodox — to the Church which will die but never surrender the minutest point which Council or Father has bequeathed to it. If we are to make the most of monasticism as a necessary model of Christian perfection, we ought not to stop short with the Grande Chartreuse, or Monte Casino, when we can have the seclusion of Mount Athos, or the exaltation of Simeon Stylites. If we are to have the ancient theory of sacramental forms carried out to its extreme limits, we must not halt half-way with a Church which has curtailed the waters of baptism, and

deferred confirmation and communion to years of dis-
cretion : we must take refuge in the ancient Eastern
ritual, which still retains the threefold immersion, which
still offers the rites of chrism and of the eucharist to
the unconscious touch of infancy.

Nay, beyond the Eastern Church itself, there is a
further East to which we must go, if wisdom is to be
sought, not in moderation, but in extremes. The Greek
Church is more ceremonial than the Latin, but the Coptic is more ceremonial than the Greek, and the Abyssinian is more ceremonial than the Coptic. In the
Church of Abyssinia we shall find the best example
of what many seek in a limited degree in the West, —
a complete sacrifice of the spirit of Christianity to the
letter.

Remember, too, that if the voice of authority is
confident at Rome, it is hardly less confident at Constantinople and at Moscow. Remember, that beyond
the Carpathians, beyond the Hæmus, beyond the Ural
range, there are unbroken successions of bishops, long
calendars of holy men unknown in the West, who can
return anathema for anathema, as well as blessing for
blessing ; who can afford to regard even Augustine and
Jerome, not as canonized saints, only as "pious Christians of blessed memory." Remember, that Athos can
boast its miraculous pictures and springs, no less than
Rimini or Assisi. Remember, that in the eyes of
orthodox Greeks the Pope is not the representative
of a faith pure and undefiled, but (I quote [1] their own
words) is "the first Protestant," "the founder of German rationalism." The Eastern patriarchs speak in their
solemn documents of the Papal supremacy as "the chief
heresy of the latter days, which flourishes now as its
predecessor Arianism flourished before it in the earlier

[1] Quelques Mots, par un Chrétien Orthodoxe, 1853, p. 40.

ages, and which, like Arianism, shall in like manner be cast down and vanish away." [1] To a devout Russian the basilica of S. Peter's seems bare and cold and profane; hardly deserving the name of church — a temple without an altar. Rome itself is chiefly interesting to him because it reminds him of Moscow, [2] but even then, as he pathetically adds, "it is Moscow without the Kremlin." The Pope of Rome has fallen out of the mystic circle of the five patriarchs; he has himself dropped the name; his vacant place has been filled by the new Patriarchate [3] of Moscow.

The fact of such wide-spread, deeply rooted feelings remains in all its length and breadth to be accounted for in any hypothesis which we choose to frame of a universal Church. Eastern Christendom, so considered, is one of the strongest bulwarks against the undue claims or encroachments of any Church or see of the West, whether at Rome, or Geneva, or London.

3. Yet again, if we may make this use of the Greek Church for purposes of war and of defence, we may also make use of it for purposes of peace and harmony. It is often observed, with regard to the most general features, of manners, geography, and history, that the West can only be perfectly understood after having seen the East. A green field, a rushing stream, a mountain clothed with verdure from head to foot, will, I believe, always assume a new interest in the eyes of one who has come from the dry, bare, thirsty East. We trace a distinctness, a vividness, a family likeness in these features of Western Europe which, until we have seen their opposites, almost escape our notice.

Illustration of the unity of Western Christendom.

[1] Encyclic Epistle of the Eastern Patriarchs, 1848, § 5. (See Neale, ii. 1195.) Compare a similar Epistle, 1723, addressed to the English Nonjurors (Lathbury's History of the Nonjurors, p. 350.)

[2] Mouravieff, Questions Religieuses, p. 270.

[3] See Lecture X.

Like to this is the additional understanding of our own
portion of Christendom, gained by a contemplation of
its counterpoise in the Oriental Churches. However
great the differences between the various Western
Churches, there are peculiarities in common which imply deeper elements of consanguinity and likeness than
those which unite any of them to the communities of
the East. The variety, the stir, the life, the turmoil, the
" *drive*," as our American brethren would call it, is, in
every Western Church, contrasted with the immobility,
the repose, the inaction of Greece, of Syria, and of Russia. It is instructive for the stanch adherents of the
Reformation to feel that the Latin Church, which we
have been accustomed to regard as our chief antagonist,
has after all the same elements of Western life and civilization, as those of which we are justly proud; that,
whatever it be as compared with England or Germany,
it is, as compared with Egypt or Syria, enlightened,
progressive, — in one word, Protestant. It is instructive
for the opponents of the Reformation to see that in the
Eastern section of the Christian Church, vast as it is,
the whole Western Church, Latin and German, Papal
and Lutheran, is often regarded as essentially one; that
the first concessions to reason and freedom, which involve by necessity all the subsequent stages, were made
long before Luther, in the bosom of the Roman Church
itself; that the Papal see first led the way in schism
from the parent stock in liberty of private judgment;
that some of the most important points in which the
Latin is now distinguished from the Greek Church,
have been actually copied and imported from the new
Churches of the Protestant West. To trace this family
resemblance between the different branches of the
Occidental Church is the polemical object of an able
treatise by a zealous member of the Church of Rus-

sia:[1] to trace it in a more friendly and hopeful spirit is a not unworthy aim of students of the Church of England.

4. But it would be unjust to our Eastern brethren to draw from them lessons merely of contrast and disparagement. There are those, no doubt, who look on the Oriental Church merely as the dead trunk, from which all sap and life *Advantages of the Eastern over the Western Church.* have departed, fit only to be cut down, because it cumbers the ground. But it is also, beyond doubt, the aged tree, beneath whose shade the rest of Christendom has sprung up. We may ask whether its roots have not struck too widely and too deeply in its native soil to allow of any other permanent form of religious life in those regions which does not in some degree engraft itself on that ancient stem.[2] We may thankfully accept even the sluggish barbarism and stagnation which have, humanly speaking, saved so large and so venerable a portion of the Christian world from the consolidation of the decrees of Trent, and from the endless subdivisions of Augsburg and Geneva. We may reflect with satisfaction that should ever the hour come for the reawakening of the Churches of the East, there is no infallible pontiff at Constantinople, no hierarchy separated from the domestic charities of life, to prevent the religious and social elements from amalgamating into one harmonious whole. We may gratefully remember that there is a theology in the

---

[1] Quelques Mots, par un Chrétien Orthodoxe, 1853 and 1854.

[2] "Let foreigners bring us light, and we will thank them for it: but we beg of them not to bring fire to burn our house about our ears." — *Saying of a Greek bishop*, recorded in Masson's *Apology for the Greek Church*, p. 7. In quoting this little work, which, though disfigured by some personal partialities, contains much good sense and charity, I cannot forbear to express my obligations to its author. To my intercourse with him at Athens, now twenty years ago, I owe my first interest in the state of the Greek Church.

world of which the free, genial mind of Chrysostom
is still the golden mouth-piece ; a theology[1] in
which scholastic philosophy has had absolutely no
part; in which the authority alike of Duns Scotus and
of Calvin is unknown.   Doubtless the future of the
whole Church is to be sought, not in the East, but in
the West.   But there is a future also for the Church
of the East.   Have we not known characters, venerable
from age or station, who, with the most immovable adherence to ancient hereditary forms of belief and practice, yet, when brought into contact with the views of
a younger and more stirring generation, have by the
very distance from which they approach given it a new
turn, showed a capacity for enduring, tolerating, understanding it, such as we should have vainly sought from
others more nearly allied by pursuits or dispositions ?
Such is, to an indefinite extent, the position of the Eastern Christian towards the Western.   Kept aloof from
our controversies, escaping our agitations, he comes
upon them with a freedom and freshness, which in the
wear and tear of the West can no longer be found.
He has the rare gift of an ancient orthodox belief without intolerance and without proselytism.   He is firmly
and proudly attached to his own Church and nation,
yet has a ready and cordial recognition to give to the
faith of others.   He knows, and we know, that although
he may become a European, yet we can by no possibility become Asiatics.   And such a knowledge engen-
ders a confidence, which between rivals and neigh-

---

1 " The Greeks of the humbler classes have a good acquaintance with the
Gospel History and the Life of our Lord ; but — they know nothing of *Substitution.*"   Such was the lamentation of an excellent Presbyterian minister
who had been long resident amongst them, in answer to the inquiry of an
English traveller on the state of religious knowledge in the East.   What was
thus said of the poor Greeks of the present day is no less true of their most
illustrious theologians in former time.

bors is almost unattainable.   He stands on the confines
of the East and West, drawn eastward by his habits, by
his lineage, by his local position; drawn westward by
the inevitable, onward, westward progress of Christianity and of civilization.   In him, therefore, we find a
link between those two incommunicable spheres, such
as can be found nowhere else.   The Greek race may
yet hand back from Europe to Asia the light which, in
former days, it handed on from Asia to Europe.   The
Sclavonic race may yet impart by the Volga or the
Caspian the civilization which it has itself received by
the Neva and the Baltic.

And we, too, with all our energy and life, may learn
something from the otherwise unparalleled sight of
whole nations and races of men, penetrated by the
religious sentiment which visibly sways their minds
even when it fails to reach their conduct, which if it
has produced but few whom we should call saints or
philosophers, has produced through centuries of oppression whole armies of confessors and martyrs.   We may
learn something from the sight of a calm strength, re-
posing " in the quietness and confidence " of a treasure
of hereditary belief, which its possessor is content to
value for himself, without forcing it on the reception
of others.   We may learn something from the sight of
Churches, where religion is not abandoned to the care
of women and children, but is claimed as the right
and the privilege of men ; where the Church reposes
not so much on the force and influence of its clergy
as on the independent knowledge and manly zeal of
its laity.

5. Yet once more, — if there is any Church which
may be expected to learn congenial and useful *Its use to*
lessons from the study of Eastern Christendom, *the Church*
of Eng-
it is our own.   I do not lay stress on the pos- *land.*

sible connection of the ancient British Church with
Eastern missionaries before the arrival of Augustine,
nor on the more certain influence of the East on the
Anglo-Saxon Church when Theodore of Tarsus sat on
the throne of Canterbury. These associations are too
slight to sustain any substantial argument. But there
are likenesses between our position and that of the
Eastern Churches, which, amidst great differences, may
render the knowledge of their history specially profitable in the study of our own. The national character
of our religion, which is at once our boast and our reproach, finds a parallel — even an exaggerated parallel
—in the Eastern identification of nationality and creed,
such as the larger ideas of continental Europe will hardly
tolerate or understand either in us or in them. The relations of Church and State, as portrayed in Hooker's
Ecclesiastical Polity, are avowedly based on those of
the ancient Church of Constantinople, and still find
their counterpart in the modern Church of Russia.
If the ecclesiastical commonwealth of our own little
island, with manifold contending principles within its
pale, and manifold sects multiplying without, can be
better understood by the sight of a like phenomenon,
reproduced on a gigantic scale, from different causes, in
the remote East, let no one grudge us this advantage
from the consideration of the double-sided, contradictory
aspect of the Eastern Churches, or the vigor and wide
extension of the Eastern sects. And if ever the question, often agitated, should be brought to issue, and any
changes should be attempted in the English Prayer-Book,
many scruples might be soothed by recurring to the model
of the Eastern Church. What has never been received into
the creeds or the services[1] of Churches venerable as those

---

[1] I allude to the passage relating to Absolution in the Ordination and Visi-
tation Services, and the adoption of the Athanasian Creed. The first two

of Oriental Christendom, cannot by any sound argument be represented as indispensable to the character of the Church of England.

"I die in the faith of the Catholic Church, before the disunion of East and West." Such was the dying hope of good Bishop Ken.[1] It was an aspiration which probably no one but an English churchman would have uttered. We may not be able to go along with the whole of the feeling involved in the thought. But it expresses a true belief that in the Church of England there is a ground of antiquity, of freedom, and of common sense, on which we may calmly and humbly confront both of the great divisions of Christendom, without laying ourselves open to the charge of ignorant presumption, or of learned trifling, or of visions that can never be realized. We know, and it is enough to know, that the Gospel, the original Gospel, which came from the East and now rules in the West, is large enough to comprehend them both.

NOTE ON THE DOCTRINE OF THE PROCESSION OF THE HOLY SPIRIT.

The question of the Double Procession furnishes so many illustrations of the points laid down in the previous Lecture, that it may be well to devote a few words to its history.

1. It brings out forcibly the contrast noticed above between the systematizing, innovating tendency of the West, and the simpler and more conservative tendency of the East. The Western

are mediæval and Latin, as distinct from ancient and catholic. (See p. 125.) The third is distinctly opposed to the Eastern Church. (See Lecture VII.)

1 Life of Ken, by a Layman, p. 509.

insertion of the words "from the Son" (*filioque*) arose in the Spanish Church, from the logical development of the Athanasian doctrine against the Arian Visigoths. The Greek refusal to admit these words arose from the repugnance to any change in the decrees or creeds laid down in the early Councils, analogous to that which animated the Russian dissenters against Nicon and Peter (see Lecture XII.).

2. It well exemplifies the double-sided aspect of most theological doctrines. Each of the two statements expresses a truth which the other overlooks or omits. In the original statement of the Nicene or Constantinopolitan Creed, which makes the Spirit to proceed from the Father alone, is the necessary safeguard of the abstract unity of the Godhead. It is urged that to make the Spirit proceed equally from both the Persons in the Trinity, is to imply two principles or originating powers in the Divine Essence. In the Western view, which associates the Son with the Father, it is maintained that the addition of the disputed words was needed to assert the identity of the Father and the Son in all the acts of redemption, and especially the identity of the Spirit of Christ with the Spirit of God. Both statements may be reconciled if the former is understood as applying to the abstract and eternal essence of the Deity, the latter to the Divine operations in the redemption of man. If the word "proceed" (ἐκπορεύεσθαι) be used in a strictly scientific, or, it may be added, biblical sense, then the Greeks are in the right. If it be used according to popular usage, then the Latins are not in the wrong.

3. It is an excellent specimen of the race of "extinct controversies." For nearly a thousand years it seemed to the contending parties to be of such importance as to justify the rent between East and West. It was probably the chief reason for cherishing the Athanasian Creed and the anathemas peculiar to that confession (see Lecture VII.). By the disputes which it engendered at the Council of Florence, it largely contributed to the fall of the Byzantine Empire. The capture of Constantinople on Whitsunday was regarded in the West as a Divine judgment on the East for its heresy in regard to the Spirit, whose festival was thus awfully vindicated. Yet now the whole question is laid completely to rest. In the West it is never seriously discussed.

In the East it is remembered, and will never, perhaps, be forgotten; but it is more as a point of honor than of faith; it is more the mode of our Western innovation, than the substance of our doctrine, that rouses their indignation.[1]

[1] For the details of the doctrine, see Adam Zernikoff, as quoted by Neale, ii. 1154. Mouravieff, Questions Réligieuses, 860.

LECTURE II.

THE COUNCIL OF NICÆA.

The Authorities for the Council of Nicæa are as follows: —

I. The original documents.

    a. The Creed.

    b. The Twenty Canons.   }   Contained in Mansi's Councils, ii. 625–701, and the historians given below.

    c. The Official Letters.

      1. Letter of Constantine, convoking the Bishops from Ancyra. (Mr. Harris Cowper, Analecta Nicæna, 21.)

      2. Letter of Constantine to the Bishops, denouncing the books of Arius.

      3. Letter of Constantine against Arius.

      4. Letter of Constantine to the Bishops, containing the decree on Easter.

      5. Letter of the Council to the Church of Alexandria, on the three points of debate.

      6. Letter of Eusebius to the Church of Cæsarea, Theod. i., explaining his subscriptions.

      7. Letters of Eusebius and Theognis, praying for re-admission.

      8. Letter of Constantine against Eusebius.

      9. Letter of Constantine to Theodotus, warning him against Eusebius.

    d. Apocryphal canons, subscriptions, letters, &c., given in Mansi's Councils, ii. 710–1071.

II. Eye-witnesses.

    a. Eusebius of Cæsarea in the Life of Constantine, iii. 4–24; and in his Letter to the Church of Cæsarea. (Theod. i. 9.)

    b. Athanasius.

      1. The Tract on the Decrees of the Nicene Council.

      2. Epistle to the Africans.

      3. Orations against Arians.

      4. On the Councils of Ariminum and Seleucia.

    c. Eustathius of Antioch. A short extract in Theod. i. 8.

    d. Auxano, a Novatian Presbyter, who had been present as a boy. He told his experience to Socrates. (H. E. ii. 1.)

e. Old people alive in Jerome's time, whom he had seen. (Adv. Lucif. c. 20.)

III. Historians of the next generation.

1. Rufinus. (H. E. i. 1–6.) A. D. 380–401.
2. Ambrose. (De Fide.) A. D. 333–397.
        (These are the only two Western authorities.)
3. Epiphanius. (Hær. lxix.) A. D. 360–401.
4. Socrates. (H. E. i. 4–14.) A. D. 380–440.
5. Sozomen. (H. E. i. 15–28.) A. D. 380–443.
6. Philostorgius. (Arian Fragments.) A. D. 350–425.
7. Theodoret. (H. E. i. 1–13.) A. D. 394–458.
8. The lost history of the Council of Nicæa (in Syriac) by Maruthas, Bishop of Tagrit or Maipherkin, in Mesopotamia (A. D. 410), "*Opus valdè aureum : sed proh dolor ! necdum inventum.*" (Asseman. Biblioth. Orient. i. p. 177, 195.)

IV. Later Historians.

1. Gelasius of Cyzicus. (Fifth century.) Acts of the Council, filled with imaginary speeches. The book professes to be founded on an old MS. in his father's house.
2. "Eutychius," otherwise "Sayd Ibn Batrik," of Cairo. A. D. 876–950. Arabic Annals of Alexandria, printed by Pococke, and partly edited by Selden.
3. Gregory the Presbyter. (Tenth century.) "Panegyric of the Nicene Fathers," printed in the Novum Auctarium of Combefis, vol. ii. p. 547.
4. Nicephorus. A. D. 1390–1450. (H. E. from A. D. 1–610.)

V. Modern Historians. — Of these may be selected :

a. English.

1. Gibbon's " Decline and Fall," c. 21.
2. Dean Milman's " History of Christianity under the Empire," vol. ii. pp. 431–448.
3. " Some Account of the Council of Nicæa," by Bishop Kaye. (1853.)

b. German.

1. Ittig's " History of the Council " (a brief documentary summary). (1644–1710.)
2. Walch's " History of Heresies," vol. ii. 385–689. (1762.)
3. Hefele's " History of the Councils," book ii. (1855.)

c. French.

1. Tillemont's " Ecclesiastical History," vol. vi. (1637–1698.)
2. Fleury's " Ecclesiastical History," book iii. (1640–1723.)
3. Albert Prince de Broglie's " History of the Church and the Empire in the Fourth Century," c. iv. (1857.)

19

THE COUNCIL OF NICÆA AND THE SEVEN GENERAL COUNCILS.

THE earliest important development of the Eastern Church is the First General Council of Nicæa. This event I propose to describe with all the particularity of detail of which it is capable; to describe it in such a way that it may remain fixed in our memories; to describe it, as it appeared to those who lived at the time. In this opening Lecture it will be my object to vindicate the place which I have assigned to it in that portion of Ecclesiastical History which I have undertaken to treat.

I. On the one hand we must consider its peculiar connection with the Eastern Church. This connection it has in common with the first Seven General Councils. The locality of these great assemblies was always Eastern; in most instances immediately in the neighborhood of the centre of Eastern Christendom, within reach of Constantinople. Their decrees were written, their debates were conducted, not in Latin, but in Greek. They are still honored by the Oriental Church with a reverence which hardly any Western Council has received in the West. The series of the Seven Councils is the constant subject of the sacred paintings in the cathedrals of Russia, in the monasteries of Athos, in the basilica[1] of Bethlehem. Each can be traced by its peculiar arrangements, or by the Emperor or Empress who presides. Once a year, on the first Sunday[2] in Lent, called Orthodox Sunday, all the Seven Councils are commemorated in one, the anniversary of the last: the service and ceremonial of the Church is made to reproduce the image of the ancient

Oriental character of the Seven General Councils,

---

[1] At Bethlehem and in Russia, they are on the south side of the nave. In Athos they are usually in the cloister or outer narthex. The most remarkable of these representations is in the Iberian monastery.

[2] Neale. Hist. of the Eastern Church, Introd. ii. 867.

synods — bishops, presbyters, and deacons, seated round in the semicircular form in which the old pictures represent them. The Eastern bishops still promise in the service of consecration to observe their decrees; and not only is their memory preserved in learned or ecclesiastical circles, but even illiterate peasants, to whom, in the corresponding class of life in Spain or Italy, the names of Constance and Trent would probably be quite unknown, are well aware that their Church reposes on the basis of the Seven Councils, and retain a hope that they may yet live to see an eighth General Council, in which the evils of the time will be set straight. The subjects discussed in the assemblies, and the occasions which called them together, were especially Eastern and Greek. This could hardly have been otherwise. The whole force and learning of early Christianity was in the East. A general Council in the West would have been almost an absurdity. With the exception of the few writers of North Africa, there was no Latin defender of the faith. With the exception of Tertullian, there was not a single early heretic of eminence in the West. The controversies on which the Councils turned all moved in the sphere of Grecian and Oriental metaphysics. They were such as no Western mind could have originated.

What may be said of all the Seven Councils, is true of the earliest and greatest of them. The Council of Nicæa was held not in a Western but an Eastern city. Of the three hundred and eighteen bishops whose subscriptions were affixed to its decrees, only eight at most came from the West. The language of its Creed is not only not Latin, but is almost untranslatable into Latin.[1] Grecized forms

and of the Nicene Council especially.

---

[1] e. g. *Usia* (for οὐσία); *Homoüsion; Dominum vivificantem* (for τὸ κύριον τὸ ζωοποιοῦν.)

have been adopted for some of its more subtle expressions. Others have been modified in order to be
accommodated to their new garb. The one phrase introduced by the Western Church, "filioque,"[1] was only
introduced gradually, irregularly, and reluctantly, in the
West, and has never been admitted into the East. In
the Western Church the ancient Latin, commonly called
the "Apostles' Creed," has been long since overlaid
by later documents: by the Creed of Pius V. in the
Church of Rome, by the numerous Confessions of Augsburg, London, Westminster, Geneva, in the Protestant
Churches. But throughout the Eastern Church the
Nicene Creed is still the one bond of faith. It is still
recited in its original tongue by the peasants of Greece.
Its recitation is still the culminating point of the service
in the Church of Russia. The great bell of the Kremlin
tower sounds during the whole time that its words are
chanted. It is repeated aloud in the presence of the
assembled people by the Czar at his coronation. It is
worked in pearls on the robes of the highest dignitaries
of Moscow. One of the main grounds of schism in the
seventeenth and eighteenth centuries from the Established Church of Russia[2] was, that the old dissenters
were seized with the belief that the patriarch Nicon had
altered one of the sacred words of the original text of
the creed. The anniversary of the Council is still celebrated on special days. Every article of the Nicene
Creed is exhibited, according to the fashion of the Russian Church, in little pictures, and thus familiarized to
the popular mind.

It is necessary to dwell on the Oriental character of
the Nicene Council and Creed, because we cannot rightly understand it without bearing in mind its peculiar
origin; and also, because, in justice to the Eastern

[1] See Lecture I. p. 141.   [2] See Lecture XII.

Church, we must remember that whatever value we attach to this venerable confession, whatever reverence we pay to this great Council, is due, not to our own sphere of Christendom, not to the Church of Rome, but to that remote region with which we have now hardly any concern. The position of the Nicene Creed in our Liturgy is a perpetual memorial of the distant East. Other like memorials remain in the "Kyrie eleison," the "Gloria in excelsis," parts of the "Te Deum," and the prayer of S. Chrysostom. But more remarkable than these, as a link uniting our worship with that of Alexandria and Constantinople, is the Creed which was elaborated by the Egyptian and Syrian Bishops at Nicæa.

II. But I have also to show that this Oriental assembly, this Greek confession, have a place in the General universal history of the world. To a certain interest of degree, and perhaps by a kind of prescriptive the Seven Councils, right, this general interest attaches, as their name would imply, to all the Eastern Councils to which by the Greek, the Latin, or the Protestant Churches the title of "general" or "œcumenical" has been conceded.

The eight Councils, as enumerated by the Latins, the seven as enumerated by the Greeks, all turned on controversies producing more important effects than have followed on any action of the Oriental Church in later times. The doctrines of the first four were raised by the Emperor Justinian to the level of the Holy Scriptures, and their decrees to the rank of Imperial laws; [1] and they have even received a limited acknowledgment in the Church of England. It is well known that in one of the earliest Acts of Elizabeth, which undoubt-

---

[1] "Dogmata, sicut sanctas scripturas, accipimus, et regulas sicut leges observamus." — *In Authenticis*, collatione ix. tit. vi. De Ecclesiasticis Regulis et Privilegiis. (Routh's Opusc. i. 363.)

edly has considerable authority as expressive of the mind of the foundress of the present constitution of our Church, the Councils of Nicæa, Constantinople, Ephesus, and Chalcedon are raised as judges of heresy to the same level as " the High Court of Parliament, with the assent of the English clergy in their convocation." [1] Even at the present day, in spite of the vast accumulation of dogmatic statements in our popular Western theology, it is acknowledged by many English churchmen that " besides the decrees of the four General Councils, nothing is to be required as matter of belief necessary for salvation." [2]

Still we cannot say that the importance of all these early Councils is fully recognized. Their official decrees have never gained a place, and are never even mentioned, in our formularies. The fifth, sixth, and seventh are rarely named by Protestant theologians. The fourth (that of Chalcedon) is, as we have seen, rejected by a large part of the East. The third (of Ephesus) is repudiated by the Chaldæan Christians, and its distinguishing formula, " the Mother of God," has never been frankly accepted by Protestant Churches. The Council of Constantinople was avowedly only an Eastern assembly. Not a single Western bishop was present; and its œcumenical character, after having been entirely passed over by the Council of Ephesus, was only tardily acknowledged by the Council of Chalcedon.

But with the Nicene assembly it is otherwise. Alone *and of the Nicene Council especially.* of all the Councils it still retains a hold on the mass of Christendom. Its creed, as we just now saw, is the only creed accepted throughout the Universal Church. The Apostles' Creed and the Atha-

1 1 Eliz. c. 1.

2 Bishop Taylor's " Advice to his Clergy," quoted in the Enchiridion Theologicum, i. 348 ; and in the Oxford Controversial Sermons of 1856.

nasian Creed have never been incorporated into the ritual of the Greek Church. But the Nicene Creed, Greek and Eastern though it be, has a place in the liturgies and confessions of all Western Churches, at least down to the end of the sixteenth century. It was regarded at the time, and long afterwards, even by Councils which chafed under the acknowledgment, as a final settlement of the fundamental doctrines of Christianity; and so in a certain sense it has been regarded by many theologians of later times.

And, if we examine the relations of this Council to the history of the period, its superiority to the later Councils will still hold good.

1. Eutychianism, Nestorianism, Apollinarianism, represent sects which, except in the remote East, have not, nor have ever had, any lasting significance. But the Arian sect, the occasion of the Nicene Council, though it also has now long been laid to sleep, yet for three hundred years after the date of its origin was a considerable power, both political and religious; and this, not only in the Eastern regions of its birth, but in our own Western and Teutonic nations. The whole of the vast Gothic population which descended on the Roman Empire, so far as it was Christian at all, held to the faith of the Alexandrian heretic. Our first Teutonic version of the Scriptures was by an Arian missionary, Ulfilas. The first conqueror of Rome, Alaric, the first conqueror of Africa, Genseric, were Arians. Theodoric the Great, King of Italy, and hero of the Nibelungen Lied, was an Arian. The vacant place in his massive tomb at Ravenna is a witness of the vengeance which the Orthodox took on his memory, when on their triumph they tore down the porphyry vase in which his Arian subjects had enshrined his ashes. The ferocious Lombards were Arians till they

began to be won over by their queen Theodelinda, at
the close of the sixth century. But the most remarkable stronghold of Arianism were the Gothic kingdoms
of Spain and Southern France. In France, it needed
all the power of Clovis, the one orthodox chief of the
barbarian nations, to crush it on the plains of Poitiers.
In Spain, it expired only in the sixth century, when it
was renounced by King Recared in the basilica of Toledo. But even in that "most Catholic" kingdom its
traces have been thought to remain in the heretical
names which elsewhere in Europe had ceased to exist.
The favorite divine of Philip II., the first librarian of
the Escurial, was "Arias Montanus." And of the intensity of the Spanish struggle between the ancient
expiring heresy and the new triumphant orthodoxy,
three memorials still remain in all Western liturgies,
including our own. One is the constant recitation
of what was then considered the orthodox formula —
" Gloria Patri, *et* Filio, *et* Spiritui Sancto " — at the close
of every psalm. Another is the practice (adopted from
the Eastern Church) of reciting the Nicene Creed in its
present place, before the administration of the Eucharist,
to guard that ordinance against Arian intruders. The
third is the insertion of the words "filioque" into the
Creed, as an additional safeguard for the Creed itself.[1]
These three innovations (as they then were) are all said
to have proceeded from the Councils of Toledo, in their
reaction from the vanquished Arianism.

It implies an immense vitality, inherent in the orthodox doctrine established at Nicæa, that it should have
won its way against such formidable antagonists, and
should have securely seated itself in the heart of the
Church for so many subsequent centuries.

[1] See Lecture VII.

Constantine, indeed, and even at intervals Athanasius himself, endeavored to moderate the zeal to which the eager partisans on both sides pursued their quarrel at the time; and looking back from later times, Erasmus [1] in the Reformation, and Bishop Kaye in our own age, have regarded the controversy as carried to a pitch beyond any bounds which faith or wisdom could reasonably sanction. But the importance of its actual effects at the time, and for some centuries afterwards, on the opinions and the feelings of Christendom, can hardly be overstated, and the final result is one of those victories which go far to justify the cause itself.

Nor has the interest of the controversy entirely ceased with the final extermination of the Arian sect by the sword of Clovis, and the conversion of Recared and Theodelinda. From that time no doubt the continuous existence of the Arian tradition was broken; and no system of opinions which has since arisen can be considered as in any true historical sense the representative of the old Alexandrian and Gothic heresy. The Arianism (as it is sometimes called) of Milton, of Whiston, and of Sir Isaac Newton, differed in three important particulars (which shall shortly be described [2] hereafter) from the system of Arius and Eusebius. Nothing is more needed in Ecclesiastical history than to guard against the illusion of inferring an identity of belief and feeling, merely from an identity of name. The Anabaptists of the nineteenth century are hardly more different from the Anabaptists of the sixteenth, than the Arians of the seventeenth century were from the Arians of the fourth.

Still the fundamental principle of the old Arianism, as separate from the logical form and the political or-

---

1 See Ittig's Council of Nicæa, § xlvii.
2 See Lecture III.

20

ganization which it assumed, has hardly ever departed from the Church.[1] It has penetrated where we should least expect to find it. The theological opinions of many who have thought themselves, and been thought by others, most orthodox, have been deeply colored by the most conspicuous tendencies of the doctrine of Arius. Often men have been attacked as heretics, only because they agreed too closely with the doctrine of Athanasius. "Ingemuit orbis et miratus est se esse Arianum," is a process which has been strangely repeated, more than once, in the course of ecclesiastical history. To track such identity under seeming differences, and such differences under seeming identity, is a duty prescribed to the Christian theologian by the very highest authority.

2. But over and above the magnitude of the question discussed between Arius and Athanasius, there are other considerations which make the first Nicene Council a fruitful field of ecclesiastical study.

It was the earliest great historical event, so to speak, which had affected the whole Church, since the *Importance of the period.* close of the Apostolic age. In the two intervening centuries there had been many stirring incidents, two or three great writers, abundance of curious and instructive usages. But all was isolated and fragmentary. Even the persecutions are imperfectly known. We are still in the catacombs: here and there a light appears to guide us; here and there is the authentic grave of a saint and a martyr, or the altar or picture of a primitive assembly; but the regular course of ecclesiastical history is still waiting to begin, and it does not begin till the Council of Nicæa. Then, for the first time, the Church meets the Empire face to face. The

---

[1] On this more general aspect of the controversy, I shall enlarge in Lecture VII.

excitement, the shock, the joy, the disappointment, the hope of the meeting communicate themselves to us. It is one of those moments in the history of the world which occur once, and cannot be repeated. It is the last point whence we can look back on the dark, broken road of the second and third centuries, of which I have just spoken. It is the first point whence we can look forward to the new and comparatively smooth and easy course which the Church will have to pursue for two centuries, indeed, in some sense, for twelve centuries onwards. The line of demarcation between the Nicene and the ante-Nicene age, is the most definite that we shall find till we arrive at the invasion of the barbarians.

The form, too, which this decisive event assumed, is memorable as the first of a series of events *The Nicene Council as* which have now become extinct. The Coun- *the first example* cil of Nicæa is the first "General Council" — *of a General Coun-* the first of that long series of eighteen synods *cil.* which ended, and in all probability has ended forever, in the Council of Trent. In the church in which was held the last session of that latest of the Councils, is a vaunting inscription, which unconsciously conveys the truth that this was the end of the succession, of which it brought up the rear: —

> " Sacra limina ingressus
>   Infra quæ *postremum*
>   Spiritus Sanctus
>   Deus æternus munificus
>   Solator ecclesiæ catholicæ
>   Per concilium magnum legitimum
>   Oracula effudit,
>   Quisquis es
>   Mitte tibi præoptari
>   *Nicæam, Constantinopolim,*

Chalcedonem, Lugdunum,
Viennam, Constantiam,
Florentiam.
Roma ipsa hoc nomine
Tibi par non majus dedit."

Wide as was the difference between the first and the last, yet still there is a family likeness, which renders each an illustration of the other; and which, therefore, renders the study of any one of them a study of all. Of all the institutions recorded in ecclesiastical history they are, or ought to be, the most significant. And, if the first Council of Nicæa be the one which, by its antiquity and its sanctity, commands the most general homage, we shall have in its sessions the advantage of observing a Council under the most favorable circumstances.

There are three characteristics which were fixed in the Council of Nicæa, and which it shared more or less with all that followed.

a) First, as its name implies, it is the earliest example of a large assembly professing to represent the voice and the conscience of the whole Christian community. Meetings and synods there had been before, but this was the first open inauguration of them, in the face of day. Its title at the time was, in contradistinction to all which had gone before — " The Great and Holy Synod."

It was the decisive sanction of the doctrine that a free and numerous assembly is the best channel for arriving at Christian truth. It is obvious that this was not the necessary or only course that might have been pursued. In heathen ages, and also in many Christian ages, decisions have been sought in particular spots or from particular persons, oracles, hermits, shrines, gifted men, sovereigns, bishops, popes.

Delibera-tive char-acter of Councils.

But none of these courses were adopted in the first times of the Church. Even as far back as the apostolic age the most important question which agitated the Christian community was determined, not, indeed, by a gathering of different Churches, but still by an assembly in some respects far more democratic than any which succeeded. The Council of Jerusalem consisted not only of the apostles and elders, but of the brethren also. It was a decision of the whole Church of Jerusalem, laity as well as clergy. This, as far as we know, was the last instance of such an extension of the legislative body of the Church. But the principle of a popular as distinguished from an individual authority was recognized in all the provincial synods, and was finally adopted on the grandest scale at the Nicene Council. Freedom and deliberation were thus proclaimed to be the best means of deciding a question of high Christian doctrine. Whether the means succeeded or not, is not now the question. But it is remarkable that in that age of despotism and political inactivity it should have been adopted at all. As it has been said that the early Christian bishops were the only likenesses of the tribunes of the ancient Roman republic, so it may be said that the Councils were the only likenesses of the ancient Roman senates. The old spirit of liberty which had died away, or been suppressed everywhere else, revived, or was continued, in the ecclesiastical synods of the Empire, just as now in France, free discussion, banished from all other places, still maintains its hold in the literary and scientific meetings of the Institute. The Christian Church is not the only religious system which has had the courage to intrust its highest interests to the decision of large and, at times, tumultuous assemblies; it is one of the curious parallels often observed between Christianity and the outward forms

of the wide-spread religion of Buddhism, that there
also general councils [1] have been called to decide questions of faith and discipline. But this is the only parallel. Nothing of the kind existed in ancient paganism,
and nothing of the kind has arisen in modern Mahom-
edanism. Whatever might be the disadvantages and
weaknesses attendant upon the institution, the Christian Church must have the credit of having made the
effort of giving to all its members a voice in the settlement of its highest interests, and of uniting all the
various elements of which it was composed, from time
to time, for one common purpose.

And they are also the first precedents of the principle
of representative government. The Nicene Council,
like those which followed, and (with the exception of
that recorded in the Acts of the Apostles) like those
which preceded, consisted chiefly, if not exclusively, of
bishops. But the bishops at that time were literally
the representatives [2] of the Christian communities over
which they presided. They were elected by universal
suffrage, and they considered themselves responsible to
their constituents, to a degree which at times reminds
us, even painfully, of the vices of modern constitutional
government. Eusebius felt himself bound to explain to
his diocese at Cæsarea the grounds on which he had
given his vote at Nicæa; and at Chalcedon, so intense
was the fear of their countrymen entertained by the
Egyptian bishops, that they threw themselves in an
agony at the feet of the Council, with the cry of, " Spare
us — kill us here, if you will — but do not send us home
to certain death. The whole province of Egypt will
rise against us." [3]

[1] For the Buddhist councils see Turnour's translation of the Mahawanso, i.
11–43. The first council was held B. C. 543 ; the second, B. C. 443 ; the third,
B. C. 309.

[2] ἐντολεῖς. Mansi, Concil. vii. 58.   [3] See Mansi, Concil. vii. 57.

b) Another characteristic of a General Council first exemplified at Nicæa is stated in somewhat polemical language, but still with substantial truth, in the well-known words of the 21st of the Thirty-nine Articles of the Church of England: " General Councils may not be gathered together but by the commandment and will of Princes."

What the Article here states controversially as against the Church of Rome, was a recognized fact and principle in the historical constitution of a General Council. It was almost implied in the meaning of the word. An " Œcumenical Synod," that is, an " Imperial gathering" from the whole οἰκουμένη, or Empire (for this was the technical meaning of the word, even in the Greek [1] of the New Testament), could be convened only by the Emperor. This was assumed as a matter of course in the case of Nicæa, and indeed of all the Eastern Councils. Not only no single bishop, but no single prince [2] (unless we take the word in its most ancient sense), was sufficient to convene a general assembly from all parts of that vast territory. A Council was part, as it were, of the original constitution of the Christian Empire; and however much disputed afterwards in the entanglement of civil and ecclesiastical relations in the West, the principle has never been wholly abandoned. When the Western Empire fell, the Eastern Emperor still retained the inalienable right, and when the Eastern Emperor became inaccessible to the needs of European Christendom, and a new " Holy Roman Empire" was erected in the West, then the Emperor of Germany (solely or, more properly, conjointly with his Byzantine brother) succeeded to the rights of Constantine.

[1] See Luke ii. 1.

[2] We must bear in mind, that in the sixteenth century, the word " prince" was used for " sovereign," as e. g. in the case of Elizabeth, and probably it was here used in its classical sense for the " Princeps" or Roman Emperor.

We shall see in the forms of the Council of Nicæa the earliest precedents, not so much of our ecclesiastical synods as of our parliaments, convened by the writ of the sovereign, opened by his personal presence, swayed by his personal wishes and advice. And if we look from the first to the fourth General Council, of which the forms are more fully preserved, and in which perhaps the independence both of the Roman citizen and of the Christian bishop had sunk to a lower pitch, we shall see in the reception of the Emperor Marcian and the Empress Pulcheria, who came with their whole court to ratify the decrees of Chalcedon, something more than a mere nominal presidency. The assembled Bishops exclaimed (and here I give the words as reported at the time)—"To Marcian, the new Constantine, the new Paul, the new David, long years— long years to our sovereign lord David. . . . You are the peace of the world, long life. Your faith will defend you. Thou honorest Christ. He will defend thee. Thou hast established orthodoxy. . . . To the august Empress, many years. You are the lights of orthodoxy. . . . Orthodox from her birth, God will defend her. Defender of the faith, may God defend her. Pious, orthodox enemy of heretics, God will defend her. Thou hast persecuted all the heretics. May the evil eye be averted from your Empire. Worthy of the faith, worthy of Christ. So are the faithful sovereigns honored. . . . Marcian is the new Constantine, Pulcheria is the new Helena. . . . Your life is the safety of all; your faith is the glory of the churches. By thee the world is at peace; by thee the orthodox faith is established; by thee heresy ceases to be: long life to the Emperor and Empress." [1]

This secular character (I use the word in no invidious sense), thus stamped upon the institution of Councils

[1] Mansi, vii. 170.

from the first, they never lost. Western Christendom, separated from the Byzantine Imperial court, and never completely subjugated to its own Imperial head in Germany, was not equally dependent on the Emperor for its general assemblies. But they were still cast in the same Imperial mould. The sanction of the Emperor was still required.[1] An appeal to a General Council was the half-temporal half-spiritual weapon which the Emperors and Kings of Europe always held in reserve as a rejoinder to a Papal interdict. Even so submissive a sovereign as Philip II. did not hesitate to use the threat to the refractory Paul IV. Even so late as the Council of Constance, the Emperor Sigismund appeared in person. In the Council of Trent, the ambassadors of all the courts of Europe were there to represent their absent masters. The Imperial ambassador sits in the highest place, the French the next, and the Spaniard, unwilling to concede the second place to any one but the most Catholic king, sits proudly aloof in the centre.

It is important to notice this control and admixture of secular and lay authority, not only allowed but courted by the highest and most venerable of ecclesiastical synods, because it may tend to reconcile sensitive churchmen of our own country to a like control over English convocations, or Scottish general assemblies.[2] It further reminds us how the Councils of the Church, in the time of their grandeur, were mixed up with the general history of the world, and thus became the expression of the age. The Council of Nicæa was, in the eyes of its

[1] The first Pope, said to have called a Council, is Pelagius II., A. D. 587. But the Epistle in which the right is claimed is a forgery. (Robertson, i. 547. 2d ed.)

[2] See "The Councils of the Church" by Dr. Pusey, — written with the express intention of allaying the alarms of English churchmen occasioned by the theological decisions of the Judicial Committee of the Privy Council.

contemporaries, far the most important gathering that had taken place in the Roman Empire in the time of Constantine, or even since the virtual suppression of the Roman senate. The Council of Constance was at least as closely interwoven with all the passions and feelings of the fifteenth century, as the Congress of Vienna could have been with those of the nineteenth. It is well also to remember that this intimate connection of the Councils with the constitution of the ancient Empire, furnishes one strong ground for the prediction, which I ventured to make just now, that in all probability a General Council will never be held again. According to the only precedents universally recognized, an Œcumenical Synod cannot be summoned except by the Emperor, and "the Emperor," in that sense of the word in which alone he could be made available, has ceased to exist. There is now no longer an Empire of the West; the modern Empire of Austria and the modern Empire of France are merely separate kingdoms under lofty titles. There is, in a truer sense, an Emperor of the East. But no one will suppose it probable that the authority of the Russian Czar would ever be recognized in the kingdoms or churches of the West, even putting aside the intense ecclesiastical animosity with which the Latin Church would regard any such attempt. General Councils were part and parcel of the Imperial Constitution of Europe — but with the dissolution of that venerable fabric they have, we may be almost sure, been laid aside in their ancient form never to reappear.

c) And this prepares us to consider the remaining portion of the somewhat harsh, but still, as I said, incontestable, description of them in the language of the twenty-first Article. " When they be gathered together" (at that time, we may here observe, the Article contemplated the recurrence of the event as not entirely impossible), "forasmuch as they be assemblies of men, whereof all be not governed with the Spirit and word of God, they may err, and sometimes have erred, even in things pertaining unto God." It is absolutely necessary to claim the freedom of criticism on which these words insist. With every disposition to honor these assemblies, — with every desire to make allowance for their weaknesses, and to esteem the results of their labors, — it is impossible to understand them rightly, or even to do justice to their merits, without remembering throughout that they were assemblies of fallible men, swayed by the good and evil influences to which all assemblies are exposed. Fallible character of General Councils.

We need not adopt the extreme language of condemnation into which Gregory Nazianzen [1] was driven, irritated, no doubt, by the excesses which he himself witnessed : — "I never yet saw a council of bishops come to a good end." "I salute them afar off, since I know how troublesome they are." "I never more will sit in those assemblies of cranes and geese." It is enough to remember, in the wise language of Dean Milman, how almost inevitable is the disappointment which we experience on finding the repulsive aspect which Christianity assumes in the very assemblies which should represent it in its best and most attractive form. "A General Council," he justly observes,[2] " is not the cause, but the consequence of religious dis- " sension. It is unnecessary, and could hardly be con- " voked, but on extraordinary occasions, to settle some " questions which have already violently disorganized " the peace of Christendom. It is a field of battle in " which a long train of animosities and hostilities is to " come to an issue. Men, therefore, meet with all the " excitement, the estrangement, the jealousy, the antip-

[1] Ep. 124, 136; Carm. xvii. 91.   [2] Latin Christianity, i. 228.

"athy, engendered by a fierce and obstinate controversy.
"They meet to triumph over their adversaries, rather
"than dispassionately to investigate truth.   Each is
"committed to his opinions, each exasperated by oppo-
"sition, each supported by a host of intractable follow-
"ers, each probably with exaggerated notions of the
"importance of the question, and that importance seems
"to increase, since it has demanded the decision of a
"general assembly of Christendom."

Let us approach the Council of Nicæa with these
humbler expectations, and we shall be agreeably surprised to find how many incidents of moderation and
charity and simplicity it contains amidst much fierce
animosity, and much pardonable enthusiasm.

There is a well-known, perhaps somewhat flippant,
passage, in which Jortin remarks on the possible motives by which such an assembly would be influenced:
— "It may be," he says, "by reverence to the Emperor,
"or to his counsellors and favorites, or the fear of offend-
"ing some great prelate (as the Bishop of Alexandria or
"of Rome), who had it in his power to insult, vex, and
"plague all the bishops within and without his jurisdic-
"tion; by the dread of passing for heretics, and of being
"calumniated, reviled, hated, anathematized, excommu-
"nicated, imprisoned, banished, fined, beggared, starved,
"if they refused to submit: by the love of peace and
"quiet; by the hatred of contention; by compliance
"with an active body and imperious spirit; by a defer-
"ence to the majority; by a love of dictating and dom-
"ineering, of applause and respect; by vanity and am-
"bition; by a total ignorance of the question in debate,
"or a total indifference about it; by private friendships;
"by enmity and resentment; by old prejudices; by
"hopes of gain; by an indolent disposition; by good-
"nature and the fatigue of attending; by the desire to

"be at home," &c. &c. &c.[1] Many of these feelings may
doubtless have been at work in the sittings of Nicæa;
indeed the passage must have been partly suggested by
the enumeration of motives in the history of Eusebius.[2]
But we have every reason to suppose that such passions
had far less control over the Council of Nicæa than over
those which followed. It would be easy to multiply
instances of the crimes and follies which disfigured the
Christian assemblies of later times. We need not dwell
on the exceptional case of the murder of John Huss at
Constance, or repeat how at the second Council of
Ephesus the Bishop of Constantinople was trampled
down and stamped to death by the Bishop of Alexandria. But it may be well to give one authentic scene
from the Council of Chalcedon, in numbers and in dignity far the most distinguished of the Seven.[3] I quote
from the Report of the Council itself. The moment
is that of the Imperial officers ordering that Theodoret, the excellent Bishop of Kars, well known as the
commentator and ecclesiastical historian, should enter
the assembly : — "And when the most reverend Bishop
"Theodoret entered, the most reverend the Bishops of
"Egypt, Illyria, and Palestine shouted out — 'Mercy
"'upon us! the faith is destroyed. The canons of the
"'Church excommunicate him. Turn him out! turn
"'out the teacher of Nestorius!' On the other hand,
"the most reverend the Bishops of the East, of Thrace,
"of Pontus, and of Asia, shouted out — 'We were com-
"'pelled [at the former Council] to subscribe our names
"'to blank papers; we were scourged into submission.
"'Turn out the Manichæans. Turn out the enemies
"'of Flavian; turn out the adversaries of the faith!'
"Dioscorus, the most reverend Bishop of Alexandria,

---

[1] Remarks on Eccl. History, i. 188.   [2] Eus. V. C. iii. 6.
[3] Mansi, vi. 590, 591.

"said—'Why is Cyril to be turned out? It is he whom
"'Theodoret has condemned.' The most reverend the
"Bishops of the East shouted out—'Turn out the
"'murderer Dioscorus. Who knows not the deeds of
"'Dioscorus?' .... The most reverend the Bishops
"of Egypt, Illyria, and Palestine shouted out—'Long
"'life to the Empress!' The most reverend the Bishops
"of the East shouted out—'Turn out the murderers.'
"The most reverend the Bishops of Egypt shouted out
"—'The Empress turned out Nestorius; long life to
"'the Catholic Empress! The Orthodox synod refuses
"'to admit Theodoret.'" Theodoret then being at last
received by the Imperial officers, and taking his place,
"the most reverend Bishops of the East shouted out—
"'He is worthy—worthy.' The most reverend the
"Bishops of Egypt shouted out—'Don't call him bish-
"'op, he is no bishop. Turn out the fighter against
"'God; turn out the Jew.' The most reverend the
"Bishops of the East shouted out—'The Orthodox for
"'the synod. Turn out the rebels; turn out the mur-
"'derers.' The most reverend the Bishops of Egypt—
"'Turn out the enemy of God. Turn out the defamer
"'of Christ. Long life to the Empress, long life to the
"'Emperor, long life to the Catholic Emperor! Theod-
"'oret condemned Cyril. If we receive Theodoret, we
"'excommunicate Cyril.'"

At this point the Imperial Commissioners who were
present put a stop to the clamor, as unworthy a meeting of Christian bishops. We shall, doubtless, agree
with them. My object in recalling so scandalous a
scene has been, first, that we may not form too high
a standard of what we are to expect from the first
Council; secondly, that we may be the better able to
do justice to its undoubted superiority over the conduct
of the later assemblies.

But we must not forget the good as well as the
evil which the Councils — and not least that of Modera-
Nicæa — shared with all large assemblies of fal- tion of
lible men everywhere; namely, the unconscious Councils.
moderation which springs up from bringing two parties
face to face with each other. No doubt violent and
extreme partisans are often exasperated against one
another by personal contact and conflict. But the vast
mass of intervening shades of opinion is by such meetings drawn more closely together. Probably no Council has separated without making some friends who
were before enemies, and some friends closer than before. Such, in an eminent degree, was the express
object and result of the Apostolic Council at Jerusalem.
No doubt even then there was the separation between
Paul and Barnabas, and the quarrel between Paul and
Peter. But on the whole the assembly brought together, instead of dividing asunder, the true servants
of Christ. It agreed to tolerate, without approving or
condemning, the differences which it was called to ad-
judge. The Jewish Apostles gave the right hand of
fellowship to the Apostle of the Gentiles. The Church
of Jerusalem determined not to lay upon the Gentiles
the yoke which it was willing to bear itself. Assemblies so minded, and so deciding, have doubtless been
very rare. But both in intention and effect the Council
of Nicæa partook largely of that first Apostolic example. The estimation in which we at this moment hold
the writings of Eusebius of Cæsarea, is a proof of the
kindly feeling which then gathered round him and his
party, and which has never since been entirely dissi-
pated. The professed object of those who directed the
decisions of the Council was to include as wide a number as possible ; and every succeeding Council and
creed (with whatever provocation or justification for

doing so) has yet been a narrowing of the basis on which the first Council took its stand.

III. Such being the general interest of the Council of Nicæa, there are several peculiarities in its history which render the study of it instructive in detail.

1. The original narratives are in great measure de-
Contemporary sources. rived from contemporary sources. The *Acts*, indeed, or Reports of the Council (such as are preserved in the case of the Councils of Ephesus and Chalcedon), never existed, or have perished. But the decrees and the official letters of the Council and of the Emperor remain ; and we have the accounts, more or less perfect, of not less than four eye-witnesses.

2. Both amongst these eye-witnesses, and amongst the
Sources on both sides. later historians, we have the help which in all history, especially ecclesiastical history, is much to be desired, of the representations of both sides. As in the history of the Council of Trent we have the double account of Pallavicini and Sarpi, so here we have the double account of Athanasius and Eusebius. Gibbon longs for a Sarpi at Nicæa. But, in fact, we have a Paul Sarpi, not indeed as regards wisdom or learning, but certainly as regards his indifference, if not hostility, to the successful party of the Council, in Eusebius himself. Without entering into the much disputed question of the precise shade of his Arianism, there can be no doubt of his leaning to that side ; and so far, therefore, it cannot be said that the defeated party have been left without a spokesman: and on the same side we must add the fragments from the avowed Arian, Philostorgius. The Meletians, in like manner, (to take a smaller section of the Council,) are represented by Epiphanius ; the Novatians, by the aged informant of Socrates. Of the three chief historians, too, of the next generation,

two (Socrates and Sozomen) are not clergymen, but laymen and lawyers; and of these, Socrates is at times
quite remarkable for his philosophical candor; and the
third, Theodoret, although a bishop and a theologian,
belonged to the moderate party in the Church, and
had at one time been himself under a grave suspicion
of heresy.

3. The legendary tales which have been formed on
the basis of the historical facts have a twofold The le-
interest. They well represent those two classes gends.
which Arnold has described in his history of Rome,[1]
" equally remote from historical truth, but in all other
" respects most opposite to each other; the one imag-
" inative but honest, playing with facts, and converting
" them into a wholly different form, but addressing it-
" self also to a different part of the mind; not professing
" to impart exact knowledge, but to quicken and raise
" the perception of what is beautiful and noble; the
" other, tame and fraudulent, deliberately corrupting
" truth, in order to minister to national or individual
" vanity, but substituting in the place of reality the rep-
" resentations of interested or servile falsehood."   To
the former of these classes belongs, in the old Roman
history, the legend of the fall of Veii; in the history
of Nicæa, the legends of the different saints who were
present. To the latter belong, in the Pagan history,
the pretended victory of Camillus over the Gauls; in
the Christian history, the inventions intended to exalt
the see of Rome, or to blacken the character of the
Arians.[2] Both are instructive. The former convey to
us a sense of the deep impression made by the Council
on the popular mind. The latter exhibit to us what
the history would have been (but is not), had it taken

[1] i. 393.   [2] Lectures III. and V.

22

place according to the theories and wishes of later times.

4. The details which, from whatever quarter, we thus *Its char-* gain of the Nicene Council are far more impor- *acters.* tant than they would be in any other Council. They disclose to us a section of the different layers of society in that period.   The effect of this is, that we share in the good fortune of those who attended the Council, and through their eyes become personally acquainted with many of the most famous personages of that age — some famous in all ages.   Most of them we shall sufficiently see in the Council itself.[1]   But there are two whose eminence so far transcends the limits of that particular event, and the understanding of whose characters is so necessary for the understanding of the whole event, as to demand a special notice.   It will be worth while to have known something of the Council, if only it enables us to take a nearer view of two men so extraordinary as Constantine[2] and Athanasius.[3]

[1] Lecture III.   [2] Lecture VI.   [3] Lecture VII.

LECTURE III.

THE MEETING OF THE COUNCIL.

In the close of the month of May, 1853, it was my good fortune to be descending, in the moonlight of an early morning, from the high wooded steeps of one of the mountain-ranges of Bithynia. As the dawn rose, and as we approached the foot of these hills, through the thick mists which lay over the plain there gradually broke upon our view the two features which mark the city of Nicæa.

Beneath us lay the long inland lake — the Ascanian Lake, which, communicating at its western ex- The present appearance of Nicæa. tremity by a small inlet with the Sea of Marmora, fills up almost the whole valley ; — itself a characteristic of the conformation of this part of Asia Minor. Such another is the Lake of Apollonius, seen from the summit of the Mysian Olympus. Such another is the smaller lake seen in traversing the plain on the way from Broussa.

At the head of the lake appeared the oblong space enclosed by the ancient walls, of which the rectangular form indicates with unmistakable precision the original founders of the city. It was the outline given to all the Oriental towns built by the successors of Alexander and their imitators. Antioch, Damascus, Philadelphia, Sebaste, Palmyra, were all constructed on the same model of a complete square, intersected by four straight streets adorned with a colonnade on each side. This we know to have been the appearance of Nicæa,[1] as founded by Lysimachus, and rebuilt by Antigonus. And this is still the form of the present walls, which, although they enclose a larger space than the first Greek city, yet are evidently as early as the time of the Roman Empire; little later, if at all, than the reign of Constantine. Within their circuit all is now a wilderness ; over broken columns, and through tangled thickets, the traveller with difficulty makes his way to the wretched Turkish village of Is-nik (εἰς Νίκαιαν), which occupies the centre of the vacant space. In the midst of this village, surrounded by a few ruined mosques, on whose summits stand the never-failing storks of the deserted cities of the East, remains a solitary Christian church, dedicated to " the Repose of the Virgin." Within the church is a rude picture commemorating the one event which, amidst all the vicissitudes of Nicæa, has secured for it an immortal name.

To delineate this event, to transport ourselves back into the same season of the year, — the chestnut woods then as now green with the first burst of summer, the same sloping hills, the same tranquil lake, the same snow-capped Olympus from far brooding over the whole scene, but, in every other respect, how entirely different! — will be my object in this Lecture.

The meeting of a General Council is, as I have elsewhere said, in ecclesiastical history, what a pitched battle is in military history, and similar questions naturally rise in speaking of each.

The occasion of the Council. — I. The first question is, Why was it fought? Two opposite forces concurred in bringing about the Council of Nicæa.

1. The Arian controversy. — 1. The first was the Arian controversy. To enter into the details of the contest would lead me too far away from the subject, and they have

---

[1] Strabo, xii. 565.

been told sufficiently in histories accessible to all. But three points must be briefly mentioned to mark its precise connection with the history of the time.

First: It was distinguished from all modern controversies on like subjects by the extremely ab- *Its abstract* stract region within which it was confined. *dogmatism.* The difficulties which gave rise to the heresy of Arius had but a slight resemblance to those which have given birth to the opinions which have borne his name in modern times. He was led to adopt his peculiar dogma from a fancied necessity arising out of the terms "Father" and "Son;"—"begotten" and "unbegotten." The controversy turned on the relations of the Divine Persons in the Trinity, not only before the Incarnation, before Creation, before Time, but before the first beginnings of Time. "There was"—the Arian doctrine did not venture to say "a time"—but "there was when He was not." It was the excess of dogmatism founded upon the most abstract words in the most abstract region of human thought.

Secondly: A serious cause of the apprehension which the Arian doctrine excited when the Orthodox *Its Polythe-* considered the ultimate consequences to which *ism.* it might lead them, was not so much its denial or infringement of the Divinity of Christ (although the controversy naturally opened into this further question), as its making two gods[1] instead of one, and thus relapsing into Polytheism. Polytheism, Paganism, Hellenism, was the enemy from which the Church had just been delivered by Constantine; and this was the enemy under whose dominion it was feared that the dividing, dogmatizing spirit of Arius might bring them back. Greece and the East, far more than Italy and the West, were

---

[1] For this "polytheism" of the Arians, see Dr. Newman's note on Athanasius's Treatises, i. p. 221, and Dr. Pusey's note on Joel iii. 9, p. 137.

the true native seats of the old Pagan idolatries, and therefore the Eastern, far more than the Western, Church was sensitive on the subject of anything that tended, even remotely, to revive the multiplication of deities. "I believe in *God*," was the usual formula of the Western creeds. But, irrespectively of the Council of Nicæa, the formula of the Eastern creeds was, "I believe in *one*[1] *God*." Whether or not the Polytheistic conclusion was fairly to be deduced from the Arian doctrine, it is certain that this was the inference which the Orthodox party feared, and to this fear peculiar significance was given by the time and place in which the Arian doctrine first arose.

Thirdly (which is the most important point in reference to the actual convention of the Council), was the intense vehemence with which the controversy was carried on. When we perceive the abstract questions on which it turned, when we reflect that they related not to any dealings of the Deity with man, not even, properly speaking, to the Divinity or the Humanity of Christ, nor to the doctrine of the Trinity, (for all these points were acknowledged by both parties,) but to the ineffable relations of the Godhead before the remotest beginning of time, it is difficult to conceive that by inquiries such as these the passions of mankind should be roused to fury. Yet so it was, — at least in Egypt, where it first began. All classes took part in it, and almost all took part with equal energy. "Bishop rose against Bishop," says Eusebius, "district against district, only to be compared to the Symplegades dashed against each other on a stormy day."[2]

Vehemence of the contest.

---

[1] See Rufinus in Symb. § 4, and the note in Professor Heurtley's Harmonia Symbolica, p. 127. The same feeling appears in the earnestness of the Eastern Church in behalf of the Single Procession. See Lecture I. p. 141.

[2] Eus. V. C. iii. 4.

So violent were the discussions that they were parodied
in the Pagan theatres, and the Emperor's statues were
broken in the public squares in the conflicts which took
place. The common name by which the Arians and
their system were designated (and we may conclude
that they were not wanting in retorts) was the Maniacs
— the Ariomaniacs, the Ariomania;[1] and their frantic
conduct on public occasions afterwards goes far to justify the appellation. Sailors, millers, and travellers sang
the disputed doctrines at their occupations, or on their
journeys:[2] "every corner, every alley of the city" (this
is said afterwards of Constantinople, but must have been
still more true of Alexandria) "was full of these discussions — the streets, the market-places, the drapers, the
money-changers, the victuallers. Ask a man 'how many
oboli, he answers by dogmatizing on generated and
ungenerated being. Inquire the price of bread, and
you are told, 'The Son is subordinate to the Father.'
Ask if the bath is ready, and you are told, 'The Son
arose out of nothing.'"[3]

2. This was one side of the scene. On the other side
arose a power and a character hitherto unknown 2. Inter-
in the Christian Church. The Emperor of the vention of
world now for the first time appeared in the the Em-peror.
arena of theological controversy. He entered upon
his relations to the Church as a traveller enters a new
country — with high expectations, with hasty conclusions, with bitter disappointments. Of all these disappointments none was so severe as that which he felt
when first he became acquainted with the fact that the
Christian as well as the heathen commonwealth was torn
by factions. It had broken upon him gradually — first

[1] See Newman's note on Athanasius's Treatises, i. 91.
[2] See Lecture IV.
[3] Greg. Nyss. de Deitate Fil. iii. 466. (Neander, iv. 61.)

at Arles, then at Rome, when the African controversy of
the Donatists was brought before him. But the culminating point was their wild outbreak, as it must have
seemed to him, in the important province of Egypt.
We know his feelings from himself. In the celebrated
letter which he addressed to the Alexandrian Church —
however much it may have been suggested or modified
by one or other of his episcopal advisers — the sentiments are so like what he expressed on other occasions,
that we may fairly adopt them as his own. He describes
(as usual, with the attestation of an oath[1]) his mission
of uniting the world under one head. He expresses the
hope with which he turned from the distracted West to
the Eastern regions of his empire, as those from which
Divine light had first sprung. " But, oh ! divine and
glorious Providence, what wound has fallen on my ears
— nay, rather on my heart ! " And then with an earnestness which it is difficult not to believe sincere, and
with arguments which modern theologians have visited
with the severest condemnation, but which the ancient
and Orthodox historian, Socrates, has not hesitated to
call " wonderful and full of wisdom ; "[2] he entreats the
combatants " to abandon these futile and interminable
disputes, and to return to the harmony which became
their common faith." " Give me back my calm days,
and my quiet nights ; light and cheerfulness instead of
tears and groans." He had come as far as Nicomedia,
the capital of the East ; he entreats them to open for
him the way to the East, and to enable him to see them
and all rejoicing in restored freedom and unity.[3] His
letter was in vain. The controversy had gone too far.
The wound could be healed only by an extraordinary

---

[1] See Lecture VI.

[2] i. 8 : θαυμαστὰ καὶ σοφίας μεστά. None of the ancient historians condemn
the letter.

[3] Eus. V. C. ii. 68–73.

remedy. That remedy the Emperor was determined to provide. With the ardent desire for enforcing unanimity on those whom he was now called to govern, he combined a vague but profound reverence for the character and powers of the heads of the Christian community. From the union of these two feelings sprang (as he himself tells us, " by a divine inspiration ") the first idea of convening a Council of the representatives of the whole Church. He may have been advised by the clergy[1] who were about him; but he declares, and his declaration is confirmed by history, that the main conception, under God, was due to himself only. And if the idea was his, still more exclusively so was its execution. Not till many years afterwards was the claim put forward, that Sylvester, Bishop of Rome, had combined with him in convening the assembly.[2] The little gatherings in each diocese, often hardly more in numbers than the meeting of the vestry of a large parish, had been called together in former times by the Bishops of the respective dioceses. But the gathering of the Bishops themselves, from all parts of the Empire, could be effected only by a central authority, which they all alike acknowledged; and in the beginning of the fourth century that authority could be found nowhere but in the Emperor. Complimentary letters, accordingly, were addressed by him to all the Bishops. One of these has been preserved. It alludes to some similar intention (of which no other record exists) on the part of a small assembly of eighteen Bishops, which had met at Ancyra, in Galatia, nine years before, and then proceeds at once to name the place where the Council should meet.[3]

His idea of the Council.

[1] Ruf. i. 1.
[2] See Mansi's Conc. ii. 637.
[3] Anal. Nic. 21, or " Syriac Miscellanies," p. 1.

II. This leads us to ask what caused the selection of the locality. In General Councils, as in battles, this has always been a very important question. Look at Trent. Its situation immediately under the Alps, yet on the Italian side, exactly expresses the peculiarity of the assembly convened there. It was to be as near the dominions of the Emperor as was possible, without being altogether out of reach of the dominions of the Pope. It was to come as close to the confines of Protestantism as it could without crossing the barriers which parted it from them. Look at Pisa. It seems, so say those concerned in the event,[1] "as if the place was made for a council;" a fertile plain, abounding in gardens and vineyards for provisions and wine; a river communicating with the sea, accessible to French, Italians, and Germans. Look at Constance. Here, again, was a frontier situation — a free city, therefore, to a certain extent, neutral between the contending parties — on the banks of a large lake, which would both furnish easy mode of access, and also assist in furnishing provisions for so great an assemblage, especially fish in time of Lent. A name, too, of happy omen — " Constantia," which alone is said to have induced the Pope to consent to the locality.

Not unlike to the motives which determined these sites of the great Western Councils, were those, as far as we can see, which determined the site of the chief Council of the East. One reason is expressly alleged by the Emperor himself—its healthy situation.[2] The mortality which took place amongst the Bishops at Ephesus, the violent disputes which raged amongst the medical authorities at Trent, as to the salubrity of the place, show the importance attached to this ground of selection. It

The selection of the place.

---

1 L'Enfant, Concile de Pise, ii. 26.
2 Syriac Misc. p. 1.

is not, however, the reason which might have been expected in the case of Nicæa.   The rich alluvial plain had
a character for insalubrity, especially in summer,[1] the very
season when the Council was assembled ; and, according
to tradition, as we shall see, two Bishops died during
the session.   But there were also political and religious
reasons.   Constantinople was not yet founded ; by the
time of the second Council, this, the capital of the Eastern Empire, was at once chosen for the gathering of
the Eastern Church.   But, although the precise locality
of the capital was not yet fixed, yet its general atmosphere, so to speak, hung already over the shores of the
Propontis.   Already this was the resort of the Eastern
Cæsars ; and Nicomedia, the ancient capital of Bithynia,
only twenty miles from Nicæa, had, since the time of
Diocletian, been chosen as the capital of the East.   Nicomedia was probably rejected for two reasons.   As in the
case of Constance and Trent, a city not actually the seat
of government would be more appropriate for the purpose of a sacred assembly.   And again, considering the
controversy at stake, it would hardly have been fitting
to have held the meeting in Nicomedia, where the
Bishop, Eusebius, had taken so active a part in defence
of one of the combatants, and had already convoked
a synod of Arian Bishops[2] in the neighborhood.   The
second capital of Bithynia, therefore, Nicæa, naturally
presented itself; its lake furnished means of access
from the Propontis, and it was sufficiently near the
Imperial residence.   " The Bishops of Italy, and from
the rest of the countries of Europe, are coming " —
these are the Emperor's own words — " and I shall be
at hand as a spectator and participator in what is
done." [3]   Finally, the name, as afterwards in the case
of Constance, was highly important.   It was " Nicæa,"

---

[1] Strabo, xii. p. 565.   [2] Soz. i. 15.   [3] Analecta Nic. 21.

the city of "victory," or. "conquest." Its coins bore a
figure of Victory. This fell in with Constantine's
favorite title and watchword.[1] He was just fresh from
the victory over his second rival, which caused him to
assume the surname of Niketes — the Victor, or the
Conqueror. The motto seen, or alleged to be seen, in
the apparition of the cross before his earlier victory,
was the same word, ἐν τούτῳ νίκα — "By this conquer;"
and Eusebius specially dwells on the strains of conquest[2]
and victory, which harmonized with the name of the
place, and regards the Council itself as a thank-offering for the victory just gained by the Emperor over
all his enemies.[3] "It was a city," he says, "fitting for
the synod — called after Victory, 'the City of Victory,'
or 'Nicæa.'"[4]

III. We are thus brought to the next point in connec-
Time
of the
Council.
tion with the convention of the Council, its date.
The year of Christ 325 was the twentieth
year of the reign of Constantine, reckoning from the
25th of July 306, when he had been proclaimed at
York. Every tenth year of an Imperial reign was
celebrated with solemn games and festivities, in recollection of the original conditions under which Augustus
accepted the Imperial power, namely, that it should be
renewed at the end of every ten years.[5] "The memory
of this comedy," says Gibbon, "was preserved to the
latest ages of the empire;" and, in the case of Constantine, it was characteristically blended with the events
following his conversion. Of the Decennalia, or celebra-

---

[1] See Lecture VI.

[2] V. C. iv. 47 : ἡ σύνοδος ἐπινίκιος ἦν . . . ἐπὶ τὴν κατ' ἐχθρῶν καὶ πολεμίων νικὴν ἐπὶ τῆς Νικαίας αὐτῆς ἐπιτελοῦσα. Compare Eus. Laud. Const.
v. 18.

[3] V. C. iii. 7 : τῷ αὐτοῦ σωτῆρι τῆς κατ' ἐχθρῶν καὶ πολεμίων νίκης θεοπρεπεῖς
ἀνετίθει χαριστήριον.

[4] V. C. iii. 6 : νίκης ἐπώνυμος, ἡ Νικαία.   [5] Dio Cass. iii. 16.

tion of his tenth year, we have no account. But the
Tricennalia, or thirtieth year, was marked by the dedication of the Church of the Holy Sepulchre at Jerusalem;[1] and the Vicennalia, or twentieth year, was expressly chosen as the time in which the solemnities of
the first Œcumenical Council might act the part usually
played by mere pomp and festivity.[2] And if under any
circumstances this would have been appropriate, much
more so was it in the peculiar conjuncture of this anniversary. It was little more than a year since Constantine, by the victory over Licinius to which I have just
referred, became Emperor of the East as well as of the
West. An Eastern Council would, in fact, have been
almost impossible before this time, and accordingly the
Arian controversy was of necessity allowed to roll on,
unchecked, for five years, till the restoration of peace
and the close of the civil war enabled the Emperor to
turn his attention to the subject, and to make his last
attempt to heal it. The year of the meeting of the
Council, therefore, of itself indicates the state of the
world at large. In place and time alike, it marks the
final victory of Constantine over his enemies, the settlement of the Eastern Empire, and the connection of that
Empire with the fortunes of the Eastern Church.

The actual month and day of the meeting are more
difficult to ascertain. The date of the opening varies
from May 20 to May 29, June 14, and June 19. It is
enough for our purpose to know that it took place somewhere near Whitsuntide, at the beginning of the summer. This was the usual time of the gathering of the
Eastern Councils,[3] and was probably fixed with a view

---

[1] Eus. V. C. iv. 47.   [2] Eus. V. C. iv. 47 ; Soz. H. E. i. 25.

[3] The Greeks call the Sunday after Ascension Day " The Sunday of the
Holy Fathers," or of the " 318 Theophori at Nicæa." Heinichen on Eus. V.
C. iii. 15. Smith, De Ecclesiæ Græcæ hodierno Statu, p. 76. The Syrians

to the reopening of the navigation of the Mediterranean, when the winter storms were over and the warm weather rendered travelling easy. In this instance the time would be further narrowed by the desire of the Emperor to combine it with the 25th of July, the anniversary of his accession, with which, as we shall see, the formal proceedings of the Council were closed, though the members appear not to have dispersed till the 25th of August.[1]

IV. It was, then, at such a time and to such a place, **Arrival of the Bishops.** with the feelings inspired by such a conjuncture as I have described, that, in the close of May or beginning of June, Nicæa was approached by the representatives of the Christian Church from every part of the Eastern Empire, and from a few spots of the Western also. The mode of their travelling must be observed, not only as characteristic of the manners of the time, but as decisive of the authority by which they were summoned.

Letters were addressed, doubtless on this as on a previous lesser occasion in the West, to the civil authorities, enjoining the supplies necessary for the journey. The posting arrangements of the Empire made such a convention far more easy than would have been the case at any period in the Middle Ages. The great lines of communication were like railroads, straight as arrows, from one extremity of the Empire to the other. From Bordeaux to Constantinople, a few years later, we have the record of two hundred post-stations ($\mu\acute{o}\nu\alpha\iota$) and ninety-one inns; an inn at the interval of every half-

---

celebrate it on July 1; the Armenians on Sept. 7; the Egyptians on Nov. 5. See Lecture V.

[1] Alexander (of Byzantium?) describes it as ending in September (Photius, Bib. 473); according to the later Greek traditions it lasted three (Phot. Bib. 473) or six years (ib. 66). See Beveridge's Synodicon, ii. 42.

day's journey.[1] Each Bishop was to have two presbyters and three slaves[2] as his retinue. They travelled partly in public carriages,[3] partly on horses, asses, and mules, provided for the purpose, both for riding and carrying baggage.[4] The precedent thus established was never dropped, and the summoning of a Council was always known throughout the Empire by the stir along the roads in every direction. At later Councils we hear of the indecent haste with which Bishops might be seen[5] galloping at full speed to reach the appointed place in time, — the horses knocked up by their impatience, — or at times detained, as would not unfrequently happen at the end of an Eastern spring, by the flooding of rivers.[6]

This (varied no doubt by the arrival in vessels across the Ascanian Lake) must have been the general aspect of the gathering of the Council of Nicæa.

Their number.

They came, says Eusebius, as fast as they could run, in almost a frenzy of excitement and enthusiasm.[7] The actual crowd must have been enough to have metamorphosed the place. It was indeed a number far below the enormous crowds which beset the later Councils. At Nicæa the highest calculation, in the distorted accounts of later times, fixes the number at more than 2000.[8] This, if we include all the presbyters and attendants, is probably correct. The actual number of Bishops, variously stated in the earlier authorities as 218,[9]

---

1 Itin. Burd. p. 548. See Dr. Newman's notes on Ath. Hist. Tracts, ii. 50.
2 Eus. H. E. x. 8.
3 Eus. H. E. x. 5 : δημόσιον ὄχημα. V. C. iii. 6 : δημόσιος δρόμος.
4 Theod. H. E. i. 6 : ὀρεῦσι καὶ ὄνοις καὶ ἡμιόνοις καὶ ἵπποις.
5 Ammian. xxi. 16.
6 As at the Council of Ephesus. (Robertson, i. 445.)
7 V. C. iii. 6 : οἷά τινος ἀπὸ νύσσης ἔθεον οἱ πάντες ἐν προθυμίᾳ πάσῃ.
8 2340 (Macrizi, 31) ; 2348 (Mansi, ii. p. 1073 ; Eutychius, Ann. i. 440).
9 Anal. Nic. 34.

250,[1] 270,[2] or 300,[3] was finally believed to have been 320 or 318,[4] and this in the Eastern Church has so completely been identified with the event that the Council is often known as that of "the 318." It is a proof of the importance of the event, that even so trivial a circumstance as the number should be made the groundwork of more than one mystical legend. In the Greek numerals it was ΤΙΗ; i. e. Τ for the cross, ΙΗ for the sacred name Ἰησοῦς.[5] It was[6] also supposed that their number was prefigured in the 318 slaves of Abraham. It became the foundation of seeking mystical numbers for the later Councils. The greatest of all the Eastern Councils, in numbers and dignity, that of Chalcedon, prided itself on being just double that of Nicæa, 636. The Council of Constantinople, which deposed Ignatius and exalted Photius in the ninth century, prided itself on being exactly the same number, 318. The Alexandrians, after two Arabian historians,[7] giving the sum total of the Council as 2348, represent the mob as the grand gathering of all the heretics of the world, Sabellians, Mariolaters, Arians, — and that the 318 were the Orthodox and steadfast minority. Two still stranger stories in connection with the number will appear as we proceed.[8]

But it was the diversity of the persons, and the Diversity of characters. strongly marked characters dividing each from each, which, more than any mere display of numbers, constituted their peculiar interest. In the

---

[1] Eus. V. C. iii. 8.

[2] Eustathius (apud Theod. i. 8), who, however, adds that he had not examined the matter closely.

[3] Athan. Hist. Monach. c. 66; Apol. c. Arian. c. 23, 25; De Synod. c. 43.

[4] Athan. ad Afr. c. 2; Soc. i. 8; Soz. i. 17; (320) Theod. i. 7.

[5] Ambrose, De Fide, i. 18.   [6] Ibid. i. 1.

[7] Macrizi, 31; Eutychius, Ann. i. 440.   [8] Lecture V.

conventional pictures of the Council, such, for example,
as that which still exists at Nicæa, the figures are almost
indistinguishable from each other, with the exception of
the small knot of Arians, who are represented as grouped
together in the centre, bearing the marks of their dis-
comfiture in their looks of extreme disgust, and the
sign of their heresy in the coal-black color of their com-
plexions.   But this was far from being the true aspect
of the assembly as it was first seen, before the theological differences had been fully developed, and whilst
the natural differences were the most prominent.   Eusebius, himself an eye-witness, as he enumerates the various characters, from various countries, of various age
and position, thus collected, compares the scene either
with the diverse nations[1] assembled at Pentecost, or
with a garland of flowers gathered in season, of all
manner of colors, woven together as a peace-offering
after the tranquillization of the Empire;[2] or with a
mystic dance, in which every actor performs a part of
his own,[3] to complete a sacred ceremony.   There were
present, the learned and the illiterate, courtiers and peasants, old and young, aged bishops on the verge of the
grave, beardless deacons just entering on their office;[4]
and it was an assembly in which the difference between
age and youth was of more than ordinary significance;
for it coincided with a marked transition in the history
of the world.   The new generation had been brought
up in peace and quiet.   They could just remember the
joy diffused through the Christian communities by the
edict of toleration published in their boyhood; but they
had themselves suffered nothing.   Not so the older, and
by far the larger part of the assembly.   They had lived
through the last and worst of the persecutions, and they

[1] V. C. iii. 7.   [2] Ibid. iii. 7.
[3] Ibid. iii. 8, 9.   [4] Ibid. iii. 8.

now came like a regiment out of some frightful siege or battle, decimated and mutilated by the tortures or the hardships they had undergone.   There must have been some of the aged inhabitants of Nicæa who remembered the death [1] of the two martyrs, Tryphon and Respicius, who, in the reign of Decius, had been dragged through the streets of the city, bleeding from their wounds, in the depth of winter.   There must be some who retained from their grandfathers the recollection of that still earlier and more celebrated persecution in Bithynia, recorded by Pliny in his letters to Trajan.   Most of the older members must have lost a friend or a brother. Many still bore the marks of their sufferings.   Some uncovered their sides and backs to show the wounds inflicted by the instruments of torture.   On others were the traces of that peculiar cruelty which distinguished the last persecution, the loss of a right eye, or the searing of the sinews of the leg,[2] to prevent their escape from working in the mines.[3]   Both at the time and afterwards, it was on their character as an army of confessors and martyrs,[4] quite as much as on their character as an Œcumenical Council that their authority reposed.   In this respect no other Council could approach them, and, in the whole proceedings of the assembly, the voice of an old confessor was received almost as an oracle.

V. They assembled in the first instance in one of the chief buildings of Nicæa, apparently for the purpose of a thanksgiving and a religious reunion.   Whether it was an actual church may be questioned.   Christians, no doubt, there had been in Bithynia for some generations.   Already in the second century Pliny had found them in such numbers that the tem-

First place of meeting.

---

[1] See Tillemont, iii. 33.

[2] Eus. H. E. viii. 12.

[3] Chrysostom, i. 609.

[4] Chrysostom, i. 609.

ples were deserted, and the sacrifices neglected. But it would seem that on this occasion a secular building was fitted up as a temporary house of prayer. At least the traditional account of the place where their concluding prayers were held exactly agrees with Strabo's account of the ancient gymnasium of Nicæa. It was a large building, shaped like a basilica, with an apsis at one end, planted in the centre of the town, and thus commanding down each of the four streets a view of the four gates, and therefore called "Mesomphalos," the "Navel" of the city.[1] Whether, however, this edifice actually was a church or not, its use as such on this occasion served as a precedent for most of the later Councils. From the time of the Council of Chalcedon, they have usually been held within the walls of churches. But for this, the first Council, the church, so far as it was a church, was only used at the beginning and the end.

After these thanksgivings were over, the members of the assembly must have been collected according to the divisions which shall now be described.

1. The group which, above the rest, attracts our attention, is the deputation from the Church of Egypt. Shrill above all other voices, vehement above all other disputants, "brandishing their "arguments," as it was described by one who knew them well,[2] "like spears, against those who sate under the "same roof, and ate off the same table as themselves," were the combatants from Alexandria, who had brought to its present pass the question which the Council was called to decide. Foremost in that group in dignity, though not in importance or in energy, was the aged Alexander, whose imprudent ser-

Deputies of the Egyptian Church.

Alexander, Bishop of Alexandria.

---

[1] See Strabo (xii. 565); and Gregory the Presbyter, De Patr. Nic. Conc., as quoted in Mansi, ii. 727.

[2] Theod. i. 6.

mon had provoked the quarrel, and whose subsequent
vacillation had encouraged it. He was the Bishop, not
indeed of the first, but of the most learned, see of Christendom. He was known by a title which he alone offi-
cially bore in that assembly. He was "the Pope." "The
Pope of Rome" was a phrase which had not yet emerged
in history. But "Pope of Alexandria" was a well-known
dignity. *Papa*, that strange and universal mixture of
familiar endearment and of reverential awe, extended
in a general sense to all Greek Presbyters and all Latin
Bishops, was the special address which, long before the
names of patriarch or of archbishop, was given to the
head of the Alexandrian Church.[1]

In the Patriarchal Treasury at Moscow is a very ancient scarf, or "omophorion," said to have been given
by the Bishop of Nicæa in the seventeenth century to
the Czar Alexis, and to have been left to the Church of
Nicæa by Alexander of Alexandria. It is white, and is
rudely worked with a representation of the Ascension;
possibly in allusion to the first Sunday of their meeting.
This relic, true or false, is the nearest approach we can
now make to the bodily presence of the old theologian.
The shadow of death is already upon him; in a few
months he will be beyond the reach of controversy.

[1] This peculiar Alexandrian application of a name, in itself expressing
simple affection, is thus explained: — Down to Heraclas (A. D. 230), the
Bishop of Alexandria, being the sole Egyptian bishop, was called " Abba"
(father), and his clergy " Elders." From his time more bishops were created,
who then received the name of " abba," and consequently the name of " Papa"
(*ab-aba*, pater patrum = grandfather) was appropriated to the Primate. The
Roman account (inconsistent with facts) is that the name was first given to
Cyril, as representing the Bishop of Rome in the Council of Ephesus (Suicer,
in voce). The name was fixed to the Bishop of Rome in the 7th century. It
has been fantastically explained as: — 1. *Poppœa*, from the short life of each
pope. 2. *Pa*, for Pater. 3. *Pap*, suck. 4. *Pap*, breast. 5. *Pa* (Paul) *Pe*
(Peter). 6. παπαῖ! (admiration). 7. *Papos*, "keeper" (Oscan). 8. *Pappas*,
chief slave. 9. *Pa*(ter) *Pa*(triæ). 10. *Pa*, sound of a father's kiss. See
Abraham Echellensis, De Origine Nom. Papæ, 60.

But close[1] beside the Pope Alexander is a small insignificant[2] young man, of hardly twenty-five years of age, of lively manners[3] and speech, and of bright, serene countenance. Though he is but the Deacon, the chief Deacon,[4] or Archdeacon, of Alexander, he has closely riveted the attention of the assembly by the vehemence of his arguments. He is already taking the words out of the Bishop's mouth, and briefly acting in reality the part he had before, as a child,[5] acted in name, and that, in a few months, he will be called to act both in name and in reality. In some of the conventional pictures of the Council his humble rank as a Deacon does not allow of his appearance. But his activity and prominence[6] behind the scenes made enemies for him there, who will never leave him through life. Any one who has read his passionate invectives afterwards may form some notion of what he was when in the thick of his youthful battles. That small insignificant Deacon is the great Athanasius.

Next after the Pope and Deacon of Alexandria, we must turn to one of its most important Presbyters — the parish priest of its principal church, which bore the name of Baucalis, and marked the first beginnings of what we should call a parochial system.[7] In appearance he is the very opposite of Athanasius. He is sixty years of age, very tall and thin, and apparently unable to support his stature; he has an odd way of contorting and twisting himself,

[1] Gelas. ii. 7; Theod. i. 26; Soc. i. 8.
[2] Julian, Ep. 51.
[3] Greg. Naz. Or. 219.
[4] See Lecture VII.
[5] See Lecture VI.
[6] Ath. Apol. c. Ar. 6; Soz. i. 17.
[7] It was the earliest church in Alexandria. It contained the tomb of S. Mark, and in it took place the election of the Patriarch. It stood near the sea-shore, on a spot which derived its name (Boucalia) from the pasturage of cattle. (Neale's Hist. of the Alex. Church, i. 7, 9.) Another origin of the name is given in Niceph. H. E. viii. 5.

which his enemies compare to the wrigglings of a snake.[1] He would be handsome but for the emaciation and deadly pallor of his face, and a downcast look, imparted by a weakness of eyesight. At times his veins throb and swell, and his limbs tremble, as if suffering from some violent internal complaint — the same, perhaps, that will terminate one day in his sudden and frightful death. There is a wild look about him, which at first sight is startling. His dress

Arius.   and demeanor are those of a rigid ascetic. He wears a long coat with short sleeves,[2] and a scarf of only half size, such as was the mark of an austere life; and his hair hangs in a tangled mass over his head. He is usually silent, but at times breaks out into fierce excitement, such as will give the impression of madness. Yet, with all this, there is a sweetness in his voice, and a winning, earnest manner, which fascinates those who come across him. Amongst the religious ladies of Alexandria he is said to have had from the first a following of not less than seven hundred. This strange, captivating, moon-struck giant is the heretic Arius — or, as his adversaries called him, the madman of Ares, or Mars.[3] Close beside him was a group of his countrymen, of whom we know little, except their fidelity to him, through good report and evil: Saras, like himself a presbyter, from the Libyan province; Euzoius, a deacon of Egypt; Achillas, a reader;[4] Theonas, Bishop of Marmarica in the Cyrenaica, and Secundus, Bishop of Ptolemais in the Delta.[5]

1 This description is put together from the two different, but not irreconcilable, accounts given in Epiphanius (lxix. 3), and in the letter ascribed to Constantine in Gelasius, iii. 1. (Mansi, ii. 930.)

2 The monks wore no sleeves, to indicate that their hands were not to be employed in injury. Soz. H. E. iii. 14.

3 Ἀρειμάνης, in later Greek, was a phrase for *war frenzy*.

4 For these three names see Jerome Adv. Lucif. ii. 192.

5 Theod. i. 7.

These were the most remarkable deputies from the Church of Alexandria.   But from the interior _{Coptic} of Egypt came characters of quite another _{hermits.} stamp; not Greeks, nor Grecized Egyptians, but gen-uine Copts,[1] speaking the Greek language not at all, or with great difficulty; living half or the whole of their lives in the desert; their very names taken from the heathen gods of the times of the ancient Pharaohs. One was Potammon, Bishop of Heracleopolis, _{Potam-} far up the Nile; the other, Paphnutius, Bishop _{mon.} of the Upper Thebaid.   Both are famous for the auster-ity of their lives.   Potammon [2] (that is, "dedicated to Ammon") had himself visited the hermit Antony; Paphnutius (that is, "dedicated to his God") _{Paphnu-} had been brought up in a hermitage.[3]   Both, _{tius.} too, had suffered in the persecutions.   Each presented the frightful spectacle of the right eye dug out with the sword, and the empty socket seared with a red-hot iron.   Paphnutius, besides, came limping on one leg, his left having been hamstrung.[4]

2. Next in importance must be reckoned the Bishops of Syria and of the interior of Asia; or, as they _{Deputies} are sometimes called in the later Councils, the _{from the Church of} *Eastern* Bishops, as distinguished from the _{Syria.} Church of Egypt.   Then, as afterwards, there was a rivalry between those branches of Oriental Christen-dom; each, from long neighborhood, knowing each, yet each tending in an opposite direction, till, after the Council of Chalcedon, a community of heresy drew them together again.   Here, as in Egypt, we find two

---

1 Antony could not speak Greek.   Soz. i. 13.

2 Three of that name were at Sardica.   (Ath. Apol. c. Ar. 50.)

3 ἐν ἀσκητηρίῳ.   The same word that in the Russian Church is abridged into *skeet*.   See Lecture XI.

4 Rufin. i. 4 : " Sinistro poplite succiso."   See also Soc. i. 11.

classes of representatives — scholars from the more
civilized cities of Syria; wild ascetics from the remoter

Eustathius
of Antioch. East.   The first in dignity was the orthodox
Eustathius, who either was, or was on the point
of being made,[1] Bishop of the capital of Syria, the metropolis of the Eastern Church, Antioch, then called
" the city of God." He had suffered in heathen persecutions, and was destined to suffer in Christian persecutions also.[2]   But he was chiefly known for his learning
and eloquence, which was distinguished by an antique
simplicity of style.   One work alone has come down to
us, on the " Witch of Endor."

Next in rank and far more illustrious, was his chief suf-
Eusebius of
Cæsarea. fragan the metropolitan of Palestine, the Bishop
of Cæsarea, Eusebius.   We honor him as the fa-
ther of ecclesiastical history—as the chief depositary of
the traditions which connect the fourth with the first century.   But in the Bishops at Nicæa his presence awakened
feelings of a very different kind.   He alone of the Eastern Prelates could tell what was in the mind of the Emperor; he was the clerk of the Imperial closet; he was
the interpreter, the chaplain, the confessor of Constantine.   And yet he was on the wrong side.   Two especially, we may be sure, of the Egyptian Church, were
on the watch for any slip that he might make.   Athanasius (whatever may have been the opinions of later
times respecting the doctrines of Eusebius) was convinced that he was at heart an Arian.[3]   Potammon of
the one eye had known him formerly in the days of
persecution, and was ready with that most fatal taunt,

[1] The very intricate question of the date of Eustathius's appointment to
Antioch is well discussed in Tillemont, vii. 646.   It seems most probable that
he was appointed just at this crisis.

[2] Soz. ii. 19.

[3] De Syn. c. 17.

which, on a later occasion, he threw out against him, that, whilst he had thus suffered for the cause of Christ, Eusebius[1] had escaped by sacrificing to an idol.

If Eusebius was suspected of Arianism, he was supported by most of his suffragan bishops in Palestine, of whom Paulinus of Tyre,[2] and Patrophilus of Bethshan (Scythopolis), were the most remarkable. One, however, a champion of Orthodoxy, was distin- Macarius of Jerusa-guished, not in himself, but for the see which lem he occupied—once the highest in Christendom, in a few years about to claim something of its former grandeur, but at the time of the Council known only as a second-rate Syro-Roman city — Macarius, Bishop of Ælia Capitolina, that is, "Jerusalem."

From Neocæsarea, a border fortress on the Euphrates,[3] came its confessor Bishop, Paul, who, like Paul of Paphnutius and Potammon, had suffered in the Neocæs-area. persecutions, but more recently, under Licinius. His hands were paralyzed by the scorching of the muscles of all the fingers with red-hot iron. Along with him were the Orthodox representatives of four famous Churches, who, according to the Armenian tradition, travelled in company.[4] Their leader was the James of marvel, "the Moses" as he was termed, of Nisibis. Mesopotamia, James, or Jacob, Bishop of Nisibis.[5] He had lived for years as a hermit on the mountains; in the forests during the summer, in caverns during the winter: browsing on roots and leaves like a wild beast, and like a wild beast clothed in a rough goat-hair cloak. This dress and manner of life, even after he became

---

[1] Epiph. cxviii. 7; Ath. Apol. 8.　　[2] Theod. i. 4, 7.　　[3] Ibid. i. 6.

[4] Moses Choren. ii. 87. To these must be added Maruthas, Bishop of Tagrit, namesake of the future historian of the Council. (Assem. Bibl. Or. i. 195.) See p. 145.

[5] Theod. Philoth. iii. 11–14 : οἷά τις ἀρίστευς καὶ πρόμαχος ἁπάσης φάλαγγος. See Biblioth. Patrum, v. p. clviii.

bishop, he never laid aside; and the mysterious awe
which his presence inspired was increased by the stories
of miraculous power, which, we are told, he exercised
in a manner as humane and playful as it was grotesque;
as when he turned the washerwoman's hair white, detected the impostor who pretended to be dead, and
raised an army of gnats against the Persians. His
fame as a theologian rests on disputed writings.[1]

The second was Ait-allaha ("the brought of God,"
like the Greek "Theophorus"), who had just occupied
the see of Edessa, and finished the building of the
cemetery of his cathedral.[2]

The third was Aristaces, said to be the cousin of
Jacob of Nisibis and son of Gregory the Illuminator,
founder of the Armenian Church.[3] He represented
both his father the Bishop, and Tiridates the King,
of Armenia; the Bishop and King having received a
special invitation from Constantine,[4] and sent their written professions of faith by the hands of Aristaces.

The fourth came from beyond the frontier, the sole
representative of the more distant East. "John the
Persian," who added to his name the more sounding
title, — here appearing for the first time, but revived
in our own days as the designation of our own Bishops
of Calcutta, — "Metropolitan of India." [5]

A curious tradition related that this band, including

---

[1] Theod. Philoth. iii. 1108–1116; Bibl. Patr. v. iii.–clii.

[2] Chronicon Edess. ap. Assemanni Biblioth. Or. i. 394. His name is written *Ettilaus*, *Ætholaus*, *Ætolus*, in the Nicene subscriptions, and *Authalius* in
Moses Choren. ii. 87. *Rabalas*, Chronicle of Amrou, Asseman. iii. 588.

[3] See Le Quien, Oriens Christ. ii. 1251; Bibl. Patr. v. cliii.

[4] Moses Choren. ii. 86.

[5] Eus. V. C. iii. 7: ἤδη δὲ καὶ Πέρσης ἐπίσκοπος συνόδῳ παρῆν. In Gelas.
Cyz. called John. In the Coptic version (Spicil. Solesm. 533) he is made the
Bishop of Persis, a city in Mesopotamia. (See Spicil. Solesm. 533.) Has his
name, thus emphatically stated, any connection with Prester John ?

eleven other obscure names from the remote East, were the only members of the Nicene Council who had not sustained some bodily mutilation or injury.[1]

3. As this little band advanced westward, they encountered a remarkable personage, who stands at the head of the next group which we meet —the Prelates of Asia Minor and Greece. This was Leontius of Cæsarea in Cappadocia. From his hands, it was said, Gregory of Armenia had received ordination, and from his successors in the see of Cæsarea had desired that every succeeding Bishop of Armenia should receive ordination likewise.[2] For this reason, it may be, Aristaces and his company sought him out. They found Leontius already on his journey, and they overtook him at a critical moment.[3] He was on the point of baptizing another Gregory, father of a much more celebrated Gregory, the future Bishop of Nazianzum. A light, it was believed, shone from the water, which was only discerned by the sacred travellers.

Deputies from the Church of Asia Minor.

Leontius of Cæsarea.

Leontius was claimed by the Arians, but still more decidedly by the Orthodox.[4] Others, of the same side, are usually named as from the same region, amongst them Hypatius of Gangra, whose end we shall witness at the close of these events, and Hermogenes the deacon, afterwards Bishop of Cæsarea, who acted as secretary of the Council.

Eusebius of Nicomedia, afterwards of Constantinople, Theognis of Nicæa,[5] Maris of Chalcedon, and Menophantus of Ephesus, were amongst the

Eusebius of Nicomedia.

[1] Acta SS. Jan. 13, 781.
[2] Moses Choren. ii. 87.
[3] Greg. Naz. Or. xviii. c. 12, 13.
[4] Ath. ad Episc. Æg. c. 8; Philostorgius, i. 9.
[5] Theod. i. 11.   He says: Θεόγνιος Νικαίας αὐτῆς ἐπίσκοπος.

most resolute defenders of Arius. It is curious to reflect that they represent the four sees of the four Orthodox Councils of the Church. The three last named soon vanish away from history. But Eusebius of Nicomedia, friend, namesake, perhaps even brother of the Bishop of Cæsarea, was a personage of high importance both then and afterwards. As Athanasius was called "the great" by the Orthodox, so was Eusebius by the Arians.[1] Even miracles were ascribed to him.[2] Originally Bishop of Beyruth (Berytus), he had been translated[3] to the see of Nicomedia, then the capital of the Eastern Empire. He had been a favorite of the Emperor's rival Licinius,[4] and had thus become intimate with Constantia, the Emperor's sister, the wife, now the widow of Licinius. Through her and through his own distant relationship with the Imperial family, he kept a hold on the court which he never lost, even to the moment when he stood by the dying bed of the Emperor, years afterwards, and received him into the Church. We must not be too hard on the Christianity of Eusebius, if we wish to vindicate the baptism of Constantine.[5]

Not far from the great prelate of the capital of the East would be the representative of what was Alexander of Byzantium. now a small Greek town, but in five years from that time would supersede altogether the glories of Nicomedia. Metrophanes,[6] Bishop of Byzantium, was detained by old age and sickness, but Alexander, his presbyter, himself seventy years of age, was there with a little secretary of the name of Paul, not more than twelve years old, one of the readers and collectors of

---

1 Philostorg. Fragm. i. 9.
2 See Neale's Alexandrian Church, i. 123.   3 Theod. i. 19.
4 Athan. Apol. c. Arian. 6 ; Ammian. Marcell. xxii. 9, 4.
5 See Lecture VI.   6 Photius, Biblioth. 471.

the Byzantine Church.[1]   Alexander had already corresponded with his namesake of Alexandria on the
Arian controversy,[2] and was apparently attached firmly
to the Orthodox side.

Besides their more regular champions, the Orthodox
party of Greece and Asia Minor had a few very eccentric allies. One was Acesius, the Novatian, "the
Puritan," summoned by Constantine from By- Acesius, the
Novatian.
zantium with Alexander, from the deep respect entertained by the Emperor for his ascetic character. He
was attended by a boy, Auxanon, who lived to a great
age afterwards as a presbyter in the same sect.[3] This
child was then living with a hermit, Eutychianus, on the
heights of the neighboring mountain of the Bithynian
Olympus, and he descended from these solitudes to attend upon Acesius.   From him we have obtained some
of the most curious details of the Council.

Marcellus, Bishop of Ancyra, was, amongst the Bishops,
the fiercest opponent of Arius, and when the Marcellus
of Ancyra.
active deacon of Alexandria was not present,
seems to have borne the brunt of the arguments.[4]   Yet,
if we may judge from his subsequent history, Athanasius could never have been quite at ease in leaving the
cause in his hands.   He was one of those awkward
theologians who never could attack Arianism without
falling into Sabellianism ; and in later life he was twice
deposed from his see for heresy, once excommunicated
by Athanasius himself; and in the present form of
the Nicene Creed one clause (that which asserts that
" the kingdom of Christ shall have no end ") is said
to have been expressly aimed at his exaggerated language.[5]

And now come two, who in the common pictures of

---

[1] Photius, Biblioth. 471.   [2] Neale, i. 130.   [3] Soc. i. 13.
[4] Ath. Apol. c. Ar. §§ 23, 32.   [5] Ibid. de Syn. §§ 24, 26.

the Council always appear together, of whom the one
probably left the deepest impression on his contemporaries, and the other, if he were present at all, on the subsequent traditions of the Council. From the
island of Cyprus there arrived the simple shepherd Spyridion, a shepherd both before and after his elevation to the episcopate. Strange stories were told by
his fellow-islanders to the historian Socrates of the thieves
who were miraculously caught in attempting to steal his
sheep, and of Spyridion's good-humored reply when
he found them in the morning, and gave them a ram
that they might not have sat up all night for nothing.
Another tale, exactly similar to the fantastic Mussulman
legends which hang about the sacred places of Jerusalem,
told how he had gained an answer from his dead daughter Irene to tell where a certain deposit was hidden.[1]
Two less marvellous, but more instructive, stories bring
out the simplicity of his character. He rebuked a celebrated preacher at Cyprus for altering, in a quotation
from the Gospels, the homely word for " bed " into
" couch." — " What ! are you better than He who said
" ' bed,'[2] that you are ashamed to use His words ? " On
occasion of a wayworn traveller coming to him in Lent,
finding no other food in the house, he presented him
with salted pork; and when the stranger declined, saying
that he could not as a Christian break his fast, — " So
" much the less reason," he said, " have you for scruple ;
" to the pure, all things are pure."[3]

A characteristic legend attaches to the account of his
journey to the Council. It was his usual practice to
travel on foot. But on this occasion the length of the
journey, as well as the dignity of his office, induced him

Spyridion
of Cyprus.

1 Ruf. i. 5 ; compare " Sinai and Palestine," p. 179.
2 κράββατον altered into σκίμπους. Soz. i. 11.
3 See Tillemont, vi. 688–696.

to ride, in company with his deacon, on two mules, a white and a chestnut. One night, on his arrival at a caravanserai where a cavalcade of Orthodox bishops were already assembled, the mules were turned out to pasture, whilst he retired to his devotions. The bishops had conceived an alarm lest the cause of Orthodoxy should suffer in the Council by the ignorance or awkwardness of the Shepherd of Cyprus when opposed to the subtleties of the Alexandrian heretic. Accordingly, taking advantage of this encounter, they determined to throw a decisive impediment in his way. They cut off the heads of his two mules, and then, as is the custom in Oriental travelling, started on their journey before sunrise. Spyridion also rose, but was met by his terrified deacon, announcing the unexpected disaster. On arriving at the spot, the saint bade the deacon attach the heads to the dead bodies. He did so, and, at a sign from the bishop, the two mules with their restored heads shook themselves as if from a deep sleep, and started to their feet. Spyridion and the deacon mounted, and soon overtook the travellers. As the day broke, the prelates and the deacon were alike astonished at seeing that he, performing the annexation in the dark and in haste, had fixed the heads on the wrong shoulders; so that the white mule had now a chestnut head, and the chestnut mule had the head of its white companion. Thus the miracle was doubly attested, the bishops doubly discomfited, and the simplicity of Spyridion doubly exemplified.[1]

Many more stories might be told of him, but (to use the words of an ancient writer who has related some of

---

[1] Another version of this legend (which appeared in the 1st edition of this work) ascribes the decapitation to the Arians. But the more usual version is that here given. I heard it both in Mount Athos and at Corfu, and it is told at length in an Italian MS. Life of S. Spyridion, communicated to me by the kindness of a friend in Corfu.

them) "from the claws you can make out the lion." [1]
Of all the Nicene fathers, it may yet be said that in a
certain curious sense he is the only one who has survived the decay of time.   After resting for many years
in his native Cyprus, his body was transferred to Constantinople, where it remained till a short time before the
fall of the Empire.   It was thence conveyed to Corfu,
where it [2] is still preserved.   Hence, by a strange re-
suscitation of fame, he has become the patron saint,
one might almost say the Divinity, of the Ionian
islands.   Twice a year in solemn procession he is
carried round the streets of Corfu.   Hundreds of Cor-
fiotes bear his name, now abridged into the familiar
diminutive of "Spiro."   The superstitious veneration
entertained for the old saint is a constant source of
quarrel between the English residents and the native
Ionians.   But the historian may be pardoned for gazing with a momentary interest on the dead hands,
now black and withered, that subscribed the Creed
of Nicæa.

Still more famous (and still more apocryphal, at least
Nicolas of   in his attendance at Nicæa) is Nicolas, Bishop
Myra.   of Myra.   Not mentioned by a single ancient
historian, he yet figures in the traditional pictures of
the Council as the foremost figure of all.   Type as he
is of universal benevolence to sailors, to thieves, to the
victims of thieves, to children, — known by his broad
red face and flowing white hair, — the traditions of the
East always represent him as standing in the midst of
the assembly, and suddenly roused by righteous indignation to assail the heretic Arius with a tremendous
box on the ear.[3]

[1] Photius, Biblioth. 471.
[2] It was brought by the great family of the Bulgaris, who are said to be
descendants of his sister.
[3] See Tillemont, vi. 688.   Comp. Lecture IV.

4. One more group of deputies closes the arrivals. The Nicene Council was, as I have often said, The Western Bishops. a Council of the Eastern Church; and Eastern seemingly were at least 310 of the 318 Bishops. But the West was not entirely unrepresented. Nicasius from France, Marcus from Calabria, Capito from Sicily, Eustorgius from Milan (where a venerable church is still dedicated to his memory), Domnus of Stridon in Pannonia, were the less conspicuous deputies of the Western provinces.

But there were five men whose presence must have been full of interest to their Eastern brethren. Corresponding to John the Persian from the extreme Theophilus the Goth. East, was Theophilus the Goth from the extreme North. His light complexion doubtless made a marked contrast with the tawny hue and dark hair of almost all the rest. They rejoiced to think that they had a genuine Scythian amongst them.[1] From all future generations of his Teutonic countrymen he may claim attention, as the predecessor and teacher of Ulphilas,[2] the great missionary of the Gothic nation.[3]

Out of the province of Northern Africa, the earliest cradle of the Latin Church, came Cæcilian, Cæcilian of Carthage. Bishop of Carthage. A few years ago he had himself been convened before the two Western Councils of the Lateran and of Arles, and had there been acquitted of the charges brought against him by the Donatists.

If any of the distant Orientals had hoped to catch a sight of the Bishop of the "Imperial city," they were doomed to disappointment. Doubtless, had he been there, his position as prelate of the capital would have been, if not first, at least among the first. But Sylves-

---

[1] Eus. V. C. iii. 7.   [2] Soc. ii. 41.   [3] See Lecture IX.

ter[1] was now far advanced in years; and in his place
Victor and Vincentius the Roman Presbyters. came the two presbyters, who, according to the
arrangement laid down by the Emperor, would
have accompanied him had he been able to
make the journey. In this simple deputation later
writers have seen (and perhaps by a gradual process
the connection might be traced) the first germ of *legati
a latere.* But it must have been a very far-seeing eye
which in Victor and Vincentius, the two unknown elders, representing their sick old Bishop, could have detected the predecessors of Pandulf or of Wolsey. With
Hosius of Cordova. them, however, was a man who, though now
long forgotten, was then an object of deeper
interest to Christendom than any Bishop of Rome could
at that time have been. It was the world-renowned
Spaniard, as he is called by Eusebius; the magician
from Spain,[2] as he is called by Zosimus; Hosius, Bishop
of Cordova. He was the representative of the westernmost of European Churches; but, as Eusebius of Cæsarea was the chief counsellor of the Emperor in the
Greek Church, so was Hosius in the Latin Church, as
we shall see hereafter in the darkest and most mysterious crisis of Constantine's life. With some there
present he was personally acquainted. The Alexandrian deputies had already seen him, when he had
come to their city charged with the Emperor's pacifi-
catory letter to Alexander and Arius. He and Eusebius must have been regarded as the most powerful
persons in the assembly. He had still thirty years
of life to run, yet he was already venerable with years
and sufferings and honors. He had been a confessor
in the persecutions of Maximin; he was received, Athanasius tells us, with profound reverence, as that "Abra-

---

[1] Sozomen (i. 17), by mistake, says "Julius."   [2] See Lecture VI.

hamic old man, well called Hosius,[1] the 'Holy';" and probably no one then present would have thought of inquiring whether any portion of his authority was derived from the absent Bishop of Rome. This claim for him has been set up in later times; and it is possible that, as he was certainly charged with the secrets of the Roman Emperor, so he may have been with those of the Roman Bishop. But such was not the impression produced on the contemporary witnesses of the scene; his own high character, his intimacy with Constantine, and his theological learning, were sufficient of themselves to have secured for him the position which he occupied there, as in all the other Councils of the age.

VI. It was probably by degrees that these different arrivals took place, and the lapse of two or three weeks must be supposed, for the prepar- Prelimi-nary dis-cussions. atory arrangements, before the Council was formally opened. This interval was occupied by eager discussions on the questions likely to be debated. The first assemblage had been, as we have seen, within the walls of a public building. But the other preliminary meetings were held, as was natural, in the streets or colonnades in the open air. The novelty of the occasion had collected many strangers to the spot. Laymen, philosophers, heathen as well as Christian, might be seen joining in the arguments on either side,[2] orthodox as well as heretical. There were also discussions amongst the Orthodox themselves as to the principle on which the debates should be conducted. The enumeration of the characters just given shows that there were two very

[1] Apol. Ap. Ar. 44; De Fuga, 5; Ad Mon. 42–45.

[2] Soc. i. 8 : ἐν ἑκατέρῳ μέρει συνηγορεῖν προθυνούμενοι. This disproves the representation that the philosophers were all on the Arian side, as in later historians and in the Athonian pictures.

different elements in the assembly, such indeed as will always constitute the main difficulty in making any general statements of theology which shall be satisfactory at once to the few and to the many. A large number, perhaps the majority, consisted of rough, simple, almost illiterate men, like Spyridion the shepherd, Potammon the hermit, Acesius the puritan, who held their faith earnestly and sincerely, but without much conscious knowledge of the grounds on which they maintained it, incapable of arguing themselves, or of entering into the arguments of their opponents. These men, when suddenly brought into collision with the acutest and most learned disputants of the age, naturally took up the position that the safest course was to hold by what had been handed down, without any further inquiry or explanation. A story somewhat variously told is related of an encounter of one of these simple characters with the more philosophical combatants, which, in whatever way it be taken, well illustrates the mixed character of the Council, and the choice of courses open before it. As Socrates describes the incident, the disputes were running so high, from the mere pleasure of argument, that there seemed likely to be no end to the controversy; when suddenly a simple-minded layman, who by his sightless eye, or limping leg, bore witness of his zeal for the Christian faith, stepped amongst them, and abruptly said: "Christ and the "Apostles left us, not a system of logic, nor a vain "deceit, but a naked truth, to be guarded by faith "and good works." "There has," says Bishop Kaye[1] in recording the story, "been hardly any age of the "Church in which its members have not required to "be reminded of this lesson." On the present occasion the by-standers, at least for the moment, were struck by

The theologians and the layman.

---

[1] "Some Account of the Council of Nicæa," p. 39.

its happy application, the disputants, after hearing this plain word of truth, took their differences more good-humoredly, and the hubbub of controversy subsided.

Another version of the same story, or another story of the same kind, with a somewhat different moral, is told by Rufinus and Sozomen,[1] and amplified by later writers. The disputants, or rather disputant (for one is specially selected), is now not a Christian theologian, but a heathen philosopher, to whom, in later writings, is given the suspicious name of Eulogius,[2] "Fairspeech." He was a perfect master of argument; the moment that he seemed to be caught by one of his opponents, he slipped out of their hands like an eel or a snake.[3] His opponent is, in this story, not a layman, but an aged bishop or priest (and here the later account identifies him with the shepherd Spyridion). Unable to bear any longer the taunts with which the philosopher assailed a group of Christians, amongst whom he was standing, he came forth to refute him. His uncouth appearance, rendered more hideous by the mutilations he had undergone in the persecutions, provoked a roar of laughter from his opponents, whilst his friends were not a little uneasy at seeing their cause intrusted to so unskilled a champion. But he felt himself strong in his own simplicity. "In the name of "Jesus Christ," he called out to his antagonist, "hear me, "philosopher. There is one God, maker of heaven and "earth, and of all things visible and invisible: who made "all things by the power of His Word, and by the holi- "ness of His Holy Spirit. This Word, by which name "*we* call the Son of God, took compassion on men for "their wandering astray, and for their savage condition, "and chose to be born of a woman, and to converse

The philosopher and the peasant.

---

[1] Ruf. i. 3; Soz. i. 18.   [2] Gelasius, iii. 13.
[3] Ruf. i. 3: "Velut anguis lubricus."

"with men, and to die for them, and he shall come again
"to judge every one for the things done in life. These
"things we believe without curious inquiry. Cease
"therefore the vain labor of seeking proofs for or
"against what is established by faith, and the manner
"in which these things may be or may not be; but, if
"thou believest, answer at once to me as I put my
"questions to you."

The philosopher was struck dumb by this new mode
of argument. He could only reply that he assented.
"Then," answered the old man, "if thou believest this,
"rise and follow me to the Lord's house,[1] and receive
"the sign of this faith." The philosopher turned round
to his disciples, or to those who had been gathered
round him by curiosity. "Hear," he said, "my learned
"friends. So long as it was a matter of words, I op-
"posed words to words, and whatever was spoken I
"overthrew by my skill in speaking, but when, in the
"place of words, power came out of the speaker's lips,
"words could no longer resist power, man could no
"longer resist. If any of you feel as I have felt, let
"him believe in Christ, and let him follow this old man
"in whom God has spoken." Exaggerated or not,[2] this
story is a proof of the magnetic power of earnestness
and simplicity over argument and speculation.

The tradition which identified the simple disputant
with Spyridion grew in later times into the form which
it bears in all the pictures of the Council, and which is
commemorated in the services of the Greek Church.
Aware of his incapacity of argument, he took a brick,

---

1 Ruf. i. 3: "Ad dominicum." This shows that they were outside the
building, see p. 203.

2 See a similar story of Alexander of Byzantium, who was present at the
Council (Soz. i. 17), and of S. Francis Xavier (Grant's Bampton Lectures,
p. 272).

and said, " You deny that Three can be One. Look at
" this : it is one, and yet it is composed of the three ele-
" ments of fire, earth, and water." As he spoke, the
brick resolved itself into its component parts : the fire
flew upward, the clay remained in Spyridion's hand, and
the water fell to the ground. The philosopher, or (according to some accounts) Arius himself, was so confounded, as to declare himself converted on the spot.[1]

These tales represent probably the feeling of a large
portion of the Council — the sound, unprofes- Principle
sional, untheological, lay element which lay at _{of free dis-} cussion.
the basis of all their weakness and their strength. The
historian Socrates is very anxious to prove that the
assembly was not entirely composed of men of this
kind, and he points triumphantly to the presence of
such men as Eusebius of Cæsarea. No proof was necessary. The subsequent history of the Council itself is
a sufficient indication that, however small a minority
might be the dialecticians and theologians, yet they
constituted the life and movement of the whole.
Socrates dwells with evident pleasure[2] on the circumstance that the ultimate decisions were only made
after long inquiry, and that everything was stirred to
the bottom. Gelasius, in the next century, so far from
being satisfied with the summary treatment of the disputant by the old confessor, introduces a second philosopher, of the name of Phædo, who has a pitched battle
with five Bishops,[3] Hosius included, whose arguments

---

[1] In the MS. Italian Life of S. Spyridion before quoted, the speech with
the philosopher is lengthened into a history of the Old and New Dispensations, and the miracle of the brick is reported as taking place afterwards with
Arius. But in the pictures of the Council, in Mount Athos and at Nicæa, it
is as I have represented.

[2] i. 9.

[3] Hosius, Leontius, Eusebius, Macarius, and Eupsychius (of Tyana).
(Gelas. iii. 14–23.)

are drawn out at full length. This, though fabulous in its details, is doubtless true in its substance. The frenzy of argument was too vehement to be restrained. Heretics and Orthodox alike felt themselves compelled to advance.

We may wish, with Bishop Jeremy Taylor and Bishop Kaye, that it had been otherwise. But there is a point of view in which we may fully sympathize with the course that was taken. All the elements which go to make up the interest of theology were involved : love of free inquiry, desire of precision in philosophical statements, research into Christian antiquity, comparison of the texts of Scripture one with another. Traditional and episcopal authority was regarded as insufficient for the establishment of the faith. The well-known clause of the Twenty-first Article does but express the principle of the Nicene Fathers themselves : — "Things ordained by them as "necessary for salvation have neither strength nor "authority unless it may be declared that they are "taken out of Holy Scripture." The battle was fought and won by quotations, not from tradition, but from the Old and New Testament. The overruling sentiment was, that even ancient opinions were not to be received without sifting and inquiry.[1] The chief combatant and champion of the faith was not the Bishop of Antioch or of Rome, nor the Pope of Alexandria, but the Deacon Athanasius. The eager discussions of Nicæa present the first grand precedent for the duty of private judgment, and the free, unrestrained exercise of Biblical and historical criticism.[2]

---

[1] Soz. i. 17, 25.

[2] It has been often maintained that the decisions of the Council were based on authority, not on argument. It is certain that some of the reasonings of Athanasius rest on the general reception of the Nicene doctrines, rather than on their intrinsic truth. (See the quotations and inferences in Keble's Sermons, pp. 392–394.) But the whole tenor of the narrative in Eusebius,

And now, on the morrow of the discussion between the peasant and the theologians,[1] the day arrived when the Council was to begin its work in earnest, — the day when they should at last see the great man at whose bidding they were met together, and to whose arrival many looked forward as the chief event of the assembly.[2] The Emperor was on his way to Nicæa, and would be there in a few hours to open the Council in person.

Socrates, and Sozomen points to the conclusion that the existing tradition was alleged, not as authority, but as historical evidence, and that it was alleged subordinately to the argument from the Bible itself. Compare especially the paragraph at the close of Sozom. i. 17 : οἱ δὲ ἰσχυρίζοντο — βουλῆς. Ibid. i. 25 : μετὰ ζήτησιν ἀκριβῆ καὶ βάσανον πάντων τῶν ἀμφιβόλων δοκιμασθεῖσαν. A slight reminiscence of this aspect of the Council is preserved in the picture of it in the Iberian monastery at Athos, where the heretics are represented as eagerly poring over the arguments of the Orthodox.

[1] Soc. i. 8.   [2] Eus. V. C. iii. 6.

27

LECTURE IV.

THE OPENING OF THE COUNCIL.

THE Emperor had already been at Nicæa on the 23d of May; as we happen to learn by an edict dated from that city against usurers in Palestine.[1] Probably he had come before the arrival of the Bishops, to ascertain that fit preparations were made for their reception. He had then, as it would seem, returned to Nicomedia, to celebrate his victory over Licinius. If he waited for the actual anniversary, he must have remained there till the 3d of July, and consequently could not have arrived at Nicæa till the 5th. The earlier dates, however, for the opening of the Council — the 14th or the 19th of June — are inconsistent with so long a delay. We must be content, therefore, to leave the precise day in doubt.

The first news that greeted him on his arrival must have been an unpleasing surprise. He had no sooner taken up his quarters in the Palace at Nicæa, than he found showered in upon him a number of parchment rolls, or letters, containing complaints and petitions against each other from the larger part[2] of the assembled Bishops. We cannot ascertain with certainty whether they were collected in a single day, or went on accumulating day after day.[3] It was a

Arrival of the Emperor.

Complaints of the Bishops.

---

[1] Cod. Theod. i. p. xxv.

[2] Soc. i. 8: οἱ πλείονες. This contradicts the later notion that the Arians were the only complainants.

[3] Soc. i. 8.

poor omen for the unanimity which he had so much at heart.

We may indeed make some excuses. We may remember how, even in prison, the English Reformers maintained an unceasing strife with each other on the dark points of Calvinism. We are expressly told both by Eusebius and Sozomen, that one motive[1] which had drawn many to the Council was the hope of settling their own private concerns, and promoting their own private interests. It was the practice to seize the opportunity of solemn processions[2] of the sovereigns to temples and afterwards to churches, as even now of the Sultans to mosques, in order to lay wait with petitions, as the only means of catching their attention. There, too, were the pent-up grudges and quarrels of years; which now for the first time had an opportunity of making themselves heard. Never before had these remote, often obscure, ministers of a persecuted sect come within the range of Imperial power. He whose presence was for the first time so close to them, bore the same authority of which the Apostle had said that it was the supreme earthly distributer of justice to mankind. Still, after all due allowance, it is impossible not to share in the Emperor's astonishment that this should have been the first act of the first Œcumenical Assembly of the Christian Church. Constantine received the letters in silence.[3] His reply we shall hear, when at his own time he chooses to give it.

The meetings of the representatives, which had up to this time been in the church, or gymnasium, Hall of or in separate localities, were henceforth to be Assembly.

---

[1] Eus. V. C. iii. 6; Soz. i. 17.   [2] See Dufresne, Πρόοδος.

[3] It is probably this scene (with another later incident) which led the first Regius Professor of Divinity in Oxford to describe the Nicene fathers as a set of demoniacs, driven by evil furies and malignant passions. (Peter Martyr, Comm. on 1 Kings, xii.)

solemnized in the Imperial residence itself. It is with reluctance that later controversialists, accustomed to the idea of a Council meeting only within consecrated walls, will admit of this transferrence. But the fact is undoubted, and is in accordance not only with the paramount importance of the Emperor on this occasion, but with the precedent already established in the little Council in the Lateran Palace at Rome, and afterwards confirmed by the two Councils held in the vaulted room called the "Trullus" in the palace at Constantinople. Tradition points out the spot, marked by a few broken columns, at the south-west angle of the walls, close by the shores of the lake. A solitary plane[1] tree grows on the ruins. The chamber prepared for their reception was a large oblong hall,[2] in the centre of the palace — the largest that it contained. Benches[3] were ranged along the walls on[4] each side for those of lower dignity, and seats, or chairs, for those of higher; along these were ranged the 300 prelates, perhaps with their assistant deacons and presbyters. In the centre of the room, on a seat or throne, was placed a copy of the Holy Gospels,[5] as the nearest approach to the presence of Christ Himself. Every eye was fixed on one small vacant stall or throne, carved in wood, richly gilt, such as was usually[6] occupied by the sovereign at the Circus or Hippodrome — now placed in the upper end of the hall, between the two ranges of seats.

Entrance of the Emperor.   The long-sustained disputations, the eager recriminations, were at last hushed into a deep

---

[1] I have been informed by the present Bishop of Nicæa that this tree is supposed to stand on the site of the throne.

[2] Eus. V. C. iii. 10.   [3] Theod. i. 7; Eus. V. C. iii. 10.

[4] Niceph. viii. 16.

[5] Westcott on the Canon, 496. This at least was the custom of the later Councils, as of Ephesus. (Ib. i. 175.) See Suicer, Ἐυαγγέλιον, p. 1227; and so it is in the picture at Nicæa.

[6] Eus. V. C. iii. 10: κάθισμα. See Dufresne in voce.

silence. Not a voice broke the stillness of that expectation which precedes the coming of a long wished-for, unknown spectacle, the onward march of a distant procession.[1] Presently a stir was heard, — first one, then another, and then a third, of the officers of the court dropped in. Then the column widened. But still the wonted array of shields and spears[2] was absent. The heathen guards were not to enter the great Christian assembly which had, as it were, consecrated the place where it sat. Only those courtiers who were converted to the Christian faith were allowed to herald the approach of their master. At last a signal from without — probably a torch raised by the " cursor " or avant-courier[3] — announced that the Emperor was close at hand. The whole assembly rose and stood on their feet; and then for the first time set their admiring gaze on Constantine, the Conqueror, the August, the Great. He entered. His towering stature,[4] his strong-built frame, his broad shoulders, his handsome features, were worthy of his grand position.[5] There was a brightness in his look and a mingled expression of fierceness and gentleness[6] in his lion-like eye, which well became one who, as Augustus before him, had fancied, and perhaps still fancied, himself to be the favorite of the Sun-god Apollo. The Bishops were further struck by the dazzling, perhaps barbaric, magnificence of his dress. Always careful of his appearance, he was so on this occasion in an eminent degree. His long hair, false or real, was crowned with the imperial diadem of pearls. His purple or scarlet robe

---

[1] Eus. V. C. iii. 10 : προόδου. The word always used for the Imperial processions. Dufresne in voce.

[2] The appearance of a single guard (speculator) at the Council of Tyre was the subject of much remark. (Ath. Apol. c. Arian. 8.)

[3] For the torches carried by the avant-couriers, see Eus. Paneg. i. 1.

[4] Eus. V. C. iii. 10.　　[5] See Lecture VI.　　[6] Cedrenus, i. 472.

blazed with precious stones and gold embroidery. He was shod no doubt in the scarlet shoes[1] then confined to the Emperors, now perpetuated in the Pope and Cardinals. Many of the Bishops had probably never seen any greater functionary than a remote provincial magistrate, and gazing at his splendid figure as he passed up the hall between their ranks, remembering too what he had done for their faith and for their Church, — we may well believe that the simple and the worldly both looked upon him, as though he were an angel of God, descended straight from Heaven.[2] Yet the awe was not exclusively on their side.[3] However imperfect may have been Constantine's religion, yet there can be little doubt that, as far as it went, it was devout even to superstition. It was a solemn moment for him to find himself for the first time in the midst of the representatives of the great community of which he had so recently professed himself a sincere adherent. Whatever sacredness had before in his eyes attached to flamens and augurs, now in a still higher degree he transferred to the venerable men who stood before him, and whose very looks, whose very disfigurements, bore witness to the earnestness and energy of their young and vigorous faith. The color rushed to the Emperor's cheeks.[4] We cannot forget how far more innocent and ingenuous was this first Imperial blush, than that which became memorable, ages afterwards, in the great Council of the Latin Church — the "*blush of Sigismund*," ob-

---

1 " Campagi." See Mr. Payne Smith's note on John of Ephesus, p. 56.

2 Eus. V. C. iii. 10. That this feeling was not peculiar to Eusebius, may be gathered from the expressions collected by Dr. Newman in his learned note on Athanasius's Tracts, i. 59. In the picture in the Iberian convent at Athos, the Sacred Dove hovers over the head (not of the Bishops, but) of the Emperor.

3 See Lecture VI.   4 Eus. V. C. iii. 10.

served at Constance, remembered at Worms. It was
the genuine expression of Constantine's excitement
and emotion.　As he advanced up the hall he cast
his eyes down, his steps faltered, and when he reached
the throne allotted to him, he stood motionless, till
the Bishops beckoned to him to be seated. He then
sat down, and they followed his example.

If he was still anxious as he looked round on so many
strange faces, he must have been reassured as he looked
on his right hand and his left. Which of the Bishops
occupied these places of honor has been vehemently
disputed in later times, and it is still further complicated
by the ambiguity of the use of the words. Was the
chief seat on the right-hand side of the Emperor, or the
right-hand side of the hall? Apparently, as the Emperor's seat was not permanently there, and as the
Bishops were arranged irrespectively of his entrance,
the latter of these two meanings must be adopted. The
left-hand place has been usually assigned to _{Hosius on}
Hosius of Cordova; and in a picture of the _{the left.}
Nicene Council which adorns the Escurial library, the
Church of Spain, in her zeal for this her eldest and most
distinguished son, makes the very most of him. But
Roman writers, eager to claim the first place for him,
as the supposed representative of the Papal see,[1] have
ingeniously argued that the left, and not the right, was,
with the ancient Romans, the place of honor; and
further, what is also undoubted — although inconsistent
with the argument just used — that the left-hand side
of the hall would give him the right-hand side of the
Emperor.[2] The right-hand post has been naturally more

---

[1] In ancient pictures it is observed of St. Peter and St. Paul, of the Virgin
and St. John, that St. Peter and the Virgin are on the left hand of the
Saviour. (Baronius, 52–60; Bellarmine, De Conc. i. 19; in Mansi, ii. 730.)

[2] In the Council of Chalcedon, the Legates of Rome, with the Bishops of

contested.   In the picture of the Nicene Council at
Nicæa itself, and also in the annals of the Alexandrian
Church,[1] it is filled by Alexander of Alexandria.   Theodoret[2] gives it to Eustathius of Antioch.   But there can
be little doubt that, as on one side of the Emperor sat
his Western favorite Hosius, so on the other side, his
Eusebius on the right. Eastern favorite Eusebius.   Twice over Eusebius
has himself told us so; and from him[3] we know
how, as soon as Constantine and the assembly were
seated, he rose from his place, and in metrical prose, if
not in actual verses, recited an address to the Emperor,
and then a hymn of thanksgiving to the Almighty for
the victory over Licinius, of which the anniversary
had so lately been celebrated.   Eusebius resumed his
seat, and again a deep silence prevailed.   All eyes were
fixed on Constantine.   He cast round one of those bright
glances of which he was master; and then, after a momentary self-recollection, addressed them in a short
speech, exhorting concord and unanimity.   It was in
Latin, — on so solemn an occasion he would not depart
from the Imperial language, in which long afterwards
the laws even of his new capital were written, — and,
therefore, very few of those present could have understood it.   But there was a gentleness and sweetness in
his voice which arrested the attention of all; and as

Constantinople and Antioch, sat on the left, and the Bishops of Alexandria
and Jerusalem on the right, of the Imperial officers.   But there they ranged
themselves according to their opinions.   (Tillemont, xv. 649.)

[1] Eutych. Ann. i. 444.

[2] i. 7. He must have had some ground for this; as Eustathius was evidently
one of his chief authorities for the events of the Council.

[3] Eus. V. C. i. 1; iii. 1; Soz. i. 18. A short speech, supposed to be the one
now spoken, but really written by Gregory of Neocæsarea in the seventh century, is preserved in Fabricius, Biblioth. Gr. ix. 132. Its use of the words
μία οὐσία ἐν τρίσιν ὑποστάσεσι is fatal to its genuineness. Nicephorus (viii. 16)
and Epiphanius Scholasticus (ii. 5) give the first speech to Eustathius, the
second to Eusebius.

soon as it was concluded the Imperial dragoman or interpreter translated [1] it into Greek.

" It has, my friends, been the object of my highest " wishes, to enjoy your sacred company, and " having obtained this, I confess my thankful- " ness to the King of all, that in addition to all my other " blessings He has granted to me this greatest of all — " I mean, to receive you all assembled together, and to " see one common harmonious opinion of all.   Let, then, " no envious enemy injure our happiness, and, after the " destruction of the impious power of the tyrants by the " might of God our Saviour, let not the Spirit of evil " overwhelm the Divine law with blasphemies ; for to " me far worse than any war or battle is the civil war " of the Church of God ; yes, far more painful than the " wars which have raged without.   As, then, by the as- " sent and coöperation of a higher power I have gained " my victories over my enemies, I thought that nothing " remained but to give God thanks, and to rejoice with " those who have been delivered by us.   But since I " learned of your divisions, contrary to all expectations, " I gave the report my first consideration ; and praying " that this also might be healed through my assistance, " I called you all together without delay.   I rejoice at " the mere sight of your assembly ; but the moment " that I shall consider the chief fulfilment of my prayers " will be when I see you all joined together in heart " and soul, and determining on one peaceful harmony " for all, which it should well become you who are con- " secrated to God, to preach to others.   Do not, then, " delay, my friends ; do not delay, ministers of God, and

The Emperor's speech.

---

[1] Eus. V. C. iii. 13 : ὑφερμηνεύοντος.   As late as the Council of Chalcedon, the Emperor Marcian spoke in Latin, which was then translated into Greek. (Mansi, vii. 127.)   A false speech of Constantine is given in Gelas. iii. 7.

"good servants of our common Lord and Saviour, to re-
"move all grounds of difference, and to wind up by laws
"of peace every link of controversy. Thus will you
"have done what is most pleasing to the God who is
"over all, and you will render the greatest boon to me,
"your fellow-servant."[1]

The Council was now formally opened, and the Em-

The open-
ing of the
Council.

peror gave permission to the presidents of the
assembly to commence their proceedings.

In the Egyptian traditions this was enlarged into a
formal authorization of the legal powers of the Council.
He gave to them, it was said, his ring, his sword, and
his sceptre, with the words, "To you I have this day
"given power over my empire, to do in it whatever you
"think fit for the promotion of religion and for the ad-
"vantage of the faithful."[2] This, no doubt, is a later
invention. But it is probably so far correct that the
Emperor's intention was to constitute them into an independent body for the settlement of these questions,
however much his personal influence controlled their
decisions, and his authority was needed for the ratifi-
cation of their decrees.[3]

The plural number used by Eusebius to designate the

The Presi-
dents.

presidency of the Council, renders it probable
that the two Bishops of the leading sees, Alexandria and Antioch,[4] must be amongst those intended;
the general testimony points to Hosius as another, who,
from the causes already mentioned, would naturally be
what he is expressly styled by Athanasius, leader of

---

[1] Eus. V. C. iii. 12. [2] Eutych. i. 443.

[3] Athanasius (Apol. c. Ar. c. 9) is full of horror at a count having presided
at the Council of Tyre. Technically speaking, this was inconsistent with the
precedents of Nicæa. But the Emperor's officers appeared frequently in the
Council of Chalcedon. Mansi, vi. 822.

[4] In Facundus, i. 1, xi. 1, Eustathius is president.

all the Councils; and to these, by his own account, we must add Eusebius of Cæsarea.

From this moment the flood-gates of debate were opened wide; and from side to side recrimina- *The mutual* tions and accusations were bandied to and fro, *complaints.* without regard to the Imperial presence. He remained unmoved amidst the clatter of angry voices, turning from one side of the hall to the other, giving his whole attention to the questions proposed, bringing together the violent partisans. He condescended to lay aside his stately Latin, and addressed them in such broken Greek as he could command, still in that sweet and gentle voice, praising some, persuading others, putting others to the blush, but directing all his energies to that one point, which he has himself described as his aim — a unanimity of decision.[1] We have it on his own authority, that he reckoned himself as one of the number — as a bishop for the time being;[2] and that he took an active part in the discussion. It was probably in this first session that he put a stop to those personal quarrels, of which he had already had the earliest instalment on his arrival on the preceding day.[3] We cannot doubt, from the eagerness with which their complaints had been handed in, that this must have been the uppermost thought in the minds of most of the assembly when the debates began, and their expectation would be raised to

[1] Eus. V. C. iii. 13.   [2] Soc. i. 9. (30.)

[3] In this I follow the account of Socrates, because, —

a) He is more precise in his statement of the days than the others.

b) His account is confirmed by Gelasius, and not absolutely contradicted by Rufinus and Sozomen.

c) The mention of the purple robe in Theodoret, i. 10, agrees with the Emperor's dress on the first day.

d) The incident naturally finds a place in the general scene described by Eusebius, V. C. iii. 13.

e) The impression conveyed by Eusebius, V. C. iii. 12, is that the greater part of the assembly then saw Constantine for the first time.

a high pitch when the Emperor produced, before the Council, from the folds of his mantle,[1] the petitions on

The Emperor's answer. their papyrus or parchment rolls. He pointed to them as they lay, bound up and sealed with his Imperial ring; and then, after declaring with a solemn oath[2] (his usual mode of attestation) that he had not read one of them, he ordered a brazier[3] to be brought in, in which they were burnt at once in the presence of the assembly. Three speeches are given by the different historians on the occasion, each probably expressive of three different turns which the Emperor's mind may have taken. According to Socrates, after having dwelt on the importance of dismissing those personal disputes, if they hoped to arrive at a conclusion on the great matter which had called them together, he added[4] just this one pregnant remark, as the parchments were smouldering in the flames — " It is the command of Christ that he who " desires to be himself forgiven must first forgive his " brother."[5] According to Theodoret and Rufinus there was mingled with this feeling of disgust at the want of Christian concord in them, and with the desire for it in his own mind, something of the almost superstitious awe which animated him, as we have already seen, in the presence of the Christian clergy. Perhaps, also, he may have intended a stroke of that quiet humor which was one of the happiest characteristics of his public speeches.[6] " You have been made by God priests

---

1 Rufinus, H. E. i. 2: " In sinu suo continens."

2 For his oath, see Lecture VI.

3 Niceph. viii. 17.

4 Soc. i. viii. 20 : ἐπειπὼν μόνον.

5 Dioscorus, President of the (Robber) Council of Ephesus, rejected like complaints for a very different reason. See the excellent remarks of Theodoret, Ep. 147.

6 Victor, 23 : " Irrisor potius quam blandus."

"and rulers, to judge and decide . . . . and have even
"been made Gods, so highly raised as you are above
"men; for it is written — 'I have said ye are Gods, and
"ye are all the children of the Most High;' 'and God
"stood in the congregation of the gods, and in the midst
"He judges the gods.'[1] You ought really to neglect
"these common matters, and devote yourselves to the
"things of God. It is not for me to judge of what
"awaits the judgment of God only." And as the libels
vanished into ashes, he urged them — "Never to let the
"faults of men in their consecrated offices be publicly
"known to the scandal and temptation of the multi-
"tude." "Nay," he added, doubtless spreading out the
folds of his Imperial mantle as he spoke, "even though
"I were with my own eyes to see a bishop in the act of
"gross sin,[2] I would throw my purple robe over him,
"that no one might suffer from the sight of such a
"crime."

The theological controversy which followed, though
doubtless lightened and sweetened by this abrupt dis-
entanglement of it from bitter personal grievances, was
more difficult to terminate. And we have no continuous account of the mode in which it was conducted.
We know not whether it lasted weeks or days.[3] Of
the two eye-witnesses, one (Eusebius) tells us next to
nothing; the other (Athanasius) writes with such a
special purpose, that it is hard to extract from him
the actual facts. Still certain incidents transpire, and
those, in however fragmentary a manner, I shall now
endeavor to describe.

We have hitherto viewed the Council in its national

[1] Ruf. i. 2.

[2] Theod. i. 10. That gross licentiousness was one of the complaints brought
forward may be gathered from the charges brought against Eustathius of Antioch and Athanasius.

[3] Ruf. i. 5: "Per dies singulos agitabatur conventus."

divisions, and in its arrangement of outward preced-
The theo-   ence. We now proceed to view it as it broke
logical
parties.   itself up into theological parties.[1]

The Orthodox side would be represented by the Alexandrian Bishop and his deacon Athanasius; the extreme
right being occupied by the exaggerated vehemence of
Marcellus of Ancyra.[2]

The opposite party would be represented by the three
Bithynian Bishops, Eusebius of Nicomedia, Theognis,
and Maris, with those prelates of Palestine and Asia
Minor who had committed themselves to the same view,
deepening on the extreme left into Arius himself, supported by his two boldest adherents, Theonas and Secundus.

The great mass of the assembled Bishops[3] would occupy the centre between these two extremes; shading
off on the one side through men like Leontius and Hosius
into the party of Alexander and Athanasius, and on the
other through men like Eusebius of Cæsarea and Paulinus of Tyre into the extreme Arian party of the Bithynian Bishops.[4]

[1] This is well given in Hefele, i. 273.

[2] Ath. Apol. c. Arian. 23, 32. Cyril. Alex. tom. v. pt. i. p. 4.

[3] Neander (iv. 40) well points out the unfairness of Athanasius in ignoring
this large intermediate party.

[4] The Arian bishops are thus reckoned by Philostorgius :

1. Sentianus of Boreum.	13. *Athanasius of Anazarbus.*
2. Dachius of Berenice.	14. Tarcodinatus of Ægæ.
3. Secundus of Theuchira.	15. Leontius
4. Zopyrus of Barca.	16. Longianus } of Cappadocia.
5. Secundus of Ptolemais.	17. Eulalius
6. *Theonas of Marmarica.*	18. Basil of Amasia. } Pontus.
7. Meletius of Thebes.	19. Meletius of Sebastopolis. }
8. *Patrophilus of Scythopolis.*	20. *Theognis of Nicæa.*
9. *Eusebius of Cæsarea.*	21. Maris of Chalcedon.
10. *Paulinus of Tyre.*	22. Eusebius the Great of Nicomedia.
11. Amphion of Sidon.	See Walch. i. 471.
12. *Narcissus of Irenopolis (Neronias).*	

The names in *italics* are also mentioned by Theodoret (i. 5, 7); Theodoret

The discussion was, like those which had preceded it, based on the principle of free inquiry, and not of authority. The duty — so hateful to theological adversaries — of "exact statement," "searching trial," and "hearing both sides," is repeatedly and expressly mentioned, both in the narratives and documents of the Nicene assembly.[1]

Small as the Arian minority eventually appeared to be, it is clear from the account of the debates which followed the opening of the Council, that they must have had a hope of victory.

It may have been this confidence that caused their ruin. At least it appears that the chief recoil against them was occasioned by the overweening subtlety or rashness of their own statements, which were all more or less aggressive. Arius, though as a presbyter he had no seat in the Council, was frequently called upon to express his opinions,[2] and was usually confronted with Athanasius.[3] It was now, apparently, that the Council first heard the songs which Arius had written under the name of Thalia[4] for the sake of popularizing his specu- *The Thalia of Arius.* lations with the lower orders. The songs were set to tunes, or written in metres, which had acquired a questionable reputation from their use in the licentious verses of the heathen poet Sotades, ordinarily used in the low revels or dances of Alexandria; and the grave Arius himself is said, in moments of wild excitement, to have danced like an Eastern dervish, whilst he sang these abstract statements in long straggling lines, of which about

of Heraclea is added by Gelasius of Cyzicus (ii. 7) ; and Theodorus of Laodicea, Gregory of Berytus, and Aerius of Lydda by Theodoret (i. 5).

[1] Soc. i. 9, *passim.*

[2] Ruf. i. 5.　He was there by the Emperor's command.　(Ib. i. 1.)

[3] See Lecture III. p. 189.　A fictitious "Dispute of Athanasius and Arius" is found in Athanasius's works, ii. p. 205.

[4] Soc. i. 9, 29.　Apollinarius did the same.　His songs were sung at banquets, and at work, and by women weaving.　Soz. vi. 25.

twenty are preserved to us.[1] To us the chief surprise
is that any enthusiasm should have been excited by sentences[2] such as these : — "God was not always Father ;
"once He was not Father ; afterwards He became Fa-
"ther."   But, in proportion to the attraction which they
possessed for the partisans of Arius, was the dismay which
they roused in the minds of those by whom the expressions which Arius thus lightly set aside were regarded
as the watchwords of the ancient faith.   The Bishops,
on hearing the song, raised their hands in horror, and,
after the manner of Orientals, when wishing to express
their disgust at blasphemous words, kept their ears fast
closed, and their eyes fast shut.[3]

It was doubtless at this point that occurred the incident, whatever it be, embodied in the legend
which I have before noticed, of the sudden outbreak of fury in Nicolas, Bishop of Myra, who is represented in the traditional pictures of the Council as
dealing a blow with all his force at Arius's jaw.   It is
this incident, real or imaginary, that gave some color to
the charge of violence brought by Peter Martyr against
the Nicene fathers.   But the story itself bears witness
to the humane spirit which exalts this earliest Council
above its successors.   The legend, best known in the
West, goes on to say that for this intemperate act S.
Nicolas was deprived of his mitre and pall, which were
only restored to him long afterwards by the intervention of angels ; so that in many old pictures he is represented as bareheaded, and with his shoulders uncovered.[4]   But in the East, the story assumes a more

The Le-
gend of S.
Nicolas.

---

[1] Ath. Or. c. Ar. i. 4.

[2] The extracts are given in Ath. Or. c. Ar. i. 5.

[3] Ath. Or. c. Ar. i. 7.— Ath. ad Ep. in Egypt. 13 : ἐκράτουν τὰς ἀκοάς. Conf.
Acts vii. 56 : σύνεσχον τὰ ὦτα.   This incident has given rise to the groundless
complaint of the Polish theologian, Sandius, that Arius was condemned un-
heard.

[4] Nauclerus, Chronographia, 506.   Molanus, Hist. Sacr. Imag. iii. 53.

precise and more polemical form. The Council, it is said, on Arius's appeal, imprisoned and deprived the Bishop of Myra. But in prison, the Redeemer, whose honor he had vindicated, appeared with His mother: the One restored to him the Gospel, the other the pall; and with these credentials he claimed and obtained his freedom.[1] It is not often that the contradiction between Christ as He is in the Evangelical history, and Christ as He is in the fancies of theologians, is so strongly brought out.

At this same conjuncture it must have been that the first draught of a Creed was produced in the Coun- *The Creed of Arius.* cil, signed by the eighteen[2] extreme Arian partisans. Its contents are not given. But it was received with tumultuous disapprobation; the document was torn to pieces, and the subscribers, all except Theonas and Secundus, gave up Arius on the spot, and he was removed from the assembly.

These violent attacks and explosions were however in all probability mere episodes in the assembly. The main object of the Emperor in convening the Council was not to lengthen divisions, but to secure a unanimous signature to its final report. Like our own Elizabeth, he regarded the points at issue as of less moment than the formation of one compact Imperial Church. As may be seen in public meetings and discussions of every-day occurrence, the devotion of any one leading person to this single aim is almost sure to succeed. Two powerful efforts were made for this purpose by

(Ittig, § 38.) Molanus interprets the absence of mitre and pall as an indication of the schism and degradation of the Greek Church.

[1] This version I heard in Mount Athos. The vision in the prison is a frequent subject of pictures there.

[2] Theod. i. 6. For the eighteen Bishops see p. 222. It was probably from combining this minority with the round numbers of the majority that the traditional number of 318 was attained.

the Emperor's two chief advisers — the supporters of
what I have called the central party, the cross benches
of the assembly ; and from a combination of these two
the desired result was finally brought to pass.

The solution of the difficulty was sought in the pro-
duction of an ancient Creed, which had existed before
the rise of the controversy.   Excellent and obvious as
such a solution always is, this seems to have been the
first attempt of the kind.   It was proposed by Eusebius
of Cæsarea.   He announced that the confession
of faith which he was about to propose was no
new form, — it was the same which he had learned in
his childhood from his predecessors in the see of Cæsarea[1] during the time that he was a catechumen, and at
his baptism, and which he taught for many years, as
Presbyter and as Bishop.   It had been approved by
the Emperor,[2] the beloved of Heaven, who had already
seen it.   It accorded with his own view, that Divine
things cannot be precisely described in human language.   He held strongly the modern theological doctrine, that the Finite can never grasp the Infinite.[3]

Creed of Eusebius of Cæsarea.

This Creed was as follows : — " I believe in one God,
" the Father Almighty, Maker of all things both visible
" and invisible, and in one Lord Jesus Christ, the Word
" of God, God of God, Light of Light, Life of Life, the
" only begotten Son, the First-born of every Creature,
" begotten of the Father before all worlds, by whom
" also all things were made.   Who for our salvation was
" made flesh, and lived amongst men, and suffered, and
" rose again on the third day, and ascended to the Fa-
" ther, and shall come in glory to judge the quick and
" the dead.   And we believe in One Holy Ghost.   Be-
" lieving each of them to be and to have existed, the

---

[1] Ath. de Decret. Syn. Nic. 32.   [2] Ibid.
[3] Eus. Eccl. Theol. i. 12.   (Neander, Hist. iv. 35.)

" Father, only the Father, and the Son, only the Son,
" and the Holy Ghost, only the Holy Ghost : As also
" our Lord sending forth His own disciples to preach,
" said, ' Go and teach all nations, baptizing them into
" ' the name of the Father, and of the Son, and of the
" ' Holy Ghost ; ' concerning which things we affirm
" that this is so, and that we so think, and that it has
" long so been held, and that we remain steadfast to
" death for this faith, anathematizing every godless
" heresy.   That we have thought these things from
" our heart and soul, from the time that we have known
" ourselves, and that we now think and say thus in
" truth, we testify in the name of Almighty God, and
" of our Lord Jesus Christ, being able to prove even
" by demonstration, and to persuade you that in past
" times also thus we believed and preached."

We recognize at once the basis of the present Nicene
Creed, and it is a pleasing reflection that this basis was
the Creed of the Church of Palestine.   We have Eusebius's express declaration that it was what he had
himself always been taught in his own native city of
Cæsarea in the plains of Sharon ; and the fact that this
declaration occurs in a letter to the inhabitants of that
very place is a guarantee for the truth of his statement.
An additional confirmation is supplied by its likeness
to the Creed preserved by Cyril, in the neighboring
Church of Jerusalem.   One phrase, which dropped out
of the Creed in its subsequent passage through the
Council, must have had a touching sound as repeated
amongst the hills and valleys of the Holy Land : " who
" for our salvation lived amongst men."

The Emperor had read and approved this Confession.
The Arian minority were willing to adopt it.   But this
very fact was in the eyes of the opposite party a fatal
difficulty.   They were determined to find some form of

words which no Arian could receive. They seemed to see sinister glances, to hear dark mutterings interchanged among their opponents,[1] as this or that Orthodox expression was mentioned; on every term, "God," "Image," "Power," was put some interpretation which just eluded the desired meaning. Texts were quoted from Scripture, and even from the Shepherd of Hermas, to show the large sense of the disputed words. At last the weapon which they had been seeking, to cut off the head of their enemy, was suddenly drawn from his own scabbard.[2] A letter was produced from Eusebius of Nicomedia, in which he declared that to assert the Son to be uncreated would be to say that He was "of one substance" ($\delta\mu oo\acute{v}\sigma\iota ov$) with the Father, — and therefore that to say "He was of one substance," was a proposition evidently absurd.

The letter produced a violent excitement. There was the very test of which they were in search. The letter was torn in pieces[3] to mark their indignation, and the phrase which he had pledged himself to reject became the phrase which they pledged themselves to adopt.

The decisive expression "of one substance" was not altogether unknown. It was one of those remarkable words which creep into the language of philosophy and theology, and then suddenly acquire a permanent hold on the minds of men, "Predestination," "Original Sin," "Prevenient Grace," "Atone-

The Homöousion.

---

[1] Ath. de Dec. Syn. Nic. c. 19, 20; ad Afros, 5, 6: $\tau ov\vartheta o\rho\acute{v}\zeta ov\tau a\varsigma$ $\kappa a\grave{\iota}$ $\delta\iota av\epsilon\acute{v}ov\tau a\varsigma$ $\tau o\~\iota\varsigma$ $\delta\phi\vartheta a\lambda\mu o\~\iota\varsigma.$

[2] Ambrose de Fide, iii. 15.

[3] Eustathius apud Theod. i. 7. The document here mentioned has been identified sometimes with the Creed of Arius, described in page 225; sometimes with that of Eusebius of Cæsarea in page 226. But the first supposition is disproved by the order of events, and the second by the mention of Nicomedia in the work of Ambrose de Fide, iii. 15. Comp. Neander, iv. 40.

ment; "—there is an interest attaching to the birth, the growth, the dominion of words like these, almost like that which attaches to the birth and growth and dominion of great men or great institutions. Such a phrase was the singular compound "Homöousion:" in its native Greek, though abstract, yet simple, and, in its own metaphysical element, almost natural; but in the Latin and Teutonic languages becoming less and less intelligible, though even there, as "Consubstantial," "of one substance," retaining a force, which the contemporary phrases like "Circumincession" and "Projection" have entirely lost. The history of the word is full of strange vicissitudes.[1] It was born and nurtured, if not in the home, at least on the threshold, of heresy. It first distinctly appeared in the statement, given by Irenæus, of the doctrines of Valentinus,[2] then for a moment acquired a more Orthodox reputation in the writings of Dionysius[3] and Theognostus of Alexandria; then it was colored with a dark shade by association with the teaching of Manes;[4] next proposed as a test of Orthodoxy at the Council of Antioch against Paul of Samosata; and then by that same Council was condemned as Sabellian.

On the present occasion it is said to have been first talked over at Nicomedia, when Alexander met with Hosius on his way to the Council.[5] The immediate cause of its selection in the Council we have already seen. As soon as it was put forth a torrent of invective was poured out against it by the Arians. It was,

---

[1] For a general account of it see Suicer's Thes. *in voce;* Newman's Arians, c. ii. § 4 ; Bull, Def. Fid. Nic. ii. 1, 16.

[2] Adv. Hær. i. 5, 1 ; i. 5, 5. The Dialogue of Origen contra Marcion. A. D. 230, and the treatise " Pœmander," A. D. 120, to which Bull refers as containing the expression, are by recent writers ascribed to a later age.

[3] Apud Ath. de Syn. 43.

[4] Ath. de Syn. 16.   [5] Philost. i. 7.

so they maintained, unscriptural, heretical, materialistic.
It was Sabellian. It was Montanistic. It denied the
separate existence of the Son.[1] It implied a physical
cohesion of the various parts of the Godhead.[2] On the
other hand, Athanasius and his friends retorted, that it
was not more unscriptural than the dogmatic language
of Arius himself; that if it was not found in Scripture
in the actual form in which they proposed it, it was
found at least in compound words and in roots of
words: if not ὁμοούσιος, *Homöousios*, at least there were
Periousios and *Epiousios*; if not *ousia* itself, there was
οὖσα ἀεί, "always existing."[3] If it had been used by
heretics, and been condemned as heretical, this had been
in another sense. It had been defended by at least one
Orthodox[4] writer of former times. It was found in
sense, if not in words,[5] both in Scripture and in the
Fathers. If the acceptance of it seemed to savor of
recent Sabellianism, the rejection of it seemed to involve Polytheism, and a return to the ancient Paganism.[6]

The historian Socrates,[7] looking back on this and
similar debates from the next century, compares the
combatants to two armies engaged in a battle at night,
neither knowing the meaning of the other's terms; each
agreeing in the personal existence of the Son, and acknowledging the Unity of God in Three Persons, yet
unable to agree or to rest in their common belief. Nor
was this view altogether alien from the calmer judgment
of the great Athanasius himself. He, as Bishop Kaye
has well observed,[8] rarely if ever uses the disputed word

---

[1] Soc. i. 23.

[2] As of particles of gold in a mass, of a child to a parent, of a tree to a
root. Soc. i. 8.

[3] Ambrose de Fid. iii. 15.   [4] Ath. de Syn. 43.

[5] Ibid. i. 270.   [6] Soc. i. 23.

[7] Soc. i. 23.

[8] Kaye on Nicæa, p. 57.   See Lecture VII.

in his own statements of the truth; he avoids it, as if it
had a dangerous sound; and also, with a moderation and
an insight unusual in the chief of a theological party,
he is willing, unlike the extremer partisans of his
school, to surrender the actual word if it cause offence
to weaker brethren, and if there was reason to suppose that the same sense was intended.

The course of many centuries has taken out of this
famous word alike its heretical associations and its polemical bitterness. At the time, it indicated the exact
boundary, the water-mark, which the tide of controversy
had reached. When Hosius[1] had been at Alexandria
with Constantine's letter of pacification, he had endeavored to mediate between the contending parties, by
attacking the Sabellian as well as the Arian controversialists. Two words had then come into antagonism, of
which one was closely connected with the epithet now
about to be introduced — *ousia* and *hypostasis*. The controversy
These words, which in the Greek of that time were respecting
ousia and
almost identical in meaning, and of which the *hypostasis.*
Latin language almost used the one (*sub-stantia = hypostasis*) as the translation of the other (*ousia*), were just
beginning to show the divergences which afterwards
dragged them to the opposite points of the theological
compass. When, therefore, the "Homöousion" appeared
in the Nicene debates, it seemed a favorable opportunity
for the advocates of the several meanings of these two
cognate words to press on the Council this decision also.
But the leading members of the assembly had gone as
far as they could. If Athanasius showed in youth the
same moderation on this question that he afterwards
displayed in age,[2] he must have thrown his weight into
the decision at which the Council arrived, to allow not
a word to be said on the subject. The phrase *ousia* was

[1] Soc. iii. 7.   [2] See Lecture VII.

just named in the Creed itself. But the phrase *hypostasis* was mentioned only in allusion to a condemned error, and in such a context as to confound the two terms together, and, so far as in the Council lay, to render impossible the antithesis between *ousia* and *hypostasis* (*substance* and *person*), which was made the basis of later confessions.

To the formula, as thus limited, the consent of the Emperor was now to be obtained. He would be led to acquiesce in the term Homöousion from the motives which had guided him throughout. He saw that the Creed of Eusebius could never, in its original form, gain the assent of the Orthodox, that is, the most powerful, part of the assembly. He trusted that by this insertion they might be gained, and yet that, under the pressure of fear and favor, the others might not be altogether repelled. He, therefore, took the course the most likely to secure this result, and professed himself the patron [1] and also the interpreter of the new phrase. The various sections that gathered round Eusebius of Cæsarea had, on a previous occasion, been forced into dead silence by their own divisions.[2] But now, by their acceptance of the Emperor's terms of peace, they, in their turn, checked the vehemence of their opponents ; and another silence, no less profound, fell on the chief speakers of the Orthodox party.[3] In this silence, the time was now come for the other counsellor of Constantine to come forward. On the left-hand side of the hall, Hosius of Cordova[4] rose, and announced the completion of the *Faith* or *Creed* of the Council of Nicæa. The actual Creed was written out[5] and read,

[margin note: Acquiescence of Constantine.]

---

[1] Eus. ad Cæs. in Theod. i. 12.

[2] Ath. de Dec. Nic. Syn. c. 3.

[3] Eustath. apud Theod. i. 8.

[4] Ath. ad Monach. 42 : οὗτος ἐν Νικαίᾳ πίστιν ἐξέθετο.

[5] Basil, Epp. 81 and 244. In the picture before described in the Iberian

perhaps in consideration of Hosius's ignorance of Greek, by Hermogenes, a priest or deacon of Cæsarea in Cappadocia, who appears, at least on this occasion, to have acted as secretary to the Council. In the copies shown at the Council of Chalcedon, the 19th of June was the date affixed.[1] But this does not seem to have been formally incorporated in the Creed, in order (it was said) to avoid the inference that the faith which it professed was the creation of any single month or day.[2]

[3]"We believe in one God, the Father Almighty, "Maker[4] of all things both visible and in- The Creed "visible: of Nicæa.

"And in one Lord, Jesus Christ, the Son of God, be-"gotten of the Father,[5] *only begotten that is to say, of the* "*substance of the Father, God of God,*[6] Light of Light, very "God of very God, begotten not made, being of one sub-"stance with the Father, by whom all things were made, "*both things in heaven and things in earth*—who for us men "and for our salvation came down[7] and was made flesh,[8] "and was made man,[9] suffered,[10] and rose again on the "third day ;[11] went up into the heavens, and is to come "again[12] to judge the quick and dead.[13]

convent at Mount Athos, Athanasius is represented as seated on the ground, in his deacon's dress, writing out the Creed.

[1] Mansi, vi. 957.

[2] This is contrasted with the precise date affixed by the Arians to the Creed of Ariminum. Ath. de Syn. c. 3, 4, 5.

[3] The parts which have since been added to the text of the Creed are inserted in the notes. The parts which have been since omitted are in italics. See Appendix.

[4] " of heaven and earth "

[5] " before all worlds "   [6] See p. 244.

[7] " from the heavens"

[8] " of the Holy Ghost and the Virgin Mary " See p. 236.

[9] " and was crucified for us under Pontius Pilate and "

[10] " and was buried "

[11] " according to the Scriptures "   [12] " with glory "

[13] " and of his kingdom there shall be no end."

" And in the Holy Ghost.[1]

" *But those that say, ‘ there was when He was not,’ and*
" *‘ before He was begotten He was not,’ and that ‘He came*
" *‘ into existence from what was not,’ or who profess that the*
" *Son of God is of a different ‘ person ’ or ‘ substance ’*
" *(ἑτέρας ὑποστάσεως ἢ οὐσίας [2]), or that He is created, or*
" *changeable, or variable, are anathematized by the Catholic*
" *Church.*"

In this " the Faith set forth at Nicæa," we have the
altered shape in which the Creed of Cæsarea was established as the Creed of the whole Church. Compared
with the Creed of which it is a modification, or with
the later enlargements of which mention shall be made
presently, its most striking feature is extreme abruptness
of form, which well indicates the desire of its framers
not to go a hair's-breadth beyond what was needed for
the special occasion.

To the Emperor it had been already exhibited in private, and was now doubtless exhibited publicly.
According to the Egyptian traditions,[3] the
Bishops, on presenting him with the Creed, girt on
his side the sword which he had given into their hands
at the beginning of the Council, saying : — " This Chris-
" tian Faith (or Creed) do thou now openly profess and
" defend." Fabulous as this story probably is, yet something of the kind may have occurred as the basis of a
like practice in the Russian Church when the Czar pro-
nounces the Creed at his coronation. But there was a
more substantial exemplification of the lesson which the

*The Impe-
rial confir-
mation.*

---

[1] Here follows the addition, from the words "the Lord, the Giver of Life,"
to the words " the life of the world to come. Amen."

[2] Ruf. i. 6 : " ex aliâ subsistentiâ aut substantiâ." I have used " person "
as the recognized equivalent of ὑπόστασις. The Authorized Version has
" person " in Heb. i. 3, " substance " in Heb. xi. 1.

[3] Eutychius, i. 444.

story no doubt was meant to convey. Whether from the awe which Constantine entertained for the persons of Christian Bishops, or from his desire to enforce unanimity in the Church at any cost, he, now that the Creed was determined, entirely changed his tone respecting the doctrines against which it was levelled. With the rapidity with which some remarkable men even of high intelligence and wide views throw themselves from one state of mind into another, seeing only for the time that which is immediately before them, and seeming to forget that they have ever held opposite language or opposite opinions, Constantine not only received the decision of the Bishops[1] as a divine inspiration, but issued a decree of banishment against all who refused to subscribe the Creed, denounced Arius and his disciples as impious, and ordered that he and his books should follow the fate of the Pagan Porphyry; that he and his school should be called Porphyrians, and his books burned, under penalty of death to any one who perused them.[2]

In the Council itself the feelings which the recitation of the Creed excited must have been various. To the more simple and illiterate of the assembly it probably conveyed the general impression of a noble assertion of the greatness and divinity of the Saviour of mankind. But the more learned disputants of Alexandria probably fixed their attention on the three debated points, (two of which have since dropped out of the Creed altogether,) namely, the Homöousion, the definition of the words "only begotten," and the anathema. To see how these portions would be received by those against whom they were aimed was now the critical question.

As the Creed of Nicæa is the first deliberate composition of Articles of Faith, so the signatures at Nicæa form the first example of subscription to *The subscriptions.*

[1] Ruf. i. 5; Soc. i. 9, 30. [2] Soc. i. 9, 31, 32.

such articles. The actual subscriptions remained till the beginning of the next century,[1] and some imperfect lists have been preserved in various forms. At the head of all these lists is Hosius of Cordova: "So I believe, as "above written;" followed by the Bishop of Rome as represented by his two presbyters. "We have sub-"scribed for our Bishop, who is the Bishop of Rome. "So he believes as above is written."[2]

But the main question was whether those who would have been satisfied to adopt the Creed of Eusebius without these additions, could be satisfied to adopt it with them. There was much hesitation. It is impossible at this distance of time, and with the imperfect accounts of the transaction, to judge how far the recusants were influenced by an attachment to the positive dogma of Arius, or how far they were sincerely scandalized by an expression which appeared to them to savor of Sabellianism or Manicheism; or again how far their reluctance was occasioned by scruples of their own, or from fear of offending their constituents. Eusebius

The subscription of Eusebius of Cæsarea. describes in his own case what probably took place more or less in the case of many others. He took a day for consideration.[3] He determined to consult what we should call the "animus imponentis" — the mind of the imposer. This was easy enough. It was his own master, the Emperor. Constantine declared that the word, as he understood it, involved no such material unity of the Persons in the Godhead as Eusebius feared might be deduced from it. In this sense, therefore, the Bishop of Cæsarea adopted the test, and vindicated his adoption of it in a letter to his diocese. The anathemas against the dogmatic statements

1 Epiph. Hær. lxix. 11 ; Jer. adv. Lucif. 20 (ii. 193).
2 Spicil. Soles. i. 516.
3 Ath. de Dec. Nic. Syn. 3.

of Arius presented perhaps a more serious difficulty. But here again Eusebius wrote to his Syrian flock that there was a sense in which he could fairly condemn the use of these expressions, even though he might agree in the truth which they had been intended to express. They were none of them scriptural terms, and as such were (so the Orthodox party themselves had justly pointed out) liable to the same objections as those which Eusebius and his friends had brought against the *homöousion*. And in this view he was further fortified by the suggestion of the Emperor, that in two of the expressions ("there was when He was not," and "before He was begotten He was not"), taken literally, there was a contradiction with the doctrine held even by Arius himself, "that the Son was begotten before all "worlds, and that there must have been a potential exist-"ence even before the actual creation." With these reasonings, which much resembled those which reconciled the Jansenists to the Papal Bull condemning the opinions of Jansenius, Eusebius satisfied himself, and hoped to satisfy his excitable congregation in Palestine. Others of the same, or even more extreme, views, including Paulinus, Menophantus, Patrophilus, and Narcissus, followed his example. They even sprang forward in eager repudiation of the condemned [1] dogma.

Eusebius of Nicomedia, with the two other Bithynian Bishops of Nicæa and of Chalcedon,[2] was less accommodating; indeed he had committed himself more deeply, both to Arius personally and to the condemnation of the test. In this difficulty he consulted not the Emperor, but his own special patroness, the Princess Constantia, widow of Licinius,

The subscription of Eusebius of Nicomedia.

---

[1] Eustath. apud Theod. i. 8 : προπηδήσαντες ἀναθεματίζουσι τὰ ἀπηγορευμένον δόγμα. Rufinus (i. 5) makes seventeen the first, and six the final, recalcitrants.
[2] Soc. i. 8.

then living at Nicomedia. No doubt her views, though more decidedly Arian[1] than her brother's, leaned to the same general conclusion of a wish for uniformity; and she persuaded them to comply, urging (what, it is said, the Bishops themselves urged some years afterwards to Constantine himself) that they must be unwilling by their individual scruples to protract a controversy which had already caused him so much anxiety, and which, they feared, might, if continued, have the effect of driving him back in disgust to his original Paganism.[2]

There were two stories circulated in after-times respecting this signature, which cannot both be literally true, but which curiously represent the feelings of the time. One, apparently proceeding from the Orthodox party, described how, in later years, Eusebius and his friends had bribed the keeper of the Imperial archives to let them have access to the documents of the Council, in order to erase their names;[3] and that Eusebius had then openly repudiated the *homöousion*, and in the presence of the Emperor torn off a piece of his dress, and said, "What I thus see divided I will never believe "to be of the same substance." Another story proceeded from the extreme Arian party, savoring of that peculiar bitterness with which the more eager partisans of a failing cause attack its more moderate and more conciliating adherents. According to them, the advice of Constantia took a more precise form. The fact, remarked by Gibbon, that the controversy between *homöousion* and *homoiousion* turned upon the use of a single letter, would naturally occur (so it was said) to the quick mind of the Princess, not merely as a mental, but as a physical and literal solution of the difficulty; and accordingly Eusebius, Theognis, and Maris satisfied

[1] See Lecture VI.   [2] Soz. iii. 1, 9.   [3] Ibid. 21.

their consciences, and the wishes of their Imperial patron and patroness, by dexterously inserting an iota into the text of the Creed,[1] and then subscribing it without scruple.

They still, however, refused their assent to the anathemas, on the ground already noticed, that though the opinions condemned were false, they were not the opinions held by Arius, as they knew from personal knowledge of the man himself. This partial assent, however, did not satisfy the Emperor. Against Eusebius of Nicomedia there was, besides, a personal grudge, as having favored the rebel Licinius. He and Theognis, therefore, were deposed from their sees, Amphion and Chrestus were substituted for them, and the edict of banishment was issued. Once more they entreated the powerful favor of Constantia, or of her party, with the Emperor; and, on their sending to the Council a final submission and explanation of their difficulties, were received and subscribed all the decrees. The date of this last act it is not easy to ascertain, but it must have been before the close of the Council.[2]

Banishment of Eusebius.

There remained[3] only the extreme section of the Arian party — the Bishops Theonas and Secundus, Arius himself, the deacon Euzoius, the reader Achillas, and the presbyter Saras. Secundus seems to have agreed in the general doctrine of the Creed, but refused to sign the anathemas. He

Banishment of Arius and his companions.

---

[1] Philost. i. 8.   Sulp. Severus (ii. 40) says, probably from this story, that the Arians generally satisfied the Council by substituting ὁμοι- for ὁμον-ούσιον.

[2] Soc. i. 14 (42); Theod. i. 19.   The long negotiations about these Bishops seem to imply that at least a month must have passed between the drawing up of the Creed and the dissolution of the Council.

[3] The tradition of a distinction between the mass of the Arian party, and a few obstinate impenitents, is preserved in a picture of the Council in the Iberian convent at Mount Athos.   A crowd of heretics are represented as being admitted to re-union; whilst a smaller band is driven into a tower or prison by an Imperial officer armed with a stout club.

left the Council after an indignant remonstrance against
Eusebius of Nicomedia, for his first subscription. "Thou
"hast subscribed to escape banishment, but within the
"year thou shalt be as I am." His prediction was only
partially fulfilled. The five companions were banished,
indeed, in pursuance of the Imperial decree, to Galatia
and Illyria. But in the rapid turns of fortune or of
disposition which seem to have accompanied the decision of the Nicene Council, not unlike those at the
period of the English Reformation — they were, before
the close of the assembly, recalled,[1] and were favorably
received after subscription to the Nicene decrees. So
we are informed by Jerome,[2] on the authority of old
men still living in his time, who had been present at
the Council, and of the authentic acts of the Council,
where their names were still to be seen.

Arius himself disappeared before the close of the
Council. His book, Thalia, was burnt on the spot;
and this example was so generally followed, that it became a very rare work. Sozomen had heard of it, but
had never seen it.[3] Constantine, also, if the letter be
really his, condescended to an invective against him,
mixed in almost equal proportions of puns on his name,
of jests on his personal appearance, of eager attacks
upon his doctrine, and of supposed prophecies against
him in the Sibylline books; and his letter (or documents
corresponding to it) was posted up in the different
towns of the Empire.[4] Yet the immediate fate of Arius

[1] It is not expressly stated that Theonas and Secundus were recalled before the end of the Council. Philostorgius (i. 8) says they were recalled
afterwards when the Emperor became Arian. But the name of Secundus
appears amongst the signatures. (Godef. ad 1.)

[2] Adv. Lucif. c. 20. So also Socrates justly infers from the letter of Eusebius and Theognis (i. 14).

[3] Soz. i. 22.

[4] Broglie (i. 398) places this letter before the Council, relying on Epiphanius (Hær. lix. 9). But Epiphanius's account is evidently a confusion of the

himself is involved in mystery. In the official letter of
the Council to the Alexandrian Church, it is studiously
concealed. In the traditions of the remote East, he was
believed to have died on the spot, under the curse of
Jacob of Nisibis.[1] But, in fact, he was allowed to return, to be received with Theonas and Euzoius, either
before the conclusion of the Council, or shortly after,
with no further penalty than a prohibition against returning to Alexandria.[2] A singular custom in Alexandria commemorated this prohibition. There, alone, in
Christendom, no presbyter was allowed to preach.[3]

This general amnesty, after such a struggle, and after
the announcement of measures in appearance so severe, is to be ascribed to two causes. The _The Am-_
nesty.
first is that feeling of good-will which I before[4] described, as the almost necessary result of any general
gathering of men not wholly devoured by faction. The
distance between Arius and Marcellus, on the two extremes, was so broken by the intervening stages of
opinion, that it was probably found almost impossible
to refuse to one shade of opinion what had been granted
to another. In this respect the clemency of the Council
of Nicæa stood out in strong relief against the severity
of later Councils; the savage treatment of Nestorius
at Ephesus, or of Huss at Constance; and remained a

---

earlier with the later relations of the Emperor to Arius, and the testimony of
Socrates (i. 9, 15) is decisive the other way: Πανηγυρικώτερον γράψας πανταχοῦ
κατὰ πόλεις προσέθηκε, διακωμῳδῶν καὶ τῷ τῆς εἰρωνείας ἤθει διαβάλλων αὐτόν. This
passage (1) confirms the genuineness of the Emperor's letter; (2) gives some
explanation of it, as a mere ironical and rhetorical display; and (3) shows
that it was written _after_ the Council.

[1] Biblioth. Patr. v. p. clv.

[2] Hieron. c. Lucif. 20, ii. 192; Soc. i. 14, 2; Soz. ii. 16.

[3] Soc. v. 22 (298). Philostorgius (ii. 1) says that Alexander was induced
by Constantine to subscribe a formula renouncing the _homöousion;_ that on
this Arius communicated with him; but that Alexander once more returned
to his former position.

[4] See Lecture II. p. 167.

31

standing protest, to which S. Jerome could justly appeal, against the harsh intolerance of the Luciferians, who, rather than receive a single Bishop tainted with Arianism, would have excommunicated the whole Christian world.

But there was also another reason which facilitated the amnesty in the case of the Nicene Council. It is evident that both at the time and long afterwards their decision of the orthodox faith was looked upon as final. When, indeed, the Mussulman chroniclers [1] imagine that the doctrines of Christianity, unsettled before, were settled once for all at Nicæa, this is an exaggeration. But it is certain that the Creed of Nicæa was meant to be an end of theological controversy. The "Word of the Lord which "was given in the Œcumenical Council of Nicæa," says Athanasius, "remaineth forever." Those who had drawn it up were emphatically the *fathers* of Nicæa. To it was applied the text "Remove not the ancient "landmark which thy fathers have set." [2] No addition was contemplated; it was of itself sufficient to refute every heresy.

They believed, and their immediate successors believed, that they were, under Constantine, beginning the final stage of the Church's history. This belief continued, even after the growth of new controversies and the convention of new Councils might have seemed to call for a new Profession of Faith. Particular Churches retained their special Creeds. But the Nicene Creed remained the one public confession. The Council of Sardica declared that it was amply sufficient, and that no second Creed should ever appear.[3] When the next General Council met in 381

The finality of the Nicene Creed.

Sanctioned by the Council of Sardica, by the Council of Constantinople,

[1] Hist. Pat. Alex. 76.

[2] Dr. Newman's note on Athanasius's Treatises, i. p. 19.

[3] Ath. Tom. ad Antioch, 3, 4.

at Constantinople, although it had to confront two new
heresies — those of Apollinarius and Macedonius, it did
not venture to do more than recite the original Creed
of Nicæa.   The additions which now appear in that
Creed, and which are commonly ascribed to the Fathers of Constantinople, did, probably, then make their
appearance.   But they were not drawn up by that
Council.   They are found seven years before in the
writings of Epiphanius;[1] and although they may have
been put into the exact form in which we now see
them at the Council, perhaps by Gregory of Nyssa,[2]
they were not set forth as its Creed, and are first
called by that name when quoted by the Imperial
officers at Chalcedon in 431.[3]

The divines of Ephesus showed their sense of the
finality of the Nicene Creed still more strongly.   After
reciting it aloud in its original simple form, by the
Council of
they decreed, as if foreseeing the alterations to Ephesus.
which the growing spirit of controversy might lead,
that henceforward no one should "propose, or write,
"or compose any other Creed than that defined by
"the Fathers in the city of Nicæa," under pain of deposition from the clerical office if they were clergy,
and of excommunication if they were laymen.   It was
not till the next Council, the Fourth General Broken by
Council, at Chalcedon, that the original exclu- the Council
of Chalce-
sive supremacy of the old Nicene Creed was don.
impaired.   Then, for the first time, amidst much remonstrance,[4] the additions of Constantinople were formally acknowledged, and the enlarged Creed, in its
present form, was received, though not as superseding

---

[1] Epiph. Ancor. 120.   [2] Niceph. H. E. xii. 3.

[3] See the case clearly put in Tillemont, ix. 494.

[4] The remonstrances are given in Mansi, vi. 630, 631, 641 ; the adoption of
the new Creed, vi. 958, vii. 22, 23 ; the principle of its adoption, vii. 114, 115.
The difficulties are well given in Tillemont, xiv. 442.

the original Creed of the First Council, with a protest against any further changes. It is said that the ancient Eastern sects, both Monophysite and Nestorian, still bear witness to the fact, that no additions had, up to this time, been made. The Creed, as they recite it, is that of Nicæa alone. In the West, even as late as the seventh century,[1] it was retained in the Church of Spain. But the principle was broken through, and the way was opened for still further modifications. The Constantinopolitan Creed, as set forth at Chalcedon, gradually rose, from its coördinate position, into the place and name of the Creed of Nicæa. The original Arian controversy was now so far in the distance, that the polemical elements were regarded as unnecessary. It not only dropped some of the emphatic phrases defining the term "begotten of the Father," but also abandoned the anathemas against the condemned dogmas.[2] On the other hand, the expressions which it added concerning the Incarnation and Passion, though at the time not intended for more than mere amplifications, contain germs which in later ages have fructified into vast dogmatic systems. And the enlarged description of the attributes of the Spirit gave an opening to the deliberate addition of the words "and the Son" to the doctrine of the Procession which rent asunder the Churches of East and West.

In the Western versions of the Creed, besides this one important alteration, others appeared of less moment, but not to be overlooked. "God of God," was reinserted from the old Nicene Creed. "By the Holy Ghost of the Virgin Mary" was another variation. The ab-

---

1 Mansi, x. 778.

2 The only Church in the East, which, whilst adopting the Constantinopolitan Creed, retains the anathemas of the Nicene, is said to be the Armenian. Their last appearance in the West is in the Creed of Gregory of Tours. (Greg. Tur. i. 1.)

stract neutrality of the original (τὸ κύριον, τὸ ζωοποιοῦν) was transformed into " Dominum vivificantem " in the Latin, and " the Lord and Giver of Life " in the English version. " Holy," as an epithet of the Catholic Church, probably from inadvertence, has been omitted in the English.

Such have been the changes of the most unchangeable of all the Creeds. So slight a check has even the solemn decree of the Council of Ephesus been able to place on the growth of controversy, and the modification of the work of the Council of Nicæa. That decree has often been quoted as a condemnation of the numerous confessions of faith which have in later times been introduced : the so-called " Athanasian," in the seventh century ; the Tridentine, Lutheran, Reformed, and Anglican Articles in the sixteenth. So far as these confessions are regarded as terms of communion, they no doubt (as Burnet urged in the case of the Athanasian Creed [1]) run counter to the spirit of the Council of Ephesus. But the substitution of the Creed [2] as set forth at Chalcedon for that set forth at Nicæa, though a less important, is a more direct, as it is a more universal, violation of the Ephesian decree. We might, if we chose, vex ourselves by the thought that every time we recite the Creed in its present altered form we have departed from the intention of the Fathers of Nicæa, and incurred deprivation and excommunication at the hands of the Fathers of Ephesus. We might insist on returning to the only Catholic form of the Creed, such as it was before it was corrupted at Constantinople, Chalcedon, Toledo, and London. But there is a more

1 Macaulay's England, iii. 473. (English ed.)
2 That the Ephesian decree applied to the Constantinopolitan (or Chalcedonian) additions, was perceived by Cardinal Julian at the Council of Ferrara. (Jenkins' Life of Cardinal Julian, p. 291.)

religious, as well as a more rational, inference to be drawn from this long series of unauthorized innovations. Every time that the Creed is recited, with its additions and omissions, it conveys to us the wholesome warning, that our faith is not of necessity bound up with the literal text of Creeds, or with the formal decrees of Councils. It existed before the Creed was drawn up; it is larger than the letter of any Creed could circumscribe.[1] The fact that the whole Christian world has altered the Creed of Nicæa, and broken the decree of Ephesus, without ceasing to be Catholic or Christian, is a decisive proof that common sense, after all, is the supreme arbiter and corrective even of Œcumenical Councils.

[1] This is well put in Bishop Thomson's " Lincoln's Inn Sermons " (xii.), and Dr. Temple's Essay on " The Education of the World," p. 41.

LECTURE V.

THE CONCLUSION OF THE COUNCIL.

Two questions remained for the decision of the Council, now nearly forgotten; but one of them, at the time, occupying almost an equal share of attention with the theological controversy just concluded; the other, no doubt, to those who were specially concerned, as interesting, as to us it is tedious and trivial.

I. The first of these, in importance, if not in order of discussion, was the question of Easter. It was The Paschal Controversy. the most ancient controversy in the Church. It was the only one which had come down from the time when the Jewish and Christian communities were indistinguishable. It was the only one which grew directly out of events in the Gospel history. Its very name (the "Quartodeciman," the "Fourteenth-day," controversy) was derived, not from the Christian or Gentile, but the Jewish, calendar. The briefest statement of it will here suffice. Was the Christian Passover (for the word was still preserved, and by the introduction of the German word "Easter" we somewhat lose the force of the connection) to be celebrated on the same day as the Jewish, the fourteenth day of the month Nisan; or on the following Sunday? This was the fundamental question, branching out into others as the controversy became entangled with the more elaborate institution of the Christian fast of forty days, as also with the astronomical difficulties in the way of fixing its relations to the vernal equinox. On one side were the old, historical, apostolical traditions; on the other side, the new, Christian, Catholic spirit, striving to part company with its ancient Jewish birthplace. The Eastern Church, at least in part, as was natural, took the former, the Western the latter, view. At the time when the Council was convened at Nicæa, the Judaic time was kept by the Churches of Syria, Mesopotamia, Cilicia, and Proconsular Asia; the Christian time by the Churches of the West, headed by Rome, and also, as it would seem, the Eastern Churches of Egypt, Greece, Palestine, and Pontus. It was a diversity of practice which probably shocked the Emperor's desire for uniformity almost as much as the diversity of doctrine. The Church appeared (this was the expression of the time) "to go halting on one leg." [1] "The sight of some Churches fasting on the same day "when others were rejoicing, and of two Passovers in "one year, was against the very idea of Christian unity." "The celebration of it on the same day as was kept by "the wicked race that put the Saviour to death was an "impious absurdity." The first of these reasons determined that uniformity was to be enforced. The second determined that the older, or Jewish, practice must give way to the Christian innovation.

1. We know nothing of the details of the debate. Probably the combined influence of the Churches of Rome and of Egypt, of Hosius and of Eusebius, backed by the authority of the Emperor, was too great for resistance. It was sometimes said afterwards that the Council had made the selection of the day a matter of principle. But this was not the case. The only principle which had really guided them was, that, in a matter of indifference, the minority must give way to the

[1] Ath. ad Afros, c. 5 : ἐχώλευε.

majority.[1] In one point the form of the Decree on
Easter agreed with that of the Creed : no date The Decree.
was affixed. In another point it differed. Whereas
the Creed was prefaced with the words, " So believes the
" Catholic Church," — the Decree was prefaced with the
words, which are also found in Constantine's letter,[2] " It
" has been determined by common consent " (ἔδοξε κοινῇ
γνώμῃ), apparently to show that this was a matter of
mere outward arrangement. And it was probably
couched in this form, in order to avoid the necessity
of imposing penalties on those who were at first reluctant to give up their ancient customs.[3]

The Decree took more immediate and undisputed
effect than the Creed. Arianism, as we have seen,
lingered long, both in the Empire and in the surrounding nations. But the observance of Easter, from that
time, was reduced to almost complete uniformity. Cilicia had already given way before the Decree was issued.
Mesopotamia and Syria accepted the Decree at a solemn
Council held at Antioch within twenty years.[4]

Three small sects,[5] indeed, in each of those provinces,
still maintained their protest against the innovation of
the Nicene Council as late as the fifth century, almost
after the fashion of the modern Dissenters of Russia ;
abjuring the slightest intercourse with the established
Churches which had made the change, and ascribing
the adoption of the Nicene Decree to the influence of
the Emperor Constantine, fixing the day to suit the
Emperor's birthday, much as the corresponding com-

---

[1] Soc. v. 22 (64) ; an admirable and instructive passage.
[2] Eus. V. C. iii. 18.
[3] See Ideler, Technische Chronologie, ii. 204.
[4] Tillemont, vi. 666.
[5] The Novatians of Constantinople (Soc. v. 21), the Audians in Mesopotamia (Epiph. Hær. 70), the remaining Quartodecimans in Asia Minor
(ib. 50). See Hefele, i. 320, 321.

munities in Russia ascribe the alterations [1] against which they protest to the influence of Peter. But these were isolated exceptions. Through the rest of the Church the Jewish observance died out. Whatever subsequent troubles arose concerning the observance of Easter had no connection with this original diversity; and the Nicene Council may fairly claim the credit of having extinguished at least one bitter controversy, which had once seemed interminable, and of laying down at least one rule, which is still observed in every Church, East and West, Protestant and Catholic.

2. Even in details the mode of observance which still prevails was then first prescribed. Besides the original and more important question, whether the Paschal Feast should be observed on the Jewish or the Christian day, had arisen another question, occasioned by the difficulty of rightly adjusting the cycle of the lunar year; from which it resulted that, even amongst those who followed the more general Christian practice, Easter was observed sometimes twice or three times, sometimes not at all. It was now determined, once for all, that the Sunday should be kept which fell most nearly after the full moon of the vernal equinox. For the facilitation of this observance two measures were taken; one of which is remarkable as still guiding the calculations of Christendom, the other as having given rise to an important custom long since obsolete.

What English child has not at odd moments turned

The table for discovering Easter. over the leaves of his Prayer-book, to wonder at the table of the Golden Number, and the directions for finding Easter-day? That table first originated in the Council-chamber of Nicæa; perhaps in the desire of the Emperor Constantine to soothe the wounded feelings of his favorite counsellor.

---

[1] See Lecture XII.

When the task of adapting the cycle of the lunar year to the Paschal question was proposed, the Council would naturally turn to the most learned of its members to accomplish the work.   That member was unquestionably Eusebius of Cæsarea.[1] He had paid special attention to chronology; and his general knowledge was such as, in the eyes of the historian Socrates, of itself to redeem the assembly from the charge of illiterate ignorance.[2] He had just been sorely tried by the insertion of the unwelcome Homöousion into the Creed which he had proposed to the Council; he was probably suspected of having given but divided assent to the Creed as it now stood.   It is creditable to the justice and the wisdom of the Council, that they should not have allowed their recent disputes and wide theological differences to stand in the way of intrusting this delicate task, as they must have thought it, to the man who, on general grounds, was most fitted to undertake it.

He devoted himself to the work, and in the course of it composed an elaborate treatise on the Paschal Feast, which he presented to his Imperial master, who gratefully acknowledged it as a gigantic, almost inconceivable, enterprise;[3] and gave orders that, if possible, it should be translated into Latin for the use of the Western Church.

3. Whilst this work was preparing, and also for the sake of those whose arithmetical powers were unequal to the calculation which it might involve, the Council looked to another quarter for immediate and constant help. If Eusebius of Cæsarea was the most learned individual at hand, the most learned body represented at Nicæa was the Church of Alexandria. It is interesting to see how the ancient

The Festal Letters of Alexandria.

---

[1] Tillemont, vi. 668.   [2] See Lecture II.   [3] Eus. V. C. iv. 34, 35.

wisdom of Egypt still maintained its fame, even in
Christian theology.   By a direct succession, the Bishops
of Alexandria had inherited the traditions of astronomical science, that first appear in the fourteenth century
before the Christian era, on the painted ceilings of the
temples of Thebes.   On them, therefore, was imposed
the duty [1] of determining the exact day for the celebration of each successive Easter ; and of announcing it for
each following year, by special messengers sent immediately after the Feast of Epiphany, to all the towns
and monasteries within their own jurisdiction, as well as
to the Western Church through the Bishop of Rome,
and to the Syrian Church through the Bishop of Antioch.

So absolute was their authority in this matter, that,
even though they were certainly proved to have made
erroneous calculations and fixed the festival wrongly,
the Roman Bishop had no redress, except by appealing
to the Emperor, and entreating him to admonish the
Bishop of Alexandria to use more caution, and so to
preserve the whole Christian Church from falling into
error.   The first result of this arrangement is known to
us in the " Festal," or " Paschal," Letters of Athanasius,
who succeeded to the see of Alexandria the year after
the decision of the Council.   From that year, for a
period of thirty years, these letters (preserved to our
day by the most romantic series [2] of incidents in the
history of ancient documents) exhibit to us the activity
with which, amidst all his occupations, Athanasius carried out the order which he had heard, as a deacon, enjoined by the Council on his aged master Alexander.

The Coptic Church still looks back with pride to the

---

[1] It had already existed as a custom.   See Neale's Alexandrian Church,
i. 68.

[2] Dr. Cureton's Preface to " The Festal Letters of Athanasius."

age when its jurisdiction was thus acknowledged by all
Christian sees. Gradually the high position of the most
learned of Churches has drifted to other regions. The
Bishops of Rome, who once received from the Popes of
Alexandria decrees unalterable even by the Roman see,
in their turn became the depositaries of science, and
in their turn accordingly reformed the calendar of the
Christian world, and imposed it, gradually, but success-
fully, on the reluctant Churches, even of the Protestant
confessions. And now the wave of learning in its onward movement has left Rome high and dry, as it
had left Alexandria before; and, if similar problems of
mixed philosophy and religion have again to be imposed on the world by the most learned of its representatives, those representatives will now certainly not
be found either in Italy or in Egypt.[1]

II. Another question which the Council had to settle
was that of the Melitian [2] schism. " I have not The Meli-
" leisure," says Gibbon, " to pursue the obscure tian Schism.
" controversy which seems to have been misrepresented
" by the partiality of Athanasius, and the ignorance of
" Epiphanius." Every one who has looked into the
matter will feel the force of this remark. But, as there
must have been a small knot of persons in the Council
who were vehemently agitated by the question, we must
briefly enter into its merits.[3] It began in one of those
numerous difficulties belonging to a generation which,
at the time of the Council, was passing away. We

[1] There is one point in regard to the settlement of the Paschal question,
which seems entirely to have escaped the Nicene Fathers, but which, probably, owing to their want of foresight, will, with each succeeding century,
widen the divergence between civil and ecclesiastical usages. How many
collisions and complications might have been avoided, had Easter been then,
once for all, made a fixed, instead of a movable, festival!

[2] Μελίτιος is the name in Athanasius, Μελήτιος in Epiphanius.

[3] The three classes of documents on which this controversy rests are well
set forth by Hefele, i. 337, 338.

often hear it said that the period of persecution was a period of purity in the Church. This, unfortunately, must be taken with considerable reservation. Whilst one class of evils was repressed, another class was provoked and aggravated. In the Christian world of the third century, a controversy arose out of the persecutions, which tended to embitter every relation of life, namely, the mode of treating those who, in a moment of weakness, had abjured or compromised their faith. No weapon of polemics, even in the Nicene Council itself, was so pointed as the charge or suspicion of having "lapsed." No allies were so important, even in the support of abstract theological or chronological speculations, as those who had "confessed" and suffered for the faith. The Novatian, the Donatist, and finally the Melitian schisms were so many phases of this excited feeling. Melitius was Bishop of Lycopolis (Osioot), the present capital of Upper Egypt. He had taken the severer view of the cases of the lapsed, whilst his episcopal brother of Alexandria, Peter, had leaned to the milder side. The quarrel had broken out in prison. Peter, stretching out his episcopal mantle like a sail, had caused his deacon to proclaim, " Those who are for " me, let them come to me ; those who are for Melitius, " to Melitius." Each set up his own Church and succession of Bishops. Peter's communion in Alexandria retained the title of the " Church Catholic." [1] Melitius's, in distinction, was styled the " Church of the Martyrs." His orthodoxy was undoubted, and he had the credit of having first called attention to the heresy of Arius. He was probably one of those men who spend their lives in picking holes in the conduct or opinions of their neigh-

---

[1] The word was here probably used in its more restricted sense of " parochial," " established," Church. See Pearson on the Creed (note on Art. 9).

bors, and who have so keen a scent for the weaknesses
and the errors of others, that they never attend to their
own.   He became, with his following of independent
Bishops, the head of a Nonjuring community, a thorn
in the side of the Bishops of Alexandria hardly less
vexatious than Arius; and as years rolled on, and as
increasing troubles made strange bedfellows, the Melitian schismatics and the Arian heretics,[1] once deadly
enemies, became sworn allies against their common
enemy Athanasius.

This, however, was still far in the distance.   The
Council had to decide only on the facts of the case
as they then were.   They were gifted neither with the
divine insight into coming events which could have
enabled them to anticipate the future, nor with the
wicked desire to push to their possible extremities all
the tendencies of an innocent sect.   They acted according to what at the time appeared the dictates of charity
and prudence, and if, during the next thirty years, their
judgment might seem to have been a mistake, by the
end of the next century the total extinction of the sect
ratified its real and permanent wisdom.   Melitius was
to retain his title and rank in his own city, but not to
ordain.   Those ordained by him were to resume their
functions after a second ordination, and to take their
places below those ordained by the Bishop of Alexandria.   Any future ordinations were to be made with the
consent of the same authority.[2]

Melitius and his party belong to that prying, meddle-
some, intolerant class, who least of all men have a right
to claim toleration at the hands of their opponents or
at the hands of posterity.   Yet even characters such as

---

[1] It is said, however, that before this (Epiph. Hær. 69) Theonas had
been appointed by Melitius.
[2] Soc. i. 9.

these must receive the just allowance which they deny to others; and we may well admire the liberal treatment which they received from the Council of Nicæa. By what means it was brought about we know not. But we cannot err in supposing that it was agreeable to the general temper of Constantine; and we may also conjecture that it was accelerated by the general respect for the venerable confessor Paphnutius, himself an adherent of the Melitian party.

One person present must have been deeply mortified by this result. Athanasius, who up to this point had carried all before him, now saw a blow aimed at the supremacy of the see of Alexandria, which, both as the archdeacon of its Bishop, and the champion of its faith, he had so strenuously defended. Afterwards, if not at the time, he revenged himself by the taunt,[1] which we now know to be the reverse of the truth, that Melitius had compromised himself by compliance with heathen sacrifices: "O that Melitius had never been received by "the Church! By some means or other," he says, with an unmistakable bitterness,[2] "the Melitians were re-"ceived, but the reason I need not tell." He was clearly in a minority in the Council. However much in his later life we may rejoice that Athanasius stood firm against the world, we may fairly rejoice that on this occasion Athanasius stood alone against the Church, and that the Church stood and prevailed against Athanasius.

III. The main grievances of the Christian world, all more or less connected with the Church of Egypt, had been remedied. There still remained the correction of abuses such as have ever since occupied, in name at least, the chief attention of every General Council. Little as is the notice that these regulations attract, compared with

---

[1] See Hefele, i. 331.   [2] Athan. Apol. c. Arian. 58, 71.

the special controversies which called the Council together, they have a peculiar interest of their own.
They give us an insight into the customs and morals
of the age ; and the extent to which they are observed
or neglected now, gives us a measure of the nearness
or of the distance of our relations to the Council.

The Apocryphal Canons of Nicæa fill forty books.
They are translated into Arabic, and are re- The Apo-
ceived by the Eastern Church as binding with Canons.
the validity of Imperial laws.   They are, in fact, a collection of all the customs and canons of the Oriental
Church, ascribed to the Nicene Council, as all good
English customs to Alfred.[1]   But the authentic Canons
are only twenty in number, filling only three or four
pages.   There are, indeed, a few points mentioned in
connection with the Council, which are not contained
in these Canons.   Four such usages are thus cited by
the writers of the next two generations, namely : the
injunction to offer the Eucharist fasting ; the permission of appeal from episcopal jurisdiction to the higher
"apostolical" sees ; the revision of the decrees of former
Councils by those that followed ; the prohibition of
second marriage to the clergy, and of two bishops in
the same see.[2]

According to an old tradition, the Canon of Scripture
was now fixed.   The Canonical and the Apocry- Decision of
phal books were placed together near the Holy the Canon
                                                of Scrip-
Table, with a prayer that the canonical might be ture.
found above and the others below.[3]   This was no doubt a
mere popular representation.   It is a mark of the wisdom of the Nicene, and indeed of all the early Councils,
that they never ventured to define the limits of the
sacred books.   But that some discussion on the subject

[1] Hefele, i. 344–350.
[2] See the question discussed, Mansi, ii. 734 ; Broglie, ii. 428.
[3] Mansi, ii. 749.

33

took place, may be inferred from Jerome's belief[1] that
The Book of Judith. the Book of Judith was there and then recognized as canonical. Such a recognition, or even the belief in such a recognition, probably had great weight in determining for many centuries the reception of that most doubtful of all the Apocryphal writings. Nor has its reception been barren of results. It has answered the purpose of opening the minds of thoughtful theologians in the Church of Rome to the shades and degrees of canonicity and inspiration. In France, its perusal as a sacred book nerved the hand of Charlotte Corday to the assassination of Marat.

From these doubtful points we proceed to the consideration of the twenty Canons, so far as they bear on the history of the Council.

They may be divided, for convenience, into four groups : —

1. Those which relate to clerical jurisdiction bring
Canons on Clerical Jurisdiction. out, more forcibly perhaps than any others, the inequality of observance which those ancient decrees have received. They are the 4th, 5th, 6th, 7th, 15th, 16th, and 18th.

The fifth Canon breathes an air of Ante-Nicene sim-
The fifth Canon. On Provincial Councils. plicity. It is intended to act as a check on the tyranny of individual Bishops, to guard against the unjust exclusion of any one from the Church through the party-spirit (φιλονεικία), or the narrow-mindedness (μικροψυχία), or the personal dislike (ἀηδία), of the Bishop of any particular diocese. To remedy this, all questions of excommunication are to be discussed in Provincial Councils to be held twice a year, once in the autumn, once before Easter, in order that the offerings at the Easter communion might be made with good consciences and good-will towards each other. The whole

---

[1] Epist. iii.

of this machinery has necessarily passed away.[1] But the Decree renders a striking testimony to the care with which the rights of individuals were guarded, and to the belief in the ancient Evangelical doctrine of forbearance and forgiveness.

The fourth Canon is still observed through the greater part of Christendom. It enjoined that, at the consecration ("ordination," as it was then termed) of a Bishop, no less than three Bishops should be concerned, as representing the absent Bishops of the province, who might be detained by pressing business or the length of the journey. On the observance of this Canon in the consecration of Archbishop Parker of Canterbury, on its neglect in the consecration of Archbishop Petersen of Upsala, depends the different degree of validity and regularity which is attached by scrupulous churchmen to the orders of the Church of England and of the Church of Sweden. *The fourth Canon. On the Ordination of Bishops.*

The 6th, 7th, 15th, and 18th Canons, could we but look under their surface, each probably represents a fierce debate, in which we almost seem to see the very combatants engaged. The two highest dignitaries in the Council were Alexander of Alexandria, and Eustathius of Antioch. The jurisdiction of the former had been assailed, as we have seen, by Melitius. It was this, probably, which led to the sixth Canon, confirming to him and to his brother Metropolitans whatever ancient privileges they had possessed over the Bishops in their respective provinces. *The sixth Canon. On the Privileges of Metropolitans.* In this Canon we see the first germ of the yet undeveloped Patriarchates of the East; and, in the one precedent selected for such a jurisdiction, we see the

---

[1] An attempt to revive " this pearl of reformatory decrees," as it has been called, was made in the Council of Basle. See the Life of Cardinal Julian, by the Rev. R. Jenkins, p. 227.

organization already formed of what was to become
the Patriarchate of the West. "This," the Council
says, " is to be laid down as is the custom in *the parallel
"case of the Bishop of Rome.*"[1]

In later times, and especially at the Council of Chalcedon, this decree was made the ground of exalting the
primacy of the Roman see above that of Constantinople,
which of course had not been mentioned at Nicæa. But
it is a remarkable instance of the cautious and deliberate
spirit of the Nicene Council that the settlement of the
jurisdiction refers to no grounds, historical or doctrinal,
for its decision, but simply appeals to established usages,
in words which have since become almost proverbial,
" Let ancient customs prevail " (τὰ ἀρχαῖα ἔθη κρατείτω).

This confirmation, limited as it was, of long *prestige,*
naturally led to a claim on the part of another see,
which was itself soon to aspire to an equality with the
others, but now only sought a humble recognition of

Seventh
Canon.
Relations
of Jerusa-
lem and
Cæsarea.

its former grandeur. The seventh Canon ran
thus, and it discloses a slight passage at arms
between Eusebius of Cæsarea and Macarius of
Ælia Capitolina, not yet "Jerusalem :" — "As
" custom and ancient tradition have obtained that the
" Bishop of Ælia should be honored, let him bear his
" proper honor," — so far Macarius gained his point, —
but (and here we cannot mistake the intervention of
his superior, the Metropolitan of Cæsarea,) " always sav-
" ing the rights of the metropolitan." So closely was
the ecclesiastical organization framed on the arrangements of the Empire, that even the parent Church
of Christendom could not take precedence, even in
the Holy Land, of the merely secular seat of the Ro-

---

[1] Rufinus (i. 6) adds : " ut vel ille Ægypti, vel hic suburbicariarum eccle-
siarum solicitudinem gerat." By " suburbicariarum " was meant the churches
of the Italian prefecture, specially under the vicariate of Rome, viz. Southern
Italy and the islands. Greenwood, l. 188.

man government. It was the same spirit which guided
William the Conqueror in his selection of the Norman
fortresses, rather than the Saxon sanctuaries, as the
sees of the bishoprics of England. But in this case we
catch the relation of the sees of Cæsarea and Jerusalem
on the very edge of their turn. Before another ten
years, Ælia Capitolina had not only become Jerusalem,
but the Holy Sepulchre had been discovered, and Macarius was more than compensated for any concessions he
may have made to Eusebius at Nicæa; and by the next
century his see had become a patriarchate, whilst Cæsarea remained an inferior bishopric.

The fifteenth Canon struck at a custom which prevailed, as it would seem, largely even at that Fifteenth
early time, and which, in spite of this canon, Prohibition
was continued, and probably will continue as tion. of Transla-
long as the Church itself. It prohibits absolutely the
translation of any Bishop, Presbyter, or Deacon, from
one city to another. There were at least two high personages in the Council who must have winced under
this decree, the orthodox Eustathius of Antioch,[1] and
the heterodox Eusebius of Nicomedia. But they would
have had their revenge, if they could have seen how
soon the decree would have spent its force. Eusebius
himself, who had subscribed this very decree, was translated a few years afterwards from Nicomedia to Constantinople,[2] and it was thought so heroic a virtue in
Eusebius of Cæsarea to have declined a translation to
the see of Antioch, that Constantine declared him in
consequence fit to be a Bishop, not of a single city, but
of the whole world.[3] By the close of the century it
was set aside as if it had never existed, and there is

---

[1] Eustathius had been translated from Berrhœa, and Eusebius from Berytus. See Hefele, i. 404.
[2] Theod. i. 19.   [3] Soz. ii. 19.

probably no Church in Europe in which the convenience or the ambition of men has not proved too strong
for its adoption. If the translation of Bishops has now
become the exception, yet the translation, the promotion, of Presbyters and Deacons from place to place has
been so common as to escape all notice.

The eighteenth Canon, on the other hand, touches
an evil which has vanished, and hardly left a
trace behind. Later ages have been accustomed to the domination of Popes, Bishops, Presbyters.
But the Church of the Nicene age was vexed with the
peculiar presumption of the order of Deacons. Being
usually the confidential attendants of the Bishops, they
were in the habit of taking their place among the Presbyters, and of receiving the Eucharist even before the
Bishops themselves. This the Council of Nicæa
strongly reproves, and glances at certain places
and cities where the reproof was specially needed. One
young Deacon, we know, there was present in the
Council, whose prominent activity on this occasion provoked the envy of many of his superiors. But it is
probable that the place specially alluded to was not
Alexandria, but Rome. The Bishop Sylvester, as we
have seen, was absent. But his two Presbyters, Victor
and Vincentius, were present. We learn from Jerome
how the Roman Deacons took especial advantage of
their master's dignity to lord it over the Roman Presbyters, and it is not too much to suppose that the two
aggrieved Presbyters took the opportunity of urging
what in the Bishop's presence would have been unnecessary or inexpedient.

2. One regulation alone, the twentieth Canon, related
to worship: that which enjoins that on every
Sunday, and in daily worship between Easter
and Pentecost, the devotions of the people shall

(margin notes: Eighteenth Canon. Restraint of the Power of Deacons. Twentieth Canon. Prohibition of kneeling on Sundays.)

be performed standing.   Kneeling is forbidden.   The almost universal violation of this Canon in Western Churches, at the present day, illustrates our remoteness from the time and country of the Nicene Fathers.   To pray standing was, in public worship, believed to have been an apostolical usage.   It is still the universal practice in the Eastern Church, not only on Sundays, but week-days.   But in the West kneeling has gradually taken its place ; and the Presbyterians of Scotland, and at times the Lutherans of Germany, are probably the only Occidental Christians who now observe the one only rubric [1] laid down for Christian worship by the First Œcumenical Council.

3. The Canons which relate to the manners and morals of the clergy naturally carry us back to evils long extinct.   But they are all distinguished by a remarkable prudence and moderation ; namely, the 1st, 2d, 3d, and 17th.

The 1st is aimed against acts [2] of excessive asceticism, which had led to scandalous consequences.   The 2d restrains the rapid transition of converts from heathenism to baptism, and from baptism to ordination.   The 17th, with the strong feeling of those times against usury, forbids the clergy to make money by exorbitant interest.   The third Canon guarded against the scandals which might arise from the ancient practice of the intimate companionship of the clergy with religious women,[3] not bound to them by ties of close kindred, " who were not their " mothers, sisters, or aunts."   But connected with this decree was an abortive attempt, which discloses to us

The third Canon. Prohibiting Intercourse with religious Women.

[1] Rufinus (i. 6) omits it.

[2] See Bingham, xiii. 8 ; Beveridge, Synod. ad l. note 44 ; Athan. Tracts, ed. Newman, ii. 250–252.

[3] συνεισάκται, also called ἀγαπηταί. See Bingham, vi. 2, 13.

one of the most interesting scenes of the Council. A proposition was made, enjoining that all married clergy (according to one report, including even subdeacons) were to separate from their wives. It was in substance the same measure that was afterwards proposed and carried in the Spanish Council of Illiberis, and it is therefore not improbable that it was brought forward on this occasion by the great Hosius. It was also, we are told, supported by Eustathius of Antioch.[1] But every distinguished member of the Council in turn seems to have met with a rebuff. The opposition came from a most

Protest of Paphnutius against clerical celibacy.

unexpected quarter. From amongst the Egyptian Bishops stepped out into the midst, looking out of his one remaining eye, and halting on his paralyzed leg, the old hermit-confessor, Paphnutius or Paphnute. With a roar of indignation, rather than with a speech,[2] he broke into the debate: — "Lay not " this heavy yoke on the clergy. 'Marriage is honorable " in all, and the bed undefiled.' By exaggerated strict- " ness you will do the Church more harm than good. " All cannot bear such an ascetic rule. The wives them- " selves will suffer from it. Marriage itself is continence. " It is enough for a man to be kept from marriage after " he has been ordained, according to the ancient[3] cus- " tom; but do not separate him from the wife whom " once for all he married when he was still a layman." His speech produced a profound sensation.[4] His own austere life of unblemished celibacy gave force to every word that he uttered; he showed that rare excellence of appreciating difficulties which he himself did not feel, and of honoring a state of life which was not his own.

---

1 Synod. Gangr. 4. (Hefele, i. 417.)

2 Soc. i. 11 : ἐβόα μάκρα.

3 Apost. Const. vi. 17.

4 James of Nisibis (if his Sermons are genuine) took the same view, Serm. xviii. s. 9, 383. (Routh, Opusc. i. 403.)

He has been rewarded by the gratitude of the whole
Eastern Church, which still, according to the rule which
he proposed, allows and now almost enjoins marriage on
all its clergy before ordination, without permitting it
afterwards.[1] The Latin Church has rushed into the opposite extreme; but, owing to Paphnute's victory, must
have been conscious from the first that it was acting in
defiance of the well-known intention and wise moderation of the Fathers of Nicæa. The story has been
denied, and explained away. Even the candid French
layman who has last written the account of the Council
throws it into an appendix.[2] As early as the fifth century it is omitted in the one Latin historian of these
events. But its authenticity is beyond dispute;[3] and
even in the West the wise Egyptian hermit has not
been forgotten. An aged cardinal, at the Council of
Basle[4] (though, unfortunately, with less success than
Paphnutius), expressed himself so nearly in the same
way that we can hardly help supposing a reminiscence
of this incident. Yet later, in the reign of Mary, when
Hooper, Bishop of Gloucester, was tried before the
Bishops of London, Winchester, Durham, Llandaff, and
Chichester, and the question of the marriage of priests
was discussed, "My Lord Chancellor and many with him
"cried out that Master Hooper had never read the
"Councils. 'Yes, my Lord,' quoth Hooper, 'and my
"Lord of Chichester, to-day, knoweth that the great
"Council of Nice, by the means of one Paphnutius,

---

[1] It was an Egyptian tradition that the decree was carried so far as related
to Bishops, the separation having been previously enforced in regard to Patriarchs; who, however, did not exist till long after the Council. Eutych. Ann.
450.

[2] Broglie, ii. 430.

[3] For the arguments against the genuineness of the story, and a candid
and complete refutation of them, see Hefele, i. 417.

[4] Milman's Latin Christianity, vii. 562.

" decreed that no minister should be separated from
" his wife.' But such clamor and cries were used that
" the Council of Nice was not seen." [1]

4. The remaining decrees for the most part sprang
from the same agitations as those which had
produced the Melitian schism. They were the
settlements of cases of conscience which arose in dealing with those who had given way in the recent persecutions. They remind us that we are still on the border
land between the persecuted and the established age of
the Church. They steer for the most part the same
middle course, as in the case of the Melitians. On the
one hand, the offenders are rigidly excluded from the
clerical office, yet gently admitted to communion. On
the other hand, the austere Puritan or Novatian sec-
taries, who, like the Melitians, had separated from the
Church rather than communicate with their fallen
brethren, are allowed to reënter the Church with re-
ordination, or even to retain their orders in remote
cities and villages.

Cases of conscience.

In this decree we can dimly discern two characters of
the Council on opposite sides. One is Acesius,[2]
who was then a Bishop of the Novatians, and who would
doubtless defend the interests of his sect. The other is
Hypatius of Gangra. He was probably a vehement opponent of the Novatians : for, many
years afterwards, he was attacked by a gang of Novatian ruffians, in a pass near Gangra, and pelted and
stoned to death.[3] The incident is curious, as showing
the savage character of the sect. But, on this occasion,
the modified reception of the Novatians by the Council
may be considered as its final act of toleration. As
every rule admits of an exception, so even the

Acesius.

Hypatius of Gangra.

Amnesty.

1 Foxe (Wordsworth, Eccl. Biog. ii. 452).
2 See Lecture III.   3 Menolog. March 31.

general amnesty of the Council (in the 19th canon) excepted from the general favor the small sect of the disciples of Paul of Samosata. "Synodus Nicæna," says Jerome, in his argument against the Luciferians,[1] "omnes hæreticos suscepit præter Pauli Samosateni "discipulos."

The Council had now completed its labors. The settlement of the Arian and the Paschal controversies was embodied in a letter of the Emperor to the Churches generally. The settlement of the Melitian controversy was expressed in a letter of the Council to the Church of Egypt. The Creed and the twenty Canons were written in a volume, and again subscribed by all the Bishops. Some singular legends adorn this stage of the proceedings. It was believed in later times[2] that two of the 318 Bishops, Chrysanthus and Mysonius, who had entirely concurred in the views of the Council, had died before the close of its sessions, and been buried in the cemetery of Nicæa. When the day for the final subscription arrived, the Bishops took the volume to the grave of the two dead men, addressed them, as Mussulmans still address their dead saints, and solemnly conjured them, that, if now in the clearness of the Divine Presence they still approved, they would come and sign with their brethren the decrees of the Faith. They then sealed the volume, and laid it on the tomb, leaving blank spaces for the signatures, watched in prayer all night, and returned in the morning, when, on breaking the seal, they found the two subscriptions, "We, Chry-"santhus and Mysonius, fully concurring with the first "Holy and Œcumenical Synod, although removed from "earth, have signed the volume with our own hands." A bolder attempt to give a supernatural sanction to the

Marginal notes: Official letters and final subscription. — Legend of Chrysanthus and Mysonius.

---

[1] c. 26.   [2] Niceph. H. E. viii. 23.

decrees was retained in another story,[1] preserved in the Alexandrian Church, as derived from the court-iers of the Palace. "When the Bishops took "their places on their thrones they were 318; "when they rose up to be called over it appeared that "they were 319; so that they never could make the "number come right, and whenever they approached "the last of the series, he immediately turned into the "likeness of his next neighbor." This truly Oriental legend expresses in a daring figure, what was undoubtedly the belief of the next generation of the Church, that the Holy Spirit had been present to guide their deliberations aright.

Legend of the Appearance of the Holy Spirit.

We return to the actual history. The Emperor had now accomplished his wish. The three controversies had been extinguished. The Christian world, as he hoped, had been reduced to peace and uniformity. The twentieth anniversary of his accession was come round. The 25th of July, celebrated throughout the Empire with games and festivities, was appointed by him for a solemn banquet to the assembled Bishops. Not one was missing. The sight exceeded all expectation. The Imperial guards, who had not entered the chamber where the Council had been assembled, were now drawn up round the vestibule of the Palace with their swords drawn. The Bishops, many of whom had only seen the bare steel of the Roman swords in the hands of their executioners and torturers, might well have started at the sight. Eusebius thinks it necessary to tell us that they passed through the midst of them without any signs of fear, and reached the room prepared for their reception, apparently the same as that in which they had met for debate. Instead of the seats and benches, couches or chairs or mattings[2] were placed along each

---

1 Spicil. Solesm. i. 523.   2 Theod. i. 10.

side; and in the midst was a table for the Emperor, with a favored few. "It might have seemed," says Eusebius, who no doubt was one of these, "the likeness "of the kingdom of Christ — the fancy of a dream, "rather than a waking reality." The Emperor himself presided, and, as the feast went on, called to him one Bishop after another, and loaded each with gifts in proportion to his deserts. Three are specially named, as marked out for peculiar honor. James of Nisi- Commendation of James of Nisibis. bis (so ran the Eastern tale[1]) saw angels standing round the Emperor, and underneath his purple[2] robe discovered a sackcloth garment. Constantine, in return, saw angels ministering to James, placed his seat above the other Bishops, and said: "There are "three pillars of the world, Antony in Egypt, Nicolas "of Myra, James in Assyria." The two other incidents are as certainly historical, as this is legendary. Paphnutius was lodged in the Palace. The Emperor Honor of Paphnutius. had often sent for him to hear his stories of the persecution; and now it was remarked how he threw his arms round the old man, and put his lips to his eyeless socket, as if to suck out with his reverential kiss the blessing which, as it were, lurked in the sacred cavity,[3] and stroke down with his Imperial touch[4] the frightful wound; how he pressed his legs and arms and royal purple to the paralyzed limbs, and put his own eyeball into the socket. Acesius, the Novatian, Acesius, the Novatian. too, had come at Constantine's special request; in the hope, no doubt, that the genial atmosphere of the Council would soften his prejudices against the Estab-

---

[1] Biblioth. Patr. p. clv.   [2] See Lecture IV. p. 213.

[3] Theodoret (i. 10) speaks of the Emperor doing this to all who had lost their right eye; but Rufinus (i. 4) and Socrates (i. 11) fix it specially to Paphnutius. Gregory of Cæsarea (De Pat. Nic. 316) names the banquet, but extends it to all.

[4] Ruf. i. 4.

lished Church of the Empire. It was probably on the occasion of this banquet that the dialogue took place which was reported to the historian Socrates by the eye-witness Auxano. "Well," said the Emperor, "do you "agree with the Creed and the settlement of the Paschal "question?" "There is nothing new, your Majesty," replied Acesius, "in the decisions of the Council; for "it is thus that from the beginning, and from the apos-"tolical times, I have received both the definition of "the faith and the time of the Paschal Feast." "Why, "then," said the Emperor, "do you still remain separate "from the communion of the Church?" The old Dissenter could not part with his grievance; he intrenched himself within his unfailing argument; he poured forth an animated description of the doings in the Decian persecution, and of the strictness of primitive times, which the Church had surrendered. "None," he said, "who, after baptism, have sinned the sin, which the Di-"vine Scriptures call the sin unto death, have a right "to partake in the Divine mysteries. They ought to be "moved to perpetual repentance. The priests have no "power to forgive them; only God, who alone has the "right to pardon sins." So spoke the true ancestor of the Puritans of all ages, — the true mouth-piece of that narrow spirit, which thinks itself entitled to pronounce on the sins which can never be forgiven; which makes a show of charity in delivering over its adversaries to what are called, as if in bitter irony, the uncovenanted mercies of God. The Emperor, for once, was not over-awed. His natural common sense came to the rescue. He replied, with that short dry humor which stamps the saying as authentic: "Ho! ho! Acesius; plant a ladder, "and climb up into heaven by yourself." [1]

These are the last actual words which we have from

1 Soc. i. 10.

the Emperor on this solemn occasion, so characteristic, so full of instruction for the Puritans and sectarians of all times, that we might well take leave of him with those words on his lips.   But quite in accordance with their general spirit is the farewell speech, of Farewell which the substance only has been preserved Address of the Emperor. to us, made by him to the assembled Bishops, peror. on one of the days immediately before their departure. As they stood in his presence, he renewed, with the additional experience which the last month had afforded, his exhortations to mutual peace.   " Let them avoid " their bitter party strifes [here, no doubt, he looked at " the deputation from Alexandria] ; let them not envy " any one distinguished amongst the Bishops for wisdom " [here he would glance alternately at the detractors of " Eusebius of Cæsarea and of Athanasius] ; but regard " the merit of every single individual as common prop- " erty.   Let not those who were superior look down on " their inferiors [here a look at Acesius].   God only " could judge who were really superior.   Perfection was " rare everywhere, and therefore all allowance must be " made for the weaker brethren [here a glance of com- " mendation to Paphnutius] ; slight matters must be for- " given ; human infirmities allowed for ; concord prized " above all else.   Factions only caused the enemies of " the faith to blaspheme.   In all ways unbelievers must " be saved.   It was not every one who would be con- " verted by learning and reasoning [here he may have " turned to Spyridion and the philosopher].   Some join " us from desire of maintenance [this he said, in accord- " ance with a well-known principle which he was wont " to commend] ; some for preferment ; some for pres- " ents : nothing is so rare as a real lover of truth.   We " must be like physicians, and accommodate our medi- " cines to the diseases, our teaching to the different "minds of all."[1]   Finally, he begged their earnest prayers to Heaven for himself; and dismissed them on their journey to their several homes with letters to all the provinces through which they passed, with the injunction to celebrate his own twentieth year by liberal support to the returning prelates.   He also ordered that in every city a yearly allowance of provisions should be made for the widows and nuns and other sacred ministers.   This endowment lasted, though in a diminished amount, to the middle of the fifth century.[2]

Another decree ordered that corn should be exported to those countries where it was rare, for the purpose of the sacramental elements.   This led afterwards to violent recriminations between the Arians and Athanasius, as the head of the great corn-country of Egypt.[3]

Before the end of August, Nicæa was restored to its former state, but the fame of the Council still lingered on the spot.   It was said that they had met for the last time in a building in the centre of the town — probably the same as that which had received them on their first arrival — to pray for their own safe return and for the welfare of the city.   Tradition pointed out a spring, which was believed to have sprung up in consequence in the centre of the apsis.[4]   When the Arians held a synod at Nice in Thrace, it was in the hope that under the common name of the Nicene Creed their own views might receive a better reception.[5]   When the Fourth General Council was

---

[1] Eus. V. C. iii. 21.

[2] It was suspended by Julian, and reduced to one third by Jovian. Theod. i. 11.

[3] See Lecture VII., and Tillemont, viii. 32.

[4] Greg. Cæs. 365.   For the supposed inspiration of these parting prayers and acclamations see Sarpi's History of the Council of Trent, ii. 747.

[5] Soc. ii. 29.   See Mansi, ii. 727.

summoned, it had been the Emperor Marcian's first wish
to have it, not at Chalcedon, but within the sacred walls
of Nicæa.   The last Council which has been acknowledged as œcumenical both by the Greek and the Latin
Church received no doubt additional weight from its
being held at Nicæa, the scene of the first and greatest
of them all.   It was supposed to have given the city
impregnable strength when attacked by the Persians.
When a prisoner was taken who came from Nicæa, it
was a security for his being well treated by his cap-
tors.[1]

The prelates returned, as they went, at the public expense.   Some, it is said, were specially commis- Departure
of the
sioned to carry the decrees of the Council to Bishops.
the different provinces of the Empire.   The only reception of which any detailed[2] mention is pre- Reception
of the
served, is that in the Armenian Church.   Aris- Decrees.
taces is said to have met his father Gregory and King
Tiridates at Velasabata, and delivered to them the
Nicene Canons.[3]   To these Gregory added a few rules
and then retired into a mountain cave, and never appeared again, leaving the diocese to Aristaces.   The
hymn of praise said to have been used on occasion of
this event is still preserved in the Armenian Church :[4]
" We glorify Him who was before all ages, adoring the
" Holy Trinity, and the one only Divinity of the Father,
" the Son, and the Holy Ghost, now and ever, through
" ages of ages.   Amen."

The day celebrated in the different Churches as the

---

[1] Tillemont, vi. 287.   The Council, afterwards divided into the two of
Ariminum and Seleucia, was to have met at Nicæa.   Theod. ii. 26 ; Soz.
iv. 16.

[2] The names are given in Photius, Biblioth. 471 ; Gelas. iii. 27.

[3] Moses Choren. ii. 87, 88.

[4] I am glad to refer for this quotation to the compendious but learned History of the Fourth Century, by the Rev. W. Bright, p. 27.

anniversary of the Council was probably that on which these decrees and letters were published.

Two legends, characteristic of the Churches of the East and West, mark the interest which each attached to the reception of these decrees. When they arrived at Rome, so runs the Latin story, Sylvester convened, with Constantine's consent, another Council of 277 Bishops, in which the Nicene decrees were enforced by the Pope's authority, and in which a number of minute regulations were inserted, descending even to the material of which the dress of Roman deacons was to be made.[1] It is one of the fables by which the Roman Church has endeavored to establish a precedent for its authority over Councils, as the like fables of the Donation of Constantine, and the false Decretals, were intended to establish its authority over princes and kingdoms. Like all such fables it recoils on its framers. The best proof that no such authority existed is the necessity of so manifest a fiction to supply the place of facts.

The Eastern legend is far more pleasing, and may Legend of the death of Metrophanes of Byzantium. possibly have some slight foundation of truth. Before the Bishops finally left Nicæa, Constantine, it was said, announced that he had one favor to beg. They granted it. It was that they would return with him to Byzantium to see Metrophanes, the aged Bishop of that city, whom he called his father; and to bless by their presence the new city which he was about to found.[2] They came; and on the Sunday they met both the Emperor and the Bishop of the future capital of the Eastern Church. The Emperor then adjured the aged prelate to name his successor.

---

[1] Anast. Vit. Pont. p. 36.

[2] "Which he had founded," is the version in Photius. "To make it a patriarchal city," Hist. of Alex. Patr. 79.

Metrophanes replied, with a smiling countenance, that a week since it had been intimated to him in a dream, how ten days from that time his end would come, and he accordingly named Alexander of Byzantium his successor, and the boy Paul [1] to be the successor of Alexander. Then turning to the Bishop of Alexandria: "You too, my brother," he said, "shall have a good suc- "cessor." And, taking the young deacon Athanasius by the hand: "Behold," said he, "the noble champion of "Christ! Many conflicts will he sustain, in company "not only with my successor Alexander, but even with "my next successor Paul." With these words he laid his pall on the Holy Table for Alexander to take; and in seven days afterwards, on the 4th of June, expired in his 117th year. [2] Such, according to the Byzantine tradition, was the inauguration of the two next great events of Eastern ecclesiastical history, the Foundation of the City and Church of Constantine, and the Commencement of the Pontificate of Athanasius.

So ended the Council of Nicæa. There remain some general inferences to be deduced from this detailed account of its history.

1. Fragmentary as the narrative has been, every one must have observed how various are the inci- *Diversity of* dents that it embraces. Every party has had *incidents in the* its turn; every one, as the story has gone on, *Council.* must have heard something, I trust, congenial to his own predilections; something also, I trust, which has been distasteful. This is as it should be. This it is which makes us sure that we are reading, not a mere conventional legend, but a real chapter of human life; grave and gay, high motives and low, wise sayings and foolish. This also makes us feel that we are still far back in the first ages of the history of the Church. The

---

[1] See Lecture III. p. 196.   [2] Photius, Biblioth. p. 472.

elements of thought and feeling which at Ephesus, at
Chalcedon, at the Second Council of Nicæa, at Florence, or at Trent, are narrowed into a single channel,
or excluded altogether, are here all blended in one
mixed stream. Every Church feels that it has some
standing-place in the Council Chamber at Nicæa. In
this the highest sense, the Council was truly Œcumenical.

2. It is impossible not to notice the powerful influence exercised over the results of the Council
by personal character. Take away Constantine,
Athanasius, Eusebius of Cæsarea, Hosius, Paphnutius,—
and how materially its conclusions would have varied!
It is a truth enforced upon us both by history and experience, yet often put aside by theological speculations
in former days, and by philosophical speculations in the
present.

Effect of individual characters.

3. I have before spoken of the advantage of contrast-
ing the later apocryphal representations of the
Council with the earlier ones. We have now
seen what the contrasts are. The profusion of
miraculous portents, fanciful legends, and rhetorical
exaggerations in the later versions sets off the
simplicity and the vividness of the old accounts.
The claims of the Roman Church, which occupy so
large a space in the later Roman annals, have no
place in the true contemporary accounts of the Council. In the descriptions of Eusebius and Athanasius,
the Bishop of Rome is an old man kept away by illness, who would have had a high, perhaps the highest,
place, as Bishop of the capital city, if he had been
there. This is all. The later additions represent the
Council as convened by him, its decrees as confirmed
by him, and a separate Council as convoked by him
at Rome to receive them. By the difference between

Contrast of legendary and histo- rical ac- counts.

the two statements, we can judge of the difference between the earlier and the later systems. Again, in the earlier accounts, the heathen philosophers are attracted by curiosity; in the later, they are hired by the Arians : in the earlier, the mutual complaints are made by the Orthodox Bishops; in the later, they are made by the Arians. By the difference between the two accounts, we can judge of the growth of theological calumny.

4. Finally, let me briefly touch on the settlement of the general controversies which gave occasion to the Council's convention. They may have seemed, perhaps, a wearisome study, but they still leave solid lessons and truths behind. " Old " religious factions," says Burke, " are volcanoes burnt " out : on the lava and ashes, and squalid scoriæ of " extinct eruptions grow the peaceful olive, the cheer- " ing vine, and the sustaining corn." Most true is this in the present instance. The Eastern Creed of Nicæa, indeed, as compared with that of the Western Church, commonly called the Apostles', is a controversial and elaborate composition; and we may justly rejoice that it is the Apostles' Creed, rather than the Nicene, which has been chosen by the English Church as its one test of membership and communion. But as compared with almost all subsequent Creeds, — as compared even with the Creed (so called) of Constantinople;[1] still more, as compared with the precise definitions of Ephesus and Chalcedon; still more, as compared with the Creed (so called) of Athanasius; still more, as compared with the modern confessions of Roman Catholic and Protestant Churches, — the Nicene Creed is simple, moderate, and comprehensive. Only one technical word is incorporated in

[1] See Lecture IV.

its language; other words relating to the subtle controversies of the age — "Perichoresis," "Pro-
bole," "Theotocos," even "Hypostasis" (except
in a phrase which it condemns) — have no
more place in it than if they had never existed. The
anathemas, indeed, represent the passions of the time,
and as such have long been discarded. But even they
might fairly be taken, as Eusebius and Constantine took
them, as protests against the excessive definitions of
the opposite party, against the exaggerated inferences
drawn by Arius and his followers from figures and
metaphors, which, in relation to the invisible world, can
never be pressed literally without extreme danger to
the cause of truth and faith. The late Bishop Kaye
considered the distinction drawn at the Council between
Athanasians and Arians to be "the greatest misfortune
which ever befell the Christian[1] Church." But, as has[2]
been well observed, it would have been a greater misfortune had the Council given an Arian definition, or
had it defined further than it did. In hardly any subsequent age of the Church should we have fared so well.
To Calvin the very pathos and solemnity of the Creed
seemed but as a dull repetition. For *homöousios* he would
have substituted the not less dogmatic and more barbarous word, *autotheos.* The decree of Ephesus, forbidding
the introduction of any new Creed,[3] well expresses the
sense which the Church of that age entertained of
the growing dangers of theological disputation. That
decree was afterwards set aside in the letter by the
Council of Chalcedon, and in the spirit by many subsequent acts of the Church. But the decree itself

Sidenote: Nicene Creed a bulwark against dogmatism,

---

[1] "Claims of Truth," by the Rev. Charles Wodehouse, p. 15.

[2] Professor Jowett, "On the Interpretation of Scripture," "Essays and Reviews," p. 420.

[3] See Lecture IV.

remains as a venerable and sure indication of the mind
of Eastern, if not of Catholic, Christendom; and the
original Creed of Nicæa, though almost overlaid by the
Confessions of later ages, yet still, even in its altered
form, may be regarded as the standing bulwark and
protest of the Church against an excessive spirit of
dogmatism.

But the work of the Council of Nicæa has been also
justly regarded as a bulwark of the Orthodox $_{\text{and of}}$
faith. Luther, with the felicity of expression $^{\text{Orthodoxy.}}$
which so often distinguished his short sayings, described
the Homöousion as a *propugnaculum fidei*, not the faith
itself; not the actual citadel, but its outpost in the
enemy's country. Such is the light in which the word
was regarded by Athanasius himself.[1] He and those
who acted with him were eager to make a stand somewhere against the infringement of the received ideas of
the Divine Nature; and the truth, of which this particular form was an expression, and round which this
special controversy raged, was held by them to be the
central truth of Christianity. This is not the place to
discuss so grave a question as the proportion of the doctrines of religion, "the analogy of faith." First, and
above all, stand those great moral doctrines of the Gospel to which the highest place has been assigned beyond
dispute in the Gospel itself. But, next after these, ecclesiastical history teaches us that the most vital, the
most comprehensive, the most fruitful, has been, and is
still, — not the supremacy of the Bible or the authority
of its several books, not the power of the Pope or of the
Church, not the Sacraments, not Original Sin, not Predestination, not Justification, but the doctrine of the
Incarnation.[2] And it is a pregnant fact that this doc-

---

[1] So Ath. de Syn. 45: ὥσπερ ἐπιτείχισμα κατὰ πάσης ἀσέβους ἐπίνοιας αὐτῶν.
[2] See Lecture VII.

trine, and none of those just named, which have each
in their turn been by different sections of the Church
regarded as the pivots of theological controversy, was
the one which exclusively engaged the attention of the
Fathers of Nicæa.

LECTURE VI.

THE EMPEROR CONSTANTINE.

The authorities for the Life of Constantine are as follows : —

I. Ancient.
    1. Lactantius. (De Mort. Persec.) A. D. 250–330.
    2. Eusebius. A. D. 264–340.
        a. Life of Constantine.
        b. Panegyric on Constantine.
        c. Constantine's Address.
    3. The Letters and Treatises of Athanasius. A. D. 296–373.
    4. Eumenius. (Panegyric at Treves.) A. D. 310.
    5. Nazarius. (Panegyric at Rome.) A. D. 321.
    6. Julian. (Cæsars.) A. D. 331–363.
    7. Eutropius. A. D. 350?
    8. Aurelius Victor. (Epitome.) A. D. 370 ?
    9. Zosimus. A. D. 430 ?

II. Modern. Of these may be mentioned specially :
    1. (German.) "The Life of Constantine the Great," by Manso. (1817.)
    2. (French.) "The Church and the Empire," by Albert Prince de Broglie ; of which the Life of Constantine is the most remarkable portion.

In describing the Council of Nicæa, I spoke of two celebrated men, each a pillar of the Eastern Church, each claiming also a place in general ecclesiastical history. One was the Emperor Constantine, the other was the Archdeacon Athanasius.

36

The Emperor Constantine is one of the few to whom has been awarded the name of "Great." Though this was deserved rather by what he did, than by what he was; — though he was great, not among the first characters of the world, but among the second; great like Philip, not like Alexander; great like Augustus, not like Cæsar; great with the elevation of Charlemagne or Elizabeth, not with the genius or passion of Cromwell or of Luther; — yet this gives us a stronger sense of what the position was which could of itself confer such undoubted grandeur on a character less than the highest. "It is "one of the most tragical facts of all history," says Mr. Mill, "that Constantine, rather than Marcus Aurelius, "was the first Christian Emperor. It is a bitter thought "how different the Christianity of the world might have "been, had it been adopted as the religion of the em- "pire under the auspices of Marcus Aurelius, instead "of those of Constantine."[1] The whole history of the fourth century should be read in the light of that sad reflection, because it serves both to hold up to us the ideal of what the Christian Church and Christian theology might have been, and to remind us of what, under the existing conditions, it must have been, and actually was.

Historical position of Constantine.

But although Constantine was not Marcus Aurelius, nor S. Louis, nor Gustavus Adolphus, yet there is a profound interest in his imperfect complex character, which renders it peculiarly interesting as a subject of theological study. Over his virtues and vices the Pagans and Christians quarrelled during his lifetime. "You may believe safely," says the candid Fleury, "whatever Eusebius the bishop has said in his "blame, or Zosimus the heathen in his praise." The

Subject of theological criticism.

[1] Essay on Liberty, p. 58.

Orthodox and the heretics have each claimed him; and
a great writer[1] in our own time, though in one of his
least remarkable works, has even gone so far as to avow
that the services of Constantine to the Church ought to
have closed the door against all censures of his character, had not his patronage of heresy restored to us
the right of freedom of speech.   In the estimate of his
character the Greek and Latin Churches have each a
stake.   The Eastern Church, regarding him as especially
her own, has canonized him as a saint, " equal to the
Apostles." The Latin, at least the modern Latin, Church
prides herself on superior discernment.   Yet she also
has, as we shall see, a dark corner in the story of Constantine; and, if the Eastern Church were to recrimi-
nate,[2] there would be no difficulty in finding parallel
blots in the founder of Western (as Constantine was
of Eastern) Christendom, the " beatified," though not
" canonized," Charlemagne.

Nor is his life without a special connection with the
history of our own Church.   To English students I
cannot forbear recalling that he was, if not
our fellow-countryman by birth, yet unquestionably proclaimed Emperor in the Prætorium at York.
He probably never visited our shores again.   Yet the
remembrance of that early connection long continued.
It shaped itself into the legend of his British birth, of
which, within the walls of York, the scene is still shown.
His father's tomb was pointed out in York till the suppression of the monasteries.   His mother's name lives
still in the numerous British churches dedicated to her.
London wall was ascribed to him.   One argument
pleaded by the English ecclesiastics for precedence in

---

[1] Newman, History of the Arians, p. 138.
[2] See Mouravieff, Question Religieuse, ii. 16.

the Councils of Constance and Basle was that Constantine had been a born Englishman.

I have already described him as he appeared in the Council of Nicæa. Handsome, tall, stout, broad-shouldered, he was a high specimen of one of the coarse military chiefs of the declining Empire. When Eusebius first saw him,[1] as a young man, on a journey through Palestine before his accession, all were struck by the sturdy health and vigor of his frame; and Eusebius perpetually recurs to it, and maintains that it lasted till the end of his life. In his later days his red complexion and somewhat bloated appearance[2] gave countenance to the belief that he had been affected with leprosy. His eye was remarkable for a brightness,[3] almost a glare, which reminded his courtiers of that of a lion. He had a contemptuous habit of throwing back[4] his head, which, by bringing out the full proportions of his thick neck, procured for him the nickname[5] of *Trachala*. His voice was remarkable for its gentleness and softness.[6] In dress and outward demeanor the military commander was almost lost in the vanity and affectation of Oriental splendor. The spear[7] of the soldier was almost always in his hand, and on his head he always wore a small helmet. But the helmet was studded with jewels, and it was bound round with the Oriental diadem, which he,[8] first of the Emperors, made a practice of wearing on all occasions. His robe was remarked for its unusual magnificence. It was always of the Imperial purple or scarlet, and was made of silk,

His personal appearance.

---

[1] V. C. i. 19, 20.   Compare Lact. de Mort. Persec. c. 18.
[2] Cedrenus, 269.   [3] Ibid. 269.
[4] Aurelius Victor, Epit. 224 ; Manso, p. 412.
[5] Cedrenus, 269: παχὺς τὸν τράχηλον.
[6] Eus. V. C. iii. 9.
[7] Ibid. iv. 30.   See p. 306, infra.
[8] Aurelius Victor, Epit. p. 224 ; Cedrenus, 295.

richly embroidered with pearls and flowers worked in gold.[1] He was especially devoted to the care of his hair,[2] ultimately adopting wigs of false hair[3] of various colors, and in such profusion as to make a marked feature on his coins.[4] First of the Emperors, since Hadrian, he wore a short beard.

He was not a great man, but he was by no means an ordinary man. Calculating and shrewd as he ⎫ His char-was, yet his worldly views were penetrated by ⎭ acter. a vein of religious sentiment, almost of Oriental super-stition. He had a wide view of his difficult position as the ruler of a divided Empire and divided Church. He had a short dry humor which stamps his sayings with an unmistakable authenticity, and gives us an insight into the cynical contempt of mankind[5] which he is said to have combined, by a curious yet not uncommon union, with an inordinate love of praise. He had a presence of mind which was never thrown off its guard. He had the capacity of throwing himself, with almost fanatical energy, into whatever cause came before him for the moment. One instance, at least, he showed of consummate foresight and genius.

We have seen from his dress, and we see also from his language, that he was not without the wretched affectation which disfigured the demeanor of the later Emperors.[6] Against one great old Roman vice, that of voracious gluttony, he struggled, but struggled in vain.[7] The Christian accounts all speak of his continence. Julian alone insinuates the contrary.[8] It was only as despotic power and Eastern manners made inroads into the original self-control of his character that he was be-

---

[1] Eus. Laud. Const. c. 5.   [2] Cedrenus, 209.
[3] Julian, Cæs. 335, 336.   [4] Eckel, viii. 72.
[5] Eus. Laud. Const. c. 5 ; Aurelius Victor, Epit. p. 224.
[6] See Lect. IV. p. 213.   [7] Julian, Cæs. 329, 335.   [8] Ibid.

trayed into that disregard of human life, in his nearest
and dearest relationships, which, from the same causes,
darkened the declining years of the Grecian Alexander
and the English Henry.

It will be my object in the following Lecture to trace
this character through three epochs of his ecclesiastical
life: as the first Christian Emperor; as the first example of the intervention of a sovereign power in the
internal affairs of the Church; and as occupying peculiar relations towards the Western and Eastern Churches.
These aspects are in fact more or less represented by
the three periods of his reign, according to a somewhat
severe proverb which spoke of him as excellent for the
first ten years, as a robber for the next twelve, as a
spendthrift for the last ten.[1]

I. Every student of ecclesiastical history must pause
for a moment before the conversion of Constantine. No conversion of such magnitude had
occurred since the apostolic age. None such
occurred again till the baptism of the several founders
of the Teutonic and Sclavonic kingdoms.

His con-
version,
A. D. 312.
(Oct. 20?).

Like all such events, it had its peculiar preparations,
and took its peculiar coloring from the circumstances
of the time and the character of the man. He had the
remembrance of his father Constantius — just such a
"devout" believer in Divine Providence as we find so
common in the Roman army several generations earlier,
in the many good centurions of the New Testament.
He had a lively recollection of the Christian arguments
used before Diocletian. His rival Maxentius was a
fierce fanatical Pagan, armed with magical arts, as was
supposed, against which any counter supernatural influences were much to be cherished. He was approaching Rome for the first time, and was filled with the awe

---

[1] Aurelius Victor, Epit. p. 224.

which that greatest of earthly cities inspired in all who
named its name, or came within its influence. It is
needless to repeat at length the story which Eusebius
gives on the testimony of the Emperor himself. That
he was in prayer on his march; — that " about noon, as
the day was declining," [1] a flaming cross appeared in the
sky with the words " In this conquer; " — that in the
night which followed he saw in a dream the figure of
Christ bearing a standard, such as in Christian pictures
is represented in the Descent to the departed spirits; —
that on consultation with Christian clergy in the camp
he adopted this sacred banner instead of the Roman
eagles, and professed himself a disciple of the A. D. 312.
Christian faith. This differs materially from the several
narratives of the Christian Lactantius, the Pagan Na-
zarius, and the Arian Philostorgius. Yet those His vision.
stories (the former speaking of a dream in which the
monogram of the name of Christ was ordered to be inscribed on the shields of the soldiers, the latter of flaming armies in the sky) point to some fact of the same
kind: and it is not often in ancient history that we have
a statement so immediately at first hand, as this of
Eusebius from Constantine. That the Emperor attested
it on oath, as the historian tells us, is indeed no additional guarantee for the Emperor's veracity; because,
like princes professing piety in modern times, he appears to have been in the constant habit of adding an
oath [2] to almost every asseveration. But this very circumstance is an additional guarantee for the veracity
of Eusebius in his version of the story. And further,
that some such change, effected by some such means,
took place at this crisis, is confirmed by the fact, not

[1] See the explanation of this expression in the Notes to Lactantius, c. 44
(i. 315).
[2] See Lectures III. p. 176, IV. p. 220.

only of Constantine's adoption of the Christian faith immediately afterwards, but by the specific introduction of the standard of the cross into the army, in great measure, though not entirely, agreeing with the indications in the narrative.

If we suppose that the appearance was seen by others besides Constantine himself, it may well have been some such natural phenomenon as is known by the name of a "parhelion," which in an afternoon sky not unfrequently assumes almost the form of a cross. The impression produced may be compared to the effect of the Aurora Borealis which appeared in November, 1848, and which was interpreted in the various countries of Europe according to the feeling uppermost at the moment, much as we may imagine that any like appearance would be by the army of Constantine. In A. D. 312. France, it was regarded as forming the letters L. N., in prospect of the Presidential election then impending. In Oporto, it was regarded as the fire descending from on high to visit the crimes of a profligate city. In Rome, it was believed to be the blood of the murdered Rossi gone up to heaven to cry for vengeance against his assassins.

If we suppose, on the other hand, that it was an appearance to Constantine alone, there is nothing more surprising than in the vision which effected the conversion of Colonel Gardner, and which was related by himself to Dr. Doddridge, as that of Constantine to Eusebius.[1] The conversion of Colonel Gardner was doubtless more complete, and his convictions more profound; but there is nothing in Constantine's character to prevent the possibility of such an occurrence. He

---

[1] Dr. Doddridge's version of the story, in spite of its contradiction by Dr. Carlyle (Autobiography, p. 19), appears, in its main points, to be well founded.

was far from being the mere worldly prince of a worldly age. Not he only, but his whole family, were swayed by a strong religious sentiment, bursting out in different channels, — in the pilgrimages of Helena, in the Arianism of Constantia and Constantius, in the Paganism of Julian, — but in all sincerely, as far as it went. To Constantine himself, dreams, visions, and revelations were matters, as he and his friends supposed, of constant recurrence. His knowledge of the conspiracy of Maximin against his life, of the approach of the army of Licinius; the conception of the statue representing a dragon overthrown, before his palace; the discovery of the Holy Sepulchre; the dedication of Constantinople, are all ascribed by Eusebius to direct intimations from heaven.[1] He was a prophet to those around him, no less than a sovereign. We should not be surprised at the story of such a vision in the life of Cromwell, neither ought we to be in the life of Constantine, even were the issues which hung upon it less momentous than they really were.

The victory of the Milvian Bridge is one of the few battles that have decided the fate of the Church no less than of the world. It was not without cause that in the results of the engagement, as well as in its details of the entanglement of men and horses in the eddies of the Tiber, Christians should have been reminded[2] of the great deliverance of the Jewish Church, when "the horse and his rider "were thrown into the sea," and Israel came out free from the bondage of the Egyptian Pharaoh. It was the first fulfilment, as it seemed, of the motto which Constantine had seen in his vision — *Conquer;* and from this and his subsequent victories, which followed in rapid succession, over his several rivals, he acquired

The Battle of the Milvian Bridge, Oct. 28, A. D. 312.

---

[1] Eus. V. C. i. 27, 28, ii 12, iii. 3, 29.　　　[2] Eus. V. C. i. 38.

the name of *Conqueror*, which, both in its Latin and
Greek form (*Victor*, *Nicetes*,) passed almost into a
proper name, and is held up as the omen of his
career by his Christian eulogists. This victory ended
the age of persecutions, and ended also the primitive
period of ecclesiastical history. The seven-branched
candlestick of Jerusalem was lost, it is said, on that
day in the waves of the Tiber. On that day, too,
was lost the simpler ruder form of the Christianity
of the three first centuries. From that day onwards,
the 28th of October, in the year 312, began the
gradual recognition of the Christian faith by those
ambiguous measures which have invested the career
of Constantine with such a peculiar difficulty of interpretation.

The triumphal arch which bears his name, and
which was erected as a trophy of the Battle
of the Milvian Bridge, is a standing monument, not only of the decay of art which had
already made itself felt, but of the hesitation of the
new Emperor between the two religions. The dubious
inscription on its front well marks the moment of
transition. "Instinctu Divinitatis et mentis magni-
tudine" are the two causes to which the senate
ascribes the victory. "Divinitas," or Providence, is
the word[1] under which, in his public acts, he
veils his passage from Paganism to Christianity. His
statues, in like manner, halted between the two opinions. That erected at Rome held in its hand the
Emperor's well-known spear, but the spear bore the
form of a cross. That at Constantinople was in the
image of his ancient patron deity Apollo; but the
glory of the sunbeams was composed of the emblems
of the Crucifixion, and underneath its feet were buried

*Ambiguous
religion of
Constan-
tine.*

A. D. 312.

---

1 This is well brought out by Broglie, i. 234–239.

in strange juxtaposition a fragment of the "True Cross" and the ancient Palladium of Rome. His coins bore on the one side the letters of the name of Christ; on the other the figure of the Sun-god, and the inscription "Sol invictus," as if he could not bear to relinquish the patronage of the bright luminary which represented to him, as to Augustus and to Julian,[1] his own guardian deity.

The same tenacious adherence to the ancient God of light has left its trace, even to our own time, on one of the most sacred and universal of Christian institutions. The retention of the old Pagan name of "*Dies Solis*," or "Sunday," for the weekly Christian festival, is, in great measure, owing to the union of Pagan and Christian sentiment with which the first day of the week was recommended by Constantine to his subjects, Pagan and Christian alike, as the "venerable day of the Sun." His decree, regulating its observance, has been justly called[2] "a new era in the history of the Lord's day." It was his mode of harmonizing the discordant religions of the Empire under one common institution.

These ambiguities, though in part the growth of Constantine's own peculiarities, lose much of their Ambiguous' religion of strangeness and gain in general interest, when the age. viewed in the light of the age of which they were a part. In the change from Roman Catholicism to Protestantism in the English Reformation, it would be easy to adduce parallels of persons who wavered so constantly between the two, that it is difficult to know exactly what place to assign to them. Elizabeth herself may suffice as a specimen. This may prepare us for finding that even in the much greater change from Paganism to Christianity the boundary lines were less abrupt than at this distance we are apt to fancy. Orpheus and Pan

[1] Julian, Ep. 51.   [2] Dr. Hessey's Bampton Lectures, pp. 77–89.

appear as representing our Saviour in the Christian catacombs. The labors of Hercules are engraven on the chair — undoubtedly old, possibly authentic — of S. Peter. The Jordan appears as a river god in the baptistery at Ravenna. Some of the epitaphs in the Christian catacombs begin with the usual Pagan address to the gods of the grave. Even in the fifth century, a Pope was suspected of consulting the Etruscan auguries in the terror of Alaric's siege. In the sixth century, whether Boethius was a Christian or a Pagan is still matter of dispute; and Bishops of that age in the neighborhood of Antioch were accused of being present at a human sacrifice.[1]

We may remember the striking remarks of Niebuhr:—"Many judge of Constantine by too severe a "standard, because they regard him as a Christian; but "I cannot look upon him in that light. The religion "which he had in his head must have been a strange "jumble indeed. . . . . . . He was a superstitious man, "and mixed up his Christian religion with all kinds of "absurd superstitions and opinions. When certain Ori- "ental writers call him 'equal to the Apostles,' they do "not know what they are saying; and to speak of him "as a saint is a profanation of the word."[2]

This is true in itself. But, in order to be just, we must bear in mind that it probably describes the re- A. D. 313.   ligion of many in that time besides Constantine. And it is indisputable, that, in spite of all these inconsistencies, he went steadily forward in the main purpose of his life, that of protecting and advancing the cause of the Christian religion. The Paganism of Julian, if judged by the Paganism of Cicero or of Pericles, would appear as strange a compound, as the Christianity of

[1] Ecclesiastical History of John of Ephesus, iii. 29.
[2] Lectures on Roman History, v. 449.

Constantine, if judged by the Christianity of the Middle Ages or of the Reformation. But Julian's face was not set more steadily backwards than was Constantine's steadily forwards. The one devoted himself to the revival of that which had waxed old, and was ready to vanish away; the other to the advancement of that which year by year was acquiring new strength and life.

It is not necessary to do more than enumerate the acts of Constantine's ecclesiastical legislation, in order to see the vastness of the revolution of which he was the leader. *Constantine's Christian legislation.*

In the year after his conversion was issued the Edict of Toleration. Then followed in rapid succession, the decree for the observance of Sunday in the towns of the Empire, the use of prayers for the army,[1] the abolition of the punishment of crucifixion, the encouragement of the emancipation of slaves, the discouragement of infanticide, the prohibition of private divinations, the prohibition of licentious and cruel rites, the prohibition of gladiatorial games. Every one of these steps was a gain to the Roman Empire and to mankind, such as not even the Antonines had ventured to attempt, and of those benefits none has been altogether lost. Undoubtedly, if Constantine is to be judged by the place which he occupies amongst the benefactors of mankind, he would rank, not amongst the secondary characters of history, but amongst the very first.

II. From Constantine's Christian legislation for the Empire, we naturally pass to his intervention in the affairs of the Church itself. Of this the most direct example was that which we have already seen in the Council of Nicæa. But that event was only the chief manifestation of the new relations *His intervention in the affairs of the Church.*

_____

1 These contained one germ of " Te Deum."   Eus. V. C. iv. 39

which he introduced, and which to Eusebius appeared
no less than the fulfilment of the Apocalyptic vision
of the New Jerusalem.

Here, also, the conflict of his own personal character
has left its marks even to this hour.   On the one hand,
he never forgot, nor did the ecclesiastics ever forget,
that he was the consecrated Emperor of the world; and
that, even in their company, he regarded himself as the
Bishop of Bishops.   That General Councils are
called, maintained, and controlled by the Imperial power, was first laid down by Constantine, and
is still one of the established maxims of the Eastern
Churches, and also of the Church of England.[1]
On the other hand, he always felt a mysterious
awe in the presence of the clergy,[2] which probably first
awakened in them the sense of their position as a
distinct order in the State ; and which, although less
prominent in the East, became in the West the germ
of the Papal and hierarchical system of the Middle Ages.
But his leading idea was to restore peace to the Church,
as he had restored it to the Empire.[3]   In the execution
of this idea two courses of action presented themselves
to him, as they have to all ecclesiastical statesmen ever
since.   He stands at the head of all, in the fact that
he combined them both in himself.   In him both the
latitudinarian and the persecutor may find their
earliest precedents, which were both alike approved by the ecclesiastics of that age, though in later
times he has been as severely condemned for the one as
he has been praised for the other.   No scheme of com-
prehension has been broader, on the one hand, than
that put forward in his letter of advice to Alexander
and Arius ;[4] and on the other, when this failed, he

Margin notes:

A. D. 325.
General
Councils.

Established
hierarchy.

Latitudina-
rianism.

---

1 See Lecture II. pp. 160–162.   2 See Lecture III. p. 177.
3 " Quietis Instaurator."   4 See Lecture III. p. 176.

still pursued the same end, with the same tenacity, by the directly opposite means of enforcing uniformity, to us long familiar, but first introduced by him into the Church, — the hitherto unknown practice of subscription to the articles of a written Creed, and the infliction of civil penalties on those who refused to conform. Subscription to Creeds.

These were his public measures, natural in a half-educated soldier suddenly awakened to a sense of a position of almost unprecedented political importance, yet complicated by the contradictions in which such a man, so placed, was almost certain to be involved. Legislators and ecclesiastics in later times have followed in his footsteps, without the same excuse; and, on the whole, with no greater success.

What his personal convictions may have been, in regard to the peculiar doctrines which he successively attacked and defended, it is impossible to determine. But we cannot doubt his sincere interest in some at least of the questions which were raised. Like his nephew Julian,[1] although with a far ruder education and less fantastic mind, he threw himself into the disputations of the time as a serious business of Imperial state. Not only did he at the festival of Easter spend the night in prayer with every appearance of devotion, and even preside at the most sacred ceremonies, but he alternately, as student or teacher, took part in Christian preaching.[2] The extravagant adulation of his followers hardly left him any choice. Eusebius attributes to him little less than inspiration: — "We do not instruct thee, who hast been made wise by "God. We do not disclose to thee the sacred myste-"ries, which long before any discourses of men God "Himself revealed, not of men nor by men, but through His devotions.

1 Broglie, iii. 281.   2 Eus. V. C. iv. 39.

"our common Saviour, and the Divine vision of Him-
"self which has often shone upon thee." [1] If he did
His attendance on sermons. listen to the sermons of others, it was regarded
as an act of the highest condescension. Euse-
bius has left us an account of one which he himself delivered to "the marvellous man," as he calls him, on the
Church of the Holy Sepulchre. It was in the Palace.
There was a crowded audience. The Emperor stood
erect the whole time; would not be induced to sit
down on the throne close by; paid the utmost attention; would not hear of the sermon being too long;
insisted on its continuance; and, on being again entreated to sit down, replied, with a frown, that he
could not bear to hear the truths of religion in any
His preaching. easier posture.[2] More often he was himself
the preacher. One such sermon has been pre-
served to us by Eusebius. These sermons were always
in Latin; but they were translated into Greek by interpreters appointed for the purpose. On these occasions a general invitation was issued, and thousands
of people flocked to the Palace to hear an Emperor
turned preacher. He stood erect; and then, with a
set countenance and grave voice, poured forth his address; to which, at the striking passages, the audience
responded with loud cheers of approbation, the Emperor
vainly endeavoring to deter them by pointing upwards,
as if to transfer the glory from himself to heaven.

He usually preached on the general system of the
Christian revelation; the follies of Paganism; the Unity
and Providence of God; the scheme of redemption;
the judgment; and then attacked fiercely the avarice
and rapacity of the courtiers, who cheered lustily, but
did nothing of what he had told them. On one occasion he caught hold of one of them, and drawing on

---

1 Laud. Const. c. 11.   2 V. C. iv. 32.

the ground with his spear the figure of a man, said: " In this space is contained all that you will carry with " you after death." [1]

III. If Constantine was intoxicated by his success at Nicæa, and by the enthusiasm of his ecclesiastical admirers, he can hardly be blamed. It is probably to this, and to the demoralizing influence of his Oriental habits, that we must ascribe the melancholy fact that he was, by general consent, a worse prince at the close of his reign than at its beginning, when he was little better than a Pagan.[2]

On this the third part of his career, where the incidents of his life and the indications of his character were more closely connected, we now enter. It has been lately drawn out with a skilful eloquence, perhaps in its details beyond the strict warrant of facts, but in its general outline sufficiently justified.[3]

In the year following the Council of Nicæa, Constantine visited Rome for the first time since his declared conversion. Two events marked this fatal visit.

The first brings before us in a striking form the decay of the old religion and the rise of the new. The Emperor arrived at Rome a short time before the Ides of Quintilis, the 15th of July. That day was the anniversary of the battle of the Lake Regillus, when the twin gods, Castor and Pollux, had fought for Rome, and brought the glad tidings of victory to the city. On this day a grand muster and inspection of the Equestrian order formed part of the ceremony, in honor of the two equestrian gods.[4] All the knights, clad in purple and crowned with olive, rode in state to the Forum. It was con-

The Procession of the Equestrian order.

A. D. 326.

---

[1] V. C. iv. 29, 30. Probably addressed to Ablavius. (See Broglie, ii. 83.)

[2] Eutrop. x. 7; Aurelius Victor, Epit. 224.

[3] Broglie, ii. 93–114.   [4] See Zosimus, ii. 2.

sidered one of the most splendid pageants of Rome.
The cavalcade sometimes consisted of 5000 horsemen.
It is this festival which Lord Macaulay has celebrated
in his Lay on the Battle of the Lake Regillus. A few
of his lines will place us more in the presence of the
spectacle which Constantine saw, than any lengthened
prose description : —

A. D. 326.

> " Ho, trumpets, sound a war-note !
>   Ho, lictors, clear the way !
> The Knights will ride, in all their pride,
>   Along the streets to-day.
> To-day the doors and windows
>   Are hung with garlands all,
> From Castor in the Forum
>   To Mars without the wall.
> Each Knight is robed in purple,
>   With olive each is crown'd ;
> A gallant war-horse under each
>   Paws haughtily the ground.
> While flows the Yellow River,
>   While stands the Sacred Hill,
> The proud Ides of Quintilis
>   Shall have such honor still.
> Gay are the Martian Kalends :
>   December's Nones are gay :
> But the proud Ides, when the squadron rides,
>   Shall be Rome's whitest day."

Of this august ceremonial the shadow still remained,
and its great recollections endeared it to the Roman
populace ; but its meaning was passed away ; and Constantine not only refused to take part in the rights of
worship which it involved, but, as the procession rode
by, could not restrain the sarcastic humor for which he
was renowned, and openly indulged in jest at the sham
knights and the empty pomp.

The Roman people were furious. A riot broke out
in the streets. He remained impassive. It was probably on this occasion that he uttered one of those cold
dry sayings that have come down to us. A courtier

rushed in to announce that stones had been thrown at the head of one of the Emperor's statues. The Emperor passed his hand over his face, and said with a smile : "It is very surprising, but I do not feel in the "least hurt."[1]

But the disgust which this incident awakened in his mind against the city and religion of Rome Crimes of the Imperial rankled deep within, and side by side with it family. we dimly trace a tragedy, which, in its mysterious interest, and in the consequences to which it led, ranks with any to which history or fiction has been ever devoted. The Imperial family consisted of various heterogeneous elements.[2] There were, first, the off-spring of the two marriages of Constantius Chlorus : Constantine, the son of the low-born Helena ; and his three half-brothers, sons of Theodora, who was daughter of the Emperor Maximian. Next were in like manner the double offspring of Constantine himself : Crispus, the son of the obscure Minervina ; Constantine, Constantius, and Constans, the sons of Fausta, sister of Theodora ; and thus aunt to her husband's three half-brothers. Thirdly, there was Constantia, sister of Constantine, wife of Constantine's rival, the Emperor Licinius, and mother of a young prince of the same name. Every one of these characters contributes to the drama which has met with a parallel twice over in European history : the story of Philip II., Isabella, and Don Carlos ; the story of Peter the Great and his son Alexis.[3] It is easy to imagine the animosities and partialities of Helena, the Empress-mother ; of Fausta, the reigning Empress ; of the two lines of Imperial Princes against

---

[1] Broglie, ii. 95.   [2] See the Genealogy, p. 321.

[3] The parallel of Don Carlos must be received with the qualifications which later discoveries have introduced into the story. It is in its older form that it so nearly resembles the murder of Crispus. That of Alexis is still unshaken.

each other.   Out of this vortex of mutual suspicion
emerge three dark crimes faintly known at the time,
hardly mentioned above a whisper even in the next
generation, passed over without a word from the courtly
Eusebius, glanced at without the names by Chrysostom;
yet in some form or other incontestably true, and connected more or less certainly with Constantine's last
Crispus.   visit to Rome.   Crispus, the heir to the throne,
— suspected of high-treason, says one tradition; of in-
trigue with his step-mother, says another, — is, by his
Licinius.   father's orders, put to death at Pola.   The
A. D. 326.   young Licinius, apparently as part of the same
plan, is torn from the arms of his mother Constantia,
and murdered in the remote East.   If the party of
Fausta for a moment triumphed in the destruction of
these two youthful rivals, their hopes were soon overcast.   The Empress Helena,[1] furious at the loss of her
favorite grandson, turned the dark suspicions of her
son into another quarter, and the next victim was
Fausta.   Fausta herself.[2]   She was accused of unfaith-
fulness with one of the Imperial Guards;[3] according
to the Byzantine tradition of the next century, exposed to starvation on the top of some desert mountain;[4] according to the more usual story, suffocated
in the vapors of the Imperial bath.

However secret these horrors might be, yet enough
transpired to rouse the popular feeling of Rome, already
wounded by the Emperor's neglect of the sacred rites
of the city.   An inscription was found one day over
the gates of the Palatine, catching at once the two weak
points of Constantine's character, his Oriental luxury
and his cruelty:

---

[1] Zos. ii. 29; Aurel. Vict. Epit. 224.

[2] For all the authorities see Clinton's Fasti Romani, A. D. 326.

[3] Philost. ii. 5.   [4] Chrysostom, in Philipp. Hom. xv.

> " Saturni aurea sæcla quis requirit ?
> Sunt hæc gemmea, sed Neroniana."

From this black period of Constantine's life flow, in a sequence more or less remote, four great results of ecclesiastical history.

1. The foundation of the Papal Power in Rome.

In the Emperor's passionate remorse (so the story ran in the Pagan circles of his subjects) his thoughts turned back to the old religion which he had deserted. He applied to the Flamens at Rome for purification.[1] They proudly declared that for such crimes their religious ritual knew of no expiation. He turned (so another version reported) to philosophy. He sought for relief from Sopater,[2] the chief of the Alexandrian Platonists, and from him also the same stern answer was received. In this extremity (and here Pagan and Christian accounts to a certain extent coincide) he sought refuge in the new religion which he had taken under his protection. There was an Egyptian magician from Spain, well known among the ladies of the Imperial court, who assured him that in the Christian Church were mysteries which provided purification from any sin, however great. Through this Spanish Egyptian, or Egyptian Spaniard, according to Zosimus, the conversion of Constantine took place. Taken literally this cannot be true. The conversion of the Emperor had taken place long before. His baptism, as we shall see, took place long after. But the story is not, therefore, to be rejected as wholly false. That Spanish counsellor, we cannot doubt, was the well-known Hosius, Bishop of Cordova, the Em-

Story of the absolution of Hosius.

---

[1] Cf. Julian, Cæs. 336.

[2] He assisted in the dedication of Constantinople, but is said to have been afterwards put to death by Constantine, to prove the sincerity of his own creed. Soz. i. 5 ; Zosimus, ii. 40 ; Suidas *in voce*.

peror's counsellor in the West, as Eusebius of Cæsarea in the East. He would be on the spot with Helena and her suite. He, as the confidential adviser of Constantine, would be the very person that the Empress would most naturally consult; and he would in all probability give the very answer which to Pagan ears seemed so monstrous: "There are no sins so great, but "that in Christianity they may find forgiveness." It is a doctrine, which, according to the manner in which it is presented to us, is indeed the worst corruption or the noblest boast of the Christian religion. "In Christian-"ity there is forgiveness for every sin." This may be the hateful Antinomianism which, in the Protestant Church, has taken shelter under the Lutheran doctrine. of "Justification by Faith only," in the Roman Catholic Church, under the scholastic doctrine of Priestly Absolution. But it may also be the true message of the Gospel; the reception of the prodigal son, of the woman who was a sinner, and of the thief on the cross; the doctrine that the Divine forgiveness is ever at hand as soon as man turns to be forgiven. Of this interven-

Story of the absolution of Sylvester. A. D. 326.

tion of her great Hosius, the Church of Spain has made the most. But there was yet another version of the story, of which the Church of Rome has made still more. According to Sozomen,[1] it was not Hosius but Sylvester, Bishop of Rome, who thus received the penitent Emperor, and who gave him not only consolation, but the actual rite of baptism. And such a representation is curiously in accordance with the easy reception of gross sinners of which Tertullian complains in earlier Bishops of Rome, probably Callistus.[2]

1 Soz. i. 5.
2 Tert. de Pudicitia, i.: "Pontifex Maximus, quod est Episcopus Episcoporum edicat: Ego et mœchiæ et fornicationis delicta pœnitentia functis dimitto. O edictum cui non ascribi potuit Bonum factum!"

Out of this version, in part certainly false, in part founded on truth, arose the portentous fable of the Donation of Constantine, which, as an example of all such fictions, ought never to be forgotten by students of ecclesiastical history. In the seventh year of his reign (so, omitting all mention of his crimes, the legend runs), Constantine was struck with leprosy. He consulted all physicians in vain. Jews recommended to him the blood of infants.[1] The magical arts of the heathen sorcerers gave way before the sanctity of the Roman Bishop. He heard that the aged Sylvester was living in concealment on the heights of Mount Soracte, where the convent stands which bears Sylvester's name. He sought him out. He was baptized by him in the Lateran Palace. He gave him the palace which had witnessed the baptism. He gave him the dominion over the city of Rome, over Italy, over the Western Empire.

> "Ah! Constantine; to how much ill gave birth,
> Not thy conversion, but those rich domains
> That the first wealthy Pope received of thee!"[2]

So Dante wrote, in the bitterness of his heart, of what he believed to be the origin of the Pope's temporal sovereignty. And even when the progress of criticism had taught the next great Italian poet to place the donation of Constantine in the moon amongst the things which have never been, the ecclesiastical historians of Rome still clung to such shreds of truth as the story contained, even at the risk of making the Papal power the price of an absolution for the murder of a son, a nephew, and a wife.

But though the actual transaction of the baptism and of the donation is fabulous, there was a slight

---

[1] Cedrenus, 271.   [2] Inferno, xix. 115; Milton, Prose Works, i. p. 11.

connection of fact between the crime of Constantine and the early rise of Roman ecclesiastical grandeur.

There is every probability that remorse, taking the form of devotion, as in the princes and prelates of the Middle Ages, should have led to the building of churches at Rome, and the attachment of certain privileges to the see of Rome. It is false that Constantine gave the Roman States. But it may possibly be true that he gave (to use the modern phrase) "a "palace and a garden;" and there is little doubt, that the Lateran Palace, which had actually belonged to the Empress Fausta, and had been already assigned by him to ecclesiastical purposes, was formally made over by him to the Roman see. Parts of the building — especially the baptistery — are actually of his time, and it must be from some strong historical reason that the Palace and Church of the Lateran, rather than St. Peter's and the Vatican, form the nucleus of Christian and Papal Rome. Here, and not in St. Peter's, have all the Roman Councils been held. This, and not St. Peter's, is the Cathedral Church of Rome, the mother Church of Christendom:

> " *Dogmate Papali datur ac simul Imperiali,*
> Quod *sim cunctarum mater caput ecclesiarum.*"

Here, and not in the Vatican, was the early residence, A. D. 326. and still take place the enthronization and coronation, of the Popes. On the throne of the Lateran, and not on the chair of S. Peter, is written the proud inscription:

> " *Hæc est Papalis Sedes et Pontificalis.*"

This, if we may so apply Ariosto's words, as translated by Milton, —

> " This is that gift, if you the truth will have,
> Which Constantine to good Sylvester gave." [1]

---

[1] Orlando Furioso, xxiv. 80.

2. There is yet another particle of truth in the story of the Donation. According to the fable of Syl- Foundation
of Constan-
tinople. vester, Constantine retired to Greece,[1] in order to leave Italy for the Pope.

> " *Per cedere al Pastor si fece Greco.*" [2]

So said the legend. And it was undoubtedly the case, that by retiring to the East he left the field Retirement
from Italy. clear for the Bishops of Rome. In the absence of the Emperors from Rome, the chief Christian [3] magistrate rose to new importance. When the barbarians broke upon Italy, the Pope thus became the representative of the ancient Republic. It is one of the many senses in which the famous saying of Hobbes is true, that the Papacy is but " the ghost of the deceased " Roman Empire, sitting crowned upon the grave " thereof."

His retirement from Rome may well have been in part occasioned by remorse for the crimes which he had there sanctioned. The belief in such a connection was perpetuated in the story that the first monument erected in his new city was the golden statue of Crispus, underneath which was written : " To my " innocent and unfortunate son." More certainly his retreat was caused by a revulsion from the Roman Paganism. For Rome was Pagan. He and her Pagan customs had come into collision on the Ides of Quintilis in a manner never to be forgotten. He determined to make a new Rome elsewhere. A striking parallel is found in the case of another great potentate of the Eastern Church. Moscow, the centre of old Russia,

---

[1] See, for all the authorities, Gieseler, ii. 336.

[2] Dante, Paradiso, xx. 55.

[3] Compare the importance of the position which the Patriarch of Constantinople, as representative of the Byzantine Church and Empire, now holds under the Sultan.

was to Peter the Great, as Rome, the centre of old
Paganism, was to Constantine;[1] and he founded his
new capital at *Peters*burg (the very adoption of the
name is exactly analogous) as Constantine at Constantinople.

Of all the events of Constantine's life, this choice

Choice of
Constanti-
nople.
A. D. 330.

is the most convincing and enduring proof of
his real genius.   No city, chosen by the art
of man, has been so well chosen, and so permanent.   Alexandria is the nearest approach.   All the
others erected by the fancy or policy of individual
sovereigns are miserably inferior, Berlin, Madrid, and
even Petersburg.   He had thought of other spots in
the neighborhood : Sardica in Mœsia[2] ("my Rome is,"
he said, "at Sardica"); or Troy, following the old
tradition against which Horace had protested.   But,
when at Chrysopolis (Scutari) and Nicæa, he had seen
Byzantium.   As his conversion was ushered in by the
story of a preternatural apparition, so was his choice of
this, as it may well be called, predestinated capital.   An
eagle flew from the opposite shore to mark the spot.
Sopater, the Neoplatonist, assisted with his heathen
ceremonies at the consecration.   He himself, in solemn
procession, traced the boundaries of the city with his
well-known spear, and when asked to halt in the immense circuit, replied, "I shall go on till He who guides
"me stops."   "*Jubente Deo*" are his own words in describing his choice.[3]

The situation is indeed unrivalled.   It stands, alone

Its situa-
tion.
A. D. 330.

of the cities of the world, actually on two continents.   It has the advantages of the confluence
as of two rivers, and of a splendid maritime situation
besides ; for such is the effect, both in appearance and
reality, of the Bosphorus and the Golden Horn, and the

---

[1] See Lecture XII.   [2] Broglie, ii. 144.   [3] Broglie, ii. 154.

deep waters of the Propontis. As in the combination
of these advantages, narrow straits, deep inlets, numerous islands, prolonged promontories, Europe is the
miniature of the civilized world; and Greece, with its
Ægean Sea, is the miniature of the geography of
Europe; so the local peculiarities both of Greece and
Europe are concentrated and developed to the highest
degree in Constantinople. It is impossible to look down
from the Galata Tower on the complication of sea and
land, island and mainland, peninsula and promontory,
strait and continent, and not feel that the spot is destined to be, what it seems more and more likely to be
both historically and politically, the Gordian knot of
the world.

And this situation is further designed by nature, not
merely for a great city, but for a capital of the most
imposing aspect, nay more, for a second Rome. As truly
a city of the sea as any of the maritime cities of the
West, it has the advantage of being raised aloft on a
line of hills, towering high above the level waters of
the Bosphorus. These hills, too, are seven in number,
— seven, not like the hills of old Rome, indistinctly
and confusedly, but each following each in marked and
august succession, — each crowned even now, and probably crowned always, by magnificent buildings (mosques
now, churches then), closing in the mass of verdure
which gathers round the buildings of the palace on the
extreme eastern point.

And this glorious city, "*the City*," as it[1] alone is called,
is but the crowning scene which rises in the midst of
the three other quarters, Galata, Pera, Scutari, each with
its own towers and forests; and the whole intervening
space between and around is now, and probably A. D. 330.

---

[1] *Stamboul* is εἰς τὴν πόλιν, being itself a corruption of *Istambul*, which,
however, has again been corrupted into *Islambul*.

was always since its foundation, alive with skiffs and boats and ships and flags of all the nations of the world. In the Apocalyptic vision of Babylon, which brings together in one the various images of earthly greatness, there are features taken from the ancient Tyre, which are vainly sought in the old Rome beside the Tiber. Constantinople alone unites them all. Few would pretend to say that she was designed, however remotely, in the prophet's vision. But it is a proof of what she is, that she, and she alone, in her union of traffic, and ships, and splendor, and her seat of seven hills, comes up to the highest local images of earthly grandeur as therein presented to our view.

What of the ancient empire may have been within the city is now almost entirely perished. Considering how all the world was spoiled to adorn the city of Constantine, and what vast treasures old Rome still possesses, it is remarkable how meagre are the Imperial remains of Christian Constantinople. But the immediate neighborhood still recalls the glories of what has been, and what might be, a great capital. The Bosphorus with its palaces is the very ideal of the suburban retreats of an Imperial aristocracy. The walls, which still surround the city of Stamboul with their threefold circuit, broken through and through, overgrown with the rank vegetation of neglected centuries, yet still stand to tell the sad story of the twenty-seven times besieged and thrice captured city of Constantinople, the fourth city in the world ; fourth, because second only in importance to Jerusalem, Athens, and Rome.

I need not go further into detail. It has been fully described by two of the most remarkable historians of modern times. Gibbon has been inspired by it with a new life. Thrice in his history he describes it at length, as if he had seen it. The greatness of Constantinople forms the centre of the second part, almost as much as the fall of Rome of the first part, of his ma- _{A. D. 330.} jestic work. Von Hammer, author of the "History of the Ottoman Empire," has devoted to it an exhaustive treatise, such as no other ancient city, except those I have just mentioned, has called forth.

But the place of Constantinople in the history of the Church must be briefly indicated.

It was the first Christian city.   There were the spoils of heathenism within it, and there were some First of those mixed forms of Christianity and of Christian city. heathenism which I have already noticed. But its differences from the old Rome were marked by two significant changes of outward feature.   Instead of temples it had churches.   Except during the short reign of Julian, no column of sacrificial smoke has ever gone up from the Seven Hills of Constantinople.   In the place of the amphitheatre of the Colosseum, with its brutal spectacles, was the comparatively innocent Hippodrome, with those chariot races, of which the blue and green factions even interwove themselves with the passions of theological hatred and the course of ecclesiastical history.

It became the ecclesiastical city of the East.   To it was transferred the preëminence of the Apostolic Chief ecclesiastical see of the neighboring Ephesus.   Before its city of the presence the Primacy of the more distant Alex- East. andria died away.   Its Patriarch was the first to assume, and still exclusively retains, the title of "Œcumenical." Its see still bears the lofty name of "the Bishopric of "New Rome," "the Great Church of Christ." [1]   Its monasteries and schools became the refuge of Christian and

---

[1] See Gregory's Vindication of the Jurisdiction of Constantinople over Bulgaria, p. 150.

secular learning, when the West had almost relapsed into barbarism.

It has been powerfully described,[1] how, when the life Effects on the Reformation. of Europe would have been arrested under the Latin hierarchy but for the intervention of some foreign element, "Greece arose from the dead "with the New Testament in her hand." Most true. But Greece and the Greek Testament were preserved for that great crisis by the Empire and Church of Constantinople. It may have been a tomb; but in that stately tomb the sacred light was kept burning till the moment came for it to kindle a new fire elsewhere. To A. D. 453. the Greek exiles from the fallen city of Constantine we owe the purest and the most enduring elements of the Reformation, namely, the New Testament in its original language, and the revival of Greek learning, which gave us critics and commentators to unfold its meaning. Long after the effects of Luther's work shall have been exhausted, the effects of Erasmus's work will remain, and the work of Erasmus, humanly speaking, could not have been achieved without the scholars of Constantinople.

3. It is only by the coincidence of dates that we can Foundation of the Holy Places of Palestine, A. D. 327. trace any connection between the tragical visit to Rome and the foundation of the Holy Places of Palestine. Yet it is so natural a conjecture, that we may at least take advantage of it for Pilgrimage of Helena. briefly touching on this aspect of Constantine's life. If it was not in order to seek expiation for her son's crimes, and consolation for her own sorrows, that Helena made her famous journey to the Holy Land, it was immediately consequent upon them. Of the sacred relics which Helena found in Jerusalem, two were specially sent to her son: the nails which, as it

---

[1] Lecture on the Study of History, by Professor Goldwin Smith.

was believed, had fastened the Saviour's hands to the
Cross.   The use to which he applied them is so like
himself and his age, and so unlike our own, as to require
special notice.   One was turned into the bit of his war-
horse, the other into an ornament of his helmet.   It is
impossible in this appropriation of those sacred fragments not to recognize the fierce military Emperor of
the old Pagan age, even though the Christian historians
of the time strove to see in it a direct fulfilment a. d. 327.
of the prophecy, "In that day shall be written on the
"bells of the horses, Holiness unto the Lord."[1]   On the
churches erected by Helena's instigation, and at Constantine's cost, over the caves at Bethlehem, Olivet, and
Jerusalem, and on the modern controversy which rages
over the most sacred of them, I need not dwell here at
length.[2]   This pilgrimage was the last act of the Empress Helena.   She died on her return home, at her
birthplace in Asia Minor.   Rome and Constantinople
dispute her remains.   At Constantinople she was long
known simply as "the Empress" — "Augusta;" and in
the calendar of the Eastern Church she and her son
are always united.   To him also the Eastern Church
ascribes the honor of the first religious foundations in
Mount Athos.   To have thus fixed on this hitherto un-
occupied peninsula as the site of institutions so singularly appropriate to the scene is a trait worthy of the
man who selected Byzantium for his capital.

4. The restoration of Arius and his party was more
certainly connected with Constantine's crimes. Restoration
The Princess Constantia, whose husband and of Arius.
son had both perished by her brother's orders, was now
on her death-bed at Nicomedia.   She entreated to see
the Emperor once more.   He came; and her parting
request, backed by the influence of her chaplain

[1] Zech. xiv. 20 ; Theod. i. 38.   [2] See Sinai and Palestine, ch. xiv.

Eustocius,[1] was that he would recall the Arian leaders, and restore unity to the Church and Empire. This request fell in with Constantine's own troubled conscience, and with his long cherished desire for the union of the different parties in the Church. Amidst the many contradictions with which the history is here involved, the main facts are indisputable. Arius and the Nicomedian Eusebius are recalled. The troubles of Athanasius begin. The Council of Tyre, which marked the thirtieth, as the Council of Nicæa had marked the A. D. 335. twentieth, year of the reign of Constantine, marks also the changed relations of parties and events since the earlier assembly. Many of the same persons were then assembled, but Athanasius was now the defendant instead of Arius. Paphnutius and Potammon were there, as before, but on the losing side. The hero of the day was no longer Hosius or Eustathius, but Eusebius of Cæsarea; and under his auspices, and those of his partisans on the Arian or semi-Arian side, was dedicated the Church of the Holy Sepulchre at Jerusalem. It is one of the curious complications of ecclesiastical history, that this solemn event should be passed over without a word by the orthodox Athanasius, and that its only contemporary record should be from the heretic Eusebius, who assisted as Metropolitan of Palestine.

It must have been during this period that Constantine said of the Gothic missionary Ulfilas, who had led his people across the Danube at the age of twenty-six, "He is the Moses of the Goths." [2] To us who know what these Goths have been to us, and what the Bible of Ulfilas was to them, this speech shows the same kind of prophetic discrimination which marked the choice of

---

[1] Photius, Biblioth. 661.
[2] Philostorgius, ii. 5. For his general mission see Lecture X.

Athos and of Constantinople for their respective purposes, or the selection of Lactantius to be the preceptor
of his son, and of Eusebius and Hosius to be his own
ecclesiastical advisers.

The moment at last arrived when the union which
the Emperor had so much at heart was to be decided.
Athanasius was removed from the fury of his enemies
by an honorable exile at Treves. Arius was to be re
ceived in triumph at Constantinople. Such was the
Emperor's determination, and it is characteristic of the
position which he occupied in the Church, that in spite
of the reluctance of the Orthodox party to acknowledge the heretic, yet there seemed to them no alter-
native but to obey. "Let me or Arius die before to-
"morrow," was the prayer of Alexander, the Bishop of
Constantinople. That there was the third course of
refusing to admit him never seems to have occurred
to any one, after the Emperor's will had been made
known. It is one of the few occasions in history where
a difficult crisis has been solved by an unexpected
death. That the sudden illness and decease of the
aged Arius was a Divine judgment in behalf of the
doctrine which he had opposed, will now be held
by no one who has any regard to the warnings of
Christ himself against any such inference. That it was
the effect of poison, is contradicted by the actual circumstances of his end. Like most ecclesiastical wonders of this kind, it was neither a miracle nor a crime;
it was a natural coincidence, and no more.

It was, however, the passing away of one of the
chief actors in the Council of Nicæa; and now was
come the end of the chiefest of all. There is no act
of the life of Constantine so deeply instructive as his
death.

It was Easter, in the year 337. In the Church of
40

the Apostles at Constantinople he had passed the night,
The mortal illness of Constantine. with more than his usual devotion, in preparation for his Persian expedition. An illness supervened; he went to Helenopolis to try the mineral waters in the neighborhood. The illness increased; a sinister suspicion [1] of poison stole through the palace. He felt that it was mortal, and now at last he determined on taking the step, long delayed, but not yet impossible, of admission to the Christian Church.

A. D. 337.

Incredible as it may seem to our notions, he who had
His baptism. five and twenty years ago been convinced of the Christian faith; he who had opened the first General Council of the Church; he who had called himself a Bishop of Bishops; he who had joined in the deepest discussions of theology; he who had preached to rapt audiences; he who had established Christianity A. D. 337. as the religion of the empire; he who had been considered by Christian bishops an inspired oracle and apostle of Christian wisdom,[2] was himself not yet received into the Christian Church. He was not yet baptized; he had not even been received as a catechumen. A death-bed baptism was to the half-converted Christians of that age, what a death-bed communion often is to those of our own. In later ages, as we have seen, it was endeavored to antedate the baptism of the Emperor by ten or twenty years. But at that time it was too common to attract any special notice. Good and bad motives alike conduced to the same end, and of all of these Constantine was a complete example. He, like many of his countrymen, as has been indicated, united, after his conversion, a sincere belief in Christianity with a lingering attachment to Paganism. He, like some even of the noblest characters in the

---

[1] Philost. ii. 4.　　　[2] Eus. Laud. Const. c. 2, 11.

Christian Church, regarded baptism, much as the Pagans regarded the lustrations and purifications of their own religion, as a complete obliteration and expiation of all former sins; and therefore, partly from a superstitious dread, partly from the prudential desire, not peculiar to that or any age, " of making the best of " both worlds," he would naturally defer the ceremony to the moment when it would include the largest amount of the past, and leave the smallest amount of the future.   To him, as to all Christians of those times, baptism still preserved much of its original significance, which it has inevitably lost in the course of ages.   It was still regarded as the solemn passage from one state of life to another; from the darkness and profligacy of the heathen world to the light and the purity of the Christian society; a step taken not as the natural accompaniment of birth and education, but as a serious pledge of conviction and of profession.   The baptism of infants, no doubt, prevailed, just as the com- A. D. 337. munion of infants prevailed also.   But each of the sacraments must often have been deferred to a time when the candidates could give their whole minds to the subject.   If, even a century later, such men as Ambrose and Augustine, born in Christian families, and with a general belief in the main truths of Christianity, were still unbaptized, the one in his thirty-fourth the other in his thirty-second year, we may be sure that the practice was sufficiently common in the far more unsettled age of Constantine, to awake no scruple in him, and to provoke no censure from his ecclesiastical advisers.

The whole event is related in the utmost detail.   In the Church at Helenopolis, in the unusual posture of devotion, that of kneeling, he was admitted to be a catechumen by the imposition of hands.   He then moved to a palace in the suburb of Nicomedia, and

then calling the Bishops around him, amongst whom
the celebrated Arian, Eusebius, was chief, — announced
that once he had hoped to receive the purification of
baptism, after our Saviour's example, in the streams of
the Jordan ; but God's will seemed to be that it should
be here, and he therefore requested to receive the rite
without delay. " And so," says his biographer, " alone
" of Roman Emperors from the beginning of time, was
" Constantine consecrated to be a witness of Christ in
" the second birth of baptism." The Imperial purple
was at last removed ; he was clothed instead in robes
of dazzling whiteness ; his couch was covered with
white also : in the white robes of baptism, on a white
death-bed, he lay, in expectation of his end. If the
strict doctrine of Athanasius were pressed, Constantine
even at this moment failed of his wishes ; for his baptism was from the hands of an Arian Bishop, which,
according to Athanasius,[1] was no baptism at all. But
these theories are happily never pressed home to in-
A. D. 337.   dividuals. Constantine's baptism has always
been considered as valid both in the East and West.
The Arian baptism and the " Orthodox " canonization
must be left to neutralize each other. One act he is
said to have performed on his death-bed, which raises
Recall of   him above the sphere of both parties. In spite
Athana-
sius.   of the opposition of Eusebius,[2] he ordered the
recall of the exiled Athanasius ; and thus, as Theodoret
observes, illustrated in his last hours the sacred but
often forgotten duty of turning one of our two ears
to hear the side of the accused party. The Arian influence, though it was enough to make him content
with Arian consolations and Arian sacraments, was not
enough to make him refuse justice at that supreme
moment to the oppressed chief of the opposite party.

[1] Ath. Orat. c. Ar. i. 42, 43.   [2] Theod. i. 31.

His own delight at the accomplishment of the ceremony was excessive; and when the officers of Death of
his army entered the chamber of death, with Constantine.
bitter lamentations, to make their last farewell, he bade
them rejoice in his speedy departure heavenwards. He
gave his will into the custody of the Arian chaplain
Eustocius, who had consoled the last hours of his sister
Constantia, with orders that it should be given to his
son Constantius.[1] At noon on Whit-Sunday, the 22d
of May, in the sixty-fourth year of his age, and the
thirty-first of his reign, he expired. A wild wail of grief
arose from the army and the people, on hearing that
Constantine was dead. The body was laid out in a
coffin of gold, and carried by a procession of the whole
army,[2] headed by his son Constans, to Constantinople.
For three months it lay there in state in the palace,
lights burning round, and guards watching. During all
this time the Empire was without a head. Constans,
the youngest son, was there alone. The two elder sons
had not arrived. He was still "Augustus." All went
on as though he were yet alive. One dark shadow from
the great tragedy of his life reached to his last end, and
beyond it. It is said that the Bishop of Nicomedia, to
whom the Emperor's will had been confided by Eustocius, alarmed at its contents, immediately placed it
for security in the dead man's hand, wrapped in the
vestments of death. There it lay till Constantius arrived, and read his father's dying bequest. It was
believed to express the Emperor's conviction that he
had been poisoned by his brothers and their children,[3] and to call on Constantius to avenge his death.
That bequest was obeyed by the massacre of six out
of the surviving princes of the Imperial family. Two

[1] Soc. i. 39.   [2] Theod. i. 32.   [3] Philost. ii. 18.

alone escaped. With such a mingling of light and darkness did Constantine close his career.

When the tidings reached Rome, the old metropolis steadily ignored the revolution that had passed over the world in the person of the deceased Emperor. He was regarded but as one in the series of the Cæsars. He was enrolled, like his predecessors, as a matter of course, amongst the gods of the heathen Olympus. Incense was offered before his statue. A picture of his apotheosis was prepared. Festivals were celebrated in his honor.[1]

But in his own Christian city of Constantinople he had himself arranged the altered celebration of his death. Not amongst the gods and heroes of heathenism, but amongst those who now seemed to him the nearest approach to them, the Christian Apostles, his lot was to be cast. He had prepared for his mausoleum a church, sometimes, like that which he had founded at Rome, called "the Church of S. Peter,"[2] but more usually "the Church of the Apostles," or by a name truly indicating the mixture of Pagan and Christian ideas which led to its erection, the "*Heroön.*" Twelve pillars commemorated them, six on each side, and between them was his own tomb. He would not be "Divus;" he would be "Isapostolos" (equal to the Apostles). This is the title by which he is canonized, and this title expresses the precise point of transition from the old to the new religion.

Thither the body was borne.[3] Constantius was now present; and as it reached the church the Prince (for he too was still an unbaptized catechumen) withdrew with the Pagan guards, and left the Imperial corpse alone, as it lay aloft in the centre of the church in its

---

[1] See Beugnot, Hist. de Paganisme.   [2] Chrysost. Hom. 26 on 2 Cor.
[3] See Theod. i. 34.

sarcophagus of porphyry.[1] Prayers were offered for his
soul; he was placed amongst the Apostles; and he formally received the names which he had borne in life,
and which then became so purely personal that they
descended to his sons, " Victor, Maximus, Augustus."

"If any one doubts what I have said of him," says
Theodoret, "let him look at what is still done at his
"sepulchre and his statue." Lights were burned before
him; prayers were offered up to him; miracles believed
to be wrought by him.[2] So passionate was the attachment of the people of Constantinople to the tomb of
their founder, that the attempt to remove it for safety
to another church whilst its own was being repaired,
provoked a sanguinary riot.[3]

The church became the royal burial-place of the Byzantine Emperors.[4] There they all lay in Imperial state
till in the fourth crusade the coffins were rifled and the
bodies cast out.[5] The church itself remained till the
capture of the city by Mahomet II.,[6] on whom its ancient associations had still so much power that, though
he destroyed it, he built close upon its site the magnificent mosque which bears his name, and in which he
himself is buried, the founder of the second series of
Byzantine sovereigns, as Constantine had been of the
first.[7]

So passed away the first Christian Emperor, the first
Defender of the Faith — the first Imperial patron of the

---

[1] Cedrenus, i. 519.   Chrysostom (Hom. 26 on 2 Cor.) says that the coffin
was in the vestibule, to show his inferiority to the Apostles.

[2] See Philost. ii. 19 and notes.

[3] Soc. ii. 38.

[4] The bodies of S. Andrew and S. Timotheus and S. Luke were trans-
ported thither to increase its sanctity.   Philost. iii. 2.

[5] Theod. i. 34.   A sarcophagus, called "of Constantine," still remains in
the museum in the Seraglio.

[6] Von Hammer, i. 390.   [7] Ib. i. 387, 400.

Papal see, and of the whole Eastern Church, — the first founder of the Holy Places, — Pagan and Christian, orthodox and heretical, liberal and fanatical, not to be imitated or admired, but much to be remembered, and deeply to be studied.

GENEALOGY OF CONSTANTINE.

[The names printed in italics are of those put to death.]

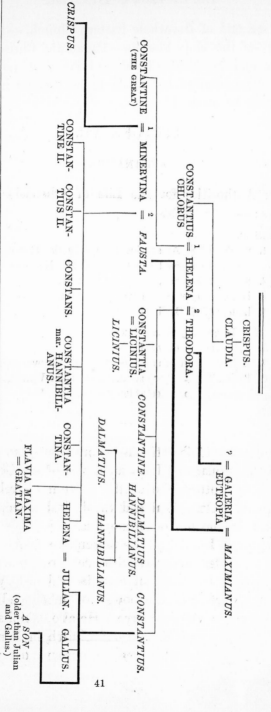

306. Proclamation at York.
312. Conversion and Battle of Milvian Bridge.
313. Edict of Milan.
323. Battle of Adrianople and defeat of Licinius.
325. Council of Nicæa.

326. Visit to Rome. Death of Crispus.
327. Death of Fausta. Pilgrimage of Helena
328. Death of Helena.
329. Death of Constantia. Recall of Arius.
330. Dedication of Constantinople.

335. Dedication of the Church at Jerusalem.
     Council of Tyre.
336. Exile of Athanasius. Death of Arius.
337. Baptism and death of Constantine.

41

LECTURE VII.

ATHANASIUS.

THE Authorities for the Life of Athanasius are as follows : —

I. Ancient.
    1. Works of S. Athanasius (especially the Historical Tracts, with the learned annotations of Dr. Newman.
    2. Socrates, Sozomen, Theodoret, Rufinus.
    3. 21st Oration of S. Gregory Nazianzen.
    4. Letters of S. Basil.

II. Of the Modern may be selected :
    1. Tillemont. (vol. viii.)
    2. Möhler. (" Athanasius, the Great : " German and French.)
    3. Bishop Kaye. (" Some Account of the Writings of Athanasius : " appended to the work cited p. 145.)

As the life of Constantine represents what may be called the secular and Imperial aspect of the Church of the fourth century, and of the Eastern Church generally, so its ecclesiastical and theological aspect is represented in the life of Athanasius. Like Constantine, although in a less degree, he presents to us one of those mixed characters which require such powers of discrimination as, in the study of ecclesiastical history, are at least as important as the powers of unbounded admiration or unmeasured invective. He also exhibits the peculiar tendencies of his age and Church, in forms more likely to impress themselves on our memory than we

could find in any other ecclesiastic of the Eastern
Church, with the single exception of Chrysostom.   And
his course is so much the more significant than that of
Chrysostom, as it includes a wider range of events and
involves far more lasting consequences.   As in the case
of Constantine, I shall take for granted a general knowledge of the history of Athanasius, and shall dwell only
on those points which bring out clearly the sentiments
of the time, the impression which he made on his contemporaries, and the permanent examples and warnings
that he has left to the Church.   What is thus to be
noticed may be placed under three heads : —

I. His connection with the Church of Egypt, including his early life and episcopal career.

II. His contests with the Emperors, including the chief
actions of his middle life and his general character.

III. His peculiarities as a theologian, including also
the close of his course.

I. He is the most remarkable representative of the
Church of Egypt.   So he is still regarded by As Egyp-
the Coptic Church, and so he must have been sentative.
at the time.   What his own race and lineage may have
been it is difficult to determine.   We know that he
himself wrote and spoke in Greek, but he also was
able to converse in Coptic.   His personal ap- His appear-
pearance throws but little light on this ques- ance.
tion.   He was of very small stature, a dwarf rather
than a man (so we know from the taunt of Julian[1]);
but, as we are assured by Gregory Nazianzen, of almost angelic beauty of face and expression.[2]   To this
tradition adds that he had a slight stoop in his figure ;
a hooked nose, and small mouth ; a short beard, which
spread out into large whiskers; and light auburn hair.[3]

[1] Ep. 51 : μηδὲ ἀνήρ, ἀλλ' ἀνθρωπίσκος εὐτελής.   [2] Orat. xxi. 9.
[3] Acta Sanctorum, May 2, c. 33.

This last characteristic has been found on the heads of Egyptian mummies,[1] and therefore is compatible with a pure Egyptian descent. His name might seem to indicate a Grecian parentage; but the case of "Antony," who was an undoubted Copt, shows that this cannot be relied upon.

His first appearance is in a well-known story,[2] which, *His childhood.* though doubted in later times from its supposed incongruity with the dignity of a great saint, has every indication of truth.[3] Alexander, Bishop of Alexandria, was entertaining his clergy in a tower or lofty house overlooking the expanse of sea beside the Alexandrian harbor. He observed a group of children playing on the edge of the shore, and was struck by the grave appearance of their game. His attendant clergy went, at his orders, to catch the boys and bring them before the Bishop, who taxed them with having played at religious ceremonies. At first, like boys caught at a mischievous game, they denied; but, at last, confessed that they had been imitating the sacrament of baptism; that one of them had been selected to perform the part of Bishop, and that he had duly dipped them in the sea, with all the proper questions and addresses. When Alexander found that these forms had been observed, he determined that the baptism was valid; he himself added the consecrating oil of confirmation; and was so much struck with the knowledge and gravity of the boy-bishop that he took him under his charge. This little boy was Athanasius; already showing the union of seriousness and sport

---

[1] Morton, Crania Hieroglyphica, 4to., p. 22; and the account of a mummy unrolled by Mr. Birch of the British Museum.

[2] Rufinus; Socrates; Sozomen.

[3] The chronological difficulty of the day on which the event occurred is not material.

which we shall see in his after-life. That childish game
is an epitome of the ecclesiastical feelings of his time
and of his country. The children playing on the shore,
the old man looking at them with interest; these, indeed, are incidents which belong to every age of the
world. But only in the early centuries could have
been found the immersion of the baptized, the necessity of a Bishop to perform the ceremony, the mixture
of freedom and superstition which could regard as serious a sacrament so lightly performed. In the Coptic
Church is there the best likeness of this Eastern reverence for the sacred acts of children. A child still draws
the lots in the Patriarchal elections. By children is
still performed the greater part of their innocent
child-like services.

From this incident arose the connection of Athanasius
with the aged Alexander. He became his Arch- Archdeacon, an office very different from that which deacon of
Alexan-
is called by the same name amongst ourselves. dria.
It was then literally what the word implies, " the chief
" of the deacons," the head of that body of deacons
whose duty it is to attend upon the Bishop. Of this
kind is the office which still bears the name in the
Eastern Church, and which is rendered illustrious to
Eastern Christians by the two great names of Arch-
" deacon Stephen " and " Archdeacon Athanasius." It
was in this capacity that he followed his Bishop to the
Council of Nicæa, and defended the Orthodox cause
with an energy which already awakened the jealousy
and the admiration of all who heard him.[1] In a few
weeks after the close of the Council Alexander died,
and Athanasius succeeded to the vacant see. It His conse-
was a marked epoch, in every sense, for the cration.
Egyptian Primacy. Down to this time (according to

[1] See Lecture III.

the tradition of the Alexandrian Church itself [1]) the election to this great post had been conducted in a manner unlike that of the other sees of Christendom. Not the Bishop, but twelve Presbyters, were the electors, and nominators,[2] and (according to Eutychius) consecrators.   It was on the death of Alexander that this ancient custom was exchanged for one more nearly resembling that which prevailed elsewhere.   Fifty Bishops of the neighboring dioceses were convened for the first time, and proceeded to the election.   Athanasius had been named both by the dying Primate and by the people as the new Bishop.   He, setting an example which has since become a fixed rule in the Coptic Church, endeavored to escape election by concealment or absence.   To this day the formalities which accompany the election of his successors in the see of Alexandria are intended to indicate the same reluctance. The future Patriarch is brought to Cairo, loaded with chains and strictly guarded, as if to prevent the possibility of escape.

According to the Arian tradition, the Bishops were assembled in great numbers, when Athanasius suddenly appeared late in the evening, secured two of the Bishops within the church of S. Dionysius, barricaded the building against the majority outside, and so, in spite of their remonstrances, and even anathemas, was conse-

---

[1] Jerome speaks of the custom as having lasted only till the Bishops Heraclas and Dionysius (Ep. ad Evangel. 85).   But the tradition of the Alexandrian Church, as preserved in Eutychius (i. 331), maintained that it lasted till Alexander.   The change which he ascribes to Heraclas is another, which may have led to Jerome's statement; viz. that down to that time there had been no Bishop in Egypt except the Bishop of Alexandria. The whole question is well set forth in Le Quien, Oriens Christianus, ii. 342.

[2] "Nominabant" is the word used by Jerome.   This, though it does not contradict, does not necessarily imply the more detailed account which Eutychius gives of the actual imposition of hands and blessing.

crated; and afterwards, as if by a letter from the municipality of Alexandria, procured the Imperial confirmation of the act.[1] The extraordinary and mysterious circumstances, which on any hypothesis attended the appointment of Athanasius, may account for the variations in the history.

Alexandria had already numbered many famous theologians in her catechetical school, but, with the exception perhaps of Dionysius, Athanasius was her first distinguished Bishop, the first who in power and character was worthy of the situation.

The see of Alexandria was then the most important in the whole Church. Alexandria, till the rise of Constantinople, was the most powerful city in the East. The prestige of its founder still clung to it.[2]

Egypt, even in the Pagan parts of the Empire, was still regarded as the ancient nurse of religious mysteries, and the possession of the Temple of Serapis made Alexandria the chief sanctuary of Egypt. The Alexandrian Church was the only great seat of Christian learning. Its episcopate was "the Evangelical see,"[3] as founded by the Evangelist S. Mark. "The chair of "S. Mark" was, as it still is, the name of the Patriarchal throne of Egypt. Its occupant, as we have seen, was the only potentate of the time, who bore the name of "Pope."[4] After the Council of Nicæa he became the "Judge of the World," from his decisions respecting the celebration of Easter;[5] and the obedience paid to his judgment in all matters of learning, secular and sacred, almost equalled that paid in later days to the ecclesias-

1 Philost. ii. 11.
2 Julian, Ep. 51. Comp. Sharpe's Egypt, c. 16.
3 Neale's History of Alexandrian Church, i. 6.
4 Lecture III.   5 Neale, i. 113.

tical authority of the Popes of the West. The "head
" of the Alexandrian Church," says Gregory Nazianzen,[1]
" is the head of the world."

In his own province his jurisdiction was even more
extensive than that of the Roman Pontiff. The Episcopate of Egypt, which had but a doubtful existence in
early times, always remained subordinate to the Alexandrian Patriarch, beyond what was the case in any
Church of the West. Not only did he consecrate all
the Bishops throughout his diocese, but no other Bishop
had any independent power of ordination. The Egyptian Bishops at Chalcedon protested with tears and cries,
that, till a Patriarch was given them, they were power-
less to do anything commanded by the Council.[2]

In civil affairs the chief of the Alexandrian Church
carried himself almost like a sovereign prince. "At a
" distance from court, and at the head of an immense
" capital, the Patriarch of Alexandria had gradually
" usurped the state and authority of a civil magistrate,
" . . . and the Prefects of Egypt were awed or provoked
" by the Imperial power of these Christian Pontiffs."[3]

Not only in name and office, however, but in fact,
Athanasius was the representative of the Egyptian
Church.

1. In his Pontificate the Church of Alexandria re-
Conversion ceived its only important accession. A trav-
of Abys-
sinia.   eller presented himself from the distant and
then almost unknown Abyssinia. His story was simple
and touching. It was one of the earliest instances of a
Christian mission following in the wake of scientific
discovery. A philosopher of Tyre, Moripius by name,
had embarked on a voyage of investigation down the
Red Sea. He had taken with him two children, rela-

---

[1] Orat. 21.   [2] Neale, i. 111, 112.
[3] Gibbon, c. xlvii; Neale, i. 112.

tions of his own, to teach on the journey. On his return the vessel touched for water at a port of Ethiopia. The savage inhabitants attacked them and massacred all the crew. The two boys, Frumentius and Edesius, faithful to the purpose for which they had been brought, were sitting under a tree by the sea-shore, learning their lessons. The savages were touched by the sight, took them to the king of the country, where they gradually rose into his confidence and that of his widow, as the instructors of his son. When the prince came of age, the two Christians returned. But Frumentius determined to bring news of this opening for Christianity to the great centre of Christian civilization (like an earlier Livingstone), unfolded his tidings to Athanasius, and then, layman and stranger as he was, was at once consecrated to the episcopate.

He returned, and under his new name of Salama became the founder of the Church of Abyssinia.

> " Hail him with the voice of joy,
>   Sing praises to Salama;
> The door of pity, of mercy,
>   And of pleasant grace." [1]

2. There was another offshoot of the Coptic Church with which Athanasius was in the closest rela- The Egyptian hermits. tions. Egypt was the parent of monachism, and the monks and Athanasius were inseparable allies. In his early youth he had been himself for a short time a hermit. In later life he poured forth to them the news of the outer world. Of Antony, the founder of the monastic system, he was the bosom friend and biographer. He had often sought him out in the desert waste, and according to the practice still pursued in the East, as a mark of deference from an inferior to a supe-

[1] Harris, Highlands of Ethiopia, iii. 89.

42

rior (as in the case of Elisha and Elijah), poured water over his hands as he washed.[1]

Antony, though unable to speak Greek, or to read or write,[2] entered with the liveliest interest into the theological controversies of the young Bishop. In the most critical moment of the struggle of Athanasius, he appeared suddenly in Alexandria to give the sanction of his mysterious presence. Heathens, as well as Christians, ran to see "the man of God,"[3] as he was called. Athanasius escorted him to the gate of the city as he departed.

In the next generation the attachment of the monks of the desert to the see of Alexandria became a fixed political institution, like the armed military orders of the Middle Ages, like the Jesuits in the sixteenth century. But in the time of Athanasius, it was the innocent, natural, enthusiastic devotion of man to man, friend to friend, disciple to teacher, and teacher to disciple. Paul, the companion of Antony, wished to be buried in the mantle given by Athanasius to Antony, in order to assure himself that he had died in communion with Athanasius. Ammon, the Egyptian monk, accompanied Athanasius to Rome, and astonished every one by the eagerness with which, regardless of all the other wonders of the great city, he ran, like a dervish of the present day, to throw himself before the tombs of S. Peter and S. Paul.

In the caves of the hermits, along the banks of the Nile, Athanasius was received whenever his residence in the capital was rendered insecure. As he approached, and saw the innumerable crowds issuing from their cells, he burst forth into the Prophet's exclamation: "Who "are these that fly as a cloud, and as doves to their "cotes?" whilst they, with thousands of blazing torches,

[1] Vit. Ant. Præf.   [2] Vit. Ath. 74, 75.   [3] Vit. Ant. 70.

their Abbot leading his ass, escorted him to their impregnable retreats.[1]

3. There was yet a third close bond of connection between Athanasius and the Coptic Church. The Arian
party at Alexandria was essentially Greek. The Orthodox party, or, as it was called by its enemies, the Sabellian, and afterwards the Eutychian, party, was essentially
national. "S. Chrysostom," as it has been truly said,
"could never have been a Monophysite, nor S. Cyril a
"Nestorian." [2]

To this national or Egyptian party belonged the great
body of the hermits and monks, who, as their names
and their ignorance of Greek indicate, were genuine
Copts. To this party belonged the Christian populace
of Alexandria. Of this party, or rather nation, Athanasius was the representative; and to him and to his
doctrine the nation clung with a tenacity which went
on increasing with the lapse of years. The Imperial
Government at Constantinople, with its Greek adherents at Alexandria, was gradually set more and more
at defiance.

When the Council of Chalcedon condemned what the
Egyptian Church believed to be a legitimate inference
from the doctrine of Athanasius,[3] the breach was final.
The adherents of the Council were contemptuously
called Synodites or Imperialists. The Egyptian Church,
with its sister communions in Syria, gloried in the exclusive title of Orthodox.[4] Rather than be reconciled
to the heterodox adherents of the Empire (as it deemed

---

[1] Vit. Pachom. (quoted in Vit. Ath., Opp. i. p. lxxiv.)

[2] Neale, Alex. Church, i. 36.

[3] In the treatise of Athanasius quoted by Cyril (Athan. ii. 1), the single
nature of Christ is expressly asserted. Its genuineness has on this account
been vehemently questioned, but apparently with no other reason against it
(See Robertson's History of the Church, i. 436.)

[4] See the history of John of Ephesus, passim.

the Greek Church to be), it surrendered itself and them
into the hands of the Saracens. To this day the old
feud still continues. Their hatred of the Greek Church
makes them of all Christian Churches the most intolerant of other Christians. They will never intermarry
with them. They prefer Mahometanism. The whole
Nubian Church became Moslem, rather than join the
Church of Constantinople.[1]

Thus strong was the union of religious and national
feeling which already in his lifetime rallied round Athanasius, and assisted in making him formidable to his opponents. No fugitive Stuart in the Scottish Highlands
could count more securely on the loyalty of his subjects,
than did Athanasius in his hiding-places in Egypt count
upon the faithfulness and secrecy of his countrymen.
Sometimes it was the hermits who afforded him shelter
in their rocky fastnesses; sometimes his fellow-townsmen
supported him as he lay hid in his father's tomb outside
the walls of their city; sometimes it was the beautiful
Alexandrian maiden who, in her old age, delighted to
tell how, when he had suddenly appeared at midnight
wrapped in his short tunic and red cloak, she had concealed and tended him in her house, with provisions and
books, till he was able, as suddenly, to reappear amongst
his astonished friends.[2] His whole course was that of
an adventurous and wandering prince, rather than of a
persecuted theologian; and, when in the brief intervals
of triumph he was enabled to return to his native city,
his entrance was like that of a Sovereign rather than
of a Prelate.

One such scene, thoroughly Egyptian in character, is
recorded by Gregory Nazianzen, which lingered in the

---

1 Lane's Modern Egyptians, ii. 312, 333; Harris's Ethiopia, iii. 68.
2 Palladius, c. 135, 150. Athanasius told her that he was directed to her
by a special revelation : see page 344.

recollections of all who had seen it, as the most splendid
spectacle of the age.   It seems to have been Entrance
his first return after the death of Constantine. andria.
There was more than delight; there was awe, almost
amounting to consternation, at the greatness of the
event.   The population of Alexandria poured forth, as
was their habit on such occasions, not in the indiscriminate confusion of a modern populace, but in a certain
stateliness of arrangement.   Each trade and profession
kept its own place. The men and women, as in Oriental
countries, were apart.   The children formed a mass by
themselves.   As the mighty stream rolled out of the
gates, it was (this was the truly Egyptian figure
that suggested itself) as if the Nile, at the height of its
flood, scattering fertility as it went, had turned in its
course and flowed backwards from Alexandria towards
the first outpost of the city.   As now, so then, the usual
mode of moving to and fro along the roads of Egypt
was on asses.   Gregory, as he describes Athanasius so
approaching, is carried into an extravagance of comparison and of symbolism.   He thinks of the triumphal
entry into Jerusalem; he thinks that the asses typified
the heathen population whom Athanasius had loosed
from their ignorance.   Branches of trees were waved
aloft; carpets of all the gayest colors and richest tex-
tures of Alexandria were spread under his feet.   There
was a long unbroken shout of applause; thousands of
hands clapped with delight; the air was scented with
the fragrant ointments poured out; the city at night
flashed with illuminations; public and private entertain-
ments were given in every house. In a wild enthusiasm
of devotion, women became nuns, men became hermits;
children entreated their parents, parents urged their
children, to sacrifice themselves to the monastic life.[1]

[1] Greg. Nazianz. 28.

In a still nobler sense of a Christian revival, the hungry and the orphans were sheltered and maintained, and every household by its devotion seemed to be transformed into a Church.[1]

Long afterwards when a popular Prefect of Alexandria was received with vast enthusiasm, and two bystanders were comparing it with all possible demonstrations that they could imagine, and the younger had said: "Even if the Emperor Constantius[2] himself were "to come, he could not be so received;" the elder replied with a smile, and an Egyptian oath: "Do you "call that a wonderful sight? The only thing to which "you ought to compare it is the reception of the great "Athanasius."

II. This leads us to the second aspect in which we must consider the life of Athanasius. It is not merely as the Egyptian saint, but as the antagonist of the whole Church and Empire of the time, that his career has been invested with such singular interest, as that, of all the saints of the early Church, he is the only one who has actually kindled the cold and critical pages of Gibbon into a fire of enthusiasm.

His contests with the Emperors.

He had, as we have seen, the support of his own party and his own nation behind him. Still it is evident that he was one of those strong characters who render to others a stronger support than others can ever render to them.

In the Nicene Council[3] he had almost stood alone against the majority, which, in spite of his remonstrances, received the Melitians. In the events which occupied the rest of his life, he was al-

His isolation.

---

1 Ath. Hist. Arian. § 25.

2 Greg. Nazianz. 29. This expression shows that the return spoken of was that after Constantine's death.

3 See Lecture V. p. 256.

most the only high ecclesiastic who stood firm against
the Arians.   We must bear in mind how completely
the Arian party had taken possession of the court, the
dignities, even the Councils, of the time.   Such rapid
revolutions in the decline and rise of theological parties
in royal or popular favor are amongst the most usual
phenomena of all ecclesiastical history.   And it is by
its solitary protest against subservience to the religious
fashion of the age, that the life of Athanasius has acquired a proverbial significance, which cannot be too
often impressed on theological students.   " Scripture,"
it has been well said, "nowhere leads us to suppose that
" the circumstance of all men speaking well of us is any
" ground for supposing that we are acceptable in the
" sight of God.   The jealousy or fear of some, the reti-
" cence of others, the terrorism of a few, have really
" nothing to do with the questions at issue in theologi-
" cal controversy.   They cannot have the slightest in-
" fluence on the meaning of words, or on the truth of
" facts.   There is a deeper work for theologians, which
" is not dependent on the opinions of men, and which
" can hardly expect to win much popular favor, so far
" as it runs counter to the feelings of religious parties.
" But he who bears a part in it may feel a confidence
" which no popular caresses or religious sympathy could
" inspire, that he has, by a Divine help, been enabled to
" plant his foot somewhere beyond the waves of time."

    This, whether we agree or whether we disagree with
the objects of Athanasius, is the permanent lesson which
his life teaches.   It is the same as that which we are
taught by the life of Elijah in the history of the Jewish
Church, and by the lives of some of the early Reformers in the Christian Church.   It is the special point
which Hooker [1] has brought out in the splendid passage

---

[1] Eccl. Pol. v. 42.

which, though well known, I cannot forbear to quote,
as giving in a short compass the events of the period in
the life of Athanasius, during which the doctrine of the
Arians had become the religion of the Government and
of the Church : —

"Athanasius, by the space of forty-six years, from the
"time of his consecration till the last hour of his life in
"this world, they never suffered to enjoy the comfort
"of a peaceable day. The heart of Constantine stolen
"from him ; Constantius his scourge and torment by all
"the ways that malice, armed with sovereign authority,
"could devise and use ; under Julian no rest given him ;
"and in the days of Valens as little. Crimes there
"were laid to his charge many. . . . His judges were
"evermore the self-same men by whom his accusers
"were suborned. . . . Those Bishops and Prelates who
"should have counted his cause theirs . . . were sure
"by bewraying their affection towards him to bring
"upon themselves those maledictions whereby, if they
"would not be drawn to seem his adversaries, yet others
"should be taught how unsafe it was to continue his
"friends. Whereupon it came to pass in the end that
"(very few excepted) all became subject to the sway of
"time ; saving only that some fell away sooner, some
"later ; . . . some were leaders in the host, . . . and
"the rest . . . either yielding through fear, or brought
"under with penury, or by flattery ensnared, or else
"beguiled through simplicity, which is the fairest ex-
"cuse that well may be made for them. . . . Such was
"the stream of those times that all men gave place
"unto it. . . . Only of Athanasius there was nothing
"observed through that long tragedy, other than such
"as very well became a wise man to do, and a right-
"eous to suffer. So that this was the plain condition
"of those times ; the *whole world against Athanasius,* and

" *Athanasius against it.* Half a hundred years spent in
" doubtful trial, which of the two in the end would pre-
" vail; the side which had all, or else the part which
" had no friend but God and death; the one a defender
" of his innocency, the other a finisher of his troubles."
It is probably from the Latin version of this celebrated
passage, that we derive the proverb, *Athanasius contra
mundum;* a proverb which, as I have observed on other
occasions, well sets forth the claims of individual, private, solitary judgment, against the claims of general
authority as set forth in the other equally well-known
maxim, *Quod semper, quod ubique, quod ab omnibus.* It is
a proverb which, though few are worthy to claim for
themselves, yet all may well take to heart as a warning
against confounding popularity with truth, or isolation
with heresy, or temporary depression with lasting defeat.

The contest successively waged with Constantine,
Constantius, Julian, and Valens, has been briefly and
powerfully told by Gibbon, and elaborately worked out
by Tillemont. Its details are as tedious and complicated, as its general interest is exciting and instructive.

But there are a few points which may be selected as
characteristic either of the man or the age.

1. His contest with the Imperial power, and the long
struggles which it cost the successive Emperors Contest
to cope with him, are proofs of the freedom with the Emperors.
and independence of the Christian Church, in the midst
of the general decay of those qualities in all the other
institutions of the Empire.

The general effect of this new principle[1] of life in
institutions of the Church has been already pointed
out; but of individual instances of this new and dis-

---

[1] See Lecture II. p. 159.

turbing force, which would never again let the world
subside into its dull stagnation and inaction, Athanasius is the first grand example. The "meddling dema-
"gogue,"[1] "the odious Athanasius,"[2] "the audacious
"conspirator, elated by his characteristic rashness,"[3] are
the expressions by which Julian designates his rival
in Egypt. "Although," says Gibbon, "his mind was
"tainted by the contagion of fanaticism, Athanasius dis-
"played a superiority of character and abilities which
"would have fitted him far better than the degenerate
"sons of Constantine for the government of a great
"monarchy."[4]

2. The contest, however, did not resemble those which
in the Middle Ages set the spiritual against the
Personal,
not eccle-   civil authority. In this respect Athanasius strict-
siastical
opposition. ly preserves the character of the Oriental hierarchy,[5] which I have more than once noticed. The spiritual and the secular were hardly ever, as such, directly
opposed.[6] During the whole of the first part of the
quarrel, nothing can exceed the deference of Athanasius to the Imperial authority ; and the subsequent vehemence of his language is personal, rather than official.
The accusations against him were also personal. It was
not for heresy or orthodoxy that he was convened before the Council of Tyre, but for the murder of Arsenius, for breaking a sacred chalice, for imposing a tax on
sacred vestments, for conspiring against the Emperor, for
consecrating a church without the Emperor's permission,
for preventing the exportation of corn from Alexandria
(a purely Egyptian charge) ; for procuring his reinstate-
ment from an Imperial decree, after his deposition by a

---

1 Julian, Ep. 51.   2 Ibid. 6.   3 Ibid. 26.
4 Decline and Fall, iii. 355.   5 See Lectures I., X., XI.
6 The nearest approach to such a collision is the charge brought against
him by Julian of baptizing Alexandrian ladies, Ep. 6.

Council; for refusing to leave Alexandria without an express command from the Emperor; for corresponding with the rebel chief Magnentius. All of these charges were repudiated by Athanasius; and of all, in the judgment of posterity as well as of his own time, he has been acquitted, though in the last century Sir Isaac Newton condescended to use his great intellect in reviving them, for the purpose of undermining the character of a theological opponent. True or false, however, they were such as had no ecclesiastical significance, except from the person against whom they were brought.

3. But though Athanasius was not formally attacked for heresy, and was therefore not, technically speaking, a sufferer for the sake of his religious creed, yet there can be no doubt that the annoyances and dangers to which he was exposed originated in theological enmity, and thus furnish the first signal instance of the strange sight of Christians persecuting Christians. We can hardly suppose that his opponents really believed him to be guilty of the murder of Arsenius, or of the detention of the Egyptian corn. But these were convenient blinds for a theological hostility which they dared not openly avow. And it is important to observe that this wide persecution arose, not from the Orthodox against the heretics, but from the heretics against the Orthodox. This is a sample of what has often occurred since. We cannot deny or palliate the intolerance of established Churches, but we must never forget that it has been shared to the fullest extent by the intolerance of sects and heresies of every kind. Indeed, wherever it exists, it is a proof that sectarianism has eaten its way into the vitals of the Church itself. Whatever provocations had been given by the Orthodox party were far surpassed by the violence and unrelenting bitterness of the Arians. A single scene will suffice, as indicating at

once the character of Athanasius and of the persecutions. He had been urged to retire from Alexandria; but with the reverential obedience which, as we have seen, he kept up, at least in appearance, for the Imperial authority, he refused to leave his post without an express warrant from the Emperor. What his enemies could not effect by law, they determined to effect by violence. A mob has, in all ages and amongst all shades of ecclesiastical party, been a ready instrument for theological agitators against their opponents. Of all mobs the Alexandrian, whether heathen or Christian, was the most terrible. On this occasion it was united with the soldiers. The chief of the police was present, but apparently took no part in restraining the outrages.[1]

On the night of Thursday the 9th of February 358, Athanasius with his congregation was, after the manner of the Coptic Church, keeping vigil through the whole night in the Church of S. Theonas, in preparation for the Eucharist of the following day. Suddenly, at midnight,[2] there was a tumult without. The church,[3] which was of unusual size, was surrounded with armed men.[4] The presence of mind for which he was famous did not desert the Bishop. Behind the altar was the Episcopal throne. On this he took his seat, and ordered his attendant deacon to read the 136th Psalm, which has for every verse the response, " For his mercy endureth forever." It was while these responses were being thundered forth by the congregation, that the doors burst open, and the Imperial general and notary entered at the head of the soldiers. The soldiers were for a moment terror-struck by the chanting of the Psalm.[5] But as they pressed forward a shower of arrows flew through the church.

Attack on the Church of S. Theonas.

---

[1] Protest of the Alexandrians, § 5.   [2] Ibid. § 3.
[3] Apol. Const. § 19.   [4] Protest, § 3.   [5] Soc. ii. 1.

The swords flashed in the light of the sacred torches, the din of their shouts mingled with the rattle of their arms. The wounded fell one upon another, and were trampled down; the nuns were seized and stripped; the church was plundered. Through this mass of horrors, the two Imperial officers and their attendants passed on to the screen [1] before the altar. Athanasius had refused to go till most of the congregation had retired. But now he was swept away in the crowd.

In his own version [2] of the story, he is at a loss to account for his escape. But his diminutive figure may well have passed unseen; and we learn, besides, that he was actually carried out in a swoon,[3] which sufficiently explains his own ignorance of the means of his deliverance. The church was piled with dead, and the floor was strewn with the swords and arrows of the soldiers. He vanished, no one knew whither, into the darkness of the winter night.

This scene well introduces us to the consideration of another and more general side of the character of Athanasius. The qualities that most forcibly struck his contemporaries seem rather to have been the readiness [4] and versatility of his gifts. An Oxford poet, in the "Lyra Apostolica," has sung of

His general character.

> " The royal-hearted Athanase,
> With Paul's own mantle blest."

Whatever may have been the intention of this comparison, it is certain that there was a resemblance between the flexibility of Athanasius and the many-sided character of the Apostle whose boast it was to have " made himself all things to all men." None such had occurred before, and none such occurred

His versatility.

---

[1] Protest, § 3.
[2] De Fuga, 24.
[3] Ibid. 4.
[4] Julian, Ep. 51 : ἐντρέχεια.

again till the time of Augustine, perhaps not till the time of Francis Xavier.

The hyperbolical language of Gregory Nazianzen shows the deep impression made by this, as it seemed, rare peculiarity. "He was," so Gregory describes him,[1] " a just distributer of praise and blame, according as " the case might be; *awakening* the *sluggish, repressing* " *enthusiasm;* equally alert in prevention or in cure; " *single in his aims, manifold in his modes of government;* " wise in his speech, still *wiser in his intentions;* on a " level with the most ordinary men, *yet rising to the* " *height of the most speculative;* uniting in himself" (the expression is worth preserving as one that could only have been used in that transitional state between heathenism and Christianity, which was described in my last Lecture) " the various attributes of all the " heathen gods. Hospitable, like [Jupiter] Philoxenius; " listening to suppliants, like [Jupiter] Ikesius; averting " evils, like [Apollo] Apotropæus; binding men together, " like [Jupiter] Zygius; pure, like [Pan] Parthenius; a " peacemaker, like [Jupiter] Irenæus; a reconciler, like " [Jupiter] Diallacterius; a conductor to the shades be- " low, like [Hermes] Pompæus."

Amongst the traits which may be especially selected, His humor. as bringing this part of his character before us, and also as being too much overlooked in the popular notions of him, the first is the remarkable quickness and humor of his address.

Take his clever retort to Constantius, who, at the instigation of his Arian persecutors, had asked him to open a church for the Arians at Alexandria. " I will " grant a church to the heretics at Alexandria, as soon " as you grant a church to the Orthodox at Antioch." It is just the one retort, obvious indeed, but unanswer-

1 Orat. c. 36.

able, that may always be made to an intolerant faction. They always shrink from the test.

Take again the well-sustained and pointed irony of the scene in the Council of Tyre, where he produces the man whom he is accused of having murdered, and whose right hand he is supposed to have cut off. The muffled figure is introduced; he shows the face first, and asks all round: "Is this Arsenius, whom I mur- "dered?" He draws out from behind the cloak, first one hand, and then the other: "Let no one now ask "for a third; for two hands, and two only, has every "human being received from the Creator of all things." It has been often said that a man who can provoke or enjoy a laugh is sure to succeed with his fellow-creatures. We cannot doubt that such was Atha-nasius.[1]

Not less efficacious is the power of making use of a laugh or a jest, instead of serious argument. The grave Epiphanius ventured one day to ask Athanasius what he thought of the opinions of his dangerous supporter, the heretic Marcellus. Athanasius returned no answer; but a significant smile broke out over his whole countenance. Epiphanius had sufficient humor to perceive that this meant "Marcellus has had a narrow "escape."[2]

So again, when he was asked his opinion on the common practice of death-bed baptisms, he replied with an apologue which admitted of no rejoinder. "An angel "once said to my great predecessor: 'Peter [the Bishop "'of the see before Alexander], why do you send me "'these sacks [these wind-bags] carefully sealed up, "'with nothing whatever inside?'"[3]

---

[1] Theod. i. 30.

[2] Epiph. Hær. lxxii. 4: διὰ τοῦ προσώπου μειδιάσας ὑπεφῆνε. See Lect. III.

[3] Tillemont, Athan. c. 117.

Another trait makes itself felt in the widespread belief entertained that he was the great magician
of his age.   It was founded no doubt on his
rapid mysterious movements, his presence of mind, his
prophetic anticipations ; to which must be added a
humorous pleasure in playing with the fears and superstitions which these qualities engendered.

His magical
reputation.

The Emperor Constantine is entering Constantinople
in state.   A small figure darts across his path in the
middle of the square, and stops his horse.   The Emperor, thunderstruck, tries to pass on ; he cannot guess
who the petitioner can be.   It is Athanasius, who comes
to insist on justice, when thought to be leagues away
before the Council of Tyre.

The Alexandrian Church is dismayed by the accession
of Julian.   But Athanasius is unmoved ; he looks into
the future ; he sees through the hollowness of the reaction.   " It is but a little cloud," he says, " that will soon
" pass away."

He is pursued by his enemies up the Nile.   They meet
a boat descending the stream.   They hail it with the
shout[1] so familiar to Egyptian travellers on the great
river : " Where is Athanasius ? "   " Not very far off," is
the answer.   The wind carries on the pursuers ; the
current carries down the pursued.   It was Athanasius,
who, hearing of their approach, took advantage of a
bend in the stream, to turn, and meet, and mislead, and
escape them thus.

He is passing through one of the squares of Alexandria.   The heathen mob are standing around ; a crow
flies over his head.   They, partly in jest, partly in
earnest, ask him to tell them what its croaking meant.
He laughs in his sleeve, and answers : " Do you not
" hear ?   It says *Cras, Cras*, which is in Latin ' to-mor-

---

1 Soc. iii. 14.   Sozomen makes this a divine intimation.

" ' row,' which means that *to-morrow* something untoward
" will befall you; for *to-morrow* your Pagan festival will
" be suppressed by an Imperial decree." So it came to
pass, and few would care to ask how he really had
gained the information.[1]

Of all these incidents the secret springs are to us
sufficiently clear; his ubiquitous activity, his innumerable
sources of knowledge, his acute observation. But whilst
to his friends they seemed to imply supernatural aid, to
his enemies they suggested suspicions of the blackest
witchcraft. When the murdered man with both his
hands was produced alive, there were those who maintained that it was an optical illusion, caused by the
glamor which Athanasius had cast over the Council.
Even an enlightened Pagan was convinced that his
knowledge of the future was derived from arts of
divination, and from the auguries of birds.[2] And this
belief of the Pagans and heretics has curiously forced
itself back into the Church. Whatever may be thought
of the real origin of the legend of S. George the martyr
of Cappadocia, there can be no doubt that it has been
incorporated with an Arian legend of the Arian George,
Bishop of Alexandria, and murdered by the Alexandrian
mob; and that from this union has sprung the story in
its present popular form. In this story, the contest of
S. George is for the Empress Alexandra (in whom we
can hardly fail to see the type of the Alexandrian
Church), and his enemy is the magician Athanasius.[3]
As time rolls on, and the legend grows in dimensions,
George becomes the champion on his steed, rescuing
the Egyptian princess, and Athanasius the wizard sinks

---

[1] Soz. iv. 10.　　　　　　　　[2] Ammianus, xv. 7.

[3] Acta SS., April 23, 120–123. The addition that the magician was a
friend of Magnentius identifies him beyond any doubt with Athanasius. See
p. 339.

into the prostrate dragon; and, in the popular representations of the story, still acted by Christmas mummers
in the North of England, the transformation is into a
lower form still; and the only image which Cheshire
peasants have seen of Athanasius is the quaint and
questionable figure who appears under the name and in
the guise of Beelzebub. It is the last expiring trace of
the revenge of the Arians on their great adversary.

III. From the active life of Athanasius we pass to his
The chief more speculative aspect, as the chief theolo-
theologian
of the time, gian of the age, in one sense of all ages.

It may indeed be doubted whether, in his own age,
there was not one of still higher authority in the theological world, Hosius of Cordova. But his was one of
those brilliant reputations which have expired with the
life of the holder; whereas that of Athanasius grew in
the next generation to the height that secured for him
finally the title of "great," which Hosius enjoyed only
during his lifetime. "Whenever you meet with a
"sentence of Athanasius," was the saying of the sixth
century, "and have not paper at hand, write it down
"upon your clothes."

1. He was one of the few theologians whose fame
in the was common both to East and West. What he
West as was in the East I need not here further specify.
well as in
the East. But he left his footprint in the West also, to a
degree far beyond what is the case with any other
Eastern Father. He visited Rome and Treves. He
learned Latin to converse with the Roman Bishop.
He introduced to the Romans the strange hermits from
Egypt. He brought monasticism into Germany. His
very remains were gradually removed westward, from
Alexandria[1] to Constantinople, to Venice, to France,
to Spain.

[1] Acta SS., May 2, i. 35.

The close argumentative style of his writings was better calculated to win the attention of the Western theologians [1] than the more rhetorical and imaginative works of most of his countrymen; and of this harmony in thought, as well as of the deep impression left by his character in Western Christendom, the most remarkable proof is the ancient hymn, " Quicunque vult," which, throughout the Middle Ages and by our own Reformers, was believed to be the Creed of S. Athanasius. The learned world is now fully aware that it is of French or Spanish origin. It not only contains words and phrases which to Athanasius were unknown, but it distinctly and from the first asserted the doctrine of the Double Procession of the Spirit, which never occurs in the writings of Athanasius,[2] and which, in all probability, he would have repudiated with his Oriental brethren of later times. But its partial resemblance to his style, and the assumption of his name, have given it an immense support.

2. He was the father of all Theology, in a more precise sense than either as the oracle of the ancient Churches, or the writer of the chief theological Creed of the West. He was the founder of Orthodoxy.[3] Before his time, and before

Athanasian Creed.

The founder of Orthodoxy.

---

[1] See Lecture I. p. 111.

[2] The nearest approach to the Double Procession in the writings of Athanasius is in Ep. ad Serapion. i. 20. On the other hand, the Single Procession was maintained as against the doctrine of the *creation* of the Spirit. (Neander, iv. 106–109.) See Lecture I. That a chief motive for cherishing the Athanasian Creed in the Latin Church was its assertion of the Double Procession, is evident from "the ancient testimonies" cited by Waterland (iv. 150), which mostly turn on this very point, A. D. 809 to 1439. It has, indeed, in later times found its way into the Psalters both of Greece and Russia, though not of the remoter East. But it has never been recognized as an Eastern Creed, and the clause for which it was so highly valued in the West has been omitted. (Renaudot, Hist. Patr. Alex. 98.) Salig. (De Eutych. ante Eutych. 131).

[3] τοῦ πατρὸς τῆς ὀρθοδοξίας. Epiph. Hær. lxix. c. 2.

the settlement of the Nicene Creed, in which he took so large a part, it might be said that the idea of an Orthodox doctrine, in the modern sense of the word, was almost unknown. Opinions were too fluctuating, too simple, too mixed, to admit of it. It is a word, even to this day, of doubtful repute. No one likes to be called "heretical," but neither is it a term of unmixed eulogy to be called "orthodox." It is a term which implies, to a certain extent, narrowness, fixedness, perhaps even hardness, of intellect, and deadness of feeling; at times, rancorous animosity. In these respects its great founder cannot be said to be altogether free from the reproach cast on his followers in the same line. His elaborate expositions of doctrine sufficiently exemplify the minuteness of argument which perhaps may have been the cause of his being regarded as a special pleader or jurisconsult.[1] His invectives against the Arians prove how far even a heroic soul can be betrayed by party spirit and the violence of the times. Amongst his favorite epithets for them are: "Devils, Antichrists, maniacs, Jews, polytheists, "atheists, dogs, wolves, lions, hares, chameleons, hydras, "eels, cuttlefish, gnats, beetles, leeches."[2] There may be cases where such language is justifiable, but, as a general rule, and with all respect for him who uses them, this style of controversy can be mentioned as a warning only, not as an example.

But the zeal of Athanasius for Orthodoxy, if it hurried him at times beyond the limits of Christian moderation in language, rarely, so far as we know, tempted him into unchristian violence in deeds. We can here speak with the more certainty from the

His polemical vehemence.

Compared with Cyril.

---

[1] Sulp. Sev. ii. 390; Gibbon, c. 22.

[2] See these epithets collected in a note to Athanasius's Historical Treatises (Newman's ed. ii. 34).

contrast which his life presents with that of another great prelate of the next generation. Just as, in the history of our own Church, Anselm's virtues can be appreciated only by comparison with Becket, or Ken's by comparison with Sancroft; so Athanasius, in the fourth century, may be fairly judged in the light of his own successor, Cyril of Alexandria, in the fifth. The bribery which is certainly traced to Cyril is at least doubtful in Athanasius.[1] There is good reason to acquit Athanasius of any share in the murder of George;[2] but Cyril was suspected,[3] even by the Orthodox, of complicity in the murder of Hypatia. Cyril was active in procuring the cruel banishment of the blameless Nestorius; Athanasius was concerned in no persecutions except those in which he himself suffered. It was a maxim of Athanasius that "the duty of Ortho- "doxy is not to compel but to persuade belief;" Cyril carried his measures by placing himself at the head of bands of ferocious ruffians,[4] and by canonizing the assassin. No graver reproach rests on the memory of Athanasius than that of being a powerful magician; Cyril's death suggested to one who has left his feelings on record the reflection that "at last the reproach of "Israel was taken away; that he was gone to vex the "inhabitants of the world below with his endless dog- "matism: let every one throw a stone upon his grave, "lest perchance he should make even hell too hot to "hold him,[5] and return to earth." But the excellence

---

[1] The charge is only found in Philostorgius, iii. 12.

[2] Philost. vii. 2. The silence of Julian acquits him.

[3] The direct charge of Damascius is not contradicted by Socrates, vii. 15. See Valesius ad h. l.

[4] Soc. vii. 13, 14.

[5] Theod. Ep. 180. The genuineness of the Epistle and its intention have been disputed, but mainly on the supposed improbability that Theodoret should so have designated Cyril.

of Athanasius, like that of every theologian, must be measured, not by his attack upon error, but by his defence of truth. Judged, indeed, by the hard and narrow standard of modern times, his teaching would be pronounced lamentably defective. But it is his rare merit, or his rare good fortune, that the centre of his theology was the doctrine of the Incarnation. His earliest treatise His defence is on that special subject, before it had become of the Incarnation. embroiled in the Arian controversy; and it contains his calm statement of the doctrine, and of its practical effects on the world, unembittered by the polemics of his middle life. And though the forms, both of the errors which he opposed and of the truths which he maintained, have varied in later times, it may be worth while briefly to point out how his teaching reaches far beyond his own time, and extends into those manifold applications which form one of the best tests of truth.

a) I have before spoken of the polytheistic tendencies of which Arianism was the partial development. The Unity of the Father and the Son, which Athanasius maintained against these tendencies, is still needed as the basis of sound representations of the Divine acts. It is a standing witness, that in Scripture and theology, no less than in philosophy and conscience, there is a marked repugnance to the forced oppositions between the justice of the Father and the mercy of the Son, which run through the popular systems of the Redemption, adopted since the Reformation. Amongst the various figures which Athanasius uses to express his view, one is that of "Satisfaction." But this is introduced incidentally and in entire subordination to the primary truth, that the Redemption flowed from the Indivisible Love of the Father and the Son alike, and that its object was the restoration of man to union with God.

b) It was a favorite position of Arius[1] that the finite
mind of man could never comprehend the Infinity of
God. Such notions have been sometimes pushed to a
still further development in the form of representing
the Divine morality as altogether different from the
human. But it is a profound remark of a gifted member of the Eastern Church, that one grand result of
the Nicene decision was the reassertion of the *moral*
nature, the *moral* perfection, of the Divinity.[2] In the
Athanasian declaration that only through the image
of perfect humanity can perfect Divinity be made
known to us, is the true antidote to any such erroneous or sceptical representations of the Divine character.

c) The Athanasian doctrine of the Divine relations
possesses an element of permanence shared by no other
theories of that time.[3] It recognizes only two intelli-
gences in the world, God and man. These are two
simple ideas which will last as long as the human race
itself. But the Arian theories introduce into the subject the hypothesis of beings intervening between the
Divine and human, such as belong to the transitory
and dubious province which lies between Religion and
Mythology. If the controversy had ended by fixing
in the centre of the Christian Creed a being like the
angels or Æons of the early heretics, or the superhu-
man saints of the Latin Church, the departure from
the simplicity and sobriety of Christian faith would
have been far wider than can be the case in any true
statement of the doctrine of Athanasius.

1 According to Philostorgius (ii. 3), "Arius everywhere asserted that God
was unknown, incomprehensible, and inconceivable, not only by men, but by
the only-begotten Son Himself. But in this error the greater part of his followers joined." Compare to the same effect Eusebius, Eccl. Theol. i. 12.

2 Quelques Mots (1857), 32, 69, 79.

3 I am indebted for this remark to the Rev. J. B. Mozley.

d) The importance ascribed by Athanasius to the doctrine of the Incarnation, almost requires "the in-"communicable preëminence"[1] which the most philosophical theologians, as well as the simplest believers, have always assigned to the Four Gospels above all other portions of the sacred volume. This preëminence has often been disputed by the sectarian or the half-informed polemics of modern times. But it is not less necessary to Athanasian theology, than it is to a right adjustment of the proportions of Scripture.

3. There was a still "more excellent way" of Ortho-

His discrim- doxy in which Athanasius was conspicuous.
ination   He had firmly grasped the idea that it was a Christian duty to reconcile imaginary differences, and distinguish the essential and unessential. "Whilst," says Gregory Nazianzen, "he was a fire which burns "away as a forest the noxious vegetation, and a sword "which cuts up evil by the roots, so he was a husband-"man's winnowing fan to separate the light chaff from "the solid grain of the wheat. Whilst he went along "with the sword of the conqueror, he was also the "breath of the quickening spirit."[2]

Four signal instances of his discriminating judgment are recorded :

a) He healed the jealousies of the two monastic

in the quar- orders, the monks (or Cœnobites) and the her-
rels with
the monks mits, which threatened to break up the Eastern
and her-
mits,   Church, as the quarrels of the Franciscans and Dominicans in later times disturbed the tranquillity of the Western Church; the one representing the more purely devotional, the other the more intellectual, form of religion. He lived equally with both; sometimes

---

[1] Remains of Alexander Knox, ii. 335 ; an admirable passage, quoted in Dr. Ogilvie's Bampton Lectures, p. 230.
[2] Orat. 21, c. 7.

in the cell of the contemplative anchorite, sometimes
in the community of the more social convent. Here,
as elsewhere, (I again quote the strong language of
Gregory,) "he showed himself the reconciler and me-
"diator of the age, imitating Him who by His own
"blood set at peace those who had parted asunder;
"showing (with the hermits) that religion was able
"to become philosophical, and (with the monks) that
"philosophy stood in need of the guidance of re-
"ligion."[1]

b) Both in discipline and in doctrine he gave proof
that he was willing to sacrifice the letter in clerical
to the spirit. A solemn decree of the Nicene discipline,
Council, one of the few still observed in the West,
required the presence of three Bishops for Episcopal
consecration, and the usage of the Egyptian Church
required that all such appointments should take place
at Alexandria. When a young active layman had been
consecrated by a single Bishop, and without consulting
the see of Alexandria, Athanasius acquiesced in the
appointment, though "against all the rules received
"from antiquity," and, yet further, "bent to the neces-
"sities of the time," and promoted him to the metropolitan see of the province.[2]

c) In doctrine he gave a yet more startling proof
of this same disposition. If there was any one in the use
object which he might seem to have at heart and disuse
more than any other, it was the word *Homö-* of the Ho-
ousion,[3] which he had been the means of introducing
into the Council of Nicæa. The truth which he believed to be expressed by the word he did indeed
defend through life and death. But the word itself
he was willing to waive, when he found that it was

---

[1] Orat. 21, c. 19.   [2] See Synesius, Ep. 67.
                    [3] See Lecture IV.

45

misunderstood.[1] We may think, with Bishop Kaye, that he might have come earlier to this conclusion. But that he should have come to it at all, shows that he possessed a rare qualification of a great theologian. It is an edifying instance of the power of appreciating identity of doctrine under different, or even opposite, forms of speech.

d) Yet one more important task of this kind was reserved for the close of his life; namely, to reconcile the divisions of the East and West, which threatened to break out, as they did afterwards, into open rupture on these verbal questions. The Council of the Apostles at Jerusalem is the only one of which the direct object was not an enforcement of uniformity, but a toleration of diversity. That which, in later times, approached most nearly to it in this respect was the Council held at Alexandria, under the presidency of Athanasius, in the year 362. It consisted of the Bishops returning home from banishment, after the struggle with the Arians, and was intended to reunite, by an act of amnesty, the broken fragments of the Church. Those who had lapsed into Arianism were now on submission to be received again.[2] Lucifer of Cagliari, the fierce Sardinian, alone protested, and the long discord was healed.

Amongst other questions brought before it was the dispute which had arisen in the Council of Nicæa on the meaning of the word *hypostasis*, and which had now reached its height. The Latins still used it in the sense in which it was used in the Nicene Creed, as identical with *ousia*, which they trans-

in the Council of Alexandria, A. D. 362.

Controversy on "Person" and "Substance."

---

[1] Ath. de Syn. 41.

[2] Basil had to defend himself for having done so. Athanasius's letters, saying that he was to receive them without hesitation, were his warrant. Ep. 204, § 6 (306.)

lated by *substantia,* the etymological equivalent of *hypos-tasis.* But the Greeks had begun to use it in the sense of *prosopon* ("person"), and taunted the ignorant Latins with Sabellianism, whilst the Latins retorted with the charge of Arianism. Others, in the hope of stifling the quarrel, proscribed the use of both words.[1] " The con-" troversy," says Gregory, " had reached to such a pitch " that the two quarters of the world were on the point " of being torn asunder by a difference of syllables. " When Athanasius of blessed memory saw and heard " this, he, like a true man of God, like a grand steward " of souls, determined that this absurd and irrational di-" vision of the Divine Word was not to be endured; and " the remedy, the charm, which he had in his own char-" acter and mind, he brought to bear on the disease. " How did he effect this ? He called both sides to-" gether. He addressed them gently and kindly. He " explained in exact terms the sense of what was in-" tended, and when he found that they agreed, and had " no difference in what they meant, he granted freely " to each the use of their words and names ; whilst he " bound them together by the things and facts which " the words represented. This was more profitable than " all the long labors and discourses, in which perhaps " there may have been an element of ambition and " vanity. This is more honorable than all the sleep-" less nights and hard couches, of which the advan-" tage ends with the endurance. This was worth all " his famous wanderings and exiles ; for this was the " object for which he bore those sufferings, and to " which he devoted himself after those sufferings were " over."

---

[1] Soc. iii. 7. The difficulty of properly adjusting these terms continued even to the Middle Ages. See a learned note on this subject in Remusat's Life of Anselm, p. 517.

The Council of Alexandria was the last public occasion on which Athanasius appeared. It is pleasing to reflect that, as in the old age of Baxter, the last public acts of Athanasius's life were of wisdom, discernment, and charity.

In Goethe's Faust, the counsel given by Mephisto-

Things, pheles is to pay no attention to *things* in the-
not words. ology, but to dwell solely on *words*. This is the Devil's advice to theological students; and, alas! by too many, in every age of the world, most faithfully has it been followed. The advice and the example of Athanasius are exactly the contrary. Words no doubt are of high importance in theology. Both in ecclesiastical history and in the interpretation of Scripture, the study of their origin and meaning is most fruitful. Athanasius himself introduced into our confessions one of the most famous of them. But this gives the greater force to his warning when he bids the contending parties ascertain first of all what is the meaning of the terms they use, and then, if the meaning on both sides is the same, to fix their attention not on the *words* respecting which they differ, but on the *things* respecting which they are agreed.

One further final glimpse we catch of Athanasius. It

Relations is the sight, seldom witnessed, of a cordial salu-
with Basil,
A.D. 370. tation and farewell between the departing and the coming generation. This is what we see in the correspondence of the aged Athanasius and the active Basil, just entering on the charge of his new diocese in Asia Minor. The younger Prelate, suspected of heresy, eagerly appeals to the old oracle of Orthodoxy, and from him receives the welcome support which elsewhere he had sought in vain. " His accusers torment themselves " without reason," replied Athanasius. "He has but con- " descended to the infirmities of the weak. Think your-

" selves happy to have received as your pastor a man so
" full of wisdom and of truth."   Basil longed to see the
great reconciler face to face.[1]   This was not to be.   But,
amidst the distracting perplexities of the time, he consoled himself by writing to him, and by delineating the
venerable figure of the representative of the former age.
" His head," so Basil [2] describes him, " is now white with
" years. . . He has lived from the happy days before the
" Nicene Council, when the Church was at peace, into
" these mournful days of boundless controversy. . . He is
" the Samuel of the Church, the revered mediator be-
" tween the old generation and the new.   He is the
" skilful physician for the manifold diseases with which
" the Church is laboring.[3] . . He stands," — such is the
expressive image drawn no doubt from the light-house
(Pharos) of Athanasius's own city, — " he stands on his
" lofty watch-tower of speculation, seeing with his ubiq-
" uitous glance what is passing throughout the world.
" He overlooks the wide stormy ocean, where there is a
" vast fleet at sea, tossed and foundering in the waters,
" partly by the external violence of the sea, still more
" by the mismanagement and misunderstanding of the
" crews of the several ships, running each other down,
" and thrusting each other aside. . . With this image,"
says S. Basil, " I will conclude what I have to say.   It is
" all that the wisdom of Athanasius will require to be
" said ; it is all that the difficulties of the time will per-
" mit me to say."

With this image too let me conclude.   Our view
over the sea of ecclesiastical history, past and present and future, is as it was then.   The tempest still
rages ; the ships which went out of the harbor have
never returned.   They are still tossing to and fro, and

---

[1] Basil, Ep. 69, § 2 (52).   [2] Ep. 68, § 1 (48).

[3] Ep. 82.

beating against one another in the waves of controversy.

It may have been an advantage to have gazed for a
moment over this scene through the eyes and with the
experiences of Athanasius the Great.

312. CONSTANTINE.
Athanasius's play with the children.

318. *Oratio contra Gentes.*
De Incarnatione Verbi Dei.

325. Council of Nicaea.

326. Election and consecration of Athanasius.

335. Council of Tyre.

336. Banishment to Treves (first exile).
Death of Arius.

337. CONSTANTINE II. ⎫
CONSTANS ⎬ WEST.
CONSTANTIUS, EAST. ⎭
Return to Alexandria.

341. Council of Antioch.
Flight to Rome (second exile). Gregory, Bishop of Alexandria.
Encyclica ad Episcopos Epistola.

347. Council of Sardica.
Return to Alexandria.

350. CONSTANTIUS SOLE EMPEROR.
Apologia contra Arianos.

352. *De Decretis Synodi Nicenae.*
De Sententia Dionysii.

356. Expulsion of Athanasius by Syrianus (third exile). George, Bishop of Alexandria.
Flight to the Desert.
Death of Antony.
Epistola ad Episcopos Aegypti et Libyae.

358. *Apologia ad Constantium.*
Apologia de Fuga.
Epistola ad Monachos.
Orationes contra Arianos.
Epistola ad Serapionem de Spiritu Sancto.

359. *De Synodis.*
Council of Rimini.

361. JULIAN.
Death of Hosius.

362. Return to Alexandria.
Council of Alexandria.

363. Flight from Julian (fourth exile).
Return.

JOVIAN.

364. VALENTINIAN, WEST.
VALENS, EAST.

365. *De Incarnatione Dei Verbi et contra Arianos.*

367. Flight and return (fifth exile).
Vita Antonii (?).

369. *Epistola ad Afros.*

370. Basil, Bishop of Caesarea.

371. *Ad Epictetum Episcopum Corinthium.*

372. *Contra Apollinarium.*

373. Death.

LECTURE VIII.

MAHOMETANISM IN ITS RELATIONS TO THE EASTERN CHURCH.

There are few historical subjects on which the changes of our degrees of knowledge are so readily appreciable as in the case of the religion of Mahomet.[1] In the time of the Crusaders, Mahometans were vulgarly regarded as Pagan idolaters: it is now known that they abhor idolatry even more than we do. The very name of " Mahomet" ("Mawmet" or "Mummet") was then taken for a graven image: it is now known that he absolutely forbade the use of any material representation. It was then believed that the name of Christ was held accursed in the eyes of Mussulmans: it is now known that He is held to be one of the greatest, almost the greatest, of their prophets. It was believed till the last century that Mahomet rested his claims on false miracles: it is now known, and indeed urged as an argument against him, that he laid claim to no miracles at all. Voltaire, no less than Prideaux and Gagnier, believed him to be a wicked impostor: it is now known that, at least for a large part of his life, he was a sincere reformer and enthusiast. The gross blunders formerly made in his Western biographies, from an insufficient knowledge of Arabic,[2] are now rec-

---

[1] Of the authorities, the following may be selected:—

On the Life of Mahomet:
1. " The Koran." (Either Sale's translation into English or Kasimirsky's translation into French, or Lane's Selections.)
2. Caussin de Percival's " Histoire des Arabes." (1848.)
3. Weil's " Mohamed der Prophet." (1843.)
4. Sprenger's " Life of Mohamed." (1851.)
5. Muir's " Life of Mahomet." (1858, 1861.)

On Mahometan Customs:
1. Burckhardt's " Notes on the Bedouins." (1831.)
2. Lane's " Modern Egyptians." (1836 : singularly accurate.)
3. Burton's " Pilgrimage to Mecca and Medineh." (1856.)

[2] A signal instance is the version of the famous speech of Ali as given by Gibbon and others, from Gagnier's translation of Abu-l-Fida's Life of Mo-

tified; and yet further, the reaction which took place in his favor about fifty years since has been checked by increased information from original sources. The story of his epileptic fits, a few years ago much discredited, seems now to be incontrovertibly reëstablished; and we have a firmer ground than before for believing that a decided change came over the simplicity of his character after the establishment of his kingdom at Medina.

But there still remain two works unfinished, or not yet begun, before the completion of which any thorough representation of the rise of Mahometanism must be impossible to a Western student.

1. We need an edition and translation of the Koran which shall give two points hitherto almost unattempted, yet both almost indispensable to its right appreciation. First, the chronological arrangement of its chapters.[1] Secondly, a version which shall represent, not merely its matter, but the form of its rhymed diction.[2]

2. Two remarkable works on the life of the Prophet lately have appeared. Mr. Muir's biography (of which only the earlier portion had appeared when the first edition of this work was published) has now been completed, and adds details of the greatest interest to those which were known before. But of Dr. Sprenger's "Life of Mohamed" we have still only the fragment published at Allahabad in 1851, and the first volume (just appeared) of his larger work. This work, when finished, will contain the whole biography, and will have been founded on a wider collection of traditions than has ever been brought before the eyes of any single critic.

I trust, however, that the following brief remarks on the general connection of this subject with the history of the Church may be of service to the ecclesiastical student, and will justify the place which is assigned to it in these Lectures.

hamed: — " O Prophet, I will be thy vizier. I will beat out the teeth, pull out the eyes, rip up the bellies, and break the legs of all who oppose you."

This speech, so unlike the gentle character of Ali, is now known to have run thus: — " O Prophet, I will be thy vizier; though I am the youngest of them in years, and the weakest of them in eyes, and the biggest of them in belly [the invariable characteristic of an Arab child], and the most slender of them in legs, I, O Prophet of God, will be thy vizier over them." — *Lane's Selections from the Koran*, p. 62.

[1] An approximation to this may be found in Weil's Mohamed, p. 364, and thence in Dr. Macbride's Mahometanism, p. 108. The clue furnished even thus far is invaluable as a guide through the chaos in which the book at present lies.

[2] A few instances are given in Sprenger, pp. 121, 122. A metrical, though not a rhymed, version has since been published by Mr. Rodwell.

46

I. As the Eastern Church ought always to be
regarded as the background of the Western
Church, so Mahometanism, at least for the first
eight centuries of its existence, is the background of
both. The sword of the Saracen, the Turk,
and the Tartar constantly hung over the eastern confines of Christendom; and down to the
final repulse beneath the walls of Vienna, by John
Sobieski and the Duke of Lorraine, checked the policy
and restrained the passions of the Churches and nations
of Europe. The Crusades, the most important event
of the Middle Ages, owe their origin entirely to the
conflict with Islam. The Spanish Church and
monarchy rose out of a crusade of its own. Of that
crusade the traces have been left, not only in the Oriental manners and architecture of the Spanish nation,
but in the fierce bigotry of the Spanish Church; in
the Inquisition; in the union of chivalry, devotion,
and fanaticism which marks the Spanish institution of
the Society of Jesuits. The "tabula rasa"
which the ancient kingdom of Hungary presents, stripped of all its historical and ecclesiastical
monuments, is the lasting scar which the Turkish invasion and long occupation of that country have left on
the face of Europe. The agitations of the Reformation were constantly arrested by the terror
of the Sultan of Constantinople. Even our Prayer-book
has one mark of the importance of this panic, when,
in the collect for Good Friday, the name of "Turk"
was added to those of "Jews, Heretics, and Infidels,"
for whose conversion in earlier days prayers had been
offered up. Nor can it be forgotten that it is
the only higher religion which has hitherto
made progress in the vast continent of Africa. Whatever may be the future fortunes of African Christian-

ity, there can be no doubt that they will long be affected by its relations with the most fanatical and the most proselytizing portion of the Mussulman world in its negro converts.

II. But with the Eastern Church Mahometanism has a more direct connection. Not only have the outward fortunes of the Greek, Asiatic, and Russian[1] Churches been affected by their unceasing conflict with this their chief enemy, but it and they have a large part of their history and their condition in common. Spring-with the ing out of the same Oriental soil and climate, doctrines of the Eastern if not out of the bosom of the Oriental Church Church, itself, in part under its influence, in part by way of reaction against it, Mahometanism must be regarded as an eccentric heretical form of Eastern Christianity. This, in fact, was the ancient mode of regarding Mahomet. He was considered, not in the light of the founder of a new religion, but rather as one of the chief heresiarchs of the Church. Amongst them he is placed by Dante in the "Inferno."

Yet more than this, its progress, if not its rise, can be traced directly to those theological dissen-with the sions which form the main part of the ecclesias-ruin of the Eastern tical history of the East. We are told by Dean Church. Prideaux, that he originally undertook the "Life of Mahomet," as part of a "History of the Ruin of the Eastern Church," to which he was led by his sad reflection on the controversies of his own time in England;[2] and the remarks, deeply instructive and pathetic now as then, with which he opens his design, well express the connection between the two events: —

[1] See Lecture IX.

[2] Pref. to Prideaux's Life of Mahomet, pp. vi.–xvi. He gave up the plan from a fear of seeming to underrate the importance of the Trinitarian controversy, which, after he had begun his work, began to be agitated in England. Ibid. pp. xvii. xviii.

" Notwithstanding those earnest expectations and strong hopes, which we entertained of having our divisions healed, and all those breaches which they have caused in the Church again made up ; finding those of the separation still to retain the same spirit on the one side, and some others to be so violently bent on the other, against everything that might tend to mollify and allay it, as to frustrate all those excellent designs which have been laid in order thereto ; I thought I could not better let those men see what mischief they both do hereby to the common interest of Christianity, than by laying before them the grievous ruin and desolation, which from the like cause happened to the Churches of the East, once the most flourishing of the whole earth.　For they, having drawn the abstrusest niceties into controversy which were of little or no moment to that which is the chief end of our Holy Christian religion, and divided and subdivided about them into endless schisms and contentions, did thereby so destroy that peace, love, and charity from among them, which the Gospel was given to promote, and instead thereof continually provoked each other to that malice, rancor, and every evil work, that they lost the whole substance of their religion, while they thus eagerly contended for their own imaginations concerning it, and in a manner drove Christianity quite out of the world by those very controversies in which they disputed with each other about it. So that at length having wearied the patience and long-suffering of God, in thus turning this holy religion into a firebrand of hell for contention, strife, and violence among them, which was given them out of his infinite mercy to the quite contrary end, for the salvation of their souls, by living holily, righteously, and justly in this present world, he raised up the Saracens to be the instruments of his wrath to punish them for it ; who taking advantage of the weakness of power, and the distractions of councils, which these divisions had caused among them, soon overrun with a terrible devastation all the Eastern Provinces of the Roman Empire.

" And when the matter came to this trial, some of those who were the hottest contenders about Christianity became the first apostates from it ; and they, who would not afore part with a nicety, an abstruse notion, or an unreasonable scruple, for the peace of the Church, were soon brought by the sword at their throats, to give up the whole in compliance to the pleasure of a barbarous and savage conqueror.

" And no wonder that such, who had afore wrangled away the substance of their religion in contention and strife against each other, and eat out the very heart of it by that malice and rancor which they showed in their controversy about it, became easily content when under this force to part with the name also.

" A sad memento to us ; for of all Christian Churches now remaining in the world, which is there that hath more reason than we at this present, to learn instruction from this example, and take warning therefrom ? "

III. There were also direct points of con- Connection between the religion of Mahomet and between the Eastern Church which may be briefly no- etan and Christian ticed. teaching.

1. The rise of his power was considerably aided by a circle in Mecca, amongst whom was the favorite slave Zeyd, who were predisposed to accept a purer Zeyd. faith than the Paganism of Arabia. This predisposition they undoubtedly derived from intercourse with Eastern Christians, either from Abyssinia or Syria.[1]

2. Through the conflicting stories and legends of Mahomet's early life emerges one dark figure, of whom the little that is said only serves to stimulate our curiosity. There are not a few mysterious characters of history, who have done more than the world will ever know or acknowledge, more than they themselves expected or desired. Bahari, Bahyra, Sergius, George, what- Bahari. ever be the name of the Syrian or Nestorian monk of Bostra, is one of these. It seems impossible to refuse all credence to the manifold traditions which represent him as conversing with Mahomet on his first journey with the camel-drivers, as welcoming the youthful

[1] Sprenger, 38, 41 ; Muir, ii. 7, 50 ; Koran, c. 85.

Prophet with a presage of his coming greatness, and entering into the innermost circle of Mahomet's companions as the first and favorite friend.[1] In that case, we can hardly doubt that the Eastern Church, through this wandering heretical son, exercised a powerful control over the rising fortunes of Islam.

3. The local legends of the Syrian or Arabian Christians, whether as communicated by Bahari or by others, form the groundwork of Mahomet's knowledge of Christianity, or at least of those parts of Christianity which he incorporated with his own religion. It is in this manner that one branch of ecclesiastical or sacred literature, little studied and with but slight influence in Christendom itself, has acquired an importance not sufficiently appreciated. The genuine canonical Gospels were almost unknown to Mahomet.[2] But the apocryphal Gospels, which enshrine so many of the traditions of Palestine and Egypt respecting the localities of the sacred story, and which no doubt circulated widely in the lower classes both of the East and West, were quite familiar to him. From these, with the total ignorance of chronology which besets an Oriental mind, he compiled his account of " The Lord " Jesus." Hence came his description of the Holy Family ; the family of Amran, as he calls it, from a confused identification of Mary with Miriam the sister of Moses. Hence came the only conception which he

The apocryphal Gospels.

---

[1] See Prideaux, 41–48 ; Muir, i. 35. As an instance of the permanence of Oriental traditions respecting Bahari, I may mention that I heard from the lips of an Egyptian Arab the identical story respecting Bahari's death which was told to Maundeville in the fourteenth century (c. xii.), and to Schwarz, the collector of Jewish traditions, in this century (p. 346).

[2] The two exceptions are : 1. The assumption to himself of the name of the Paracletus, under the distorted form of Paraclytus, the " illustrious." The word, as far as we know, is only found in the canonical writings of S. John. 2. The account of the birth of John the Baptist, which seems to be taken from S. Luke. (Muir, ii. 313, 278.)

was able to form of the character and miracles of Christ;
a conception how inferior to the true one those only can
tell who have compared the grotesque puerility of the
apocryphal, with the grand sublimity of the canonical,
narrative.[1] The same excuse that has been made for
much of the unbelief of the West, must also be made for
the misbelief of the East. As we forgive the sceptics
of the last century for a hatred to Christianity which
they only knew as represented by the corrupt monarchy
and hierarchy of France, so may we still more forgive
Mahomet for the inferior place which he assigned
amongst the Prophets to Him whom he knew not as
the Christ of the Four Evangelists, but as the Christ
of the Gospel of the Infancy or of Nicodemus.

4. Some few of his doctrines and legends are remarkable, not only as having been derived by him The Im-
from Christian sources, but as having been re- maculate
ceived back from him into Christendom. One tion.
is the doctrine of the Immaculate conception of the
Virgin Mary. The assertion of her entire exemption
from all stain of sin first appears, so far as is known, in
a chapter in the Koran.[2] Another is the story The Seven
of the Seven Sleepers at Ephesus. It is, as Gib- Sleepers.
bon observes,[3] the most widely diffused, as it is the most
suggestive, of all ecclesiastical legends, and a large part
of its diffusion it owes to its adoption in the Koran. A
third is the belief in the mysterious personage " El
" Khudr," the " Green one," the counterpart, El Khudr.
from a better side, of the legend of the Wandering
Jew, but by Mussulmans identified partly with the
Christian S. George, partly with the Hebrew Elijah ;
the strange visitant of immortal youth, who appears
to set right the wrong, and solve the obscure.[4] The

---

[1] See Muir, ii. 288.   [2] Koran, iii. 31, 37.
[3] c. 33.   [4] Jelaladdin, 128, 406, 537.

story of El Khudr in the Koran is the earliest origin
of the moral apologue well known to English readers
through Parnell's poem of the Hermit and the Angel.

IV. Through the peculiar circumstances of its ap-
Compari-   pearance in Arabia, Mahometanism furnishes
son with
the Biblical a storehouse of illustration to Christian eccle-
history.   siastical history, such as can be found in none
of the heathen religions of the world. Its Eastern
origin gives to all its outward forms and expressions
a likeness to the corresponding terms and incidents of
the Old and New Testaments, which renders it invaluable as an aid to the Biblical commentator and historian.
Its rise and growth present parallels and contrasts to the
propagation of the Christian religion, and to the different
forms of the Christian Church, which can be found nowhere else. The comparison of its first beginnings with
those of Christianity, if it could be done without exaggeration on either side, would supply by its resemblances
an admirable commentary on the historical details, and
by its contrasts an admirable evidence to the Divine spirit
of the Gospel narrative. The circle of devoted disciples
gathered round their Master ; the jealousy and suspicion
of the Arabian hierarchy ; "the house of Arcam" where
their earliest meetings were held, as in " the house " and
" the upper room " of the Gospels and the Acts ; the constant recruitment of the new society from the humblest
classes, especially from slaves ;[1] the peculiarities of the
leading followers, especially the energy and zeal of the
last and most reluctant convert, Omar the persecutor
changed into Omar the devoted preacher and caliph,[2]
are parallels which help us at every turn to understand
the like passages in the story of the Gospels and the
Acts ; whilst the immeasurable contrast between the

[1] Sprenger, 159.
[2] For the comparison of Omar to S. Paul, see Muir, ii. 168.

Character which forms the centre of the one group, and that which forms the centre of the other, reveals to us the incommensurable difference between the faith of Christianity and the faith of Islam.

Or again, we can trace, with a clearness which throws a strong light on either side, the parallel be- Comparitween the confessedly natural part of the sub- son with ecclesisequent growth of the two ecclesiastical systems. astical history. In each case there is a marked descent from the vigor and purity of the first followers to the weakness and discord of those who succeed. In each case the Church is broken up into divisions large and small, and is developed into systems of which its first framers knew nothing. Even the wide rent between Eastern and Western, and yet more between Catholic and Protestant, Christendom, finds its instructive likeness in the rent between the Sonnees and Shiahs of the Mussulman world. The exaltation of S. Peter or of the Virgin Mary in the Roman Catholic Church, beyond the position which they occupied in the earliest ages, is met by the corresponding elevation of Ali amongst the Shiahs. The Pope was hardly more hateful in the eyes of Luther and Calvin, or the Greek Church in the eyes of the Pope, than Abubekr, Omar, and Othman have been in the eyes of the Persian and Indian Mahometans, who anathematize them as impostors and usurpers.

V. The Koran has special claims on our attention as the sacred book of the world which can best be The Koran compared with our own,[1] and which, by that compared with the comparison, furnishes not merely an evidence Bible. to the Divine supremacy of the Bible, but also brings into the strongest relief the true character of the con-

---

[1] M. de St. Hilaire (Journal des Savants, Aug. 1860, p. 460) adds the Veda. But the relations of the Veda to the Bible are so much more distant, as to make the comparison less easy.

tents and authority of the Scriptures, in contradistinction to the modern theories which have sometimes been
formed concerning them.

1. In its outward form there are two resemblances to
different portions of the Bible.   First, its chapters are stamped by a peculiarly fragmentary
and occasional character, written as they are at
different periods of Mahomet's life, suggested
by special incidents, modified by the successive
exigencies of the time, revealing the struggles of his
own inward feelings, and indicating the gradual progress
of his career.   These features of the book, which form
its chief charm and its chief difficulty, also furnish the
best proof of its genuineness.   Something of the same
charm, the same difficulty, and the same evidence is afforded by the Pauline Epistles.   The
force of Paley's argument in the "Horæ Paulinæ" may
be tested by its application to the Koran.   The difficulty
which we find in the Koran from the contravention of
the chronological order in the chapters, of which the
earliest in time are the latest in position, and some of
the latest in time amongst the earliest in position, is
parallel to the confusion introduced into the study of
S. Paul's Epistles by the disregard of their natural order,
which has placed the Epistles to the Thessalonians nearly at the end, and the Epistle to the Romans at the beginning, of the series.   Happily, in the case of the Pauline Epistles, the disarrangement has not yet become
irretrievably stereotyped, as in the Koran, and we are
therefore still able to reap the benefit of their true historical sequence without difficulty.

The other resemblance is of a totally different kind,
and to a totally different part of the Scriptures.   The
position which the Koran has assumed in the Mahometan world corresponds more nearly than that of any

Marginal notes:
Their resemblances.

The occasional character of the Koran,

and of the Pauline Epistles.

other book or system to the Law or Pentateuch in the
Jewish Church. It contains the civil as well *The legal*
as the moral and religious code of the nations *character*
of the
which it governs. Its precepts are regarded as *Koran and*
of the Pen-
binding in the same literal sense as was the case *tateuch.*
with the Mosaic ordinances. It has given birth to an
order or profession of men exactly similar to the Jewish
Scribes. The clergy, if we may so call them, of the
Mahometan Church are also its lawyers. The chief ecclesiastical functionary of Constantinople is also the
chief legal officer. His duty is to expound the text
of the Koran, and furnish such interpretations of it as
will facilitate its application to the changes of modern
times. The difficulty which arose in the Jewish Church,
from the expansion and diffusion of the Jewish system
beyond the pale of Palestine and of the chosen nation,
has also arisen, though not to the same degree, in Islam.
In Judaism the difficulty was solved by the submergence
of the narrower dispensation of the Law in the freedom
of the Gospel. In Mahometan countries it is solved by
forced interpretations, bending the sacred text to circumstances which it never contemplated, and which it
cannot truly cover.

2. But the contrasts are far greater than the resemblances. I do not speak of the acknowledged *Their con-*
superiority of the Christian doctrine, morals, or *trasts.*
philosophy. For this let a single instance suffice. What
is there in the Koran that can be named for a moment,
as a proof of inspiration, in comparison with S. Paul's
description of charity? I confine myself to the contrast of form between the two books. The Koran shows
us what the Bible would be if narrowed down to our
puny measurements, and what in its own divine and
universal excellence it actually is. In the comparison
between the two we clearly see how the Koran is

marked by those attributes which we sometimes falsely ascribe to the Bible ; how the peculiarities which we are sometimes afraid of acknowledging in the Bible are exactly those excellences which most clearly distinguish it from the Koran.

a) The Koran is uniform in style and mode of ex-
Uniformity pression. It is true, as I have just remarked,
of the
Koran.   that when chronologically arranged it exhibits to us, though in an indistinct form, the phases through which the mind of that one person passed. It is, as Mahomet's followers called it, "his character." It is, in this respect, as the Old Testament might be if it were composed of the writings of the single prophet Isaiah or Jeremiah, or the New Testament if it were composed of the writings of the single Apostle S. Paul. It is what the Bible as a whole would be, if from its pages were excluded all individual personalities of its various writers, all differences of time and place and character. But
Variety of the peculiarity both of the Hebrew and of the
the Bible. Christian Scriptures is, that they are not confined to one place or time or person. They abound in incidents so varied, as to give to the whole book that searching application to every condition and character of life which has been a principal source of its endless edification. The differences between the several prophets and historians of the Old Testament, between the several evangelists and apostles of the New Testament, are full of meaning. On the face of each book we see what each book was intended to be and to teach. In each portion of each book we see what is prose, and what is poetry ; what is allegory, or parable, or drama, or vision, or prophecy ; what is chronicle, or precept, or narrative. The Bible is in this way not only its own interpreter, but its own guide. The styles of Scripture are so many heaven-planted sign-posts to set our feet in

the right direction.　There is no other book which, within so short a compass, contains such " many-colored [πολυποίκιλος] wisdom," such a variety of minds, characters, and situations.

b) The Koran represents not merely one single person, but one single stage of society.　It is, with a few exceptions, purely Arabian.　It is what the Bible would be, if all external influences were obliterated, and it was wrapt up in a single phase of Jewish life.　But in fact the Bible, though the older portion of it is strictly Oriental, and though the latest portion of it belongs not to the modern, but to the ancient and now extinct, world, yet even in its outward forms contains within it the capacities for universal diffusion. Emanating from Palestine, the thoroughfare of the Asiatic and European nations, itself a country of the most diverse elements of life and nature ; it contains allusions to all those general topics which find a response everywhere.　Whilst the Koran (with a very few exceptions) notices no phenomena except those of the desert, no form of society except Arabian life, the Bible includes topics which come home to almost every condition of life and almost every climate.　The sea, the mountains, the town ; the pastoral, the civilized, the republican, the regal state ; can all find their expression in its words.　Women emerge from their Oriental seclusion and foreshadow the destinies of their sex in European Christendom.　And not only so, but Egypt, Chaldæa, Persia, Greece, Rome, all come into contact with its gradual formation ; so that, alone of sacred books, it avowedly includes the words and thoughts of other religions than its own ; alone of Oriental books, it has an affinity of aspect with the North and the West ; alone almost, of religious books, its story is constantly traversing the haunts of men and cities.　The Koran

[margin notes:] Narrowness of the Koran. Universality of the Bible.

"stays at home." The Bible is the book of the world, the companion of every traveller; read even when not believed, necessary even when unwelcome.

c) The Koran prides itself on its perfection of com-

Purity of style and text in the Koran.

position. Its pure Arabic style is regarded as a proof of its divinity. To translate it into foreign languages[1] is esteemed by orthodox Mussulmans to be impious, and when it is translated its beauty and interest evaporate. The book is believed to be in every word and point the transcript of the Divine original, Mahomet to have been literally "the sacred penman." No various readings exist. Whatever it once had were destroyed by the Caliph Othman. Such is the strength of the Koran. In far other and opposite quarters lies the strength of the Bible; and Christian missionaries, who are, I believe, constantly assailed by Mussulman controversialists with arguments drawn from this contrast, ought to be well grounded in the knowledge that in what their adver-

Variations and peculiarities of the text of the Bible.

saries regard as our weakness is in fact our real strength. Its language is not classical, but in the Old Testament uncouth, in the New Testament debased; yet, both in the Old and New, just such as suits the truths which it has to convey.[2] The primitive forms of Hebrew are as well suited for the abrupt simplicity of the prophetic revelations, as they would be ill suited for science or philosophy. The indefinite fluctuating state of the Greek language at the time of the Christian era, admirably lends itself to the fusion of thought which the Christian religion produced. Its

---

1 The only exceptions to this rule are such versions as unite paraphrase with translation.

2 This is well drawn out by Professor Pusey in regard to the style of the Prophets (Commentary on Hosea, pp. 5, 6), and by Professor Jowett in regard to the Greek of the New Testament (Commentary on S. Paul, i. p. 135; Essay on Interpretation, p. 390).

various readings are innumerable, and, in the New Testament, form one of the most instructive fields of theological study. Its inspiration is not, as in the Koran, attached to its words, and therefore is not, as is the Koran, confined to the original language. It is not only capable of translation, but lends itself to translation with peculiar facility. The poetry of the Old Testament, depending for the most part, not on rhyme or metre, but on parallelism, reappears with almost equal force in every version. The translations of the New Testament, from the superiority of most modern languages to the debased state of Greek at the time of the Christian era, are often superior in beauty of style and diction to the original. The Apostles themselves used freely a rude version of the Old Testament. We use, without scruple, conflicting and erroneous versions of both. The essence of the Bible, if the essence be in its spirit, and not in its letter, makes itself felt through all.

d) The Koran claims a uniform completeness of materials. It incorporates, indeed, some of the earlier Jewish, Christian, and Arabian traditions, but it professes to be one book. It has no degrees of authority in its several chapters, except in the few instances of direct abrogation of precepts. With these exceptions, it is entirely stationary. It has no progress, and therefore no sequence, and no coherence. The Bible, in all these respects, stands on what some modern writers would deem a lower level, but on what is in fact a far higher one. Its composition extends over two thousand eventful years. In most of its books are imbedded fragments of some earlier work, which have served to keep alive and to exercise the industry and acuteness of critics. It is not one Testament, but two. It is not one book, but many.

Monotony of the Koran.

Multiplicity of the Bible.

The very names by which it was called in early times
indicate the plurality of its parts. The word "Bible,"
which by a happy solecism expresses the unity of its
general design, is of far later date and lower authority
than the words "Scriptures, The Books, *Biblia Sacra*," [1]
by which it was called for the first twelve centuries of
the Christian era, and which expressed the still grander
and bolder idea of its diversity. The most exact definition which it gives of its own inspiration is, that it is
" of sundry times and in divers manners." [2] In the fact
and in the recognition of this gradual, partial, progressive nature of the Biblical revelation, we find the best
answer to most of its difficulties and the best guarantee
of its perpetual endurance.

e) The Koran contains the whole religion of Ma-
The exclu-   homet. It is to the Mussulman, in one sense,
siveness of
the Koran.   far more than the Bible is to the Christian. It
is his code of laws, his creed, and (to a great extent)
his liturgy. The Bible, on the other hand, demands for
its full effect, the institutions, the teaching, the art, the
society of Christendom. It propagates itself by other
means than the mere multiplication of its printed or
written copies. Sacred pictures, as is often said, are
the Bibles of the unlettered. Good men are living
Bibles. Creeds are Bibles in miniature. Its truths
are capable of expansion and progression, far beyond
the mere letter of their statement. The lives and deeds,
and, above all, the One Life and the One Work which

---

[1] For the original neuter plural of Biblia Sacra (the Sacred *Books*), the
feminine singular (whence is derived our word " Bible," Die Bibel, La Bible,
La Bibbia, &c.) first appears in the 13th century. See Ducange in voce
Biblia Sacra ; Smith's Dict. of Bible under *Bible.*

[2] Heb. i. 1. I have elsewhere had occasion to enlarge on the manifold
instruction conveyed by this Scriptural definition of Scripture revelation.
Precisely this same use of the passage was made, in my hearing, by the
present venerable metropolitan of Moscow, in answer to difficulties suggested by parts of the Old Testament.

it records, spread their influence almost irrespectively of the written words in which they were originally recorded. It is not in the close limitation of the stream to its parent spring, but in the wide overflow of its waters, that the true fountain of Biblical inspiration proves its divine abundance and vitality.

> "Mohamed's truth lay in a holy book,
>   Christ's in a Sacred Life.

> " So while the world rolls on from change to change,
>   And realms of thought expand,
>   The letter stands without expanse or range,
>   Stiff as a dead man's hand.

> " While, as the life-blood fills the growing form,
>   The Spirit Christ has shed
>   Flows through the ripening ages fresh and warm,
>   More felt than heard or read." [1]

VI. It would be irrelevant to enter into any detailed comparison of the doctrines and practices of Islam with those of Christianity. But they contain points of special contact or contrast which illustrate the course of Christian theology and ecclesiastical usages, as the peculiarities of the Koran illustrate the position of the Bible and the course of Christian exegesis.

1. On the one hand it is the extreme Protestantism, or Puritanism, of the East. Whether or not the Iconoclasm of the seventh century in Constan- *Likeness to Puritanism.* tinople had any direct connection with the nearly contemporaneous rise of Mahometanism, there can be little doubt that the two movements had rise in the same feeling of reaction against the excessive attention to outward objects of devotion. In the case of Mahomet, there was superadded the sentiment, whether imitated from the Hebrew Scriptures or instinctive in the Arabian

---

[1] Milnes's Palm-Leaves, 38. The Preface contains an excellent summary of the better side of Mahometanism.

branch of the Semitic race, which returned with all its
Its Icono-
clasm. force to the belief in the One Unseen God. The
Iconoclasm of Mahomet far exceeds that either
of Leo the Isaurian or of John Knox. The Second
Commandment, with Mussulmans, as with the Jews, was
construed literally into the prohibition of all representations of living creatures of all kinds; not merely in
sacred places, but everywhere. The distinction drawn
in the West, between churches and houses, between objects of worship and objects of art, was in the simpler
East unknown. The very form and name of "Arabesque"
ornamentation, always taken from inanimate, never from
animated nature,[1] tells the shifts to which Mahometans
were driven, when civilization compelled them to use an
art which their religion virtually forbade. The one exception in the Alhambra (the same that occurred in the
Palace of Solomon) is an exception that proves the rule.
The rude misshapen "lions" that support the fountain
in that beautiful court which bears their name, show
how unaccustomed to such representations were the
hands which to all other parts of the building have
given so exquisite a finish.

Other points of resemblance to the Reformed branches
Its simpli-   of the Christian Church —the more remarkable
city and its
preaching. from the excessive ritualism of the Eastern
Churches, and their almost entire neglect of preaching
— are the simplicity of the Mussulman ceremonial, and
the importance attached to sermons. The service of
their sacred day, Friday, is, like Puritan worship, chiefly
distinguished by the delivery of a discourse.[2] In the
pilgrimage to Mecca, the delivery of the sermon is said
to be the most impressive of all the solemnities. There
are few Christian preachers who might not envy the

---

[1] See Burton, ii. 157.

[2] An example is given in Lane's Modern Egyptians, i. 100.

effect described by one[1] not given to exaggerate religious influences :

" The pulpit at Meccah is surmounted by a gilt polygonal
pointed steeple, like an obelisk.   A straight narrow staircase
leads up to it.   It stands in the great court of the Mosque.
When noon drew nigh, we repaired to the harem for the sake
of hearing the sermon.   Descending to the cloisters below the
Gate of Ziyadah, I stood wonderstruck by the scene before me.
The vast quadrangle was crowded with worshippers sitting in
long rows, and everywhere facing the central black tower ; the
showy colors of their dresses were not to be surpassed by a garden of the most brilliant flowers, and such diversity of detail as
would probably not be seen massed together in any other building upon earth.   The women, a dull and sombre-looking group,
sat apart in their peculiar place.   The Pacha stood on the roof
of Zem-Zem, surrounded by guards in Nizam uniform.   Where
the principal Ulema stationed themselves, the crowd was thicker;
and in the more auspicious spots nought was to be seen but a
pavement of heads and shoulders.   Nothing seemed to move but
a few dervishes, who, censer in hand, sidled through the rows
and received the unsolicited alms of the faithful.   Apparently in
the midst, and raised above the crowd by the tall pointed pulpit,
whose gilt spire flamed in the sun, sat the preacher, an old man
with snowy beard.   The style of head-dress called the Taylasan
(a scarf thrown over the head, with one end brought round
under the chin and passed over the left shoulder) covered his
turban, which was as white[2] as his robes, and a short staff supported his left hand.   Presently he arose, took the staff in his
right hand, pronounced a few inaudible words (' Peace be with
you, and the mercy of God, and his blessings,') and sat down
again on one of the lower steps, whilst a Muezzin, at the foot of
the pulpit, recited the call to sermon.   Then the old man stood
up and began to preach.   As the majestic figure began to exert
itself, there was a deep silence.   Presently a general ' Amin '

[1] Burton's Pilgrimage, ii. 314 ; iii. 177.

[2] In former times, the preacher was habited from head to foot in black, and
two muezzins held black flags fixed in rings, one on each side of the pulpit,
with the staves propped upon the first step.

was intoned by the crowd at the conclusion of some long sentence. And at last, towards the end of the sermon, every third or fourth word was followed by the simultaneous rise and fall of thousands of voices. I have seen the religious ceremonies of many lands, but never — nowhere — aught so solemn, so impressive as this spectacle."

2. But in spite of the likeness to the more modern and northern forms of Western Christianity, Mahometanism after all has far more affinity to the older, and especially to the Eastern forms of the Christian Church.

Likeness to Catholicism.

Most of the peculiarities that characterize the Greek or the Latin Church, have their counterparts in the Mahometan system.

a) In one instance, the Jewish element survives almost unaltered. "The Mahometan religion," says Gibbon, as if in praise of its purity, "has "no Priest and no Sacrifice." This statement must be considerably qualified. Sacrifice, though it forms no part of the daily worship in the mosque, yet on solemn occasions is an essential element of the Mussulman ritual. It is generally, if not universally, of the nature of a thank-offering, and, as in the case of most ancient sacrifices, is combined with an act of benevolence to the poor. To the Bedouin Arabs it is almost their only act of devotion. It was only under the pretext of sacrificing on the tomb of Aaron that Burckhardt was able to enter Petra. The railroad, recently opened from the Danube to the Black Sea, was inaugurated by the sacrifice of two sheep. The vast slaughter [1] of victims at Mecca is the only scene now existing in the world that recalls the ancient sacrifices of Jew or Pagan. In short, it might be said that, so far from Mahometanism being the only religion without a sacrifice, it is the only

Its sacrifices.

[1] See Burton, iii. 303, 313.

civilized religion that retains a sacrifice, not spiritually or mystically, but in the literal ancient sense.

b) Although a priesthood, in the sense of an hereditary or sacrificing caste, is not found in the Mahometan world, yet a priesthood in the sense in which it is found in Protestant or Catholic Christendom, a powerful hierarchy, possessed of property and influence, and swaying the religious feelings of mankind, exists in Mahometan even more than in Christian countries. The identification of the Koran with the Law at once raises the order of the interpreters of the Koran to a level with the highest legal dignitaries of the West. The office of Scribes, as we have seen, is exactly reproduced. The Sheykh-el-Islam, the great ecclesiastical functionary at Constantinople, who unites in himself the functions of the Primate and the Lord Chancellor, is, or at least was till lately, as considerable a personage as any prelate in Christendom, short of the Pope. The Sheykh-el-Bekr, at Cairo, the lineal descendant of Abu-Bekr, the administrator of the property of the mosques, is at least as high in popular estimation as Archimandrite, Abbot, or Dean, in East or West. The Muftis[1] and the Dervishes are a body as formidable to Mussulman rulers and laymen as any body of ecclesiastics or monks would be to the same classes amongst ourselves. To the dervishes the same blame and the same praise might be awarded as to the friars of the Western, or the hermits of the Eastern Church.[2]

Its priesthood.

c) If it is startling to find this system of earthly mediation in a religion which we are often taught to consider as allowing no intervening obstacle

Veneration for saints.

---

[1] This importance does not attach to the Imams, or the Preachers. They are mostly persons of humble condition and attainments, and combine their office with some other occupation.

[2] See Lecture X.; and comp. Wolff's Life, i. 483.

between man and the One True God, still more are we
surprised to find that the same system of celestial mediation in the form of the worship or veneration of
saints,[1] which prevails through the older portions of
Christendom, has overspread the whole of the Mahometan world. Bedouins who go nowhere else to pray,[2]
will pray beside the tomb of a saint. The " Welys," or
white tombs of Mussulman saints, form a necessary feature of all Mussulman landscapes. It is a significant
fact, that the westernmost outpost of Mahometan worship — the last vestige of the retiring tide of Turkish
conquest from Europe — is the tomb of a Turkish saint.
On a height above the Danube, at Buda, the little chapel
still remains, visited once a year by Mussulman pilgrims,
who have to thread their way to it up a hill which is
crowned with a Calvary, and through a vineyard clus-
tering with the accursed grape. The Arabian traveller
of the Middle Ages, who visits Thebes,[3] passes over all
the splendor of its ruins, and mentions only the grave
of a Mussulman hermit. The sanctity of the dead
man is attested by the same means as in the Eastern
Churches,[4] generally by the supposed incorruptibility of
the corpse. The intercession of a well-known saint is
invested with peculiar potency. However much the
descendants of a companion of the Prophet plunder or
oppress, they are secure in the celestial protection of
their ecclesiastical ancestor.

These features it has in common with the doctrines

---

[1] Compare Wolff's Life, i. 505.

[2] Comp. Sprenger, 107. It was against the wish of Mahomet himself. See
Burton, ii. 71.

[3] " I went to the town of Luxor, which is small but pretty. There one
sees the tomb of the pious hermit of Abou l'Hagag, near which is a hermitage." — *Ibn Batoutah*, p. 107. This is all that he says of Thebes. Ap.
p. 33.

[4] Burton, ii. 111.

and practices of the Latin, as well as the Greek Church. They show, on the one hand, that such points being the products of a religion outside the pale of Christendom, they cannot be regarded as essentially and peculiarly Christian; and, on the other hand, that, being the natural growth of human feeling everywhere, they may be regarded calmly, and without the terror or the irritation which is produced when they are looked upon as the heritage of a near and rival Church or sect.

3. There are yet other points in which Mahometanism, as being essentially an Oriental religion, approaches most nearly to the forms of Eastern Christendom, though retaining some defects and some excellences of the East, which even Eastern Churches have modified or rejected. *Its Eastern character.*

a) The legal, literal, local, ceremonial character of the religion of Mussulmans is, in spite of its simplicity, carried to a pitch beyond the utmost demands either of Rome or of Russia. What their ideas of the Koran are, compared even with the narrowest ideas of the Bible, we have already seen. Prayer is reduced to a mechanical as distinct from a mental act, beyond any ritual observances in the West. It is striking to see the figures along the banks of the Nile going through their prostrations, at the rising of the sun, with the uniformity and regularity of clockwork; but it resembles the worship of machines rather than of reasonable beings. Within a confined circle of morality the code of the Koran makes doubtless a deeper impression than has been made on Christians by the code of the Bible. But beyond that circle there is but little of the vivifying influence which the Bible has unquestionably exercised even over the unconscious instincts and feelings of Christendom. Morality and religion, which stand sufficiently far asunder in the practice of Oriental Chris- *Its ceremonial.*

tianity, stand further still apart in the practice of a large part of Islam.

b) The absence of religious art which we have already observed in Eastern, as distinct from Western, Christendom, is carried to the highest point by Mahometans. Partly this arises from the iconoclastic tendency before mentioned; but mainly it is the result of that carelessness of artistic effort which belongs to all Oriental nations. However tedious is the monotony of the Christian Churches of the East, that of Mahometan mosques is still more so.

c) But if art is banished from their worship, reason is no less banished from the creed, at least of the vulgar. The reckless extravagance of credulity which strikes us in Oriental Christians, strikes us still more in Mahometans. There are no miracles in the Koran; but this only brings out into stronger relief the insatiable avidity with which any expression that could bear such a meaning has been magnified and multiplied into the wildest portents. It is the childish invention of the Arabian Nights let loose upon the unseen world. " I knew a man in Christ above fourteen " years ago," says S. Paul,[1] " (whether in the body or " out of the body I know not, God knoweth); such an " one caught up into the third heaven. . . . How that " he was caught up into paradise, and heard unspeak- " able things which it is not lawful for man to utter." Neither Scripture nor tradition says one word further to break this silence thus imposed upon himself by the Apostle. Contrast with this the endless stories told (as it would seem from his latest biographer[2]) by Mahomet, after his vision of the nocturnal flight from Mecca, to his inquiring disciples, of the wonders of Paradise, of the peculiarities of the gigantic Borak, of the personal

Absence of art.

Credulity.

---

[1] 2 Cor. xii. 2–6.　　　　[2] Sprenger's Mohamed, i. 126, 136.

appearance of each of the departed prophets, of the
leaves of the tree of life, of the immeasurable distances
between the heavenly spheres.

d) The frantic excitement of the old Oriental religions still lingers in their modern representatives. Excite-
The mad gambols of the Greek and Syrian pil- ment.
grims round the Chapel of the Holy Sepulchre have
been sufficiently told.   But they ought in justice to
be compared with the still wilder frenzy of the Mussulman dervishes.   Both are Eastern ; both belong to
those wild forms of religion which S. Paul labored to
restrain amongst the first Christian converts.[1]   But the
Mahometan shows in excess what the other shows in
comparative moderation.   Of all modern ceremonials,
none probably comes so near the description of the
priests of Baal, cutting themselves with knives and
lancets, leaping on and around the altar, and shouting
from morning till evening, "O Baal, hear us !" as the
celebration of the Prophet's birth-day at Cairo,[2] when
the dervishes, by the constant repetition of the name
of "Allah, Allah," are worked into a state of uncon-
sciousness, in which they plant swords in their breasts,
tear live serpents with their teeth, eat bottles of glass,
and finally lie prostrate on the ground for the chief of
their order to ride on horseback over their bodies.

e) As in these extravagances, so also in some of its
noblest aspects, we see the same spirit reappearing in
Mahometanism that we have already noticed in the
Churches of the East.

That manly independence which knows no false
shame or reserve in professing its religion in Indepen-
the face of the world, is the noble heritage of dence.

---

[1] 1 Cor. xiv. 26–40.

[2] I write from my own recollections.   An accurate description is given in
Lane's Modern Egyptians, ii. 200–222.

the Turk and the Arab, as much as of the Greek or the
Russian. It is this which renders the Mussulman, even
more than the Christian layman of the East, a priest to
himself, independent of the instructions and the influence of the hierarchy, whom he yet regards with profound veneration. It is this (combined no doubt with
the mechanical nature of their prayers, to which I have
before alluded) that renders their devotions so natural, so easy, so public. It is this which lends to every
Oriental congregation, but especially to every Mussulman congregation, its main distinction from every Western congregation, namely, the immense preponderance
of men over women. In many Western Churches the
man is the exception amongst the worshippers; in all
Eastern mosques the exception is the woman.

The gravity and the temperance of the Mussulman
Gravity
and tem-
perance.
are doubtless congenial to the dignity and simplicity of Oriental life. In these respects, both
Western and Eastern Christianity, though gaining more,
have lost much. "An Eastern city has no exhibitions
" of paintings, no concerts, no dramatic representations,
" only recitations of tales in prose and verse in coffee-
" houses; and the prohibition of games of chance ex-
" cludes cards and dice. Wine can only be drunk in
" private. . . . Gravity, not dissipation, is, at least in
" public, the characteristic of a Mahometan nation." [1]

Finally, the Mussulman preserves to the world the
Resigna-
tion.
truest and most literal likeness of that ancient
Jewish faith which is expressed in the word
"Islam," "Resignation" to the will of God. However
distorted it may be into fatalism and apathy, yet it
is still a powerful motive both in action and in suffering. God is present to them, in a sense in which
He is rarely present to us amidst the hurry and con-

1 Dr. Macbride's Mahometanism, p. 179.

fusion of the West.   If "the love of God" is a feeling
peculiar to Christendom, yet the "fear of God" within
a narrow circle may be profitably studied, even by
Christians, in the belief and the conduct of the followers of Islam.

These are the qualities which, being not so much Mahometan or Arabian, as Oriental, primitive, Semitic, and
(in the best sense of the word) Jewish, no Christian can
regard without reverence, even in their humblest form;
nor can he abandon the hope that if ever the time
should come for the gathering of the followers of Mahomet within the Christian fold, gifts like these need
not be altogether lost to the world and the Church in
the process of that transition; that the habits of temperance, devotion, and resignation, which Mussulman
belief encourages, may be combined with the grace,
the humility, the purity, the freedom of the Gospel.

LECTURE IX.

THE RUSSIAN CHURCH.

THE main accessible authorities for the history of the Russian Church are, as far as I have been able to ascertain them, the following: —

1. Nestor, the Monk of Kieff. A. D. 1116. 5 vols. (Edited by Schlözer. German. 1802.)
2. Karamsin's "History of Russia." 11 vols. 8vo., to 1618. (Translated into French.)
3. Oustralieff's "History of Russia." 5 vols. to 1815. (Translated, not published, by the Rev. R. W. Blackmore.)
4. Strahl's and Hermann's "History of Russia." 6 vols., to 1815. (German.)
5. Mouravieff's "History of the Russian Church." 1 vol. 8vo., to 1710. (Translated by the Rev. R. W. Blackmore.)
6. Strahl's "Contributions to the Russian Church History." 1 vol. 8vo. (German.) It contains: —
    a. A Catalogue Raisonnée of the Documentary History of the Russian Church.
    b. A Chronological Summary of Ecclesiastical History in Russia.
    c. A History of the Russian Sects.
    d. A Chronological List of the Russian Hierarchy.
7. "Doctrines of the Russian Church." 1 vol. 8vo. (Translated by the Rev. R. W. Blackmore.)
8. "History of the Church of Russia." (An able summary in the Christian Remembrancer, vol. x. p. 245. By the Rev. James B. Mozley.)
9. Adelung's "Catalogue Raisonnée of Travellers in Russia."
10. "Monumenta Historiæ Russicæ." 2 vols. 8vo. (Being a collection of foreign State Papers bearing on Russia.)
11. Haxthausen's "Researches in Russia." (German and French.)

THE third great historical manifestation of the Oriental Church is the formation of the Russian _{The Russian Church.} Church and Empire.

Before I enter upon its leading divisions, let me give the main reasons why a history so obscure in _{Its importance.} itself, and in some of its features so repulsive, deserves to be specially noticed in connection with the history of the Eastern Church, and why it is fitly considered before we cross the threshold of the history which most concerns ourselves, the history of the Western Church generally, and of the English Church in particular.

I. The Russian Church is the only important portion of Eastern Christendom which presents any con- _{Its history continuous and national.} tinuous history. The two other epochs which we have noticed, although highly instructive in themselves, are yet isolated events, rather than long sustained movements. They represent particular phases of Eastern religion. They do not represent it in its active organization, in its effects on national character, or its relations to the ordinary vicissitudes of men and of Empires. Western ecclesiastical history would lose more than half its charms, if it had not for its subject the great national Churches of Europe. And in like manner Eastern ecclesiastical history must fail of its purpose, unless it can find some field in which we can trace from century to century, and in their full-blown development, those principles and practices of the Oriental Church which have been already unfolded in general terms.

This field is presented in the Russian Church. In it alone we trace a growth and progress analogous to that which Western or Latin Christianity found in the Teutonic tribes of Europe. And, although the Northern and Sclavonic elements form the basis of the Church and Empire of Russia, yet by its situation, by its origin, and by the singular powers of imitation with which its members are gifted, it is essentially Asiatic and Oriental. And, further, through the gradual incorporation of Russia into the commonwealth of Western nations, the Eastern Church has acquired a voice or speech, which it has lost, or has never gained, elsewhere. The feeling which the native Russians entertain towards the Western world is a likeness of the feeling which we ourselves entertain towards the Eastern world. The Russian word for a foreigner, but especially for a German, is "the dumb," "the speechless;" and it has happened within the experience of an English traveller, that Russian peasants, passing by and seeing a conversation going on in a foreign language, have exclaimed in astonishment, — "Look at those people; they are "making a noise, and yet they cannot speak!" Very similar to this is the way in which, as a general rule, we regard, almost of necessity, the Eastern Churches generally. To us, with whatever merits of their own, they are dumb. Their languages, their customs, their feelings, are unknown to us. We pass by and see them doing or saying something wholly unintelligible to us, and we say, — "Look at those people; they are "making a noise, and yet they cannot speak!" In a great measure this difficulty severs us from the Russian Church, as well as from the other branches of Oriental Christendom. Still, in Russia, if anywhere in the East, we can from time to time listen and understand with advantage. The Sclavonic power of imitation opens a door which elsewhere is closed. The Western influences which from the age of Peter have streamed into Russia, though they have often undermined the national character, have yet, where this is not the case, given to it the power, not only of expressing itself in Western languages, but of understanding Western ideas, and adapting itself to Western minds. A Russian alone presents, amidst whatever defects and drawbacks, this singular interest; that he is an Asiatic,[1] but with the sensibility and intelligence of a European:[2] that he is, if we will, a barbarian, but with the speech and communications of civilization. "Scratch him," said the Prince de Ligne, "and you will always find the Tartar underneath." Most true; but it is just that superficial coating of civilized life which brings "the Tartar" into contact with us, whom else we should never catch at all. "The Tartar," the Oriental, who in the Armenian, the Syrian, or the Abyssinian Church eludes our grasp altogether, in the Russian Church is within our touch, within our questioning, within our hearing.

II. Another peculiarity of the history of the Church of Russia is that it enables us within a short compass to go through the whole field of ec- clesiastical history, which in the West, whilst familiar to us in detail, is too vast to be comprehended in any one survey. With many differences, produced by diverse causes, of climate, of theology, of race, the history of the Russian Empire and Church presents a parallel to the history of the whole European Church, from first to last, not merely fanciful and arbitrary,

Its parallel to Western Christendom.

[1] A few of their Eastern customs may be mentioned, to which, doubtless, any one better acquainted with the country could add many more. 1. The practice of taking off the shoes on entering any great presence. This, though now discontinued, was till lately commemorated by the picture of Joshua taking off his shoes at the entrance of the Hall of the Kremlin. 2. The corner of a room is still the place of honor. The sacred picture is always in the corner. The Czar, at the coronation banquet, sits in the corner. The corners of the Patriarchal church are occupied by the most illustrious tombs. 3. The seclusion of women lasted till the time of Peter, and still is kept up (in church) in the Russian sects. 4. The Orientalism of ecclesiastical usages they share with the rest of the Eastern Church.

[2] " They look as if they had had a Turk for their father and a Quaker for their mother." — *Princess Dashkoff's Memoirs*, ii. 318.

but resulting from its passage through similar phases, in which the likenesses are more strongly brought out by the broad differences just mentioned. The conversion of the Sclavonic races was to the Church of Constantinople, what the conversion of the Teutonic races was to the Church of Rome. The Papacy and the Empire of Charlemagne had, as we shall see, their dim reflection on the throne of Moscow. Russia, as well as Europe, had its Middle Ages, though, as might be expected from its later start in the race of civilization, extending for a longer period. The Church of Russia, as well as the Church of Europe, has had its Reformation, almost its Revolution, its internal parties, and its countless sects.

The events are few; the characters are simple; but we shall read in them again and again, as in a parable, our own shortcomings, our own controversies, our own losses. The parts of the drama are differently cast. The Eastern element comes in to modify and qualify principles which we have here carried out to their full length, and beyond it; but it is this very inversion of familiar objects and watchwords which is so useful a result of the study of ecclesiastical history, and which is best learned where the course of events is at once so unlike and so like to our own, as in the Church of Russia.

III. In Russian history, the religious aspect, on which Its national our thoughts must be fixed in these Lectures, character. is on the one hand that part of it which is the least known, and yet on the other hand is full of interest, and not beyond our apprehension. It has been sometimes maintained by writers on political philosophy, that, however important in the formation of individual life and character, Religion cannot be reckoned amongst the leading elements of European prog-

ress and civilization. I do not enter into the general
discussion; but the great Empire of which we are speaking, if it has not been civilized, has unquestionably been
kept alive, by its religious spirit.   As in all the Eastern
nations, so in Russia, the national and the religious
elements have been identified far more closely than in
the West, and this identification has been continued,
at least outwardly, in a more unbroken form.   Its religious festivals are still national; its national festivals
are still religious.   Probably the last great his- The French
torical event which in any European state has invasion.
externally assumed a religious, almost an ecclesiastical,
form is nearly the only event familiar to most of us
in Russian history, namely, the expulsion of the French
from Moscow.   From the moment when Napoleon, according to the popular belief, was struck to the ground
with awe at the sight of the thousand towers of the
Holy City, as they burst upon his view when he stood
on the Hill of Salutation, to the moment when the
tidings came of the final retreat " of the Gauls and
" of the thirty nations," as they are called, the whole
atmosphere of the Russian resistance is religious as
much as it is patriotic.   The sojourn of the French
in the Kremlin is already interwoven with religious
legends, as if it had been an event of the Middle
Ages.   A magnificent cathedral has been added to the
countless churches already existing in Moscow to commemorate the deliverance.   " God with us " is the motto
which adorns its gate-way, as it was the watchword of
the armies of the Czar.   The sects, on the other hand,
regarded Napoleon as their deliverer.   Some of their
most extravagant fanatics formed a deputation to him
at Moscow.   According to them he was a natural son
of Catherine II., was brought up in a Russian university, and still lives concealed in Turkey, but will re-
50

appear as a chosen vessel in the moment[1] of their triumph. The services of Christmas Day are almost obscured by those which celebrate the retreat of the invaders on that same day, the 25th of December, 1812, from the Russian soil; the last of that long succession of national thanksgivings, which begin with the victory of the Don and the flight of Tamerlane, and end with the victory of the Beresina and the flight of Napoleon. "How art thou fallen from heaven, O "Lucifer, son of the morning!" This is the lesson appointed for the services of that day. "There shall "be signs in the sun, and in the moon, and in the stars, "and upon the earth distress of nations with perplex-"ity. Look up and lift up your heads, for your re-"demption draweth nigh." This is the Gospel of the day. "Who through faith subdued kingdoms, waxed "valiant in fight, turned to flight the armies of the "aliens." This is the Epistle.

I have dwelt on the religious aspect of this crisis, both because it may serve to remind us that there is at least one event in the history of the Eastern Church with which we are all acquainted; and also because, coming as it does at the end of a series of similar deliverances and celebrations, it brings before us one special interest which the Russian ecclesiastical history possesses; namely, its relation, both by way of likeness and illustration, to the history of the Jewish Church of old. Hardly in any European nation shall we so well understand the identity of the religious and national life in the ancient Theocracy, as through the struggles of the Russian people against their several invaders; the keenness with which they appropriate the history of the Old dispensation is but the natural result of their (in many respects) analogous situation. In the

[1] Revue des Deux Mondes, xv. 611.

sculptures of the cathedral of which I have just spoken
as the monument of the deliverance of Moscow, it is
the execution of one and the same idea, when the
groups from Russian history alternate with scenes from
the story of Joshua's entrance into Palestine, of Debo-
rah encouraging Barak, of David returning from the
slaughter of Goliath, of the coronation and the grandeur of Solomon.

For these reasons, amongst others, I propose to give
a rapid view of the main characteristics of the history
of the Russian Church. Its doctrines, its ritual, and its
actual condition have been virtually described in connection with the rest of Oriental Christendom, and to
repeat this, or to represent as peculiarly Russian what
is common to the whole East, would be at once superfluous and misleading.

The story of the Russian Church divides it- Periods of
self into four periods : — the history
of the Rus-
sian Church.

I. The period of its foundation, from the close of the
10th century to the beginning of the 14th.

II. The period of its consolidation, from the beginning of the 14th century to the middle of the 17th.

III. The period of its transition, from the middle of
the 17th century to the beginning of the 18th.

IV. The period of its reformation, from the beginning of the 18th century to the present time.

We begin, then, with the foundation of the Church
in the conversion of the Russian nation.

It is a standing reproach cast by the Latin Church in
the teeth of her elder sisters of the East, that Constantinople and its dependencies have never been centres
of missionary operations comparable to those which
have emanated from Rome, or from England.

The truth of the reproach must, in a great measure,

be conceded, and arises from causes of which I have spoken before. But still it must not be accepted without considerable modifications. It was not without reason that Gregory Nazianzen,[1] in a passage which has been happily applied of late to our own country, describes Constantinople, even as early as the fourth century, as "a city which is the "eye of the world, the strongest by sea and land, the "bond of union between East and West, to which the "most distant extremes from all sides come together, "and to which they look up as to a common centre and "emporium of the faith." Even on the Teutonic races one irregular attempt was made by the Byzantine Church, which, had it succeeded, would have changed the face of Christendom. The mission of the Greek Bishop, Ulfilas, to the Gothic tribes, wrought wonders for a time.[2] Down to the conversion of Clovis, whatever Christianity they had received was from this source; and when Augustine, in his great work on the "City of God," celebrates the charity and clemency of Alaric and his followers during the sack of Rome, we must remember that these Christian graces were entirely due to the teaching of Oriental missionaries, heretics though they were. The very word "Church," as used throughout the Teutonic tribes, was often in former times, and is still by some learned scholars, derived from the adaptation of the Greek word κυριακή, as received from the Byzantine preachers. But the rapid changes of events in the West swept away any permanent traces of the work of Ulfilas. It has now nothing but a philological interest. Its chief memorial is

Missions from Constantinople to the Teutonic tribes,

---

[1] i. 755. Quoted in a remarkable sermon on the "Evangelization of India," by the Rev. G. H. Curteis, p. 35.

[2] The whole of the complicated question of the mission of Ulfilas is well discussed in Professor Müller's Lectures on the Science of Language, 181–186.

the venerable volume of his translation of the Bible
into the Gothic tongue, the parent, so to speak, of all
the Teutonic versions of Scripture, — the silver-lettered
manuscript, fitly deposited in the chief library of the
Scandinavian people, in the University of Upsala.[1]

It is not in the Teutonic but in the Sclavonic race
that the Eastern Church has reaped the richest to the
harvest.   The conversion of the Sclavonic tribes tribes. Sclavonic
on the confines of the Byzantine Empire is not to be
altogether overlooked.   One name at least of European
significance has been contributed to ecclesiastical history from this quarter.   John Huss of Bohemia was a
genuine son of the Sclavonic family, and it is perhaps
more than a mere fancy which traces a likeness between his conceptions of reformation and those of his
more Eastern brethren ; and which derives his spiritual
pedigree, if on the one hand from our own English
Wycliffe, on the other hand, in remoter times, from the
two Greek Bishops to whom I shall have occasion again
to refer, Cyril and Methodius, the Apostles of Bulgaria
and Moravia.

But the centre and life of the Sclavonic race have
always been in those wilds of Scythia,[2] which have alternately invited or sent forth conquerors to and from
the adjacent seats of civilization in Greece or Asia
Minor.   The story of the Russian conversion Conversion
may be divided into two portions, the legen- of Russia.
dary and the historical ; and each portion in the
present instance is so characteristic of the nation, and
so illustrative of like events in the West, that I

[1] There are also fragments in the Ambrosian Library at Milan, procured
from the monastery of Bobbio.   (Ib. 184.)

[2] The name "Russ," Hebrew *Rosh*, LXX. 'Ρῶς, unfortunately mistrans-
lated in the English version "the chief Prince," first appears in Ezek.
xxxviii. 2, 3, xxxix. 1.   It is the only name of a modern nation found in
the Old Testament. (See *Gesenius*.)

will not scruple to dwell upon each of them in detail.

1. I have before spoken of the peculiar connection
Legendary
account. of Oriental Christianity with the natural features of the regions which it has traversed : and in all countries this connection is more visible in the primitive stages of nations than in their subsequent growth. The geographical and historical relations of a country so monotonous as Russia are indeed far less striking than in the diversified forms of Greece and Syria, of Egypt and Chaldæa. Endless forests, endless undulating plains, invite no local associations and foster no romantic legends. But there is one feature of Russian scenery truly grand, its network of magnificent rivers. These, important for its political and commercial interests, are the threads with which its religious destinies have been always curiously interwoven. Turn your mind's eye to the vast stream of the Dnieper, the old Borysthenes, as it rolls into the Euxine. Over the banks of that stream, five hundred miles from its mouth, hangs a low range of hills, low for any other country, but high for the level steppes of Russia, and
Voyage of
S. Andrew. therefore called Kieff, " the mountain." From that mountain, we are told, a noble prospect commands the course of the river; and up the course of that river, on his way from Sinope to Rome, came, according to the ancient legend, Andrew, the Apostle of Greece, the Apostle of Scythia : and as he rose in the morning and saw the heights of Kieff, on which he planted the first cross, he said, — " See you those hills ? " For on those hills shall hereafter shine forth the grace " of God. There shall be a great city, and God shall " cause many churches to rise within it." [1] And so he passed on by the north to Italy.

[1] See Nestor (ed. Schlözer), ii. 93. See also the strange legend which

But northward another legend meets us of more grotesque shape.   A saint of doubtful name and Voyage of origin[1] started from Italy on one of those voy- S. Antony. ages which mediæval credulity delighted to invent and to receive.   He was thrown into the Tiber with a millstone round his neck, and on or with this millstone passed out of the Mediterranean Sea into the Atlantic Ocean; through the islands of the Baltic he passed on into the Neva; through the Neva he reached the Lake of Ladoga; from the Ladoga Lake he passed into the broad Volkhoff; and from the Volkhoff, on the shores of the Lake of Ilmen, he found himself by the walls of the great Novgorod, the irresistible republic of Old Russia, the precursor of the northern capital of the New.

These are fables of which every line is a quaint lesson in geography.   But they also dimly foreshadow, even as geography itself foreshadows, the fortunes of the Empires and Churches which are founded upon them.   The Dnieper and the Neva are the two inlets by which life and light have penetrated into the vast deserts of Russia, from the East and from the West; through the race of the Norman Ruric, and through the race of the Byzantine Cæsars; through Vladimir in the first age, and through Peter in the last age, of the Russian Church.   Kieff and Petersburg form the two extremities of Russian history, ecclesiastical as well as civil.   The central sacred city of Moscow forms the point of transition, the point of contact between them, and will form the chief scene of the second and third periods of the Russian Church, as Petersburg of the fourth, and Kieff of the first.

derives the name of Russia from S. Andrew's exclamation when put into the hot-vapor bath: Ἱδρωσα, "I sweat."   Travels of Macarius, ii. 186.

[1] He was either S. Nicolas or Antony the Roman.   A cup is shown in the treasury of the Assumption Church as brought by him.   See Travels of Macarius, ii. 192, 193.

2. From this legendary beginning I pass to the actual
Historical completion of the conversion of Russia as it is
account of described by Nestor,[1] himself a monk of Kieff,
the con-
version. who occupies in the history of Russia almost
the same position as that held in our own by the Venerable Bede.

The time coincides with a great epoch in Europe, the close of the tenth century. When throughout the West the end of the world was fearfully expected, when the Latin Church was overclouded with the deepest despondency, when the Papal See had become the prey of ruffians and profligates, then it was that the Eastern Church, silently and almost unconsciously, bore into the world her mightiest offspring.

The one seed of energy and activity that had been in the ninth century scattered over Europe had also fallen
Ruric, upon Russia. The Norman race, which played
A. D. 862. so important a part in the civil and religious history of the West, as the allies or protectors of the Papal See, and as the founders of new dynasties in France, in Italy, in Sicily, and in England, had also established themselves on the throne of Russia in the
Vladimir, family of Ruric. It is to his descendant Vladi-
A. D. 980. mir that the Russian Church looks back as its founder. In the conversion of each of the European nations there is a kind of foretaste or reflection of the national character and religion, which gives to the study of them an interest over and above their intrinsic importance. The conversations of Ethelbert with Augustine, and of Clovis with Remigius, present peculiar elements characteristic respectively of the French and English people. This is eminently the case with the conversion of Vladimir. And the account has further these two special advantages. First, though not actually

[1] He lived A. D. 1050 to 1116.   (Nestor, ed. Schlözer, i. 7, 8, 9.)

by an eye-witness, it is yet by a narrator within the next generation, and is thus given with a detail which may serve to illustrate all like events. Nowhere else shall we see so clearly the mixture of craft and simplicity, of rough barbarian sense and wild superstition; of savage force bowing down before the mere display of a civilized religion. We may be grieved, as we read, that through such weak and trivial means such great results should be brought about; but every such case is a repetition on a gigantic scale, and in a various sense, of the parable of the grain of mustard seed. Secondly, the story of the conversion of Vladimir gives us an opportunity, such as we rarely possess, of a general survey of the whole of Christendom, from a contemporary point of view. He, in this position won for him by his ancestors or himself, had become the object of attention to the different forms of religion then prevailing in the world. He is approached by each in turn. He approaches each in turn. We have, if not the very words in which he and they described their mutual impressions, yet at least the words in which one who lived almost within their generation thought it likely that they would have spoken.

Let us, as nearly as possible, follow the narrative of Nestor, and apply as we proceed the remarks which I have just made.

Whatever beginnings of the Christian faith had already been imparted to Russia here and there had made but little permanent impression. Adelbert, the great Western missionary of this period, attacked the Sclavonic Pagans, not in Russia, but in the Isle of Rugen,[1] on the extreme point of which a heathen temple remained till the twelfth century. Oskold and Dir may A.D. 866. have been terrified into baptism by a storm at Constan-

[1] Neander, vi. 70.

51

tinople; Olga may have been attracted to it by a sense
A. D. 965. of policy; but her grandson Vladimir was a
ferocious prince, as much distinguished by his zeal for
the rude idolatry of his countrymen as for his savage
crimes.

To him, we are told, midway between the 6000th and
A. D. 986. 7000th year of the world according to the ancient Eastern era, in the year 986 according to the
Christian era of the West, there came envoys from the
different religions of the then known world.

First came the Bulgarian Mussulmans from the Volga.[1]
Mission "Wise and prudent prince as thou art, thou
from Bul-
garia. "knowest neither law nor religion. Believe in
"ours, and honor Mahomet." — "In what does your
"religion consist?" asked Vladimir. "We believe in
"God," they replied, "but we believe also in what the
"Prophet teaches. Be circumcised, abstain from pork,
"drink no wine; and after death choose out of seventy
"beautiful wives the most beautiful." Vladimir listened
to them for the last reason. But that which he did not
like was circumcision, the abstinence from pork, and
above all the prohibition of drinking. "Drinking is
"the great delight of Russians," he said; "we cannot
"live without it."

Next came the representatives of Western Christen-
From the dom. The question whence they came, or were
West. thought to come, wavers in the story. From
the Pope? From Germany? From the sect then widely known, now almost forgotten, premature Protestants,
the Paulicians?[2] "The Pope," they said, "begs us to
"tell you, your country is like ours, but not your re-
"ligion. Ours is the right. We fear God, who made
"the heaven and earth, the stars and the moon, and
A. D. 986. "every living creature, whilst thy Gods are of

[1] Karamsin, i. 259.   [2] Ibid. i. 260.

"wood." — "What does your law command?" asked
Vladimir.   "We fast," they said, "to the best of our
"power; and when any one eats or drinks, he does it
"in honor of God, as we have been told by our master,
"S. Paul." [1]   "Go home," said Vladimir.   "Our fathers
"did not believe in your religion, nor receive it from
"the Pope."

Next, on being informed of this, came some Jews
(who lived among the Khozars.) [2]   "We have Mission
"heard say that the Mahometans and the Chris- from the
"tians have tried to persuade thee to adopt their belief.
"The Christians believe in Him whom we have cruci-
"fied.   We believe in one God, the God of Abraham,
"Isaac, and Jacob."—"In what does your law consist?"
asked Vladimir.   "Our law requires circumcision, pro-
"hibits pork and hare, and enjoins the observance of
"Saturday."—"Where then is your country?"   "At
"Jerusalem." — "What is Jerusalem?"   "God was
"wroth with our forefathers; he dispersed us for our
"sins throughout the world, and our country has fallen
"into the hands of Christians."—"What," said Vladimir, "you wish to teach others — you whom God has
"rejected and dispersed?   If God had loved you and
"your law he would never have scattered you abroad;
"do you wish, perhaps, that we should suffer the
"same?"

In each of these answers we detect the characteristic
temper of the Russian, his love of drinking, his tenacity
of ancestral customs, his belief in the Divine right of
success.

Another agency now appears on the scene.   It is not

---

[1] Compare the expressions respecting S. Paul in Karamsin, i. 399.   For
the sect itself, see Gibbon, c. 54.   Their persecution by the Empress Theodora
is one of the worst instances of Eastern intolerance.

[2] For the Jews amongst the Khozars, see Nestor (French trans. p. 118.)

a nameless barbarian, as before. It is, so the chronicler tells us, "a philosopher from Greece." The
glory of Grecian culture still hung about its
ancient seats, and the fittest harbinger of Christian truth, even in dealing with the savage Vladimir,
was thought to be a Greek; not a priest or a missionary, but a philosopher.

Mission from Greece.

A. D. 986.

"We have heard," said he, "that the Mahometans
"have sent to lead you to adopt their belief. Their
"religion and their practices are abominations in the
"face of heaven and earth, and judgment will fall upon
"them, as of old on Sodom and Gomorrah. This is
"what they do who call Mahomet a prophet."

This calls forth the first moral spark that we have
seen in Vladimir's mind. He spat upon the ground and
said, "This is shameful."

"We have also heard," said the philosopher, "that
"messengers have come from Rome to teach you.
"Their belief differs somewhat from ours. They cel-
"ebrate the mass with unleavened bread, therefore they
"have not the true religion." Such was the point on
which the two greatest Churches of the world had been
torn asunder, and into which Vladimir did not further
inquire. He then took up the word himself and said:
"I have also had Jews here who said that the Germans
"and Greeks believe on Him whom we crucified." The
philosopher assented. "Why was He crucified?" asked
Vladimir. "If you will listen," replied the philosopher,
"I will tell you all from the beginning." "With pleas-
"ure," replied Vladimir. And the philosopher then proceeded to relate all the Divine acts and deeds from the
beginning of the world; the whole course, we may say,
of ecclesiastical history, coming to a characteristic close
in the Seventh General Council. He then defined the
true faith, and spoke of the future reward of the just

and punishment of the impious, and at the same time showed to Vladimir a tablet on which was painted the scene of the last judgment. Then, showing him on the right[1] the just, who, filled with joy, were entering into Paradise, he made him remark on the left the A.D. 986. sinners who were going into hell. Vladimir, as he looked at the picture, heaved a sigh and said, "Happy "are those who are on the right; woe to the sinners "who are on the left." "If you wish," said the philosopher, "to enter with the just who are on the right, "consent to be baptized." Vladimir reflected profoundly, and said, "I will wait yet a little while." For he wished first to be instructed about each religion. But he loaded the philosopher with presents and sent him away.

Vladimir in the next year sent for the nobles and elders, and told them of the different interviews. A.D. 987. "You know, O Prince," they said, "that no one talks "evil of his religion, but that all, on the contrary, "praise their own. If you wish to know the exact "truth, you have wise men; send them to examine the "faith of each and the manner of their worship."

We need not follow them throughout their journey. They reported that the Mussulmans prayed with their heads covered, and that their stench was insupportable; and that the German and Roman churches had no ornaments nor beauty, though better than the Mussulman mosques.

But the nobles insisted that the decision should not be made without knowing first what was the Mission to Greek religion; and accordingly the envoys Constantinople. proceeded to the city which they call Tzarogorod. In that barbarous name we recognize "the City of the

---

[1] See the corresponding story of Bogoris and Methodius. (Robertson, ii. 344.)

" Czar," or " King," the great Constantinople.[1] What it was at that period, the splendor of its ceremonial, both of Church and state, even in the most minute detail, is known to us from the nearly contemporary account of A. D. 987. the German embassy from Otho. Basil Porphyrogenitus[2] was on the throne with his brother Constantine ; and his words, in giving orders to the Patriarch to prepare for a magnificent reception of the strangers, indicate more than many treatises the importance he attached to the outward show of the ceremonial of the Church, as his grandfather had to the outward show of the ceremonial of the court. " Let them see," he said, " the glory of our God." The service was that of a high festival either of S. John Chrysostom, or of the death of the Virgin.

It was in the church — magnificent even now in its fallen state, then all gorgeous with gold and mosaics — of S. Sophia. Even had they been as far as Rome itself, they would have seen nothing equal to it. S. Peter, as it now is, was far in the future. Cologne Cathedral was not yet born. The boast of Justinian was still the masterpiece of Christian architecture.

Church of S. Sophia.

The Russian envoys were placed in a convenient position. The incense smoked, the chants resounded, the Patriarch was in his most splendid vestments. One incident is preserved in a Byzantine annalist which the Russian chronicler has omitted. " The Russians were

---

[1] According to the fragment of the Byzantine Chronicles in Karamsin (i. 393,) they went also " to the Patriarch of Rome, who is called the Pope," and returned with the hope of persuading Vladimir to join the Latin Church. The ground on which the nobles desired to hear of the Greek religion was " that Constantinople was more illustrious than Rome." Compare a (spurious) letter by Vladimir's physician. Ibid. 354.

[2] Karamsin, i. 392. Also called " Bulgaroctonus," from his savage conquest of the Bulgarians. See, for his reign of fifty years, Finlay's Byzantine Empire, bk. ii. c. ii. § 2.

"struck," he says, "by the multitude of lights and the
"chanting of the hymns; but what most filled them
"with astonishment was the appearance of the dea-
"cons and sub-deacons issuing from the sanctuary, with
"torches in their hands;" and, as we happen to know
from an earlier source,[1] with white linen wings on their
shoulders, at whose presence the people fell on their
knees and cried, "Kyrie Eleison!" The Russians took
their guides by the hand, and said: "All that A. D. 987.
"we have seen is awful and majestic, but this is super-
"natural. We have seen young men with wings, in
"dazzling robes, who, without touching the ground,
"chanted in the air, Holy! holy! holy! and this is
"what has most surprised us." The guides replied (and
the Byzantine historian repeats it without changing the
tone of his narrative, even in the slightest degree):
"What! do you not know that angels come down from
"heaven to mingle in our services?" "You are right,"
said the simple-minded Russians; "we want no further
"proof; send us home again."

It is a striking instance of the effect produced on a
barbarous people by the union of religious awe and outward magnificence, and the dexterity with which the
Byzantine courtiers turned the credulity of the Russian
envoys to account, is an example of the origin of many
of the miracles of the Middle Ages; not wholly fraud,
nor wholly invention, but a union of the two; a symbolical ceremony taken for a supernatural occurrence,
and the mistake fostered, not by deliberate imposture,
but by the difficulty of resisting the immense temptation to deception which such mistakes afforded. A like

---

[1] Quoted in Bunsen's "Christianity and Mankind," vii. 45. The same tendency to impose upon foreigners appears in the account of Luitprand's embassy, when he was received with the roaring of golden lions and the war-
bling of golden birds. (Gibbon, c. 53.)

confusion supports to this day the supposed miracle of the Holy Fire at Jerusalem.

As in many similar cases, the results far outlasted the sin or the weakness of the first beginning. " We knew " not," said the envoys on their return, " whether we " were not in heaven ; in truth, it would be impossible " on earth to find such riches and magnificence. We " cannot describe to you all that we have seen. We " can only believe that there in all likelihood one is in " the presence of God, and that the worship of other " countries is there entirely eclipsed. We shall never for- " get so much grandeur. Whosoever has seen so sweet " a spectacle will be pleased with nothing elsewhere. It " is impossible for us to remain where we are."

The rest of the story may be shortly told. With A.D. 987. some few Eastern touches, it is not unlike the A.D. 988. national conversions of the West. Vladimir, still in a state of hesitation, besieged the city of Cherson in the Crimea, and, like Clovis, vowed that he would be baptized if he succeeded. He then sent to demand from the Emperor Basil the hand of his sister Anne in marriage, under the promise of his own conversion, and under the threat of doing to Constantinople as he had done to Cherson. With some difficulty Anne was induced to sacrifice herself to the barbarian prince, in the hope of averting so great a danger and effecting so great a good. Her sister Theophano had already been established on the throne of the German Otho. She acquired a more lasting fame as the channel through which Christianity penetrated into Russia.

He was baptized [1] accordingly at Cherson, and then Baptism of issued orders for a great baptism of his people Vladimir. at Kieff. They also hesitated for a short time. But a like argument, combined with the threat of the

---

[1] For the accompanying miracle, see Mouravieff, pp. 14, 354.

Grand-Duke, convinced them also.   The huge wooden
idol Peroun was dragged over the hills at a horse's tail,
mercilessly scourged by twelve mounted pursuers, and
thrown into the Dnieper, where it was guided and
pushed along the stream till it finally disappeared
down the rapids in a spot long afterwards known as
the Bay of Peroun.   The whole people of Kieff were
immersed in the same river, some sitting on the banks,
some plunged in, others swimming, whilst the priests
read the prayers.   " It was a sight," says Nestor, " won-
" derfully curious and beautiful to see ; and when the
" whole people were baptized, each one returned to
" his own house."   The spot was consecrated by the
first Christian church, and Kieff, which had already, as
we have seen from old traditions, been the Glastonbury,
became henceforward the Canterbury, of the Russian
Empire.

Let me dwell on the points of this story which contain its singular significance as the foundation A.D. 988.
of the Russian Church.

1. Observe the immense influence of Constantinople.
The effect of the Roman ceremonial on the Teu- Influence
                                                 of Constan-
tonic barbarians was powerful ; but the effect of tinople.
the Byzantine ritual on the Sclavonic barbarians must
have been more powerful still.   They returned believing
that they had caught a glimpse of heaven itself.   They
clung to the recollections and to the support of that magnificent city, as children round the feet of a mother.   In
modern times and in political matters the connection between Russia and Constantinople has been tarnished by
baser motives, by constant suspicions, by the degradation of the one and the ambition of the other.   But in
earlier times, and in ecclesiastical matters, the relations
between the two were always preserved with filial fidelity ; the more remarkable from the reversal of their re-

spective positions in everything else. It is this which
makes the Russian Church so truly Eastern. France,
Spain, Germany, have all in diverse degrees ceased to
represent the type of the Roman Church, to which they
owe their first faith. But in the Cathedral at Moscow is
still maintained, in essential points, the likeness of the
worship which won the hearts of Vladimir's ambassadors in the Cathedral of S. Sophia; and, although the
jurisdiction of the Patriarch of Constantinople has
been gradually relaxed in proportion to the increasing
power of the Russian hierarchy and nation, yet the outward bond between the two Churches has never been
broken. The Metropolitans of Russia were for five centuries either Byzantines or closely allied to Byzantium.
Every successive change in their condition since has
been confirmed by the Church of Constantinople. The
transferrence of the see from Kieff to Moscow, the elevation of the Primacy into a Patriarchate, and finally the
transformation of the Patriarchate into a Synod, have all
been recognized by the Eastern Patriarchs themselves;
and, whatever inward jealousy they may have of their
powerful neighbor, there is no ground for the popular
Western notion that the Church of Russia is in a state
of antagonism to the other Churches of the East. Whatever its errors, or its crimes, or its excellences, it cannot
be divided from the general fortunes of Oriental Christendom. The union of Vladimir with Anne is still a
living power.

2. I have elsewhere described the inheritance of
Eastern doctrine and practice which Russia
thus received and developed in common with
other Oriental Churches. But two or three points
stand out conspicuously in the history of the conversion. One such characteristic of the Eastern Church
generally, but eminently characteristic of Russian eccle-

Veneration for sacred pictures.

siastical history, is the influence exercised over this its
first beginnings by the effect of the sacred pictures on
the mind of the Grand-Duke.   That picture of the Last
Judgment inaugurated, so to speak, the influence of its
innumerable successors of the same or of other sacred
subjects, down to the present day.   No veneration of
relics or images in the West can convey any adequate
notion of the veneration for pictures in Russia.   It is
the main support and stay of their religious faith and
practice ; it is like the rigid observance of Sunday to a
Scotchman, or the Auto da Fé to an ancient Spaniard,
or fasting to a Copt, or singing of hymns to Methodists.
Everywhere, in public and in private, the sacred picture
is the consecrating element.   In the corner of every
room, at the corner of every street, over gateways, in
offices, in steamers, in stations, in taverns, is the picture
hung, with the lamp burning before it.   In domestic life
it plays the part of the family bible, of the wedding gift,
of the birthday present, of the ancestral portrait.   In the
national life, it is the watchword, the flag, which has supported the courage of generals and roused the patriotism
of troops.   It has gone forth to meet the Tartars, or the
Poles, or the French.   It has thus been·carried by Demetrius, by Peter, by Suwaroff, by Kutusoff.   A taste,
a passion for pictures, not as works of art, but as emblems, as lessons, as instructions, is thus engendered and
multiplied in common life beyond all example elsewhere.
The symbolical representation of sacred truth extends
even to the natural world.   A dove or pigeon is considered as a living picture (" obraz ") of the Holy Spirit,
and therefore no Russian peasant will eat one.   Even a
Syrian traveller from the distant East, in the seventeenth century, observed what no less strikes an English traveller from the West in the nineteenth century,
how (to use his own words) —

"The Muscovites are vastly attached to the love of pictures, neither regarding the beauty of the painting nor the skill of the painter, for with them a beautiful and an ugly painting are all one, and they honor and bow to them perpetually, though the figure be only a daub of children, or a sketch upon a leaf of paper; so that, of a whole army, there is not a single man but carries in his knapsack a gaudy picture within a simple cover, with which he never parts, and wherever he halts he sets it up on a piece of wood and worships it." [1]

And when from common life we pass to the church, still the same peculiarity presents itself. Frequently the groups of passers-by may be seen looking at the elaborate representations of this or that Scriptural event or legendary scene, or a New Testament parable or an Old Testament miracle. One better informed than the rest will explain it to his companions, and these pictorial communications are probably the chief sources of religious instruction imparted to the mass of the Russian peasantry. Or enter within a church, at least any church such as those at Moscow, which best represent the national feeling. There the veneration has reached a pitch which gives an aspect to the whole building as unlike any European church as the widest difference of European churches can separate each from each. From top to bottom, from side to side, walls and roof and screen and columns are a mass of gilded pictures; not one of any artistic value, not one put in for the sake of show or effect, but all cast in the same ancient mould, or overcast with the same venerable hue; and each one, from the smallest figure in the smallest compartment to the gigantic faces which look down with their large open eyes from the arched vaults above, performing its own part, and bearing a relation to the whole. One only other style of sacred architecture is recalled by

1 Travels of Macarius, ii. 50.

this strange sight. It is as if four columns (for there
are but four in an Orthodox Eastern church) had been
transplanted from the mighty forest of pillars in the
great temple of Egyptian Thebes. High and massive
as these pillars do these four columns rise up, and round
and round they are painted, with ever recurring pairs,
as there of Egyptian gods, so here of Christian martyrs.
And as the walls there are hung from head to foot with
battle-pieces or sacred processions, so here with Apostles,
Prophets, Patriarchs, parables, history, legend. The
Seven Councils of the Church follow in exact and uniform order, closing on the western end with a huge
representation of the Last Judgment, such as converted
Vladimir. In one sense the resemblance to Egypt is
purely accidental. But in another sense it is almost
inevitable. Egypt and Russia are the only two great
nations in which pictures or pictorial emblems have
entered so deeply into the national life and religious
instruction of the people. Hieroglyphics and pictures
constituted more than half the learning of those grown-
up children of the ancient world; they still constitute
more than half the education of these grown-up children
of the modern world. It may be questioned whether
an uninstructed Englishman or an uninstructed Russian
would be most inclined to look upon the other as an
absolute Pagan, the one for never being able to say his
prayers without pictures, the other for never saying his
prayers with them. And when we remember that some
of these pictures have, besides their interest as the
emblems of truth to a barbarian and child-like people,
acquired the historical associations involved in the part
they have taken in great national events, it is not surprising that the combination of religious and patriotic
feelings in Russia should have raised their veneration to
a pitch by us almost inconceivable. The history of a

single picture becomes almost the history of the nation. Brought by Vladimir from Cherson, believed to have been painted by Constantine the Great, used on every great occasion of national thanksgiving and deliverance, deposited in the most sacred of Russian cathedrals, the picture, as it is called, of "Our Lady of Vladimir" represents exactly the idea of an ancient palladium; whilst the fact that it is not a graven statue vindicates it in their eyes from all likeness to a Pagan idol. It is a sentiment which, according to Western views, cannot be imitated, but which, if only in order to be avoided, must be understood and explained.

3. Another prominent feature of the conversion is the fact that alone of all the European nations (unless Spain and Hungary are counted exceptions) Russia was Christianized without the agency of missionaries, and chiefly by the direct example, influence, or command (whichever we choose to call it) of its Prince. There is Martin the Apostle of Gaul, and Augustine of England, and Boniface of Germany; but there is no Apostle of Russia except Vladimir, who bears the same title as that of Constantine, "Isapostolos;" "*Vladimir equal to an Apostle.*"

Influence of authority.

It is a remarkable example of the religious aspect of the temporal sovereign, which, though cherished everywhere in the Eastern Churches, has, as we shall hereafter see, always exercised a more powerful influence in Russia, from the peculiarly docile and yielding character of the Sclavonic race. "Our country is large and fer-"tile, but we have no order amongst us. Come amongst "us to reign and to rule over us."[1] Such was the address of the Russians to the Norman chief Ruric, their first sovereign. And in like manner the same argument of higher authority carried with it their conversion.

[1] Haxthausen, iii. 34.

"If the Greek religion had not been good," said the nobles to Vladimir, "it would not have been adopted by "your grandmother Olga, wisest of mortals." And again: "If baptism were not good," said the people of Kieff, "it would not have been adopted by our princes and "nobles." As far as the clergy were concerned, they were mere passive instruments in the hands of the prince and the people. There were no tithes, with one single exception which proves the rule. They lived, as they have lived ever since, on the free offerings of their flocks. The Russian establishment is a combination, difficult to square with our preconceived English notions, of the strictest form of a State religion with the widest application of the voluntary principle. I shall not here dwell further on this aspect of the Russian religion. We shall have occasion to return to it hereafter, and on one side of it, the most hopeful of all the peculiarities of the Eastern Church, I have dwelt before; namely, the vast weight and responsibility thrown into the hands of its laymen by the principles of the Church itself.

4. But there is another point connected with this, which helps us to a feature of the conversion not distinctly brought out in the narrative of Nestor. It appears from that narrative, and Bible. has been often observed, that, as compared with the Western nations, the spread of the Christian religion was more rapid and more easy than in any other country. No violent collision, no martyrdom, either of Christian or Pagan, marked the progress of the new religion. The docile character of the people, the outward and ceremonial nature of that form of Christianity which they received, the slight hold of their old mythology, may all account for this. But it would be wrong to omit one element in the transaction, on which much

stress is laid by later Russian historians,[1] and which undoubtedly was a matter of great moment in the mode of exhibiting Christianity to the nation.   In every country converted by the Latin Church the Scriptures and the Liturgy had been introduced, not in the vernacular language of the original or conquered population, but in the language of the government or missionaries, the Latin language of the old Empire and new Church of Rome.   Our own sense and experience are sufficient to tell us what a formidable obstacle must have been created by this single cause to the mutual and general understanding of the new faith; what barriers between the conquerors and conquered, between the educated and the vulgar, above all, between the clergy and the laity.   The ill effects of the tardy translation of our own Bible and Prayer-book into Irish amply indicate the probable results.   In the Eastern Church, on the other hand, a contrary method was everywhere followed.   The same principle which had led Jerome, in his cell at Bethlehem, to translate the Bible into what was then the one known language of the West, was adopted by the Oriental Church with regard to all the nations that came within its sphere.   Hence, in the remote East, sprang up the Syriac, Coptic, Armenian, and Ethiopic versions; hence, in the only attempt (which I have already described) made by the Eastern Church on the Western barbarians, Ulfilas immortalized himself by producing the only wide-spread translation of the Scriptures which existed in any Western language till A. D. 863.   the times of Wycliffe.   In like manner, at the approach of the Greek Church to the Sclavonic nations on the shores of the Danube, the first labor of the mis-

---

[1] For the whole of this view of the effect of the Sclavonic translation, see Oustralieff's History of Russia, c. i. § 5 (as communicated to me in a MS translation by the Rev. R. W. Blackmore.)

sionaries, Cyril or (Constantine) and Methodius, was to invent an alphabet for the yet unwritten language of the Sclavonic tribes, in order at once to render into this language the whole of the New Testament, except the Apocalypse, and the whole of the Psalter in the Old. Bulgaria, by its position on the frontiers of the Greek and Latin Churches, was a constant source of discord between them.   On this occasion the use of the version already sanctioned by Constantinople was also referred to Rome, and was allowed on grounds which in fact justify the use of vernacular translations everywhere; though it was afterwards condemned by the same authority, with that remarkable inconsistency and fluctuation which have always distinguished the policy of the Papal chair on the subject of the circulation of the Bible.   It was sanctioned on the ground that the Psalmist says, " Let everything that hath breath praise " the Lord," that is, in the different languages.   It was condemned on the ground that Methodius was a heretic, by a strange confusion between him and his Arian predecessor, Ulfilas.[1]

The translation of Cyril had been in existence for a century before the conversion of Vladimir, and *Russian language.* was thus at once ready for use by the Greek Bishops and clergy who accompanied the Princess Anne to Kieff.   Of these hardly anything is known.   But Cyril and Methodius, if any one, must be considered by anticipation as the first Christian teachers of Russia: their rude alphabet first instructed the Russian nation in letters, and by its quaint Greek characters still testifies in every Russian book, and on every Russian house or shop, the Greek source of the religion and literature of the Empire.   The Russian language was thus elevated to a dignity unknown at that time to any of the

---

[1] For the authorities, see Gieseler, 3d period, 2d sec. § 38.

barbarous dialects of Western Europe; and such as was only imparted at a much later period, by Dante to the Italian, and by Luther's translation of the Bible to the German, language. The ancient Sclavonic speech, thus attaining almost at a single bound to the perfection elsewhere reached only by slow degrees and laborious efforts, has now in turn fallen behind the growth of the modern language of Russia; and the same difficulty has arisen, or is fast arising, which besets the use of the ancient phraseology of the sacred books of all even the most vernacular languages. But the work of Cyril and Methodius gave at once a national character to the Scriptures and Liturgy, and a religious character to the literature and language of Russia, which have never been effaced; and, in the first instance, must have kept alive, before the minds of the people and clergy, both a sense of their common religious interest, and a knowledge of the leading truths of Christianity, such as could hardly have been possessed by the contemporary Churches and nations of the West.

To some such cause as this, combined with the natural vigor of the people, must be ascribed the fact that the Christianity of Russia, introduced by these purely external and formal influences, early exhibited a practical strength hardly to be recognized in the other Churches of the East, and sometimes equal even to the energetic zeal of Western Christendom.

Of this early period there are two Princes whom the Russian Church has dignified with the name of saint. The first, Vladimir, its founder in the tenth century; the second, Alexander of the Neva, so called from the A. D. 1247. victory in which he repulsed the Swedes on the banks of that river in the thirteenth century. The first has found his rest at Kieff; the other sleeps in a magnificent shrine in the capital which centuries afterwards rose beside his own Neva.   Each of them, no doubt, has his claims to veneration.   The savage character of Vladimir seems to have been tamed and softened by his conversion.   Alexander seems to have united in an eminent degree the virtues of the soldier and the pacificator.   But, as we often observe in the history both of the Western and Eastern Churches, the title of "saint" has not been the surest index of true Christian excellence; and, on the whole, there are two other Princes of this age whose memory has a better savor than that of the two royal saints just named.   One is the A. D. 1017. legislator Jaroslaff, who introduced into Russia the Byzantine system of Canon Law, and the first beginnings of Christian education.   The other is Vladimir Vladimir the Second, or as he is usually called, probably Monoma-chus, from the Byzantine Emperor of the same sur- A. D. 1113. name, Vladimir Monomachus,[1] whose date may be fixed in our minds by his marriage with Gytha,[2] daughter of our own Harold.   The details of his life can only be understood through the intricate and obscure events of his time.   But his general character may be sufficiently gathered from his own words, in the dying injunctions left to his sons.   They show that, underneath the load of Byzantine ceremonial and the roughness of Russian barbarism, there lived a spark of true manly goodness; and that he was not unworthy of the model of a just and religious ruler in the 101st Psalm, which was sent to him by the Russian Primate,[3] with an exhortation to learn it by heart, to meditate upon it, and to fashion his government accordingly.   His love of the Psalter, his rapid travelling, the turn for foreign languages, the union of fierceness and devotion, all go to make up a genuine portraiture of a Russian Christian of early days: —

---

[1] Mouravieff, p. 20.   [2] Karamsin, ii. 211.
[3] Palmer's Orthodox Communion, p. 95.

" O my children, praise God and love men. For it is not fasting, nor solitude, nor monastic life, that will procure you eternal life, but only doing good. Forget not the poor, nourish them; remember that riches come from God, and are given you only for a short time. Do not bury your wealth in the ground; this is against the precepts of Christianity. Be fathers to orphans. Be judges in the cause of widows, and do not let the powerful oppress the weak. Put to death neither innocent nor guilty, for nothing is so sacred as the life and the soul of a Christian. Never take the name of God in vain; and never break the oath you have made in kissing the crucifix. My brethren said to me, ' Help us to drive out the sons of Rostislaf, or else give up our alliance.' But I said, ' I cannot forget that I have kissed the cross.' I opened then the book of Psalms, and read there with deep emotion: — ' Why art thou so vexed, O my soul, and why art thou so disquieted within me? Put thy trust in God. I will confess my faults, and he is gracious.'

" Be not envious at the triumph of the wicked and the success of treachery. Fear the lot of the impious. Do not desert the sick: do not let the sight of dead corpses terrify you, for we must all die. Receive with joy the blessing of the clergy: do not keep yourself aloof from them: do them good, that they may pray to God for you. Drive out of your heart all suggestions of pride, and remember that we are all perishable — to-day full of hope, to-morrow in the coffin. Abhor lying, drunkenness, and debauchery. Love your wives, but do not suffer them to have any power over you. Endeavor constantly to obtain knowledge. Without having quitted his palace, my father spoke five languages; a thing which wins for us the admiration of foreigners.

" In war be vigilant; be an example to your boyards. Never retire to rest until you have posted your guards. Never take off your arms while you are within reach of the enemy. And, to avoid being surprised, always be early on horseback. When you are on horseback say your prayers, or at least the shortest and the best of all, ' Lord, have mercy upon us.'

" When you travel through your provinces, do not allow your attendants to do the least injury to the inhabitants. Entertain always at your own expense the master of the house in which you take up your abode.

"If you find yourself affected by any ailment, make three prostrations to the ground before the Lord; and never let the sun find you in bed. At the dawn of day, my father, and the virtuous men by whom he was surrounded, did thus: they glorified the Lord, and cried, in the joy of their hearts, ' Vouchsafe, O my God, to enlighten me with thy divine light.' They then seated themselves to deliberate, or to administer justice to the people, or they went to the chase; and in the middle of the day they slept; which God permits to man as well as to beasts and birds.

"For my part, I accustomed myself to do everything that I might have ordered my servants to do. Night and day, summer and winter, I was perpetually moving about. I wished to see everything with my own eyes. Never did I abandon the poor or the widow to the oppressions of the powerful. I made it my duty to inspect the churches and the sacred ceremonies of religion, as well as the management of my property, my stables, and the vultures and hawks of my hunting establishment.

"I have made eighty-three campaigns and many expeditions. I concluded nineteen treaties with the Polostzy [wandering hordes between the Kouban and the Danube — ancestors of the Nogaïs]. I took captive one hundred of their princes, whom I set free again; and I put two hundred of them to death, by throwing them into rivers.

"No one has ever travelled more rapidly than I have done. Setting out in the morning from Tchernigof, I have arrived at Kieff before the hour of vespers.

"In my youth, what falls from my horse did I not experience! wounding my feet and my hands, and breaking my head against trees. But the Lord watched over me.

"In hunting amidst the thickest forests, how many times have I myself caught wild horses and bound them together! How many times have I been thrown down by buffaloes, wounded by the antlers of stags, and trodden under the feet of elks! A furious wild boar rent my sword from my baldrick: my saddle was torn to pieces by a bear; this terrible beast rushed upon my courser, whom he threw down upon me. But the Lord protected me.

"O my children, fear neither death nor wild beasts. Trust in Providence: it far surpasses all human precautions."[1]

[1] Karamsin, ii. 202.

CHRONOLOGICAL TABLE.

A. D.

400. Mission of Ulfilas to the Goths.

862. FOUNDATION OF THE RUSSIAN EMPIRE BY RURIC.

863. Mission of Cyril and Methodius to Bulgaria, and Translation of the Bible into Sclavonic.

879. Oskold and Dir martyred as Christians by Oleg.

955. Baptism of Olga.

988. Baptism of Vladimir at Kershon, and Conversion of Russia at Kieff.

1010. Foundation of the Pechersky Monastery at Kieff.

1015. Martyrdom of Boris and Glieb.

1017. Accession of Jaroslaff I.

1054. Foundation of the Church of S. Sophia at Novgorod.

1108. Chronicles of Nestor.

1113. Accession of Vladimir Monomachus.

1246. Alexander Nevsky.

LECTURE X.

THE RUSSIAN CHURCH IN THE MIDDLE AGES.

AMONGST the special authorities for this period may be named: —

1. "The Present State of Russia." By Samuel Collins, M. D. 1671.
2. "Russia at the Close of the Sixteenth Century." (Edited by Mr. Bond for the Hakluyt Society.) 1856.

 It contains: —

 a) "A Treatise on the Russian Commonwealth." By Dr. Giles Fletcher. 1588.
 b) "The Travels of Sir Jerome Horsey." 1591.

WE have reached the period which in Russia most nearly corresponds to the Middle Ages of Europe. But, as might be expected from the much later birth of the Russian Church and Empire, this period both begins and ends much later than the corresponding epoch in the West. The consolidation of the Teutonic tribes must be carried back to Charlemagne in the ninth century; whereas the consolidation of the Sclavonic tribes, by the creation of the central capital of Moscow, dates from the beginning of the fourteenth century. The European middle age ends with the beginning of the sixteenth century. The Russian middle age continues at least till the middle of the seventeenth century, and in some sense even till the opening of the eighteenth.

These synchronisms, or anachronisms, as we might

almost rather call them, are necessary to bear in mind as illustrations of the relative positions of Eastern and Western Christendom. It is the period between these limits which I now propose shortly to describe.

Of this whole period, the local scene and the outward symbol, still surviving the events which gave it birth, is "Moscow." That marvellous city is the very personification of the ecclesiastical history of Russia. It is indeed a personification of it even in the literal sense. "Our holy mother, Moscow," is the peasant's endearing name for the city; nay, even for the road which leads to it, "Our dear mother, the great road from Vladimir "to Moscow." [1] Hallowed by no Apostolic legends, not even by any Byzantine missions; cleared out of the forests which down to the fourteenth century overhung, and still leave their names on, the banks of the Moskwa; with no other attractions than its central situation in the heart of the Russian Empire, it has yet acquired a hold over the religious mind of a larger part of Christendom than is probably exercised by any other city except Jerusalem and Rome. Look at its forest of towers and domes, springing like gaudy flowers or weeds — blue, red, green, silver, golden — from the wide field of green roofs, and groves, and gardens. It is a very Russian Rome,[2] no doubt; but still, like it, the city of innumerable churches, of everlasting bells, of endless processions, of palace and church combined, of tombs and thrones, and relics and treasures, and invasions and deliverances, as far back as its history extends. Look further at the concentration of all this in the Kremlin. In that fortress, surrounded by its crusted towers and battlemented walls, are united all the elements of the

[1] Haxthausen, iii. 151.

[2] Moscow, after the fall of Constantinople, was regarded by the Eastern Church as a "New Rome," even in the sense of "a new Constantinople." "The new Rome which is Moscow." Macarius's Travels, i. 325, ii. 57.

ancient religious life of Russia.   Side by side stand the three cathedrals of the marriages, coronations, and funerals of the Czars.   Hard by are the two convents, half palatial, half episcopal.   Overhanging all is the double, triple palace of Czar and Patriarch.   Within that palace is a labyrinth of fourteen chapels, multiplied by sovereign after sovereign, till the palace is more like the dwelling-place of the Pope than of the Emperor; whilst, still true to the well-known saying which I have quoted before, the Tartar-like building in which these chapels are imbedded, itself crabbed, ribbed, low-browed, painted within and without in the old barbaric grotesqueness of mediæval Russia, is encased with the external magnificence of modern civilization and European grandeur.

Within these walls, for the most part, lies the scene of that portion of history on which we now enter, beginning with the foundation of Moscow, and terminating with the accession of the Romanoff dynasty.   The first coincides in time with what in Europe may be called the beginning of the second portion of the Middle Ages, after the close of the great struggle between the Popes and Emperors.   The second coincides with the subsidence of the struggles of the European Reformation in the Peace of Westphalia.

In the gradual consolidation of the Church of Russia, which took place during this period, there concurred three leading institutions and two leading events. These correspond to analogous institutions and events in mediæval Europe, and thus convey similar instruction, but varied by the peculiar differences of East and West.

I. Leaving the continuous narrative to be read in the characteristic and forcible history of Andrew Mouravieff,[1] I will confine myself to the salient points.

[1] I must also express my personal obligations to the Author.

54

First is the Czar. In the West, as well as in the East,
The Czar. the framework of all religious and civil institutions was moulded on the idea of a Holy Roman Empire succeeding to the Pagan Roman Empire of former
times. But in the West this institution has signally
failed, as in the East it has signally succeeded. Charlemagne was a much greater man than any of the Russian
potentates before the time of Peter. His coronation by
Leo was a much more striking coronation than any that
has fallen to the lot even of the greatest Russian Emperors. The theory of his Empire was defended by
Dante with far more genius and zeal than ever was the
theory of the White Czar by any poet or philosopher
of Russia. But, nevertheless, the Holy Roman Empire
has faded away, whilst "the new Cæsar of the Empire
"of Orthodoxy"[1] still stands. In part this difference is
owing to the fundamental diversity of the Eastern and
Western characters. In part, however, it was fostered
by the peculiar circumstances of the Russian history,
and obtained an importance in the Russian Church and
Empire beyond what may be ascribed to the same tendency in other regions of the East. The very slowness
of the growth of the institution indicates the depth of
its roots in the national character and history. The
transformation of the Grand-Princes of Kieff, Vladimir,
and Novgorod into the Czar of Muscovy, and of the
Czar of Muscovy into the Emperor of all the Russias,
was not the work of a day or a century; it was the
necessity of the long-sustained wars with Tartars, Poles,
and Swedes; it was the craving for union amongst the
several Princes; it was the inheritance of the ceremonial
of the Byzantine Empire, through the intermarriage of
Ivan III. with the daughter of the last Palæologus; it

[1] So the Czar Alexis was formally addressed by the German Emperor.
(Travels of Macarius, 770.)

was the earnest desire for peace under one head, after the long wars of the Pretenders; it was the homogeneousness of the vast Empire, uniting itself under one common ruler. The political position of the Czar or Emperor is not within our province, but his religious or ecclesiastical position transpires through the whole history of his Church. He is the father of the whole patriarchal community. The veneration for him was in the Middle Ages almost, it is said, as if he were Christ[1] Himself. The line of Grecian Emperors, so it was said even by Orientals, had been stained with heresy and iconoclasm: never the line of the Orthodox Czars of Muscovy.[2] "He who blasphemes his Maker meets with "forgiveness amongst men, but he who reviles the Em-"peror is sure to lose his head."[3] "God and the Prince "will it, God and the Prince know it,"[4] were the two arguments, moral and intellectual, against which there was no appeal. "So live your Imperial Majesty, here "is my head;" "I have seen the laughing eyes of the "Czar:" these were the usual expressions of loyalty.[5] He was the keeper of the keys and the body-servant of God.[6] His coronation, even at the present time, The Coronation. is not a mere ceremony, but a historical event and solemn consecration. It is preceded by fasting and seclusion, and takes place in the most sacred church in Russia; the Emperor, not as in the corresponding forms of European investiture a passive recipient, but himself the principal figure in the whole scene; himself reciting aloud the confession of the Orthodox faith; himself alone on his knees, amidst the assembled multitude, offering up the prayer of intercession for the Empire; himself placing his own crown with his own hands on

---

[1] Macarius, i. 401.
[2] Ibid. ii. 45.
[3] Ibid. ii. 73.
[4] Strahl, ii. 65.
[5] Tracts on Muscovite Religion, 37.
[6] Ibid. 38.

his own head; himself entering through the sacred doors of the innermost sanctuary, and taking from the altar the elements of the bread and wine, of which then and there, in virtue of his consecration, he communicates with bishops, priests, and deacons. In every considerable church is placed a throne in front of the altar, as if in constant expectation of the sudden apparition of the Sovereign. In every meeting, council, or college, is placed the sacred triangular "mirror," "the mirror of "conscience," as it is called, which represents the Imperial presence, and solemnizes, as if by an actual consecration, the business to be transacted.

In the Cathedral of the Archangel Michael, within The Cathe- the Kremlin, lie, each in his place, their coffins dral of the Archangel. ranged around the wall, the long succession of Czars, from the founder of Moscow to the predecessor of the founder of Petersburg. Round the walls, above each coffin, are the figures painted in long white robes, each with a glory round his head, not the glory of saintly canonization,[1] but of that Imperial canonization of which I have just spoken. Twice a year a funeral service is performed for the sins of all of them. Of all those who there lie buried, under " that burden of sins," — so the service solemnly expresses it, — " voluntary or "involuntary, known to themselves or unknown," — none more strangely and insignificantly indicates the mixed character of the Russian Czar, or the hold which the office had acquired on the people, than he who, as the first crowned and anointed Czar of Muscovy, lies next the altar, in the most sacred place, Ivan or John IV., surnamed " the Terrible."

Without dwelling on the details of his life, his history Ivan the will serve the purpose of presenting to us some Terrible. A.D. 1533– peculiarities of this aspect of the Russian Church. 1584.

[1] Although it was taken for such by the Syrian travellers. Macarius, ii. 44.

His career has a dramatic interest of its own, unlike that of most of the great tyrants of the world. From a youth of barbarous profligacy he was reclaimed suddenly, and, as it would seem, entirely, by the joint efforts of his wife Anastasia, of the monk Sylvester, and of the noble Adasheff. For thirteen years under their influence he led not only a pure and good life, but a career of brilliant success long unknown in the Russian annals. " It was as if a cloud which had before con-
" cealed Russia from the eyes of Europe was suddenly
" drawn asunder, and revealed to them at the moment
" of their greatest need, against the aggressive power
" of the Ottoman Empire, a young Christian hero at
" the head of a great empire, to be the vanguard and
" support of Christendom."[1]   But this was only transient. At the end of thirteen years these good influences were partly withdrawn and partly crushed. He returned once more to far worse than his youthful vices; insanity blended itself with furious passion, and, although sparks of religion still remained, at times bursting forth into fervent devotion, although noble schemes of civilization hovered before his mind always, and kept his name in sight before the Western world, yet, if we may believe half the crimes laid to his charge, he stands unrivalled, at least amongst Christian sovereigns, in his preëminence of wickedness.

He is the first Russian Prince who comes into direct contact with the West.[2]   He corresponded with and courted our own Elizabeth.[3]   It is interesting to reflect that probably he was the first great political personage

[1] Palmer's Orthodox Communion, p. 48.

[2] It is not improbable that from him are drawn Hooker's almost contemporaneous descriptions of a prosperous but wicked potentate, delighting in the awe which he inspires, and in the thought that " the enormity of his crimes is above all reach of law." Sermon on Pride (vol. iii. pt. ii. pp. 753, 754, 787).   [3] Collins, 47.

who claimed and who received the promise of the right of asylum in England, in case of a revolution in his own country; and also that to this communication we owe the first distinct description of Russian life and religion by an Englishman, in the Journal of Sir Jerome Horsey, employed as messenger between Ivan and Elizabeth. There is something almost Shaksperian in the delineation which Horsey gives of the last time he saw the tremendous Emperor:—

"God would not leave this cruelty and barbarism unpunished. A.D. 1584. Not long after, he, the Emperor, fell out in rage with his eldest son Charrowich [the Czarovitch] Ivan for having some commiseration of these distressed poor Christians; and but for commanding an officer to give a gentleman a warrant for 5 or 6 post-horses, sent in his affairs, without the king's leave, and some other jealousy of greatness and too good opinion of the people as he thought, strake him in his fury a box on the ear or thrust at him with his piked staff; who took it so tenderly, fell into a burning fever, and died within three days after. Whereat the Emperor tore his hair and beard like a mad man, lamenting and mourning for the loss of his son. (But the kingdom had the greatest loss, the hope of their comfort, a wise, mild, and most worthy prince, of heroical condition, of comely presence, twenty-three years of age, beloved and lamented of all men: was buried in Michaela Sweat [S. Michael] Archangel church, with jewels, precious stones, and apparel, put into his tomb with his corpse, worth 50 thousand pounds, watched by twelve citizens every night by change, dedicated unto his saint John and Michael Archangel, to keep both body and treasure.)[1]

*   *   *   *   *   *   *

"The old Emperor was carried every day in his chair into his treasury. One day he beckoned to me to follow. I stood among the rest venturously, and heard him call for some precious stones and jewels. Told the Prince and nobles present before and about him the vertue of such and such, which I ob-

[1] Travels of Horsey, 178, 199.

served, and do pray I may a little digress to declare for my own memory's sake.

" ' The load-stone,' he said, ' you all know hath great and hidden vertue, without which the seas that compass the world are not navigable, nor the bounds nor circle of the earth cannot be known. Mahomet, the Persian's Prophet, his tomb of steel hangs in their Rapatta at Darbent most miraculously.'

" Caused the waiters to bring a chain of needles touched by this load-stone, hanged all one by the other. ' This fair coral and this fair turcas you see ; take in your hand ; of his nature are orient colors ; put them on my hand and arm. I am poisoned with disease ; you see they show their vertue by the change of their pure color into pale : declares my death. A. D. 1584. Reach out my staff royal ; an unicorn's horn garnished with very fair diamonds, rubies, sapphires, emeralds and other precious stones that are rich in value ; cost 70 thousand marks sterling of David Gower, from the fowlkers of Ousborghe.[1] Seek out for some spiders.'

" Caused his physician, Johannes Lloff, to scrape a circle thereof upon the table ; put within it one spider and so one other and died, and some other without that ran alive apace from it. ' It is too late, it will not preserve me. Behold these precious stones. This diamond is the orient's richest and most precious of all other. I never affected it ; it restrains fury and luxury, [gives ?] abstinence and chastity ; the least parcel of it in powder will poison a horse given to drink, much more a man.' Points at the ruby. ' O ! this is most comfortable to the heart, brain, vigor and memory of man, clarifies congealed and corrupt blood.' Then at the emerald. ' The nature of the rainbow ; this precious stone is an enemy to uncleanness. The sapphire I greatly delight in ; it preserves and increaseth courage, joys the heart, pleasing to all the vital senses, precious and very sovereign for the eyes, clears the sight, takes away bloodshot, and strengthens the muscles and strings thereof.' Then takes the onyx in hand. ' All these are God's wonderful gifts, secrets in nature, and yet reveals them to man's use and contemplation, as friends to grace and virtue and enemies to vice. I faint, carry me away till another time.'

[1] Qu. " the Fuggers [the great merchant family] of Augsburg."

" In the afternoon peruseth over his will and yet thinks not to die : he hath been bewitched in that place, and often times un-witched again ; but now the devil fails. Commands the master of his apotheke and physicians to prepare and attend for his solace and bathing ; looks for the goodness of the sign ; sends his favorite to his witches again to know their calculations. He comes and tells them the Emperor will bury or burn them all quick for their false illusions and lies. The day is come ; he is as heart whole as ever he was. ' Sir, be not so wrathful. You know the day is come and ends with the setting of the sun.' He hastes him to the Emperor: made great preparation for the bath. About the third hour of the day the Emperor went into it, solaced himself and made merry with pleasant songs as he useth to do : came out about the seventh hour well refreshed ; brought forth ; sets him down upon his bed ; calls Rodovone Bœrken, a gentleman whom he favored, to bring the chess-board. He sets his men ; all saving the king, which by no means he could not make stand in his place with the rest upon the plain board ; his chief favorite and Boris Fedorowich Goddorove and others about him. The Emperor in his loose gown, shirt and linen hose, faints and falls backward. Great outcry and stir ; one sent for aqua vitæ, another to the apotheke for ' marigold and' rose water, and to call ' his ghostly father and' the physicians. In the mean time he was strangled and stark dead."

Out of the history of this wild monster two points A. D. 1533– may be specially dwelt upon as illustrating the 1584. position of the Russian religion.

First, his union of frantic excesses of wickedness with Union of apparently sincere bursts of religious feeling fanaticism renders him, perhaps, the most remarkable in-and wick-edness. stance which history furnishes of the combina-tion of a total disregard of all the moral precepts of religion with at least an occasional observance of its ceremonial and devotional duties. Antinomianism is the reproach of the lower and coarser forms of the Protestant Church. Louis XI. is a standing disgrace to the Roman Church. But these instances are exceeded, both in the depth of their wickedness and the fervor of their zeal, by Ivan the Terrible. A single passage out of many will suffice. He retired sometimes for weeks together to a monastery which he had built for himself near Moscow. He rang the bell for matins himself at three in the morning. During the services, which lasted seven hours, he read, chanted, and prayed with such fervor that the marks of his prostrations remained on his forehead. At dinner, whilst his attendants sat like mutes, he read books of religious instruction. In the intervals he went to the dungeons under the monastery to see with his own eyes his prisoners tortured, and always returned, it was observed, with a face beaming with delight.[1]

If it be true that the Oriental forms of Christianity are more exposed than others to this danger of uniting the form of godliness with the mystery of iniquity, then the history of Ivan is a warning which should never be absent from the mind of any adherent or of any admirer of the Eastern Church. His life reads a lesson in which every Christian community is deeply concerned, but none more so than the Church and Empire of Russia.

But, moreover, terrible, loathsome, widespread as were his crimes and cruelties, he reigned not only *Influence* without personal danger, but almost, it may be *as Czar.* said, with personal popularity. When he offered to abdicate, when he drove off from the Kremlin in his sledges to his retreat at Alexandroff, the people were in despair. What would have seemed to us a deliverance beyond all hope seemed to them a calamity beyond all endurance. They could not live without a Czar; and when, as a Czar, he returned, to mangle, torture, and dishonor his subjects, he died, not by the hand of any assassin, but in the agonies of his own remorse. In

[1] Karamsin, ix. 308.

foreigners, even then, he excited dread and indignation; and the English merchant describes how he " was sump- " tuously entombed in the Archangel church, where he, " though guarded day and night, remains a fearful spec- " tacle to the memory of such as pass by, or hear his " name spoken of, who were entreated to cross and " bless themselves for his resurrection again." But this feeling was one, with his own countrymen, not of unmingled horror. The epithet which we render " Terrible," in the original expresses rather the idea of " Awful," the feeling with which the Athenians would have regarded, not Periander or Dionysius, but the Eumenides. His memory still lives amongst the peasants as of one who was a Czar indeed. The stories of his nailing the hat of the ambassador to his head, and of his driving his huge iron walking-staff through the foot of one whose attention he wished to secure, are regarded rather as the playful condescension of some great Leviathan, than as the unfeeling cruelties of a wicked prince.[1]

II. The Czar was the first person in the Church, the Metropolitan of Russia was the second. The

The Metro-
politan of
Moscow.

holy city of Kieff was, as we have seen, the earliest seat of the Russian Primacy. This was the traditional scene of S. Andrew's preaching, the ac- tual scene of Vladimir's first proclamation of the Gospel. But the ultimate and permanent seat of the Russian Primates was Moscow, which was in fact their creation. A. D. 1325. When the Grand-Prince Ivan I. was doubtfully establishing his habitation on the Kremlin hill, his deter- mination was fixed and steadied by the council of Peter the Metropolitan. " If thou wilt comfort my old age, " if thou wilt build here a temple worthy of the Mother " of God, thou shalt then be more glorious than all the

---

[1] I heard of these stories myself, but they are also given in Collins, 45.

" other princes, and thy posterity shall become great.
" My bones shall remain in this city; prelates shall re-
" joice to dwell in it; and the hands of its princes shall
" be on the neck of our enemies." [1]

The heart of Moscow is the Kremlin, and the heart
of the Kremlin is the Patriarchal Cathedral, the The Patriarchal
Church of the Assumption or Repose of the Cathedral.
Virgin. It is, in dimensions, what in the West would
be called a chapel rather than a cathedral. But it is so
fraught with recollections, so teeming with worshippers,
so bursting with tombs and pictures, from the pavement
up to the cupola, that its smallness of space is forgotten
in the fulness of its contents. On the platform of its
nave, from Ivan the Terrible downwards to this day,
the Czars have been crowned. Along its altar screen
are deposited the most sacred pictures of Russia : that,
painted by the Metropolitan Peter; this, sent by the
Greek Emperor Manuel; that, brought by Vladimir from
Kherson. High in the cupola is the chapel, where, as
at the summit of the Russian Church, the Russian Primates were elected. In the depth of the throne, behind
the altar, is the sacred picture which commemorates the
original rock of Kieff, whence the see of Moscow was
hewn. Round the walls are buried the Primates of the
Church; at the four corners, here as in all Oriental
buildings the place of honor, lie those most highly
venerated.

It was by gradual changes the Metropolitans of the
Russian Church were rendered independent of General
character
Constantinople. Jonah, in the middle of the of the
Metropol-
fifteenth century, was the first in whose ap- itans.
pointment "the Great Church" had no direct share.
And in the century after the fall of the Byzantine Empire, the Patriarch Jeremiah, in 1587, consented to turn

1 Mouravieff, 54.

the Metropolitan of Moscow into a Patriarch in the person of Job; the Patriarchate of Russia thus, according to a theory which has been advanced in the Eastern Church, supplying the place of the Patriarch of·Rome, vacated, as is alleged, by the schism[1] of the Roman Bishop.   But those external changes affected very slightly the character and bearing of those who filled the see.   An almost uniform spirit breathes through them all.   Hard by, in the neighboring convent, lies one of the earliest and most famous, Alexis the Wonderworker, whose grave is still visited by every sovereign on his entrance into Moscow.   "Whose tomb is this?" asked Davoust, in the French occupation; and on being told, he replied, "Let the old man rest." What the French general thus expressed on the impulse of the moment is the feeling with which history may regard, with one or two exceptions to be hereafter noticed, the whole series of these ancient prelates.   "Let the old men rest."

They were mostly blameless and venerable men; some had not unimportant parts to play in the leading events of Russian history. The personal veneration shown to them, as still to their successors, probably exceeded the respect attaching to ecclesiastics of the West. When the present aged Metropolitan of Moscow leaves the cathedral, it is with difficulty that he can struggle through the crowd, who, were he of pure gold and did every touch carry away a particle, could hardly press more eagerly to devour his hand with kisses, or lay a finger on the hem of his garment.   And when he drives away in his state carriage, drawn by six black horses, every one stands bareheaded in the street as he passes, and the bells of the innumerable churches and chapels

---

[1] See the Vindication of the See of Constantinople (before quoted in Lecture I. p. 103,) by Gregory, the Secretary of the Synod, p. 158.

of Moscow, as the carriage rolls by, join in an ever-increasing river of sound, tributary streams of all dimensions, from the tinkling of a brook to the roaring of a cataract, falling in and telling the course of his route long after he is out of sight.

But neither the grandeur of the office, nor the enthusiasm of the people, has ever raised the Primates of Russia to a level of political importance, I will not say with the Popes, but even with the prelates of Europe. They have always been the supporters, not the rivals, of the throne. There has been no Hildebrand, no Becket, no Anselm amongst them. Of the four who rest in the four corners of the cathedral, Peter, the first Metropolitan, has the honor of being the co-founder of Moscow with the first Ivan; Jonah was the prelate who made the see independent of Constantinople; Hermogenes died a victim to the Polish invaders; Philip alone came into collision with S. Philip. the Imperial power, and that was expressly and distinctly with the personal cruelties, not with the secular authority, of Ivan the Terrible. "As the image of the "Divinity, I reverence thee; as a man, thou A. D. 1568. "art but dust and ashes." It is a true glory of the Russian Church, and an example to the hierarchy of all churches, that its one martyred prelate should have suffered, not for any high ecclesiastical pretensions, but in the simple cause of justice and mercy. "Silence," he said, as he rebuked the Czar, "lays sin upon the "soul, and brings death to the whole people. . . . I am "a stranger and a pilgrim upon earth, as all my fathers "were, and I am ready to suffer for the truth. Where "would my faith be if I kept silence? . . . Here we "are offering up the bloodless sacrifice to the Lord; "while behind the altar flows the innocent blood of "Christian men." As he was dragged away from the cathedral, his one word was " Pray." As he received his executioners in the narrow cell of his prison in the convent of Twer, his one word was " Perform thy mis-" sion." [1] That narrow cell, now locked up and almost forgotten, is more truly deserving the name of " the " Martyrdom " than the spot where our English primate fell, with more spirit, but not with more courage, and certainly not with a better cause, nor with more meekness or charity. The death of Philip of Moscow, however obscure in ecclesiastical annals, is at least valuable as a proof that in order to secure a protest against the lust and cruelty of sovereigns, it is not necessary to have a perpetual irritation between the powers of Church and State. One such prelate occurs in the Russian history, and he more in appearance than in fact. But he, the Patriarch Nicon, lies far away from his predecessors at Moscow, and beyond the limits of the mediæval age, of which we are now speaking.

III. I pass to the third ecclesiastical power in the Russian commonwealth — the Monastic orders.

Monastic orders.

Here, as I have observed on a former occasion,[2] we must dismiss from our minds all the Western ideas of beneficence, learning, preaching, such as we ascribe to the Benedictines, Franciscans, or Dominicans ; of statecraft, energy, and policy, such as we ascribe to the Jesuits. These developments of the system are, according to the view of the Orthodox Church of the East, an infringement of the contemplative ascetic character of the anchorets and cœnobites of antiquity. In the dark forests of Muscovy, in the frozen waters of Archangel, is carried out the same rigid system, at least in outward form, that was born and nurtured in the burning desert of the Thebaid.

But, nevertheless, they have not been without their

1 Mouravieff, 176, 177, 179.   2 Lecture I. p. 113.

influence; an influence very similar to that which was exercised by their spiritual ancestors, the ascetics of Egypt.

There is no variety of monastic orders in Russia. The one name of the Black Clergy is applied to all alike. The one rule of S. Basil governs them all. But, for convenience, they may be divided into two classes: the Hermits and the Monks.

1. Even at the present day the influence of a hermit in Russia is beyond what it is in any other part of the world. Only a short time since died an ancho-ret, who for twenty years had lived in absolute solitude, except when he came out once a year to receive the Eucharist on Easter-day, and who yet, at the end of that time, was consulted in the belief of his practical sagacity far and wide through the Empire. " It was as " if by the concentration of his will he had acquired a " kind of magnetic power " — so it was described to me by one who had heard much of him — " over all who " came within his reach." In earlier times this sanctity had acquired a still stronger hold. Anthony and Theo-dosius in the caves of Kieff were the direct imitators of Anthony and Hilarion in Egypt, and their dried skeletons still attract pilgrims from the utmost bounds of Kamtschatka. The pillar hermits, imitators of Simeon Stylites, never reached the West, but were to be found in the heart of Russia.[1] But there was a further and a more noble function which these wild hermits exercised. Let me describe them as they ap-peared to English travellers of the sixteenth century.[2] " There are certain eremites, who use to go " stark naked, save a clout about their middle, " with their hair hanging long and wildly about their

The Hermits.

A. D. 1588–1591.

---

[1] Nicetas, at Peryaslav. Strahl, 138 ; A. D. 1086.
[2] Fletcher, Russian Commonwealth, 117.

" shoulders, and many of them with an iron collar or
" chain about their necks or middles even in the very
" extremity of winter. These they take as prophets
" and men of great holiness, giving them a liberty to
" speak what they list without any controlment, though
" it be of the very highest himself. So that if he re-
" prove any openly, in what sort soever, they answer
" nothing, but that it is *Po Grecum, 'for their sins.'* And
" if any of them take some piece of sale ware from any
" man's shop as he passeth by, to give where he list,
" he thinketh himself much beloved of God, and much
" beholden to the holy man for taking it in that sort.
" The people liketh very well of them, because they are
" as pasquils [pasquins] to note their great men's faults,
" that no man else dare speak of. Yet it falleth out
" sometimes that for this rude liberty which they take
" upon them, after a counterfeit manner by imitation of
" prophets, they are made away in secret; as was one
" or two of them in the late Emperor's time for being
" overbold in speaking against his government. . . . Of
" this kind there are not many, because it is a very
" hard and cold profession to go naked in Russia,
" especially in winter."

Of those thus described, three may be selected : —

" There is one at this time that walketh naked about
" the streets of Moscow, and inveigheth commonly
" against the state and government, especially against
" the Godonoffs." [That is, the high family who at that
time were " thought to be oppressors of the common-
" wealth," and of whom the chief has ever since by the
popular voice, of which this hermit was the powerful
mouthpiece, been condemned as the author of the
serfdom of the Russian peasantry.]

" Another there was, one whom they called Basil, that
" would take upon him to reprove the old Emperor

"[the terrible Ivan] for all his cruelty and oppression
"done towards the people. His body they have _{Basil of}
"translated into a sumptuous church near the _{Moscow.}
"Emperor's house in Moscow, and have canonized
"him for a saint." That sumptuous church remains, a
monument of the mad hermit. It is the cathedral immediately outside the Kremlin walls, well termed "the
"dream of a diseased imagination." It was built A. D. 1544.
according to the barbarous caprice of Ivan IV. to commemorate his conquest of Kazan. Hundreds of artists
were kidnapped from Lubeck to erect it, pagoda on
pagoda, cupola on cupola, staircase upon staircase, pinnacle on pinnacle, — red, blue, green, and gold; chapel
within chapel, altar above altar, to see how many could
be congregated under a single roof. Day by day, it is
said, he sat in the small belfry tower on the Kremlin
walls, to watch its completion; and, when it was completed, put out the eyes of the architect, that no finer
work might ever be executed. Yet in this favorite
church of a worse than Ahab was interred, as though
he and his people were unconscious of any inconsistency,
the body of one who was dreaded by him, and revered
by the people almost as a second Elijah. He lies in the
most costly of the many chapels; his iron chains and
collar hang over his bones, and his name, " S. Basil," has
superseded the earlier title which the Czar had given it,
"the Protection of Our Lady," in allusion to the conquest of Kazan, which it commemorated. Of all the
buildings in Moscow it makes the deepest impression;
it stands alone, as a fitting monument of the mad Czar
and of his mad reprover.

Another, who lived at the same time, Nicolas of
Pskoff, or Plescow, is thus described by Horsey, _{Nicolas of}
_{Plescow,}
who had himself met him. "I saw this impostor A. D. 1570.
"or magician, a foul creature; went naked both in win-

56

"ter and summer: he endured both extreme heat and
"frost; did many things through the magical illusions
"of the devil; much followed, praised and renowned
"both by prince and people. He did much good"[1]
when Ivan came to his native town of Plescow, with the
savage intention of massacring the whole population
there, as he had already done at Novgorod. It was the
early morning as the Czar approached the town. The
bells of the churches[2] — those voices of Russian religion
— were sounding for matins, and for a moment his hard
heart was melted, and his religious feeling was stirred.
The hut of the hermit was close by: Ivan saluted him
and sent him a present. The holy man, in return, sent
him a piece of raw flesh. It was during the great fast
of Lent,[3] and Ivan expressed his surprise at such a
breach of the rules of the Church. "Ivasko, Ivasko,"[4]
that is, "Jack, Jack," — so with his accustomed rudeness the hermit addressed his terrible sovereign, —
"thinkest thou that it is unlawful to eat a piece of
"beast's flesh in Lent, and not unlawful to eat up so
"much man's flesh as thou hast already?"[5] At the
same time he pointed to a dark thunder-cloud over
their heads, and threatened the Czar with instant destruction by it, if he or any of his army touched a hair
of the least child's head in that city, which God by His
good angel did preserve for better purpose than his ra-
pine.[6] Ivan trembled and retired,[7] and Plescow was saved.

I have given these instances, because they explain the
reverence of the people for the memory of those rough
messengers of unwelcome truth. They are also char-

[1] Horsey, 161.
[2] Fletcher, 118.
[3] Mouravieff, 119.
[4] Fletcher, 118.
[5] Karamsin, ix. 635.
[6] Horsey, 161, 162.
[7] One account says that he still persisted in ordering the great bell of the
church of the Holy Trinity to be moved; but that his best horse fell, according to the warning of Nicolas, and that he then retired. Strahl's Geschichte,
iii. 213.

acteristic of the truly Oriental aspect of the Russian
Church. A Dervish[1] in Arabia or India is the lowest
type of the same phenomenon; the Prophets of the
Jewish people are its highest type, not unfitly illustrated
by these its later representatives. They ought also to
be borne in mind to correct a too severe judgment of
the ceremonial character of the Russian faith. No
Prophet of old, no Reformer of modern times, could
have delivered a more striking testimony in behalf of
the true moral character of Christianity, than the wild
hermit with his raw flesh in Lent.

2. I pass to the Monasteries. Mostly they sprang
out of the neighborhood of hermitages, like The Mo-
their Egyptian prototypes; but they too gradu- nasteries.
ally acquired a peculiar mission in the Russian history
— a mission disclosed in their outward aspect and situation. We look round from the walls of the Kremlin
over the city of Moscow. What are the landmarks
which break the endless complication of domes and
cupolas in every street and square? The eye rests at
once on the towers of vast monasteries which at regular
intervals encircle the outskirts of the whole city, each
encompassed with its embattled walls, forming together
a girdle of gigantic fortresses. Or we stand on the
grass-grown walls of the great Novgorod; the ancient
city has shrunk into a mere village within their circuit;
and without, instead of the wide expanse of buildings
which fill up the view of the later capital of Moscow,
is now a desolate wilderness. Yet this one feature remains alike in both. At regular intervals, but here
isolated and in deserted solitudes, the circle of monasteries — half sanctuaries, half fortresses — preserves
the ribs of the huge skeleton from which the flesh of

[1] For an excellent description of the better and more prophet-like aspect
of the Dervishes, see Wolff's Life, i. 477.

human habitation and cultivation has long since fallen
away. This is the true aspect of the Russian monasteries. Like the convent of Sinai, like the convents of
Greece, they are the refuges of national life, or the
monuments of victories won for an oppressed population against invaders and conquerors.

IV. This brings me to what I have called the two
leading events of the mediæval age of Russia,
in which the Russian Church played so conspicuous a part.

Events
of the
Russian
Church.

1. The first was the occupation of Russia for two centuries by the Mongol Tartars. The leading
event of mediæval Europe was, undoubtedly,
the Crusades. In the Crusades Russia took no part.

Tartar
invasion.

Its separation from them is one of its most important
grounds of separation from the Western World. But in
its constant struggle against the Mussulman Tartars of
the North it had a Crusade of its own, far more close
and severe, more disastrous in its duration, and pro-
portionately more glorious in its close, than the remote
struggle of Europe with the Mussulman Turks and
Arabs of the South. With the history only of one
Western country can the history of Russia be in this
respect compared. In Spain, as well as in Russia, the
effects, partly in similar partly in dissimilar forms, are
most strongly impressed on the religious life of the nation. Civilization and consolidation must have been greatly checked. But the intensity of devotional feeling, the
close identification of the religious and the national life,
must have been immeasurably deepened by this long
struggle against foreign enemies of a different faith.

The very name for a Russian peasant, *Christianin*
(*Christian*), is a relic of the times when a Christian
was a distinctive term for a Russian. On the top of
every Russian church, in every town which was under

the Tartar yoke,[1] the Cross is planted on a Crescent.
To this is to be ascribed the strong anti-Mussulman feeling which animates the heart of every Russian peasant,
and which, whether by nature or policy, is so powerful
an engine in all the wars which have in later times been
waged against Turkey.

It was during this Tartar dominion that the clergy
showed themselves the deliverers of their country. The
post that is occupied in Europe by princes and warriors
against the several oppressors of their respective countries, is occupied in Russia against the Tartars, as in
modern Greece against the Turks, by the Clergy and
the Church. Of this fire of national and re- Foundation
ligious independence the sacred hearth is to of the
Troitza
be sought, not at Kieff or Moscow, but at a Monastery, A. D.
spot which, from this singular union of asso- 1338.
ciations, has, down to the present day, remained the
chief sanctuary of the Russian Church and nation —
the Monastery of the Troitza (" the Holy Trinity "),
which was founded at this period; the period marked,
as in Europe at large so in Russia, by the pestilence of
the Black Death,[2] and in the latter followed by the
general establishment of convents, of which that of
the Troitza was chief. About sixty miles from Moscow, in the midst of the wild forest which covers all
the uncultivated ground of the Russian soil, rises the
immense pile of the ancient convent. Like the Kremlin, it combines the various institutions of monastery,
university, palace, cathedral, churches, planted within a
circuit of walls, which by their height and strength, and
towers and trench, indicate that, over and above all

---

[1] King's Greek Church in Russia, 24.

[2] The chief year of the Black Death was 1348. It reached Russia in
1351. The Troitza was founded in 1338; but its great increase, and its
dependencies, date from 1360. Strahl, 163–165.

these other elements of life, was superadded in a predominant degree that of a camp or fortress.

Hither from all parts of the Empire stream innumerable pilgrims. Every village along the road from Moscow is consecrated by some religious or historical association. No Emperor comes to Moscow without paying his devotions there. The terrible Ivan built at least half of its stately edifices. Peter, as we shall see, twice took refuge within its sacred walls. The wicked Catherine used to go thither from Moscow with all her court, on foot, by easy stages, five miles a day; with vessels of the water of the Neva always at hand to refresh her. On foot many of the nobles of the present day have made their first pilgrimage. No presents are so welcome to their families on their return, as the memorials of sacred bread, or sacred relics, from "the Laura" or convent of the Holy Trinity. The office of Archimandrite, or Abbot, is so high that for many years it has never been given to any one but the Metropolitan of Moscow: the actual chief, the Hegoumenos or Prior, is himself one of the highest dignitaries of Russia, and lives in a style of magnificence, which is to our eyes rather like that of the heads of our grandest colleges, than of the ruler of a monastic establishment. "Whence " do you derive your support for all this state?" asked the Emperor Nicholas of the present Prior.[1] He answered nothing, but pointed to the chest which at that moment, and at all hours of the day, was receiving the offerings of the long array of pilgrims, and which has contributed in no slight degree to the necessities of the Empire.

Its present splendor stands but in remote connection with its simple beginning, to which we now return. In

---

[1] This is also told of Philaret, the Metropolitan, in regard to the offerings made before the picture at the entrance to the public place of Moscow.

the treasury of the convent we still can trace back, by gradual stages, the gorgeous vestments glittering with "barbaric gold and pearls," to the rough sackcloth of the founder; or the mass of wealth which each succeeding Czar has heaped upon the consecrated vessels, to the wooden chalice in which the first sacrament was there celebrated by Sergius of Radonegl. We may be reminded of our profound ignorance of those old Eastern worthies, and of the way in which history is often composed, by the fact that our common Western histories of Russia pass by the whole period of the times of Sergius, without even an allusion to a name at least as dear to every Russian heart, and as familiar among Russian homes, as William Tell to a Swiss, or as Joan of Arc to a Frenchman. In the depth of these then S. Sergius, A. D. 1315– impenetrable forests, with the bears for his com- 1392; canonized panions, lived, in the fourteenth century, the 1428. holy hermit Sergius. Like the lives of Western saints of the same period, his career is encircled with a halo of legend. But there is no reason to doubt the fact, which still lives in a thousand memorials throughout his grateful country. When the heart of the Grand-Prince Demetrius[1] failed in his advance against the Battle of the Don, Tartars, it was the remonstrance, the blessing, A. D. 1380. the prayers of Sergius that supported him to the field of battle on the Don, which gave him the cherished name of Demetrius of the Don. No historical picture or sculpture in Russia is more frequent than that which represents the youthful warrior receiving the benediction of the aged hermit. Two of his monks, Peresvet and Osliab, accompanied the Prince to the

---

[1] Demetrius himself was almost a saint; he went daily to church, and received the sacrament once a week in the great fasts, and wore a hair-cloth next his skin. Strahl, 171. At the battle he sang aloud the 46th Psalm. Karamsin, i. 81.

field, and fought in coats of mail drawn over their monastic habit ; and the battle was begun by the single combat of Peresvet with a gigantic Tartar, champion of the Mussulman host.[1]

The two chief convents in the suburbs of Moscow still preserve the recollection of that day. One is the vast fortress of the Donskoi[2] Monastery, under the Sparrow Hills. The other is the Simonoff Monastery, founded by the nephew of Sergius on the banks of the Mosqua, on a beautiful spot chosen by the saint himself, and its earliest site was consecrated by the tomb which covers the bodies of his two warlike monks. From that day forth he stood out in the national recollections as the champion of Russia. It was still from his convent that the noblest patriotic inspirations were drawn, and, as he had led the way in giving the first great repulse to the Tartar power, so the final blow in like manner came from a successor in his place. When Ivan III. wavered, as Demetrius had wavered before him, it was by the remonstrance of Archbishop Bassian, formerly Prior of the Trinity Convent, that Ivan too was driven, almost against his will, to the field. "Dost thou fear death?"—so he was addressed by the aged prelate. "Thou too must die as well as "others ; death is the lot of all, man, beast, and bird "alike ; none avoid it. Give these warriors into my "hand, and, old as I am, I will not spare myself, nor "turn my back upon the Tartars."[3] The Metropolitan, we are told, added his exhortations to those of Bassian. Ivan returned to the camp, the Khan of the Golden Horde fled without a blow, and Russia was set free forever.

[1] Mouravieff, 62.

[2] It commemorated, not indeed the actual victory of the Don, but the gift of a sacred picture by the Kalmucks of the Don to Demetrius (Strahl, 168), which in later times went out against the Tartars of the Crimea.

[3] Mouravieff, 88.

2. The invasion and expulsion of the Mongols form the first crisis of Russian history; the invasion and expulsion of the Poles form the second. We are so much accustomed to regard the Russians as the oppressors of the Poles, that we find it difficult to conceive a time when the Poles were the oppressors of the Russians. Our minds are so preoccupied with the Russian partition of Poland, that we almost refuse to believe in the fact that there was once a Polish partition of Russia. Yet so it was, and neither the civil nor the ecclesiastical history of Russia can be understood without bearing in mind that long family quarrel between the two great Sclavonic nations, to us so obscure, to them so ingrained, so inveterate, so intelligible. Its political effects may be here dismissed. But its ecclesiastical effect was hardly less important than that produced by the wars with the Tartars. As the vehement anti-Mussulman spirit of the nation was quickened by the one, so the vehement anti-Popish spirit received a strong impulse from the other. Poland was to Russia the chief representative of the Latin Church; Papal supremacy was in the national mind identified with the Polish conquest; and the war between the two nations became identified with a war between the two Churches.[1] The nations have now

The Polish
Invasion,
A. D. 1605.

---

[1] The following extracts from the Eastern travellers who visited Russia in the seventeenth century illustrate this feeling : —

"And why do I pronounce the Poles accursed ? Because they have shown themselves more debased and wicked than the corrupt worshippers of idols, by their cruel conduct to Christians, thinking to abolish the very name of Orthodox. God perpetuate the empire of the Turks for ever and ever ! for they take their impost and enter into no account of religion, be their subjects Christians or Nazarenes, Jews or Samaritans : whereas these accursed Poles were not content with taxes and tithes from the brethren of Christ, though willing to serve them ; but, according to the true relation we shall afterwards give of their history, they subjected them to the authority of the enemies of Christ, the tyrannical Jews, who did not even permit them to build churches, nor leave them any priests that knew the mysteries of their faith; but, on the

changed places in their relative importance, but not
more so than Spain and England since the days when
our own terror and hatred of Popery were inspired by
the Spanish Armada. As the deliverance from the Spanish Armada to the Church and State of England, so was
the deliverance from the Polish yoke to the Church and
State of Russia. It was the latter part of the seventeenth century that witnessed the crisis of the struggle.
The dynasty of Ruric came to an end in the death or
the murder of the child Demetrius, last of the race.
Pretender after pretender, false Demetrius succeeding
to false Demetrius, occupied the Imperial throne, and
the Polish Sigismund seized the opportunity of sup-
porting the armies of the impostor. Moscow was in
their hands, the Latin services were chanted in the
Kremlin, organs were heard in the Patriarchal church,[1]
anarchy spread through the country.

Once again it was the Church that saved the Empire,
Siege of the and the monastery of Sergius that saved them
Troitza Monastery, A. D. 1613. both. Hermogenes the Patriarch stood his
ground for a time, but he was starved to death,
imprisoned almost within his own cathedral. Philaret,
Archbishop of Rostoff, maintained the sinking spirit of
the people, till he too was carried off into captivity.
But now, when Czar and Patriarch had disappeared,

contrary, violated their wives and daughters, if they at all appeared abroad
in the public exercise of their religion. When the Almighty had seen their
tyranny, he made them the laughing-stock of their enemies, and laid them low
and contemptible, as we shall truly relate of them in the sequel, until he had
taken vengeance of their haughtiness." — *Macarius,* i. 165.

" O you infidels ! O you monsters of impurity ! O you hearts of stone !
what had the nuns and women done ? what the girls and boys and infant
children, that you should murder them ? If you had courage, you would
have gone to fight with the venerable old man who has set you as a laughing-
stock to the world, who has slain your princes and grandees, and annihilated
your heroes and valiant men." — *Ibid.* i. 183.

[1] Strahl, 223 ; A. D. 1605.

when the holy city of Moscow itself was in the hands of strangers and heretics, the Trinity Convent still remained erect. Its fortifications, its moat, its towers, now served a noble purpose in resisting the long siege. Its warlike traditions revived in the persons of its soldier-like monks. As Demetrius of the Don had received his blessing from Sergius, so the true patriots of this second struggle — the Prince Pojarsky, and Minin, chief of one of the guilds of Nijni-Novgorod — received their mission (as we see again and again repeated in national monuments) from the successor of Sergius, the courageous Dionysius. The soul of the movement in the convent itself was the bursar of immortal memory, Abraham Palitzin. Rude pictures still represent, in strange confusion, the mixture of artillery and apparitions, fighting monks and fighting ghosts, which drove back the Polish assailants from the walls of the beleaguered fortress. The convent was for the time the whole empire, and its victory was the deliverance of Russia. Moscow was retaken. In the townhouse of the Trinity Monastery, still bearing the same name, the Prior presided at the Council which terminated the civil war, and the bursar Abraham announced its results to the assembled people. Of the religious aspect of that great deliverance many are the memorials which remain, standing monuments of the final overthrow of the Latin Church in Russia. Every one has heard of the Sacred Gate, the Redeemer's Gate, the chief entrance to the Kremlin, through The Sacred Gate. which no Russian, not even the Emperor himself, will presume, through which no stranger is allowed, to pass with his head covered. The practice dates from this epoch. The picture of the Redeemer which hangs over the gate, and invests it with this unequalled sanctity, is that which went before Pojarsky's army when he set forth at the bidding of Dionysius. Within the church of the Archangel, amidst the tombs of the Czars, the one canonized saint, the one coffin glittering with jewels and gold, is that of the young child Demetrius, whose death or martyrdom was lamented with an everlasting lamentation, as the cause of the convulsions which followed upon it. The very existence of the present Imperial dynasty is a living tribute to the services of the Russian hierarchy at the time of their country's greatest need. Now that the race of Ruric was passed away, and that the nobles had proved unequal to the conflict, the people looked to the clergy as the class from whose ranks they should take their future chief. Philaret, once a humble parish priest, then Archbishop of Rostoff, afterwards Patriarch of Moscow, and his wife Martha, separated from her husband in the long wars, and secluded as a nun in the convent of Kostroma, were the parents of the future Czar.

The child Demetrius.

Michael Romanoff, son of Philaret, grandson of Roman, became the founder of the house of Romanoff, the ancestor of Peter and Alexander and Nicholas. So ended the period of the Middle Ages in Russia; so was wrought out the deliverance of the Empire and the Church by the monastery of Sergius.

Election of Michael Romanoff.

CHRONOLOGICAL TABLE.

A. D.

1205.
1472. } Invasion and dominion of Tartars.

1325. Foundation of the Church of Moscow. Peter, the first Metropolitan.

1338. Foundation of the Troitza Monastery by Sergius.

1354. Alexis, Metropolitan.

1380. Battle of the Don. Victory over the Tartars by Demetrius Donsky.

1395. Retreat of Tamerlane.

1448.
1461. } Jonah, first Metropolitan; independent of the see of Constantinople.

1467. Marriage of Ivan III. with Sophia of Constantinople. Building of the Cathedral of Moscow.

1472. Fall of Novgorod the Great.
Victory of Ivan III. on the Oka.

1533.
1584. } Ivan IV., or the Terrible.

1568. Martyrdom of S. Philip.

1587. Job, first Patriarch.

1598. End of the race of Ruric.

1598.
1605. } Boris Godonoff.

1606. } Wars of the Pretenders, and Invasion of the Poles.
1613. } Siege of the Troitza Convent. Expulsion of the Poles.

LECTURE XI.

THE PATRIARCH NICON.

THE accessible materials for the Life of Nicon are: —

1. " The Travels of Macarius in the 17th Century." Translated from the Arabic by the Oriental Translation Society
(see p. 458).
2. Bachmeister's " Life of Nicon." (German.)
3. Hermann's " History of Russia." (German.)
4. Mouravieff's " History of the Russian Church," c. x.–xiv.
5. Palmer's " Dissertations on the Orthodox Communion," c. v.
6. " Collins's Account of Russia." 1667–1678.

THERE has seldom been a more decisive epoch in the
history of a nation than that which witnessed the succession of the Romanoff dynasty to the throne of Muscovy. A deep calm, like that which supervened on the
Wars of the Roses in England, or on the Wars of the
League in France, succeeded to the long struggle of
the Wars of the Pretenders at the commencement of
the seventeenth century in Russia. As elsewhere, so
here, the fortunes of the Church and the nation were
inseparable. The Czar Michael and the Patriarch Philaret ruled together, an event most characteristic of the
people, and, as a Russian historian observes, " remark-
" able in the annals of the world, which has in no coun-
" try nor in any time been repeated, of a father as
" patriarch and his son as sovereign governing together
" the kingdom." The nation was freed from the Tartars
and the Poles; the Church was freed from the Mussul-

mans and the Latins; their independent existence now, for the first time, gave hope for their free development.

It is on this stage, thus newly created, that we have to witness the parallel, such as it is, which Rus- Eastern sian history presents to the Western Reforma- Reformation. tion. That event is so thoroughly a part of our existence that we can hardly imagine a Church or a Christian nation in existence which has not passed through it in some form or other. Such an exception, at first sight, seems to be found in Russia. Yet even this is not altogether an exception. It is a fact much to be observed, that the Church and the nation of all others in Europe the most tenacious of antiquity could not escape a Reformation entirely.[1] The nearest approach made in the Eastern Church to an adoption of the general doctrines of the Western Reformation was by Cyril Lucar, Cyril Greek Patriarch of Alexandria, and afterwards Lucar, A. D. 1613– of Constantinople.[2] His whole life was a com- 1638. plicated struggle against the Jesuits of the Latin, and the hierarchy of the Greek, Church, and a yearning after the Protestant, chiefly the Calvinistic, theology of Geneva, Holland, and England. Abbot and Laud both encouraged his advances, and whilst his attempts in his own Church ended with his barbarous murder at Constantinople, one monument of his intercourse with our Church still remains, in our possession of his precious gift of the "Alexandrian manuscript" of the Scriptures.

In Russia the only direct attempt at a religious revolution was that made contemporaneously with Judaisers the Reformation, and possibly in connection under Ivan III.

[1] For the Eastern view of the Reformation, see Macarius, i. 224.

[2] For Cyril Lucar, see a brief sketch in Dean Waddington's Greek Church, 173; and an elaborate, though unfavorable, account in Neale's Alexandrian Church, ii. 356–454.

with it, in the reign of Ivan III., when a secret but extensive sect of Judaisers took possession of some of the leading offices of Church and State, and at one time actually occupied the Patriarchal chair, and was totally suppressed by one of the few acts of violent persecution[1] which have stained the usual tolerance of the Eastern Church. A more serious purpose of rectifying Reforms of the abuses, at least of the outward system of Ivan IV. the Church, was conceived, and in part executed, by the awful Ivan, who, as if to make himself a warning to all Churches, Protestant as well as Papal, combined with his hideous crimes the character, not only, as we have sufficiently seen, of a religious ascetic, but also of a religious reformer. From his retreat at Alexandroff he issued a denunciation of monastic abuses worthy of Luther or Henry VIII., and Horsey describes the delight and pastime with which he brought out " seven rebellious big fat friars, one after another, with " a cross and beads in one hand, and, through the Em- " peror's great favor, a boar-spear in the other, to be ex- " posed to a wild boar, fierce and hungry, who caught " and crushed his victims, as a cat doth a mouse, tearing " their weeds in pieces till he came to the flesh, blood, " and bones, and so devoured them for a prey."[2] But Ivan was not the man to carry through a steady and deliberate plan. One only permanent work he left behind, no doubt of infinite importance in this direction, a printing-press at Moscow;[3] and the first printed Russian volume, still preserved in the Imperial Library at St. Petersburg, is the version of the Acts of the Apostles dating from his reign.

All these attempts were more or less isolated and

---

[1] See Palmer's Orthodox Communion, 142; also a Russian historical romance called " The Heretic."

[2] Horsey, 178.   [3] Strahl, 282.

abortive. It is not till the period on which we have
now entered that the true work of the Russian Reformation begins. Two leading figures fix our attention. The first, who guides us through the period of
transition from the middle of the seventeenth century
to the beginning of the eighteenth, is the Patriarch
Nicon. The second, who will guide us through the
period of completion, is the Emperor Peter.

Our present concern is with the Patriarch Nicon. In
naming his name we feel at once the immense The Patri-
disadvantage of Eastern as compared with West- arch Nicon.
ern history. How few of us have ever heard of him:
how impenetrable even to those who have heard of him
is the darkness of the original language in which his
biography is wrapped up! Yet he is unquestionably
the greatest character in the annals of the Russian
hierarchy; and, even in the annals of the Eastern hierarchy generally, there are but few who can be ranked
before him as ecclesiastical statesmen. Photius in the
ninth century, and Chrysostom in the fourth, in some
respects remind us of the career of Nicon. Indeed, the
similarity may be fairly taken as a proof of the identity
of spirit which breathed, at the interval of six centuries,
through the two main branches of the Eastern Church.
He was a Russian Chrysostom. He was also, in coarse
and homely proportions, a Russian Luther and a Russian Wolsey. But here the differences are far more
palpable than those which divide him from the Patriarch
of Constantinople. Through all the obscurity which
hangs over him, there is yet discernible a genuine
human character, combining with a wilful barbaric obstinacy, as of an overgrown spoiled child, the caustic
humor, the indefatigable energy, of a statesman of the
extremest West. In the series of portraits professing
to represent the hierarchy of ancient Russia, his is the

58

first that imprints itself on our minds with the stamp
of individual originality. In the various monasteries
over which he presided, his grim countenance looks
down upon us with bloodshot eyes, red complexion,
and brows deeply knit. The vast length of his pon-
tifical robes, preserved as relics of his magnificence, reveals to us the commanding stature, no less than seven
feet, which he shares with so many of his more distinguished countrymen. And his story, if it could be told
with the details, — many of which lie buried in the
Russian archives, but some of which have been published and translated in well-known works, — is as full of
dramatic complexity and pathetic interest, as was ever
conceived in Timon of Athens or King Lear.

I pass over the events of his early life. Born in the
troubles of the wars of the Pretenders, raised from the
ranks of the peasants to the successive dignities of
Archimandrite of the Solovetzky monastery, and Metropolitan of the great Novgorod,[1] he finally was appointed to the Patriarchate of Moscow. In that high
office he ruled the Church and State of Russia for six
eventful years.

One curious source of information we possess of this
period, which I shall frequently quote. As in
Journal of the reign of Ivan we had the advantage of the
Macarius. observations of an English eye-witness from the West,
so in the Patriarchate of Nicon we have the advantage
of a Syrian eye-witness from the East. Macarius, Patriarch of Antioch, had travelled into Russia to collect
money for his distant see, and was accompanied by his
Archdeacon Paul, who has left us a minute journal of
all that occurred, having, as he says, "roused his lan-
"guid mind to the task, and stretched towards the ob-

---

1 He had first been a married parochial priest, but on the loss of his third
child entered a convent. Levesque, iv. 65.

" ject his recoiling pen." It is valuable as giving us the impressions of a Christian from the remote East on seeing the Church of Russia, and thus enabling us to estimate the difference between the two ; and yet more as giving us the impression produced on the garrulous Archdeacon by the contrast between the shadowy Oriental prelates and the robust and vigorous character of the Patriarch of Moscow.

Nicon, as I have said, was the first Russian reformer. But we must not expect from this parallel a direct reformation of doctrine or of philosophy. Such a reformation has never taken place in any branch of the Eastern Church ; partly because it was less needed than in the West, partly because the whole character of the nations composing the Eastern Church has set in another direction. But still Nicon was, so far as we know, the first Eastern ecclesiastic, with the single exception of Cyril Lucar, who saw that the time was come for giving life to the ceremonial observances, and a moral direction to the devotional feelings of Oriental worship.

He set himself with stern severity and indomitable courage to root out the various abuses of the Russian hierarchy, especially the one crying *His reforms.* evil unfortunately not yet extinct — intemperance. To this day they remember, with a mixture of veneration and hatred, what they expressively call the " hedgehog " hand " with which he kept them down.

In his own person he exhibited a new type of pastoral virtues. Of unbounded munificence, he founded hospitals and almshouses in his successive sees for orphans, widows, and aged persons. In the famine which devastated the city of Novgorod, he showed a generosity worthy of Carlo Borromeo at Milan, or of Francke at Halle. He visited the prisons,[1] if not with

[1] Levesque, iv. 68.

the philanthropy of a Howard, at least with a prompti-
tude of justice rare in Eastern Christendom, " on his
" own personal examination releasing the prisoners if
" he found them innocent." [1]

He broke through practices, both of Church and
State, to which long custom had in Russia given an
almost religious consecration. Through his intervention, the Oriental seclusion of the female sex was first
infringed. At his injunction — still, it is true, fenced
about by many precautions — the Empress, who had
before never entered a church except under cover of
night, now appeared publicly by day. Sacred pictures
to which,[2] in his judgment, an idolatrous veneration was
shown, were taken away. The baptisms of the Western Church, of which the validity is to this day denied
by the Church of Constantinople, were by his sanction
first recognized in the Church of Russia. It was,[3] indeed, granted only after a long and stormy discussion ;
and even then conceded only to the Latin Church.
Still it was an immense advance in charity, and was
the first opening of a door of sympathy towards the
West.

From so decayed a stock as the Byzantine Church,
especially after its subjugation to the Ottoman power,
no great accession of new life could be expected. But
it was at least a pardonable feeling which led the
Russian reformer to look in the first instance to that
ancient source of the civilization of Russia, and, in earlier times, of the civilization of Europe. The advances
in education first introduced under Ivan the Terrible,
and then interrupted by the wars of the Pretenders,

---

[1] Mouravieff, 196.

[2] Levesque, iv. 76.   Strahl, 229 ; A. D. 1664.   " He is no lover of images."
Collins, 15.

[3] Macarius, ii. 85.   See Palmer's Orthodox Communion, xii. xiii.

started under Nicon into fresh life. The printing-press was again set to work. Greek and Latin were now first taught in the schools.[1] The "gross and harsh intonations of the Muscovites," as they are called by the Syrian travellers, now gave way to the sweet chants[2] of the Cossack choristers, brought partly from Poland, partly from Greece, the first beginnings of that vocal music which has since become the glory of the Russian worship. The Bible,[3] which he had profoundly studied for himself in his youth, he now sought to exhibit in the purest form of which the Sclavonic translation admitted. Deputations of learned scholars were sent to the Grecian monasteries to collect manuscripts to carry on the collations of the sacred books, which the Russian monk Maximus in the previous generation had died in attempting to accomplish.

Chiefest of all was the change, even yet hardly appreciated in his country, and entirely without an example in the rest of the East at that time, — the revival of preaching. From his lips was first heard, after many centuries, the sound of a living practical sermon. We have the impression which this revolution produced on the mind of the Archdeacon of Antioch : —

His preaching.

"Remark, brother," says the Archdeacon Paul, "what happened now, — an occurrence which surprised and confused our understandings. It was, that so far were they from being content with their lengthened services, that the Deacon brought to the Patriarch the book of Lessons, which they opened before him ; and he began to read the lesson for this day, on the subject of the Second Advent : and not only did he read it, but he preached and expounded the meanings of the words to the standing and silent assembly ; until our spirits were broken

---

[1] Levesque, iv. 76.　　　[2] Macarius, ii. 231; Haxthausen, iii. 114.
[3] Levesque, iv. 70.

within us during the tedious while. God preserve us and
save us ! " [1]

And on another occasion : —

" The Patriarch was not satisfied with the Ritual, but he must
needs crown all with an admonition and copious sermon. God
grant him moderation ! His heart did not ache for the Emperor
nor for the tender infants, standing uncovered in the intense
cold. What should we say to this in our country ? " [2]

A third example gives us at once a more pleasing
impression, and a clearer notion of his manner of
preaching. The Czar was going forth to war : —

" The Patriarch blessed him, and then stood before him, and
raised his voice in prayer for him, reading a beautiful exordium,
with parables and proverbs from the ancients, such as how God
granted victory to Moses over Pharaoh, &c. ; from modern history, such as the victory of Constantine over Maximianus and
Maxentius, &c. ; adding many examples of this nature, and with
much prolixity of discourse moving on at his leisure, like a copious stream of flowing water. When he stammered and confused his words, or made mistakes, he set himself right again
with perfect composure. No one seemed to find fault with him
or to be tired of his discourse ; but all were silent and attentive,
as if each were a slave before his master." [3]

These, or such as these, were amongst the most conspicuous of the reforms of Nicon ; very small according
to our Western notions, yet still in the only direction
suited for an Oriental Church. Let those who doubt
turn to the temperate hopes of an Eastern reformation
as expressed by one certainly not indulgent to superstition, who added to a wide range of liberal learning a
special knowledge of the Christian East.[4] Or let any
one who knows anything of modern Athens say who

1 Macarius, i. 406.   2 Ibid. 49, 51, 52.   3 Ibid. ii. 59.
4 Dean Waddington's Greek Church, chap. viii.–x.

amongst the English and American missionaries in those regions are named as the most undoubted benefactors of the Church of Greece, — those who have attempted to subvert the existing forms of faith, or those who by education and social intercourse have infused a new life into those forms?[1] Such considerations may induce us to pardon the shortcomings and hail the genuine efforts of the Patriarch Nicon. But, in carrying out his schemes, two points exhibit the rude elements both of his own individual character and also of his Church and country.

First, it is impossible not to be struck by the savage spirit in which he fulfilled his task. We are not altogether unaccustomed to rough action and speech in Martin Luther and John Knox, but we must expect something more in the Scythian atmosphere of Russia. Again I refer to the journal of Archdeacon Paul. "He was," says the Archdeacon, "a very butcher "amongst the clergy. His janissaries are perpetually "going round the city; and when they find any priest "or monk in a state of intoxication, they carry him to "prison, strip him, and scourge him.[2] His prisons are "full of them, galled with heavy chains and logs of "wood on their necks and legs, or they sift flour day "and night in the bakehouse."[3] The deserts of Siberia were filled with dissolute clergy banished there with their wives and children.[4] An instance is recorded, hardly credible, but too characteristic to be omitted, perhaps not so much of his wild severity as of his barbarian humor. It was at one of the numerous banquets attended by the Patriarch of Antioch, that Nicon, partly to show off the wonders of his master's vast dominions,

His savage manners.

---

[1] I allude, of course, to the excellent effects of the Greek school established at Athens by Mr. and Mrs. Hill.
[2] Macarius, ii. 364. [3] Ibid. ii. 76. [4] Ibid. 78.

partly to satisfy the curiosity of his own inquisitive
mind, called before him thirty chiefs of a distant Kal-
muck tribe, called, from the appearance of their physi-
ognomies, the dog-faced tribe, or (as a euphemism) the
tribe of the dog-faced saint, S. Christopher.

"As soon as they entered, the whole assembly was struck with
horror. They bared their heads, and bowed to the Patriarch
with great veneration, crouching to the ground all in a lump like
pigs. After various questions as to their mode of life, and travelling, and warfare, he said, 'Is it really true that you eat the
flesh of men?' They laughed, and answered, 'We eat our
dead, and we eat dogs; how then should we not eat men?' He
said, 'How do you eat men?' They replied, 'When we have
conquered a man, we cut away his nose, and then carve him into
pieces and eat him.' He said, 'I have a man here who deserves
death: I will send for him and present him to you, that you may
eat him.' Hereupon they began earnestly to entreat him, saying, 'Good Lord, whenever you have any men deserving of
death, do not trouble yourself about their guilt or their punishment; but give them us to eat, and you will do us a great kindness.'"

The unfortunate victim, with whom Nicon intended
to play off this experiment, was no less a person than
the Metropolitan of Mira. It happened that amidst
other "odious deformities" of himself and his companions on a recent visit to Moscow, they were found
smoking tobacco; and all, except himself, were sent
into banishment. Nicon was still, however, enraged
against him; "for," says the Syrian Archdeacon, "no
" crime with him is ever forgiven: and he now sent to
" have him brought to these savages that they might
" eat him. But he was not to be found, having hid
" himself." [1]

It may be hoped, however, that this was only a severe
practical jest; for on a subsequent occasion, when the

[1] Macarius, i. 420.

Patriarch saw the astonishment of the Syrians at the dog-faced tribe, " he came forward," says the Archdeacon, " and taking me by the hand led me before the ministers " and the assembled crowd, called the savages, as if to " eat me, that he might have his laugh and sport with " us, whilst I was shuddering and quaking with fear. " So also he did with others." One, who was a deacon, he actually delivered into their hands. As soon as they laid hold of him they tore his clothes to tatters in scrambling for him, and it was with difficulty that he was rescued, by redeeming him with fish and money, which the Patriarch gave as his price. The poor dea-con, from fright and horror,[1] lay ill for a long time after-wards.

Another still more serious instance is related. Three deacons had married again after the death of their wives by the plague. As soon as the Patriarch had heard of this, he bound them in fetters, and sent them to the Trinity Monastery, commanding that they should be confined in a wooden cell, without food, till they died of misery. The Patriarch of Antioch happened to see them on his visit, and was so much troubled by their tears and moans, that he interested himself on their be-half, and obtained their liberty.[2] We may hope that they, like the deacon just mentioned in the hands of the dog-faced tribe, were placed there rather for terror than with any deliberate intention of fulfilling the threat. But the incidents are worthy of the countrymen of Ivan the Terrible, as we have seen, and of Peter the Great, as we shall see.

The second point in Nicon's career is more important.

With all his energy and love of knowledge, he was a true son of the Eastern Church in his rigid ob- His adher-servance of its ordinances and ritual. He shared ence to the Russian

[1] Macarius, ii. 164.   [2] Ibid. ii. 151.

but little in the tolerant and indulgent feelings which have usually marked the Russian policy towards members of other Churches. Perceiving, as he passed through the streets, that the European merchants showed no marks of reverence to the sacred pictures, he drove them out of Moscow. He made a point of compelling all foreigners to appear as such, or incorporate themselves into the Russian nation by baptism. An Armenian merchant offered him a sum of fifty thousand dinars to retain his long white beard; but Nicon's only answer was, "Be baptized; become like one of us."[1] The merchant refused, and the Armenians were banished.

In one direction only his mind was entirely, even and Greek sensitively, open to receive new impressions. ritual. That direction was towards the ancient Church and Empire of Constantinople. "I am a Russian," he said, "and the son of a Russian;[2] but my faith and my "religion are Grecian."

Such a feeling was natural, even in a more civilized mind than Nicon's. The Church of Constantinople even then retained, as we may see from the relations of Cyril Lucar to the English Church, something of a European influence; and any Russian churchman of wider views would naturally turn to the ancient metropolis of his faith. But it had, in Nicon's case, this unfortunate effect. From Constantinople, as it then was, no new spiritual life could be expected; at best an antiquarian and ceremonial form of religion, which not only narrowed the horizon of the reformer who looked to it for assistance, but turned his energies into subordinate channels, and aggravated the ceremonial tendencies already existing with too much force in his own Church. With the vast field which Nicon had before him, it is mournful to see the power which might have

[1] Macarius, ii. 23.   [2] Ibid. ii. 86.

reanimated the whole ecclesiastical system employed on the correction of minute errors of ritual which can only be discovered through a microscope.

In order to understand the importance ascribed to them either by him or by his opponents, we must bear in mind the almost Chinese minuteness of the civil and ecclesiastical ceremonial of the Russian Church and Court at that time.　He saw worked in pearls on a vestment of a former metropolitan, the authentic copy of the Nicene Creed, and perceived that the word " holy " had been inserted before the words " giver of " life."　Deputations went to Athos for correct copies of the service-books.　The printing-press, lately established by him in Moscow, was set to work to circulate new rubrics.[1]　His earliest pleasure palace was an imitation of the Iberian convent in Athos ; and for him it was that the copy of the picture in that convent was bought, which still occupies the most distinguished place amongst the sacred pictures of Moscow.[2]　Stern as he was, he was constantly asking questions from the Syrian strangers, to set his own ceremonial straight.[3]　Benedictions with three fingers instead of two, a white altar cloth instead of an embroidered one, pictures kissed only twice a year, the cross signed the wrong way, wrong inflections in pronouncing the Creed,[4] — these were the points to which he devoted his gigantic energy, and on which, as we shall see, he encountered the most frantic opposition.

We are filled with surprise as we read of the contentions occasioned by these points, to us so infinitely insignificant.　But remember the controversies which have rent our own Church in the sixteenth century (and can we altogether except the nineteenth?) ; re-

1 Macarius, ii. 85.　　　　　　2 Ibid. ii. 173.
3 Ibid. ii. 414.　　　　　　　4 Ibid. ii. 85.

member the parties and the mobs which have been formed to attack or to defend a surplice, to reform or to oppose a rubric, and perhaps we shall feel that we, the descendants and the followers of the Puritans on one side, or of Laud on the other, are not entitled to cast the first stone at Nicon or his adversaries.

For the time his powerful hand repressed any overt Opposition outbreak: but some murmured inwardly; men, to his changes. such as the Syrian Archdeacon observes are to be found in every nation, " of a heavy nature and un-" derstanding, saying within themselves, ' We will not " alter our books nor our rites and ceremonies, which " we received from of old.' [1] But they had not the " force to speak openly, for the anger of the Patriarch " is not to be withstood; witness what he did with the " Bishop of Kolomna." Take two instances of these suppressed murmurs and of his mode of dealing with them, from several points of view highly illustrative of this contest.

He watched with jealousy (herein agreeing with many in the coming generation who else would have been most opposed to him) the introduction of pictures painted after the European fashion into the houses of the Russian nobles. Listen to Archdeacon Paul's account of his treatment of this subject, so closely interwoven, as we have seen, with the whole religious feeling of Russia : —

" Some of the Muscovite painters had learned to paint new pictures in the Frankish and Polish style.[2] And whereas this Patriarch is a great tyrant and loves the Grecian forms to an extreme, he sent his people and collected from every house wherein they were found such paintings as I have mentioned, even from the palaces of the grandees.[3] Then, putting out the

[1] Macarius, ii. 86.   [2] Ibid. ii. 57.

[3] A similar restriction is said to have been put on instrumental music in private parties, either to check in its growth a custom so alien to the religious

eyes of the pictures, he sent them round the city by Janissaries, publishing an Imperial proclamation in the absence of the Czar that whosoever should henceforth be found painting after such models should be severely punished. . . . When they saw, therefore, what the Patriarch had done to the pictures on this occasion, they judged that he had sinned greatly. Vowing imprecations upon him, and making a tumult, they pronounced him to be an open enemy to holy images. Whilst they were in this disposition of mind the plague appeared, and the sun was darkened on the afternoon of the 12th of August. They immediately said, 'All this that has befallen us is through the wrath of God for what our Patriarch has been committing, in contempt of our holy images.' They were all so violent against him that they made an attempt to kill him, for the Czar was absent and there were but few troops. . . . It was on the return of the Czar that the Patriarch, obtaining his first opportunity of making a discourse in his presence, proceeded at great length to show that the painting after this Frank fashion was unlawful; and he called on our Lord the Patriarch of Antioch to bear witness that certain pictures before them were on the model of the Frank paintings. [They anathematized, therefore, and excommunicated any one who should continue painting like them, and any one who should place them in his house.] Touching them with his hand one by one, and showing them to the congregation, he threw them on the iron pavement of the church to break them to pieces, and ordered them to be burnt. But as the Czar is extremely religious, and has great fear of God, and was standing near us with his head uncovered, attending in humble silence to the discourse, he entreated the Patriarch with a suppressed voice, saying, 'No, Father! do not burn them; rather bury them in the earth.' And so were they disposed of. Every time the Patriarch took up one of those pictures in his hand, he cried aloud, saying, 'This is the picture from the house of the noble such an one, or of such an one' (all grandees of the Empire). His design was to put them to shame, that the rest of the congregation might see it and take warning by their example." [1]

feelings of Russia, or because of the licentious songs and dances with which it was accompanied. Levesque, iv. 64.   [1] Macarius, ii. 50.

The next instance carries us nearer home [1] : —

"The Patriarch, out of his great love for the caps of the Greeks, had just now made for himself a new white latia, in the cut of those of the Greek monks. . . . The headdresses of the Russian monks are very ugly, covering their eyes, and with ears flapping down upon their shoulders. With difficulty can their faces be discerned, especially when they look upon the ground. As for the rest of their clothes, the filth of their dress is very great ; for they never wash their shirts, but wear them continually till they drop off. . . . The Patriarch, conscious of the great love the Czar bore him, and sensible of the advantage afforded him by the presence of the Patriarch of Antioch, mentioned the subject first to him, and then deposited, as usual, his new headdress in the sacristy secretly. Then he brought our master to intercede with the Czar that he might wear them : for he much feared the people, lest they should say that he had annulled their ancient customs and the clerical habits worn by their earliest saints. And so, indeed, it happened to him afterwards ; for when he put them on the people murmured greatly, but secretly through their fear of the Czar. Our master, therefore, approached the Czar, and said, 'We are four Patriarchs in the known world, and the dress of us all is alike : by our consent and permission this our brother has been made Patriarch in the place of the Pope of Rome ; and a token of the Pope is that he is distinguished by his white dress. If it is your majesty's pleasure, I should wish that the Patriarch should wear like us this headdress which I have newly had made for him.' The Czar, through his love for the Patriarch, was delighted at hearing this speech, and answered, 'Bascliaske Oobro !' i. e. 'Very well, Father.' Then taking the cap from our master, he kissed it, and commanded the Patriarch of Moscow to put it on. The Patriarch had no sooner done so than his face was lighted up with joy, and the Grecian headdress fitted him splendidly ; for his former cap shaded his countenance too much. . . . But when the heads of the clergy and the heads of convents, the priests and the laity then present, saw his new dress, they murmured much, saying amongst themselves, 'See how he has

[1] Macarius, ii. 227.

changed the dress of the heads of the clergy here, which they received by inspiration of the Holy Ghost, from the time we became Christians, at the hands of S. Peter, and does not the earth tremble at his act, who, having been hitherto dressed as a Muscovite, has made himself a Greek?' . . . Gradually, however," the Archdeacon proceeds, "the elegance of the Greek costume made its way. Had any of the monks of the Holy Mountain [Athos] been here with loads of headdresses, they would have sold vast numbers at a very high price. Those who obtained them showed faces brilliant with delight. They began to complain of the burdensome weight of their old latias, and threw them off their heads, saying, 'If this Greek dress were not of divine origin, the Patriarch would not have been the first to wear it.'"

We have now, I trust, formed some general conception of the character of Nicon.

I have said that he was not only an Eastern Luther but an Eastern Wolsey. His magnificence was on a scale before unparalleled. His favorite monasteries, four in number, he built anew from the ground, "some living after him, some dying with him." The Patriarchal palace in the Kremlin is his work. For three years the ablest architects in Russia were employed upon it; kitchens, stoves, chapels, such as were never seen before, rose within it. It still remains opposite to the north door of the cathedral. But it was not only in outward aspect that his history resembles that of Wolsey. We are now approaching the more human and dramatic elements of his story, which, whilst they give to it a higher than any mere ecclesiastical interest, justify us in assigning to it a place in history which the peculiarity of his ecclesiastical views would hardly sanction.

It may be supposed, from the traits already given, that Nicon's conduct had made him many enemies. His innovations, as we have seen, and as we shall see

still more clearly in the next century, touched the prejudices of the Russian people in their tenderest point.
His severity exasperated the clergy. His insolence enraged the nobles. The Syrian traveller describes how
the highest functionaries, who used to enter the presence of the Patriarch unbidden, were now kept waiting
on the threshold; and when they entered, it was with
extreme fear — fear many degrees more than they paid
to the sovereign, he sitting and they standing. "There

His friend-
ship with
the Czar
Alexis.
"was," says the Russian historian, "only one
"man who sincerely loved Nicon, and to him
"alone was the Patriarch devoted with all his
"soul, and zealous even to excess for his glory."[1] That
man was the Czar Alexis, son of Michael, and father of
Peter. He had first seen Nicon years before, when he
came up to Moscow from a distant monastery, and had
been greatly struck by his tall stature and manly eloquence and the report of his holy life, and given him
the convent of Novospasky, in which the first princes
and princesses of the Romanoff dynasty were buried.
From that time sprang up their long and close intimacy.
Whilst head of the convent he came every Friday to
the royal chapel in the Kremlin for the purpose of conversing with Alexis after the service. When raised to
the see of Novgorod he went up every winter to consult with him, and procured the gift of the Lake of
Valdai as a halting-place on the road, where he built
the Iberian monastery of which I have before spoken.
When raised at last by the entreaties of the Czar, and
by his affection for him, to the Patriarchate, they became inseparable. "They appeared," I again quote the
Russian historian,[2] "as one and the same person in all
"acts of government, passing all their days together, in
"the church, in the council-chamber, and at the friendly

[1] Mouravieff, 215.   [2] Ibid. 203.

" board.   To unite themselves still closer by the bonds
" of spiritual relationship, the Patriarch became god-
" father to all the children of his sovereign, and they
" both made a mutual vow never to desert each other
" on this side the grave."   This friendship was cemented
in the strongest manner, during the great plague which
ravaged Moscow, a few years before its appearance in
London.   The Czar, who was absent, begged the Patriarch to attend his family to the Trinity Monastery, he
himself (it is a trait not quite in keeping with his usual
spirit) living in the hills and forests, " in a tent under the
" rain and snow, with no other companion but his fire." [1]

The Syrian Archdeacon gives us glimpses of the two
men, both on festive and on solemn occasions.   The
Patriarch invited Alexis to a banquet.   First came an
interchange of magnificent presents " from the Czar to
" the Patriarch and from the Patriarch to the Czar, flow-
" ing like the Black into the White Sea, and like the
" White into the Black Sea.[2]   The Patriarch stood at
" the top of the room, and the Czar went each time [3] to
" the door to bring in the presents with his own hands,
" with great fatigue, calling to the nobles to deliver them
" quickly, and he was like a waiting slave, wonderful to
" relate. . . . Afterwards the Patriarch bowed to him,
" and expatiated on his kindness, and seated him at a
" royal table in a corner of the room [the place of
" honor]. . , . The Czar, after the banquet, rose and
" filled cups of wine for all present, to the health of the
" Patriarch, which, as the company emptied them, they
" placed inverted on their heads, to show that they had
" drunk the health complete.   In like manner the Patri-
" arch filled cups for them all to the health of the Czar,
" and these, being emptied, they placed on their heads,
" kneeling before and after."

[1] Macarius, ii. 49.   [2] Ibid. ii. 232.   [3] Ibid. ii. 231.

Another picture is that of the two friends during the sermon. " What most excited our admiration was to see " the Czar standing with his head uncovered, whilst the " Patriarch wore his crown before him ; the one with " his hands crossed in humility, the other displaying " them with the action and boldness of an orator ad- " dressing his auditor ; the one bowing his bare head in " silence to the ground, the other bending his towards " him with his crown upon it ; the one guarding his " senses and breathing low, the other making his voice " ring like a loud bell ; the one as if he were a slave, " the other as his lord. . . . When the Patriarch had " concluded his discourse with the prayer, he bowed to " the Czar, and they stood back a second time." [1]

It is from such scenes as these that Western, especial- ly English, writers have represented Nicon, some from a favorable, some from an unfavorable, point of view, as an Eastern Hildebrand or Becket, maintaining the inde- pendence of the hierarchy against the civil power, and trampling the Imperial government under his feet. It is true that there were certain points in which questions of this kind were stirred, such as that of the new code, reducing to the civil courts cases which had once be- longed to the Patriarchal courts, and restraining the accumulation of ecclesiastical property. It is true also that the devout, and in some respects childlike, or child- ish, disposition of Alexis placed him for a time under a kind of awe, inspired by the stern character and high office of Nicon, such as reminds us of our Saxon kings in the presence of Dunstan. "I fear," [2] he said, in an- swer to a deacon who entreated his permission to offi- ciate against the orders of Nicon, " I fear the Patriarch " Nicon, who would perhaps give me his crozier and say, " ' Take it and tend the monks and priests yourself : I

---

[1] Macarius, ii. 59.   [2] Ibid. ii. 249.

" do not contradict you in your command of your favor-
" ites and troops ; why then do you set yourself against
" me in the concerns of priests and monks ? ' "

It is true also that his whole conduct, when he assumed the Patriarchal chair, was that of a man who was
prepared for a vehement opposition. He had entered
on his post immediately after his removal of the relics
of Philip, the one martyr [1] of the Russian Church, to
the cathedral of Moscow, by which, possibly [2] (although
of this there is no intimation), he may have meant to
express his own anticipations for himself; and it was
only after he had taken from the Prince and people a
solemn promise of obedience to him, as their chief shepherd and spiritual father, that he consented to undertake the office.

But the whole view taken of this scene, and of
Nicon's character, by Russians themselves, and the
whole tenor of the story which I am about to relate,
forbid us to ascribe to Nicon any deliberate policy of
opposition to the sovereign power of the State, such as
that which has animated so many of the Popes, prelates,
and clergy of the West. His fears on the occasion of
his entrance on the Patriarchal see were not from his
devoted friend Alexis, but from the adherents of his
retrograde predecessor, the Patriarch Joseph, who had
already furiously denounced him as an innovator.[3] His
enmity was with a barbarous nobility and ignorant
clergy, not with the Czar ; and when at last it did reach
the Czar also, the rupture took place on purely personal
grounds. We hear enough of the civil and spiritual
conflicts in Western Europe ; let us not thrust them

---

[1] See Lecture X.

[2] Palmer's Dissertations on the Orthodox Communion, p. 56.

[3] Levesque, iv. 62. Compare Collins, p. 15 : " He began to innovate some
things, or rather reform them."

into a story of a simple and natural quarrel between man and man, with which they have little or no concern.

The nobles watched their opportunity to separate the two friends. They found it in a protracted absence of the Czar on a two years' expedition to Poland, and in the failure of a Swedish campaign which Nicon had recommended. The Czar himself had had high words with the Patriarch once before in the church, from some unexpected rudeness. Every instance of insolence, and doubtless there were many, was eagerly exaggerated. Their intercourse ceased; and, as the historian of the event observes,[1] when once a mutual misunderstanding is established between those who have once loved each other, the very recollection of their former friendship poisons the wounds of their hearts, because the change itself in their mutual relations is felt as a sort of wrong and offence by both. The nobles gained strength. Their code respecting the monastic property was reintroduced. One of them called his dog by the name of Nicon, taught it to sit up on its hind legs and to cross its paws in the offensive form of benediction which Nicon had introduced.[2] Another, in a grand procession, struck one of the Patriarch's courtiers. The Patriarch demanded satisfaction in vain. He waited for an interview with the Czar, at one of their accustomed meetings in church, on a high festival,[3] the 10th of July. The Czar was kept away, and in his stead Nicon found one of the nobles come to announce his master's absence, and to reproach the Patriarch with his insolent pomp.

Nicon felt that the crisis of his life was come, which he had forestalled in the promise of obedience exacted on his accession to the Patriarchal see.

His quarrel with the Czar.

Nicon's resignation, A. D. 1658.

---

[1] Mouravieff, 218.   [2] Levesque, iv. 75.   [3] Bachmeister, 47.

In a burst of wild indignation he came forth, after the completion of the service, from the sacred gates of the cathedral sanctuary, and, with that well-known voice which sounded like the mighty bell of the church through the whole building, announced that he was no longer Patriarch. "I leave my place," he said, "conscious of my many sins before God, which have "brought this plague and woe on Moscow."[1] He took from the Patriarchal throne the sacred staff of Peter the first Metropolitan, and laid it on the most venerable of the sacred pictures. He threw off his episcopal robes, wrote a hasty letter in the vestry to announce his intention to the Czar, and sat down on the raised platform[2] whence he had so often preached to Czar and people, awaiting the answer. The answer never came; it was intercepted by his enemies. Amidst the terrors and lamentations of the people, who tried to detain him by closing the doors of the cathedral, by taking the horses out of his carriage, by blocking up the gate of the town through which he was to pass, he went out on foot,[3] and returned no more to the Patriarchal palace, wrote once again to the Czar, entreating his forgiveness for his sudden departure, and plunged into the solitude, first of one, and then another, of his various monasteries.

In a moment of uncontrollable anger he had made a sacrifice which he could not support. But his adversaries took him at his word. The see was declared vacant, and he, having returned from his more distant place of retirement to the one which was nearest to Moscow, remained there devouring his soul in the bitter-

[1] Bachmeister, 46.

[2] Or on the lowest step of the Patriarchal throne. (Bachmeister, p. 47, who tells the story somewhat differently.)

[3] He got through by waiting for the passage of some coaches. Bachmeister, 47.

ness of a man who has made a false step, which he longs in vain to retrace. Let us follow him for a moment to the scene of these wild regrets. It is a scene eminently characteristic of the Russian Church.

The last occasion on which he and Alexis had met in friendly intercourse was at the consecration of a small wooden church on one of the Patriarchal estates, about forty miles from Moscow. They were standing together on a rising ground which overlooked a tract of hills and undulating forest, presenting a variety of foliage rare in the monotony of Russian scenery; when the Czar, who had to an unusual extent the Russian passion for imitation of sacred places, and had built in his palace and in his hunting-grounds two copies of the Holy Sepulchre, exclaimed, " What a site " for a monastery; what a beautiful place for a New " Jerusalem!"[1] Nicon caught at the thought. He had· himself already made a new Athos of his island in the Valdai Lake. " Here," he said, " there shall be indeed a " New Jerusalem. The church of the monastery shall " be the Church of the Holy Sepulchre; the river which " runs at our feet shall be the Jordan; the brook shall " be the Kedron; the hill on which we stand shall be " the Mount of Olives, the wooded mount beyond shall " be Mount Tabor." Neither Alexis nor Nicon, with all their passion for imitation, could produce the slightest resemblance between the natural features of Muscovy and of Palestine. But Nicon did what he could for the building. His agents were still in the East collecting manuscripts for a correct version of the Liturgy, and he charged them to bring back from Jerusalem an exact model of the church of the Holy Sepulchre. The result was the church of the " Resurrection " (Voskresensky), or, as it is more commonly called, of " the New Jerusa-

Convent of the New Jerusalem, A. D. 1654.

<hr />
[1] Bachmeister, 44; Mouravieff, 207.

" lem," which still remains a monument of the friendship of Alexis and Nicon. Externally it has the aspect of an ordinary Russian cathedral, still further complicated by the addition of successive chapels built by, or in honor of, the various members of the Imperial family in after-times, down to our own day. But internally it is so precisely of the same form and dimensions as the church at the actual Jerusalem, that, intricate as the arrangements of that church are, beyond probably any other in the world, a traveller who has seen the original can find his way without difficulty through every corridor, and stair, and corner of the copy; and it possesses the further interest that, having been built before the recent alterations of the church in Palestine, it is in some respects (in five [1] particulars of considerable importance) more like the old church in which the Crusaders worshipped than is that church itself. It was, amongst all the architectural works of Nicon's Patriarchate, that on which his heart was most set. Throughout it bears his impress. In the sanctuary behind the screen still remains an indication of his magnificent schemes for the Russian Church. A vast array of seats rises, tier above tier, surmounted by the five Patriarchal thrones of Constantinople, Antioch, Alexandria, Jerusalem, and Moscow, which Nicon in his days of power designed as the scene of a future General Council. A picture represents him surrounded by his disciples, amongst others the secretary Shuskerinoff seated at his feet, bending with eye-glasses over his manuscript, containing, as we may suppose, the annals of Russia,

[1] 1. There are no walls of partition such as since the fire of 1812 have been erected between the sects. 2. The dome is of larger proportions than that now existing, higher, and covered. 3. The entrance into the chapel of the Sepulchre from the antechapel has not been raised. 4. The chapels of the Sepulchre and of the Golgotha, are without altars. 5. The irregular form of the rock by the Golgotha has not been smoothed away.

called, from his superintendence, the Chronicle of Nicon.[1] Still more characteristic is the square tower,
the cell, or "skeet" (ἀσκητήριον), which he built for himself beyond the fancied Kedron, in the midst of the
pale misty birchwood that climbs the slope behind the
convent. His large black hat, his enormous clouted
shoes, his rough sheepskin,[2] bring before us his huge
figure in the costume and manner of life which he
adopted when he exchanged the Patriarchate for the
hermitage, when he fished in the river and assisted
at the drainage of the marshes like a common peasant, and worked like a common stone-mason in the
erection of the convent church. It was what he had
been of old in the monastic fortress by the Frozen
Ocean; it was what he kept before his mind even in
his greatness of state at Moscow, by inviting from
time to time to his table one of the wild enthusiasts
already described in mediæval Russia, who sat by his
side, amidst the splendor of the Imperial banquet, in
a state of absolute nudity.[3]

But neither the ideal nor the practice of solitary asceticism could enable Nicon to forget that he had been,
that he was still, except by his own rash abdication, the
Patriarch of Russia. He refused by any act or word to
A. D. 1658. acknowledge a successor in the see. He caused
a special office to be sung in the convent, in which, day
by day,[4] were repeated the curses from the 109th Psalm.
"I have not cursed the Czar," was his answer to the
commissioner who came from Moscow to complain (the
eager denial will show the contrast of his position and
that of Hildebrand), "I have not cursed the Czar, but I
"have cursed you, the nobles[5] of the Church; if you

---

[1] Levesque, iv. 75.   [2] Ibid.   [3] Macarius, ii. 266.
[4] Levesque, iv. 77.
[5] The noble referred to was Borborikina. Levesque, iv. 79.

" have a mind to stay and hear it, I will have the same
" office sung over again in your ears." For eight years
the struggle continued. At last a singular event brought
matters to a crisis. Nicon in his solitude received an
urgent entreaty from one of the few nobles who remained friendly to him that he would come unexpect-
edly to Moscow, on the festival of Peter, the first Metropolitan, and invite the Czar to join him in the cathedral, according to his former custom, as if nothing had
intervened. Meditating on this letter, yet not resolved,
he retired for his three hours' rest [1] in his hermit's tower.
At the top of the tower a stone recess in the wall is still
shown, narrow and short, which Nicon used as his bed,
and on which he must have found but scanty room to
stretch out his gigantic limbs. It is a true Fakir's resting-place. On that stone bed [2] he was sleeping, Nicon's
and he dreamed that he was once more in his dream.
own beloved cathedral, and one by one he saw rise from
their graves the whole line of his predecessors in the
Metropolitan see : Peter, whose wonder-working staff
he had laid on the sacred picture; Alexis, from the
chapel hard by, the champion of Russia against the
Tartars; Philip, murdered by Ivan the Terrible; Job,
the blind old man who had vainly struggled against the
false Demetrius; Hermogenes, starved to death by the
Polish invaders; Philaret, grandfather of the Czar Alexis : one by one, at the call of the wonder-worker Jonah,
they rose from the four corners, and from the array of
tombs beside the painted walls, and took him by the
hand, and raised him once more into his Patriarchal
throne. He woke up and left his cramped couch. He
returned by night to Moscow, on the eve of Peter's festival. At break of day he appeared publicly once more
in the cathedral, grasped once more the staff of Peter,

---

[1] Levesque, iv. 75.   [2] Mouravieff, 224.

stood erect in the Patriarch's place, and sent to the Czar to announce his arrival, and to invite him to come to the church to receive his blessing, and to assist at the prayers.

The Czar was taken by surprise. He sent to consult his nobles. To them it was a matter of life and death to prevent the interview. And they did prevent it. The Czar ordered him to return; and Nicon, in the bitterness of his heart, obeyed the command and retired from the cathedral, bearing away with him the ancient staff, which at last (it is a significant action expressive of the meaning of the whole story) he surrendered to the Czar, and to no one but the Czar. Finally, feeling that he could hold out no longer, he consented to the election of a new Patriarch.

His final retirement.

A. D. 1667.

The fall of Nicon was now inevitable. At the instigation of his enemies a Council of the Eastern Patriarchs was convened at Moscow; and thus it came to pass that the most august assembly of divines which Russia has ever witnessed, met for the condemnation of the greatest man whom the Eastern hierarchy had produced in modern times. Its general acts will be best noticed hereafter. I confine myself here to the incidents characteristic of the present story.

The trial was in the hall of Nicon's own palace. A picture of the Council of Nicæa, hung in the sacred corner of the room, still indicates, and probably then indicated, the purpose for which the hall was designed. Paisius of Alexandria and Macarius of Antioch, the same who had eight years before seen Nicon in his highest pomp, were here in person. Nicæa, Iconium, Sinai, were also represented; Georgia, Servia, Wallachia, besides the most distinguished of the hierarchy of the Russian Church itself. In front of these, still communicating with them through an inter-

His condemnation.

A. D. 1667.

preter,[1] still claiming his rank as Patriarch, and refusing
to sit as he could not seat himself on his Patriarchal
chair, stood the exiled prelate.   One last chance remained for him.   Presiding in the Council, as Constantine had presided at Nicæa, was the Czar himself.   Now,
for the first time for eight years, they stood again face
to face.   Between Nicon and his accusers all the fierceness of long pent indignation was let loose.   But between him and the Czar there was hardly anything but
an outpouring of tenderness and affection.   Tears flowed
from the Czar's eyes as he read the accusation ; and the
sight of his ancient friend standing, habited as if for a
capital sentence, so moved his heart, that to the consternation of the nobles he descended from his throne,
walked up to the Patriarch, took him by the hand, and
burst forth into a plaintive entreaty : " Oh ! most holy
" father ! why hast thou put upon me such a reproach,
" preparing thyself for the Council as if for death ?
" Thinkest thou that I have forgotten all thy services to
" me and to my family during the plague, and our for-
" mer friendship ? "   Mutual remonstrances between the
two friends led to recriminations between their attendants.   " That, O religious Czar, is a lie," was the somewhat abrupt expression of one of Nicon's clerks, on
hearing a false accusation brought against his master.[2]
In the general silence produced either by the force of
Nicon's replies or by the awful presence of the friendly
Czar,[3] when Alexis turned round to see if some of the
nobles had anything to urge, Nicon asked with his usual
bitter irony : " Why do you not bid them take up
" stones ?   *So* they would soon put an end to me ; but
" not with words, though they should spend A. D. 1667.
" nine years more in collecting them."   They parted
never to meet again.

1 Bachmeister, 86 ; Mouravieff, 227.   3 Levesque, iv. 78.
2 Palmer's Orth. Communion, p. 63.

Alexis could not bear to be present at his condemnation. The third and last meeting therefore of the Council was assembled in a small church, now destroyed, over the gates of one of the Kremlin convents. Nicon was degraded from his office to the rank of a simple monk, and banished for the rest of his life to do penance in a distant monastery.

He maintained his proud sarcastic bearing to the end. "Why do you degrade me without the pres- ence of the Czar, in this small church, and "not in the cathedral where you once implored me to "ascend the Patriarchal throne?" "Take this," he said, offering to the Bishops a large pearl from the front of his white metropolitan cowl, which they took off with their own hands from his head; "it will help to support "you under your oppressions in Turkey, but it will not "last you long. Better stay at home there than go "wandering about the world as mendicants." It was in the depth of a Russian winter, and the Czar sent him by one of the kindlier courtiers a present of money and sable furs for the journey to the far north. The impenetrable prelate sternly replied: "Take these back "to him who sent them; these are not what Nicon "wants." The courtier entreated him not to affront the Czar by his refusal; and also asked in the Czar's name for his forgiveness and blessing. "He loved not "blessing," said Nicon, in allusion to the 109th Psalm, in which he had before cursed all his enemies except the Czar, "and therefore it shall be far from him." To the nobles he shook off the dust of his feet; and on one of them sweeping it up and saying (in allusion to the goods of the Church, which they now hoped to get) that this was just what they wanted, he pointed to the A. D. 1667. comet [1] then flaming in the sky, — the "besom

His degra- dation.

---

[1] This striking story, with much else, I owe to the author of the Dissertations (so often quoted) on the Orthodox Communion.

" star," as it is called in Russ,— and said, " God's besom
" shall sweep you all away." To the people, who, in
spite of their prejudice against his reforms, flocked
round him also for his blessing, he replied in a nobler
and more Christian spirit, as Philip had done before,
this one word, " Pray." [1] The sledge was at hand to
carry him off, and he entered it with the episcopal staff
and mantle which the Patriarchs,[2] for fear of the people, had not ventured to remove. A winter cloak was
thrown over him by the pity of one of the more gentle
of the hierarchy.[3] With a dry irony he repeated to
himself : " Ah, Nicon, Nicon ! do not lose your friends.
" Do not say all that may be true. If you would only
" have given a few good dinners, and have dined with
" them in return, none of these things would have be-
" fallen you." Through the south gate of the Kremlin,
to avoid the crowds collected on the north side in the
expectation of seeing him pass, he was borne away,
with the furious speed of Russian drivers, across the
ancient bridge of the Mosqua, and rapidly out of sight
of those proud towers of the Kremlin,[4] which had
witnessed the striking vicissitudes of his glory and his
fall.

At evening, it is said, they halted in a house from
which the occupants had been ejected. In the middle
of the night, when Nicon and his attendants had been
left to themselves in the piercing cold of their destitute
condition, a trap-door in the floor of the room opened, an
old woman came up, and asked which was the Patriarch
Nicon. " I am he," said the fallen prelate. She fell at
his feet, and solemnly assured him that she had seen in
a dream the night before a very goodly man saying to
her : " My servant Nicon is coming hither in great cold

1 Palmer, 64.
2 Mouravieff, 232.

3 Ibid. 243 ; Palmer, 65.
4 Palmer, 65.

" and need of all things. Now, therefore, give him what
A. D. 1667. " thou hast by thee for his needs." [1] In this
way, — so runs the story, which is curious as showing the impression produced on the popular mind by
Nicon's career, — he was protected against the severity
of the rest of the journey, till his arrival [2] at the monastery of Therapontoff, on the shores of the White Lake.

Nine years passed away, and Nicon remained almost
His im-   forgotten in his remote prison, when a baseless
prisonment. rumor rose that he was with the insurgent
army of Stenza Razia on the Eastern frontier.[3] Alexis,
covertly or openly, sent presents and entreaties for forgiveness. Nicon, at first stern as when he left Moscow,
at last partially relented, in the hope of fulfilling the
cherished wish of his heart, to die and be buried in his
favorite monastery of the New Jerusalem, and of seeing
once more his early and only friend.[4] But before any
final reconciliation could be accomplished, Alexis was
struck with a mortal illness. On his death-bed he
sent messengers once more to Nicon, conjuring him,
even by all his former titles of Great Lord and Patriarch, to grant him full forgiveness. Verbally the
Death of   forgiveness was at last sent. But Alexis was
Alexis.
A. D. 1670. already passed away,[5] and when the tidings
reached Nicon in his solitary cell, he groaned aloud and
exclaimed : " The will of God be done ! What though
" he never saw me to make our farewell peace here, we
" shall meet and be judged together at the terrible com-
" ing of Christ." [6]

Once more, on the removal of Alexis, darkness closed
in upon the unfortunate exile. New accusations were
invented against him ; he was removed to a farther

1 Palmer, 65 ; Bachmeister, 109.   4 Palmer, 66 ; Mouravieff, 244.
2 Mouravieff, 232.   5 Palmer, 67.
3 Ibid. 240.   6 Mouravieff, 243.

monastery on the same lake, and imprisoned with still closer severity.

At the close of three years his deliverance was effected by the means which, now that his beloved master was gone, he would probably most have preferred for himself. The preceptor of the young Czar Theodore, Simeon of Polotzky, was a monk who had travelled in the West, and there, from a jumble of Latin theology and astrological divinations, conceived a wild scheme of creating four Patriarchal sees in the Russian Church, after the manner of those of the East, surmounted by one Papal throne, which he destined for the only man in Russia who was capable of filling it, the exiled but never forgotten Nicon. He worked on the mind of his royal pupil in one direction. Another older friend was the Princess Tatiana, sister of the late Czar, who had always remained faithful to Nicon, and one of whose works of devotion, an illuminated Gospel, is still shown in the treasury of the Convent of the New Jerusalem. To that beloved edifice — still in the unfinished state in which its founder had left it — she took her nephew, to visit the spot, and to receive from the monks a petition for the return of Nicon. The Czar laid it before the Patriarch Joachim, who for a time strongly resisted; but hearing at last that Nicon was preparing for his latter end, his heart was touched and he consented.

From this point the story cannot be better told than in the words of the Russian historian, whose Return of narrative here, in its simplicity and pathos, Nicon, A. D. 1681. forms a remarkable contrast to the turgid Orientalism by which, to our tastes, the general style is often disfigured. The whole story is full of that peculiar river scenery of Russia with which we were made familiar in the earlier stages of its history.

" On the very same day on which the gracious permission of
the Czar and the Patriarch arrived at the monastery of S. Cyril,
Nicon, while it was yet very early, from a secret presentiment
had prepared himself for the journey, and, to the astonishment
of everybody, ordered the religious who were in personal attendance upon himself to hold themselves in readiness.   With difficulty they placed the old man, now worn out with sickness and
A. D. 1681.   infirmity, in a sledge which took him by land to a
barge on the river Sheksna, which he descended to the Volga.
Here he was met by brethren from the monastery of the Resurrection, or New Jerusalem, who had been sent for that purpose.
Nicon gave orders to drop down the Volga as far as the point
where Yaroslaff [with its high bank crowned by monasteries]
overlooks the river.   Near one of these he put to shore and
received the communion of the sick, for he began to be exceed-
ingly feeble.   The Hegumen [or Prior] with all the brotherhood went out to meet him, accompanied by a former enemy of
Nicon, the Archimandrite Sergius, the same that during his trial
kept him under guard and covered him with reproaches, but had
since been sent to this monastery in disgrace to perform penance.
This Sergius, having fallen asleep in the refectory, at the very
hour of the arrival of Nicon, saw in a dream the Patriarch appearing to him, and saying, ' Brother Sergius, arise ; let us forgive and take leave of each other!' when suddenly at that moment
he was awakened and told that the Patriarch was actually approaching by the Volga, and that the brotherhood had already
gone out to the bank to meet him.   Sergius followed immediately, and, when he saw Nicon dying, he fell at his feet, and,
shedding tears of repentance, asked and obtained his forgiveness.

" Death had already begun to come upon the Patriarch by
the time that the barge was moving down the stream.   The
citizens of Yaroslavla, hearing of his arrival, crowded to the
river, and, seeing the old man lying on his couch all but dead,
threw themselves down before him with tears, kissing his hands
and his garments, and begging his blessing ; some towed the
barge along the shore, others threw themselves into the water
to assist them, and thus they drew it in and moored it against
the monastery of the All-merciful Saviour.

" The sufferer was already so exhausted that he could not

speak, but only gave his hand to them all.   The Czar's secretary ordered them to tow the barge to the other side of the river to avoid the crowds of the people.   Nicon was on the point of death : suddenly he turned and looked about as if some one had come to call him, and then arranged his hair, beard, and dress for himself, as if in preparation for his last and longest journey.   His confessor, together with all the brethren standing round, read the commendatory prayers for the dying ; and the Patriarch, stretching himself out to his full length on the couch, and laying his arms crosswise upon his breast, gave one sigh, and departed from this His death. world in peace.   In the mean time the pious Czar Theodore, not knowing that he was dead, had sent his own car- A. D. 1681. riage to meet him with a number of horses.   When he was informed of it he shed tears, and asked what Nicon had desired respecting his last will.   And when he learned that the departed prelate had chosen him as his godson to be his executor, and had confided everything to him, the good-hearted Czar replied, with emotion : ' If it be so, and the Most Holy Patriarch Nicon has reposed all his confidence in me, the will of the Lord be done. I will not forget him.'   He gave orders for conveying the body to the New Jerusalem." [1]

A picture in the convent represents the scene.   Down from the hill, where Nicon and Alexis had stood His when the name of " the New Jerusalem " was funeral. first suggested, the long procession descends towards the unfinished buildings of the monastery.   The Czar walks immediately before the gigantic corpse, which, on its uncovered bier, is visible to the whole attendant crowd.   So was Nicon borne to his last resting-place.   It was in the spot which he had always designed for himself, in the " Chapel of Melchizedek," at the foot of " Golgotha," close by the spot where, in the actual church of the Holy Sepulchre, lie the remains of Godfrey of Bouillon. Over the tomb were suspended, and still remain, the heavy chains which he wore round his body in the

[1] Mouravieff, 249–264.

rude hermitage. At his head is the small waxen picture which he carried about with him in all his wanderings. Amidst the copies of the sacred localities which surround the grave, it yet receives from the Russian pilgrims a share of devout enthusiasm, and awakes in the Western traveller an interest the more sincere, as being, amidst a crowd of artificial imitations, the only genuine reality. He rests, after his long vicissitudes, in the place which he had appointed for himself. He rests, all but canonized, in spite of his many faults, and in spite of his solemn condemnation and degradation by the nearest approach to a General Council which the Eastern Church has witnessed since the Second Council of Nicæa. He rests, far enough removed from the ideal of a saintly character, but yet having left behind him to his own Church the example, which it still so much needs, of a resolute, active, onward leader; to the world at large, the example, never without a touching lesson, of a rough reformer, recognized and honored when honor and recognition are too late. He closes the whole epoch of Russian history of which he was the central figure. His life as has been strikingly observed, extends itself over the whole period of the Russian Patriarchate, which was in fact the period of transition from the old Russia to the new; and already there was born to the Imperial house that still greater Reformer, who in the next generation was to carry out more than all that Nicon in his highest dreams could have anticipated, if not for the Christianization, at least for the civilization, of the clergy and people of Russia. To describe the career of that Imperial Reformer, more fortunate than his ecclesiastical predecessor, to imagine what would have been the consequence had Peter found a Nicon, or had Nicon found a Peter, either as a rival or as an ally, will be our concluding task.

CHRONOLOGICAL TABLE.

A. D.

1613. **MICHAEL ROMANOFF.**
1619. *Philaret,* Patriarch.
1633. *Joasaph I.,* Patriarch.
1642. *Joseph,* Patriarch.
1645. **ALEXIS.**
1652. *Nicon,* Patriarch.
1654. Plague. Building of the New Jerusalem.
1658. Retirement of Nicon.
1667. Deposition of Nicon.
       Joasaph II., Patriarch.
1673. *Pitirim,* Patriarch.
1674. *Joachim,* Patriarch.
1676. **THEODORE II.**
1681. Death of Nicon.

LECTURE XII.

PETER THE GREAT AND THE MODERN CHURCH OF RUSSIA.

It is needless to specify the works on the Life of Peter the Great. A catalogue of the chief of them will be found in the preface to the compendious Life of Peter the Great in the Family Library. The more special authorities for his ecclesiastical history are mentioned in the notes.

I must, however, particularly notice the Russian documents translated in "The Present State and Regulations of the Church of Russia," by Henry Consett, chaplain at the British Factory, 1727.

If the history of the first Russian Reformer suffers
Peter the Great. from our ignorance, the same cannot be said of the second. If no one has heard of Nicon, every one has heard of Peter. Let us first briefly recall his general character and career, and then transplant him into the special field of history, that of the Eastern Church, with which we are too little accustomed to associate his name.

I. Much as has been said and written of Peter the Great, yet there is a singularity in his position which always provokes afresh the curiosity of mankind. The second founder of the youngest born of European Empires, he gathers round himself all the romantic interest of a legendary hero, an Alfred or a Charlemagne; yet
His connection with Europe, he is known to us with all the exactness and fulness of recent knowledge. No prince of modern Europe is so familiar to almost every country in it, as Peter of Russia. He was, as no other

prince has been, a guest of each. Holland, Sweden,
Poland, Turkey, Prussia, Austria, Italy, knew him well
by sight or hearing as he passed to and fro on his marvellous journeys. He is ours, too, in a special with
sense. All London was alive with expectation England,
and excitement when his arrival in England was known.
Every one was full of stories of the artifices by which
the strange barbarian sought to evade the eagerness of
our national curiosity to see the prodigy. He comes directly across the path of English ecclesiastical history in
his long conversations with Bishop Burnet. He comes
for a moment even across the path of our own academical history. "Last week," says Narcissus Luttrell,[1]
" the Czar of Muscovy went privately to Ox- with
" ford ; but, being soon discovered, he imme- Oxford.
" diately came back to London without viewing those
" curiosities he intended." An honorary degree was
conferred upon him.

Strongly, however, as we are riveted by this strange
apparition in foreign lands, it is only in his own country
that he stands before us in his full proportions. Look
at him as he presents himself in the gallery of the portraits of the Czars. From Ivan the Terrible each follows each in grotesque barbaric costume, half Venetian,
half Tartar, till suddenly, without the slightest preparation, Peter breaks in amongst them, in the full uniform
of the European soldier. The ancient Czars vanish to
appear no more, and Peter remains with us, occupying
henceforward the whole horizon. Countenance, His ap-
and stature, and manner, and pursuits are ab- pearance.
solutely kept alive in our sight. We see the upturned
look, the long black hair falling back from his fine forehead, the fierce eyes glancing from beneath the over-

---

[1] Diary, iv. 368. This, I believe, is the only notice of his visit. For his
general conduct in England, see Macaulay's Hist. of England, vol. v.

hanging brows, the mouth clothed with indomitable power. We gaze at his gigantic height, his wild rapid movements, the convulsive twitches of his face and hands, the tremendous walking-staff,[1] almost a crowbar of iron, which he swings to and fro as he walks, the huge Danish wolf-dog and its two little companions which run behind him. We are with him in his Dutch house amidst the rough pieces of wood which he has collected as curiosities, the tools, the lathe, the articles of wood and ivory that he has turned. No dead man so lives again in outward form before us, as Peter in St. Petersburg. But not in outward form only. That city represents to us his whole Herculean course, more actually Hercules-like than any of modern times, and His statue. proudly set forth in the famous statue erected by Catharine II. In front of the Isaak church, built to commemorate his birthday, in the midst of the great capital which he called forth out of nothing, rises the huge granite block from Finland, up which he urges his horse, trampling the serpent of conspiracy under his feet, rearing over the edge of the precipice of the stupendous difficulty which he had surmounted, his hand stretched out towards the wide stream of the Neva, to which he looked for the regeneration of his country. Truly it is no exaggeration of what he attempted and achieved. Think of what Russia was as already described. Doubtless the two Ivans had done something; doubtless, too, his father Alexis and the Patriarch Nicon had turned their thoughts southward and westward. But, taken as a whole, it was, with many noble elements, a wild Oriental people, ruled by a court wrapped round and round in Oriental ceremonial. What must the man have been, who, born and bred in this atmosphere, conceived, and by one tremendous wrench, almost

---

[1] The only relic of the old costume of the Czars. See Macarius, i. 381.

by his own manual labor and his own sole gigantic strength, executed the prodigious idea of dragging the nation, against its will, into the light of Europe, and erecting a new capital and a new empire amongst the cities and the kingdoms of the world? St. Petersburg is indeed his most enduring monument. A spot up to that time without a single association, selected Foundation of St. Petersburg. instead of the holy city to which even now every Russian turns as to his mother; a site which, but a few years before, had belonged to his most inveterate enemies; won from morass and forest, with difficulty defended, and perhaps even yet doomed to fall[1] before the inundations of its own river; and now, though still Asiatic beyond any capital of the West, yet in grandeur and magnificence, in the total subjugation of nature to art, entirely European. And the change from Moscow to St. Petersburg is but a symbol of the revolution effected in the whole Empire by the power of Peter. For better, for worse, he created army, navy, law, dress, amusements, alphabet, some in part, some altogether, anew. Much that was superficial, much that was false, much that broke out under his successors into frightful corruption and depravity, at least of the higher classes, came in with the Western changes. But whatever hopes for the world or the Church are bound up with the civilization of the West, did penetrate into Russia through Peter and through no one else.

So unlike the rest of his dynasty — Philaret, the founder of the house, a reverend ecclesiastic; Michael, Alexis, Theodore, yielding and gentle princes — suddenly appears this man, bursting His schemes for civilizing Russia. with brutal passions, as if all the extravagances of the family had been pent up to break forth in him. And

---

[1] " Up to this point the floods have come," said an attendant, showing the mark on a tree by the river bank. "Give me a hatchet," said the angry Czar, and cut down the tree at a blow.

yet in this savage, drunken and licentious, the victim of ungovernable fury, arose this burning desire for civilization. His very violence was turned to promote his end. Literally, not metaphorically, by blows, by kicks, by cuffs, he goaded his unwilling people forwards.[1] Russia, as the Russian poet sings, was the hard anvil, and Peter was its terrible hammer. But the strangest, the most affecting, part of his career is this, that what he required from others he labored to acquire for himself. In the solitude of barbarism in which he was placed, he knew that by his own mind, by his own hands, if at all, his country was to be changed. As filthy in his habits as any Russian serf of the present day, to whom every European comfort is distasteful, he yet was able to endure the splendor of Paris and London, and, what is more astonishing, the cleanliness of Holland. Possessing in a remarkable degree the turn for mechanical pursuits, of which trophies are preserved in every part of his dominions, he yet, with a largeness of mind very rarely found in company with such pursuits (contrast the unfortunate Louis XVI.), used them all for reconstructing the fabric of his Empire. "He is mechani-"cally turned," was Bishop Burnet's observation of him, "and seems to be designed by nature rather for a ship-"carpenter than a great prince." But the Bishop was mistaken; and the remarkable point of Peter's career is that he was both.

One instance may suffice to remind us of the difficulties which he had to overcome alike in himself and in his Empire.

Inheriting — apparently it was all that he did inherit

His naval efforts.

from his family — the unhappy tendency to cataleptic fits, he was specially subject to them

---

[1] Many of the expressions here used I owe to conversation with intelligent Russians.

from his earliest years whenever he came in sight of water, in consequence of a fright which he had had when, at the age of five, he was suddenly wakened from sleep by the sound of a cascade in the river Yaousa.[1] In spite of this, in spite of all other obstacles presented by the inland character of his enormous Empire, he determined to render himself a sailor and his country a maritime power. He overcame his own infirmity by incessant efforts, first on the little stream of the Mosqua, then on the wide lake of Pereslav, then by serving as a ship-boy on board a Dutch vessel; till finally the water which had been his early terror became his natural element. The new capital on the Neva was to be built without bridges,[2] that he and his people might be always on its waters, passing and repassing. The boat[3] which he first built remains still, "The Little Grandsire," to which once a year the Russian navy does homage. "My "ships," he said, "shall make ports for themselves."[4] His own life is filled with anecdotes of hairbreadth escapes by water. In the storm in the Gulf of Finland, he reassured the terrified sailors: "Never fear! Who "ever heard of a Czar being lost[5] at sea?" On another like occasion he rebuked the ambassador who asked what account could be rendered to his master if he were shipwrecked: "Make yourself easy; if we go "down we shall all go down together, and there will "be no one to answer for your Excellency." His last illness was fatally aggravated by the generous rashness with which, on a raw winter day, he dashed into the water to save a distressed crew.

---

[1] Stahlin, § 84. For the details of this hydrophobia, see Strahlenberg's Description of Russia, 273, 274.

[2] Stahlin, § 84.

[3] Its history is given in a tract translated by Consett, 206.

[4] Stahlin, § 84.   [5] Ibid. § 110.

I dwell on these general traits of Peter's character and career, partly because we cannot understand his ecclesiastical changes without taking into account the aspect of the whole man, partly because there is something in the exhibition of such perseverance and resolution, which is in itself a part of that higher history of the Church of which we ought never to lose sight. I make no apolo- His gies for what have been only too truly called his passions Samoyedic excesses. But in considering this gross licentiousness we must remember the strong temptations of his early education; and in considering his brutal violence of temper, action, and language, the same excuses which have been offered for the violence of other reformers, of higher religious pretensions, must and diffi- also be in some degree accepted for Peter. "I culties. " know well my faults, my bursts of passion, " and therefore it is that I wish to have those near me " like my Catharine, who will warn and correct me.[1] " I can reform my people; I cannot reform myself." So he exclaimed in the penitent mood which followed one of his frenzies of lawless rage. There are many who would not have felt, much less expressed, the thought. Drinking, the fatal vice which, as we have seen, Vladimir I. had declared to be the indispensable privilege of a Russian Prince, Peter did, it is said, by the effort of his later years entirely abandon. A wild sense of justice and truth ran through even his most grotesque extravagances.

His con- II. But the question still remains, what was nection with the the true relation of the Eastern Church to this Church. extraordinary man?

It is striking to reflect that not only at the close of his career, when, in the fulsome style of Oriental eulogy, he is celebrated as the Japheth, Samson, Moses, David,

---

[1] Stahlin, § 83.

Solomon, of Russia,[1] but in his earliest years, the Russian Church seems to have claimed him as her own ; and the first recollections of his dangers and deliverances were associated with the chief sanctuary of his country. The Troitza Monastery, which has twice before figured as turning the fate of Russia, was the refuge of Peter, when still a boy of twelve years old, with his mother Natalia, from the fury of the Strelitzes. She was permitted to conceal herself, not only within the precincts of the convent, not only within the walls of the principal church, but behind the sacred screen, beside the altar itself, where, by the rules of the Eastern Church, no woman's foot is allowed to enter. That altar (still remaining on the same spot) stood between the past and the future destinies of Russia. On one side of it crouched the mother and her son ; on the other the fierce soldiers were waving their swords over the head of the Imperial child. "Comrade, not before the altar !" exclaimed the more pious or the more merciful[2] of the two assassins. At that moment a troop of faithful cavalry galloped into the court-yard, and Peter was saved. In the seclusion of that same military convent, it is said, he first learned his taste for soldiering. The tower is still shown where he shot the ducks in the neighboring stream. The ivory ball which he turned, to employ the vacant hours of his retirement, still hangs in the refectory.

His escape in the Troitza Convent.

Many, no doubt, and rude were the shocks sustained, both by Peter's orthodoxy and by the Church's loyalty ;

[1] Oration of Theophanes ; Consett's State of Russia, pp. 280–282.

[2] It is said that the recollection of that moment was the cause of his convulsions (Stahlin, § 32), and that twenty years afterwards he recognized this soldier, though disguised in a seaman's dress, and started back with an instinct of horror. He forgave him, but forbade him ever again to appear in his presence (Stahlin, § 26), as not daring to trust himself to look at the man who had once so filled him with terror.

but neither entirely failed.   As we read the account
His rela-
tions to
other forms
of religion. of his contact with the different forms of European religion, we seem to be reading again
the story of his ancestor Vladimir.   There
was the same inquiry on his side; the same solicita-
tions on the other side.   Everywhere on his journeys
through Europe he did for himself what Vladimir had
done by his envoys; heard the doctrines and attended
the worship of the countries through which he passed.
He learned the condition of our own Church in his
walks over London with Bishop Burnet, and his dinner
at Lambeth with Archbishop Tenison.   He witnessed
an ordination, and expressed his approval of the service.
He received, like his descendants, a Quaker deputation,
and attended a Quaker meeting.   He listened with profound attention to a Lutheran sermon[1] at Dantzic.   He
dashed in pieces the drinking-cup of Luther at Wittem-
berg, in vexation at not being allowed to carry away
the memorial; and observed that his monument[2] in the
church was not too splendid for so great a man.   He
ordered Dutch translations of the Bible, and loaded,
it is said, two vessels with works of Dutch theology
to enlighten his Russian subjects.   A messenger was
despatched to Rome to learn the state of religion in
the Latin Church.   He stood in motionless admiration
before the tomb of Cardinal Richelieu.   And, on the
other hand, he was, like Vladimir, the mark for all the
proselytizers and ecclesiastical agitators of the West.
The Pope was in high expectation[3] of his arrival to
effect a union between the Greek and Latin Churches.
The Gallican Church represented its claims through a
memorial of the doctors of the Sorbonne.   The Scot-

---

[1] See the story in Stahlin, §§ 12, 80.
[2] Stahlin, § 41; see also Life of Peter, p. 273.
[3] S. Simon's Memoirs, vol. xv.

tish Episcopalians[1] and Anglican Nonjurors tried to
secure through him an alliance of the Eastern Church,
as a prop to their forlorn condition. Even his unhappy
son Alexis became the subject of constant rumors from
expectants on this side and that. "Foreign letters ad-
" vise from Vienna that the Pope was in great hopes
" the hereditary Prince of Muscovy may be persuaded
" to turn Papist."[2] (June, 1710.) "Letters from Dres-
" den say that the hereditary Prince of Muscovy hath
" lately received communion there in a Lutheran
" church."[3] (Oct. 1710.)

What Peter might have been, had he lived earlier
or later, it is useless to guess. But, in fact, he His adher-
still remained at heart a Prince of the Orthodox ence to the
Church. In this respect Burnet's observation Church.
was correct, at least as regarded matters of faith. "He
" was desirous to understand our doctrine, but he did
" not seem disposed to mend matters in Muscovy." He
observed the chief Eastern fasts.[4] The blade of the
sword which he wore at Pultowa is inscribed with a
prayer,[5] and has carved upon it the figure of S. George.
In his battles he carried about always one of the sacred
pictures from the Trinity Convent. He consecrated his
new capital by transferring thither the remains of the
sainted Prince, Alexander of the Neva, who had illustrated that river by his exploits centuries before its
great destinies were unfolded. His motto in his wars
was, "For the Faith and the Faithful."[6] He had heard
much of freethinkers at Amsterdam, but he treated their
doings as mere impostures; and in the true spirit of
a Russian believer added: "They despise the Fathers

---

[1] Lathbury, History of the Nonjurors, ch. viii.
[2] Luttrell's Diary, vi. 591.
[3] Ibid. 648.   [4] Stahlin, § 109.
[5] It is preserved in the museum at Pesth.
[6] Gabriel. (Consett's State of Russia, 395.)

"of the Councils, but the least of those Fathers was
"better and wiser than they."[1]

We see signs also of more than a mere ceremonial
religion. It was said that he knew the Epistles of S.
Paul by heart.[2] His journal contains many grateful ac-
knowledgments of the good Providence which so often
had preserved him, and instructed him even by misfor-
tunes.[3] He strictly prohibited talking in church, and
working on Sunday, as marks of irreverence. "He who
"forgets God," he said, "works to no purpose."[4] In the
small wooden house where he lived to watch the erection of his capital, one of the three rooms was marked
out for his devotions, and now, fitted up as a small
chapel, and daily crowded with worshippers, is a monument at once of his own sincere faith, and of the religious associations with which his mere name is connected
by the people. At Saardam, in like manner, a small
closet in the loft of his wooden cabin answered the
same purpose; and it is a touching incident in his
life, that when he revisited Amsterdam after an interval of twenty years, during which he had carried
out almost all the great designs then still in the future, he was deeply affected on entering the cottage
at Saardam, and climbing up into the loft[5] remained
there alone a full half-hour, doubtless in devotion as
before.[6] His strong common sense and his genuine
love of truth showed themselves, not in defiance of
his religious feelings, but in unison with them. "Ora
"et labora" was the quotation with which he wound
up his address to his senators.[7] And when in a dan-

[1] Stahlin, § 54.
[2] Theophanes. (Consett, 325.)
[3] Journal de Pierre le Grand, p. 30; Narva (239), Pultowa (270), Vibourg
(295), Pruth (377), Pecklin (438), Revel (481), Petersburg (491).
[4] Stahlin, § 79.   [5] The loft is now blocked up.
[6] Life of Peter, 240.   [7] Ibid. 268.

gerous illness his life was despaired of, and he was asked, according to an ancient usage in such cases, to propitiate the Divine mercy by the pardon of criminals condemned to death, who would then pray for his recovery, he heard the charges against them, and then, in what was thought to be his death-agony, replied : " Do you think that by " arresting the course of justice I shall be doing a good " action, for which my life will be prolonged? or that God " will listen to the prayers of wretches who have for- " gotten Him ?   Carry out the sentence ; and, if any- " thing will procure from Heaven the gift of my health " and life, I trust that it will be this act of justice." [1]

His actual death-bed, as described by his two chief ecclesiastical friends, Theophanes [2] Procopovitch His death-archbishop of Plescow, and Gabriel archiman- bed. drite of the Trinity Convent, is a curious summary of the conflict of the religious experiences of his life.   One of the clergy, apparently Theophanes himself,

" made mention of the death of Christ and of the Divine bless-ings procured by it, and admonished the Emperor that now the time was come for him to think of nothing else ; that he should for his own support meditate on that which he had frequently inculcated to others.[3]   On this he sprang up and endeavored to raise himself ; and being raised a little by his attendants, with eyes and hands lifted as high as he could, though faltering in his speech, he broke out into these words : ' This it is which at length can quench my thirst ; this alone which can refresh me.'

[1] Stahlin, § 2.   A similar trait is given in Hermann's Geschichte, iv. 85.

[2] The two statements in the funeral orations of Theophanes and Gabriel are given in Consett's Regulations, 261, 360.   They contain, no doubt, much of mere eulogy, but still they represent the contemporary feeling about the dying Emperor.

[3] This appears to be said partly in allusion to Peter's habit of dwelling, in common discourse (as it would seem), on the Lutheran doctrine of justifica-tion.   " He many times copiously and learnedly discussed the question con-cerning the justification of a sinner through Christ *gratis*." — *Consett*, 260.

Just before the admonition he had moistened his mouth with julep (as he was obliged to do very often), and by way of allusion he uttered these words, and again and again repeated them. The Monitor further exhorting him that he should, without any diffidence, confide in the mercy of God, that he should believe his sins to be forgiven through the merits of Christ, and that the grace of eternal life was near at hand, to this he redoubled his reply, ' I believe and I trust.' And when the Monitor exhorted him to a prayer of faith, and produced those words which they recite who with us come to the Lord's Supper, ' I believe, Lord, now, and confess that Thou art the Son of the living God, who camest into the world to save sinners, of whom I am chief,' he added, 'I believe,[1] Lord, and confess; I believe, Lord, help Thou mine unbelief.' Shortly after he seemed to be sinking. Crowds of officers and people entered the room, and with tears and howlings kissed his hand. He lay awhile speechless, saluting every one with his looks ; then with great difficulty said, ' *Hereafter*.' Whether by this word he would have a vacant space to himself, free from molestation (for his little apartment was thronged with people), or he spoke of the time after death, is doubtful. So all retired. He continued fifteen hours afterwards in great agony, beating his side with his right hand (his left was palsied) ; yet whenever the Monitor spoke to him concerning the vanity of the world, or concerning heaven, or concerning the death of Christ, he would make effort to raise himself up, to sign the cross with his hand, or to lift it to heaven. . . He tried also to moderate his groans into accents of praise, and to cheer up his countenance, and would have embraced his Monitor. Finally, he received the Sacrament a second time from Gabriel, and soon after expired."

This was the general position of Peter towards the ancient Eastern religion, in which he had been born and bred. Something is due to a form of the Christian faith which kept its hold on such a wild ungovernable man in

---

[1] It is characteristic both of Peter and of his people, perplexed between his religion and his innovations, that the popular tradition of his last words is this expression slightly altered, " My God, I am dying! help Thou mine unbelief."

such an age. To have traversed so many foreign lands, and watched so many foreign faiths, and yet still to have retained his own traditionary belief, may be fairly ascribed to the strength inherent in that belief. And it must have been a happy circumstance, that, owing to the ancient Eastern recognition of something like the principles of toleration,[1] Peter approached them from a point of view unlike that which was familiar to the other contemporary sovereigns. To Louis XIV. those principles were odious, and to Frederick II. welcome, because to both of those princes they seemed to be irreligious. But to Peter they were little more than legitimate conclusions from the traditions of his own Church.

III. Nevertheless, though he maintained his ground as a faithful son of the Orthodox Church generally, the most instructive portion of his ecclesiastical career is the remarkable contest which, like Nicon, he maintained with one section of it, and which led to the results now to be described.

The year 1700, the first year of the eighteenth century, which was marked by his adoption of the European calendar, may also be called the year of the Russian Reformation, the boundary between old and new Russia, as in civil, so in ecclesiastical matters also. The substitution of St. Petersburg for Moscow was the sign that in both these spheres he had set his face, not Eastward, but Westward. As the ancient Pagan associations of Rome drove the first Christian Emperor of the West to Constantinople,[2] so the ancient Oriental associations of Moscow drove the first Reforming Emperor of the East to the Baltic. It is true that the reformation set on foot by Peter, like that set on foot by Nicon, was strictly in accordance with the na-

His reforms.

---

[1] See Lecture I. p. 123.   [2] See Lecture VI.

64

tional spirit. It was a revolution not of doctrines and ideas, but of customs, institutions, habits. But in this respect it went deeper than the attempts of Nicon, conducted as it was by a stronger hand, under more favorable auspices, and therefore with far more success. "We "should be guilty," he said, "of ingratitude to the Most "High, if, after having reformed by His gracious assist-"ance the civil and military order, we were to neglect "the spiritual; and if the Impartial Judge should re-"quire of us an account of the vast trust which He "hath reposed in us, we should not be able to give an "answer."[1] Increase of schools, restrictions on the growth of monasteries, and regulations respecting the monastic property, were amongst the chief practical measures by which the change was carried out. The Abolition of the Patriarchate. main constitutional alteration was that which consisted in the abolition of the office of Patriarch,[2] and the substitution of a Synod consisting of prelates, presided over by the Emperor or his secretary. We need not go through the steps by which this was carried out, the long interval by which he accustomed the people to see the chair vacant, and the savage buffoonery with which he afterwards held up the office to ridicule. But it is important to observe that here, as in the story of Nicon, we must avoid introducing Western ideas of the collision of Church and State into a measure which can only be properly understood from the Oriental point of view. The power of the Czar, or Emperor, as he was now called, was hardly altered by the change. Peter was as much or as little the head of the Church as his predecessors had been before him.[3] He had, it is true, removed out of his pathway the pos-

---

[1] Preface to Spiritual Regulations, Consett, 2.   [2] Stahlin, § 87.

[3] See the Spiritual Regulations, part i. (Consett's Present State of the Russian Church.)

sibility of a powerful rival in the State, and in a moment of passion, when asked to restore the office, he
exclaimed, as is well known, "I am your Patriarch," and
then, throwing down his hunting-knife on the table,
"There is your Patriarch." But these were expressions
which might have been used by Vladimir or Ivan, and
the office was abolished in fact, not so much because he
feared the ecclesiastical power, as because he was enraged by the retrograde obstinacy of Adrian, the last
Patriarch, because he desired to sweep away the world
of barbaric ceremonial with which the Patriarchal
throne was surrounded, and because he wished to carry
out, here as elsewhere, the principle of substituting colleges or bodies of men for the rule of individuals.[1] The
institution which thus perished was hardly more than
a century old, and its destruction was planned and approved not only by Peter himself, but by his two powerful ecclesiastical supporters, Theophanes archbishop of
Plescow, and Demetrius of Rostoff, and sanctioned by
the whole body of Eastern Patriarchs. Before the final
abolition, the question of its continuance was long kept
open. Stephen Yavorsky, the leader of the more conservative party in the clergy, was appointed its guardian; and on Stephen proposing to the Emperor that
the Patriarchal chair should either be removed from the
cathedral at Moscow or else receive an occupant, he replied: "This chair is not for Stephen to sit in, or for
"Peter to break."[2]

But there was a series of reforms to Eastern feelings
more irritating than the suspension or destruction of
the Patriarchate. There was a party in the Russian
Church which had been exasperated to the verge of

[1] Spiritual Regulations, Consett, 13–16.
[2] This I owe to the author of the " Dissertations on the Orthodox Communion."

endurance by the innovations of the Patriarch Nicon, and it was this same party which was now exasperated beyond endurance by the innovations of Peter. What Nicon had begun by introducing new customs from the South, Peter, it seemed, was about to finish by introducing new customs from the West. Even more remarkable than the direct parallels to the movement of the European Reformation are the similarity and dissimilarity of the indirect results produced by Luther and Henry VIII. in the West, and by Nicon and Peter in the East. We are sometimes accustomed to think of the ancient Eastern Church, and of the Russian Church, as free from the Western evils of division and dissent. This is not the case.[1] We have already seen that there are outside the Eastern Orthodox Church vast schismatical communities exactly analogous to those in the West, but differing in this most characteristic respect, that, whereas our Reformation rent away sects and nations because the established Churches of Europe would not change enough, the Eastern sects have arisen because the established Churches of Asia have changed too much. Such to a considerable extent are the Chaldeans, Syrians, and Copts, in relation to the Church of Constantinople; to them the Councils of Chalcedon and of Ephesus respectively present the stumbling-blocks which Protestants find in the Council of Trent. But such in the most remarkable degree are "the Separatists" — "the Rascolniks," as they are called — of the Church of Russia. Under that form indeed are included many wild sects which probably date much farther back than the seventeenth century, relics of ancient heathenism,

The Rascolniks.

1 My information is chiefly derived from what I heard on the spot, and from Haxthausen's work on Russia. There is an interesting article on this subject in the " Revue des Deux Mondes," xv. 609, based on two romances by Soltikoff, and an official report presented to the Emperor in 1851.

in the unconverted aboriginal tribes, or of the Gnostic
and Manichæan tendencies of the East, or of the secret
Judaizing conspiracy which was repressed by Ivan III.
But these, however curious in themselves, have no spe-
cial bearing on the national history of the Russian
Church, nor do they constitute the importance of the
Separatist body.   The real force, the permanent interest, of the Rascolniks lies in the eight millions of souls
who call themselves *Starovers ;* that is, " the Old The Star-
Believers."   They claim to be the one true overs.
Orthodox Church of Russia.   The ancient wandering
state of the Russian peasants is to them the mark of
true Christianity. Passports are the marks of the Beast.[1]
Huge bonfires are lit to burn any that they can lay hold
of.   They are Dissenters, but on the most conservative
principles which it is possible to conceive.   They are
Protestants, but against all reform.   They are Nonjurors
and Puritans both in one.   They use the Apocalypse as
freely as it is sometimes used amongst ourselves, but
against, not in favor of, change.   They regard the
Established Church as Babylon, themselves as the
Woman who fled into the wilderness, Nicon as the
False Prophet, the Emperor as the Great Dragon,
Peter as Antichrist himself.   Their converts from the
Established Church are solemnly rebaptized.   With
every particularity of detail these converts are required
to abjure the Niconian heresy ; to throw into the street
the dust of the room where any Niconians may have
sat ; never to eat of the same dish, nor to bathe in the
same bath, with them.[2]   Even the universal salutation
of the Russian Easter has no binding force for them :
" Christ is risen."   " Yes," they repeat, with a contemptuous smile, " *our* Christ is risen, but not yours." [3]

[1] Revue des Deux Mondes, xv. 621.
[2] Strahl, 298, 343.   [3] Ibid. 330.

And what are the grounds of this Eastern noncon-

Opposition
to Nicon. formity ?   They are grounds which all Western Churches would do well to hear, — Rome
or Geneva, England or Scotland, Conformists or Nonconformists, Free Church or Established Church, — grounds
almost equally instructive whether we recognize in them
our own likenesses or our own antipodes.   It was deemed
a mortal sin in the established clergy that they gave
the benediction with three fingers instead of two.[1]
Ecclesiastical history was ingeniously pressed into the
service, and the true cause of the separation of the
Latin from the Eastern Church was alleged to have
been, that Pope Formosus had introduced into the
world the impious and heretical doctrine of the three
fingers ; in consequence of which he had been condemned as a heretic, his body disinterred after death,
and the offending fingers cut off, by his more orthodox
successor.[2]   Their form of the cross has three trans-
verse beams instead of the Greek two or the Latin one.[3]
It was a mortal sin to say the name of Jesus in two
syllables instead of three,[4] or to repeat the Hallelujah
thrice instead of once.   The course of the sun pointed
out beyond doubt that all processions are to go from
left to right, and not from right to left.[5]   It was an innovation of the most alarming kind to read or write
a word of modern [6] Russ, to use the service books of
which the errors have been corrected by collation with
the original copies, or to use the revision by which the

---

[1] Strahl, 303.

[2] Haxthausen, i. 323.   For the true story see Robertson's Church History,
ii. 385.

[3] Strahl, 304.

[4] Ibid. 304.

[5] Ibid. 253, 303.   These practices (probably Armenian) date from the
twelfth century.

[6] Haxthausen, i. 208.

Authorized Version has been purified from the mistakes
produced through time or ignorance.   It was an act of
unpardonable rashness to erase the word " holy," which
had thus crept into the clause of the Nicene Creed
which speaks of the Giver of Life, or the interpolation
which caused them to speak in their baptismal service
of " one baptism *by fire* for the remission of sins." [1]   In
defence of this corruption of the text whole villages
of these " Fire-Baptists " have been known to commit
themselves to the flames.   It is probably (with the
exception of the somewhat similar foundation of the
practice of Suttee [2] in India) the most signal instance
of martyrdom in the cause, not even of a corrupt practice or a corrupt doctrine, but of a corrupt reading.

These were the main charges against Nicon.   But
there were others still greater against Peter. Opposition
to Peter.
It was a mortal sin to introduce into the Pictures.
churches pictures by Western artists.   All that Raphael
or Correggio ever painted are abominations in the eyes
of an ancient Russ.   It is a mortal sin to hear the services chanted in the sweet notes which were brought
by Nicon from Greece, improved by Peter from Germany, perfected by Catharine II. from Italy.   It is a
departure from every sound principle of Church Tobacco.
and State to smoke tobacco.   The ancient Czars and
Patriarchs had forbidden it, under pain of tearing out
the offending nostrils.   Peter for that very reason, and
for commercial reasons also, tried to force the abhorred
article on the now reluctant nation, and asked whether
the smoking of tobacco was more wicked than the
drinking of brandy.   " Yes," was the deliberate answer,
reaching perhaps the highest point of misquotation that

1 Strahl, 285.
2 See an interesting account of this corrupt reading of the Veda in Professor Max Müller's Essay on Comparative Mythology, p. 23.

the annals of theological perverseness present; "for it
"has been said that 'not that which goeth into a man,
"'but that which cometh out of a man defileth him.'"

Potatoes.   It is, or was till very recently, a mark of heresy
to eat the new unheard-of food of the potato, for that
accursed "apple of the earth" is the very apple of the
Devil, which was the forbidden fruit of Paradise.

Up to this time the year had always begun on the 1st
Alteration   of September, and been dated from the crea-
of Calendar.   tion of the world.   The Emperor, on the opening of the eighteenth century, conceived the daring design of giving to Russia the 1st of January as its New
Year's Day, and the nativity of Christ as the era of its
chronology.   Was not this the very sign of Antichrist,
that he should change the times and seasons?   Could
there be anything so impious as the assertion that the
world was created in January, when the ground was
covered with snow, not on S. Simon's day,[1] in September, when the corn and the fruits were ripe?   Did the
Czar think that he could change the course of the sun?

Beards.   Most serious, however, of all Peter's changes,
was the endeavor to assimilate his countrymen to the
West by forbidding the use of the beard.   The beard
was indeed one of the fundamental characteristics of
the ancient Eastern faith.   Michael Cerularius had laid
it down in the eleventh century as one of the primary
differences between the Greek and Latin Churches.
"To shave the beard" was pronounced at the Council
of Moscow in the seventeenth century, "a sin which
"even the blood of martyrs could not expiate."[2]   It
was defended, it is still defended, by texts of Scripture,
by grave precedents, by ecclesiastical history.   "The
"Levitical law commands us not to cut the hair or the
"beard."   "Man was made in the image of God: is

---

[1] Heretic, i. 43.   [2] Strahl, 282.

" the image of God to be defaced ? "   " The sacred
" pictures represent our Saviour bearded."   " But S.
" George," it may be said, " has no beard."   " Yes, but
" S. George was a soldier, and probably shaved in obe-
" dience to his commanding officer."   Even Peter, with
all his energy, quailed before the determined opposition.
The nobles and the gentry, after a vain struggle, gave
way and were shaved.   But the clergy and the peasantry were too strong for him.   Flowing locks and
magnificent beards are still,[1] even in the Established
Church, the distinguishing glory of the clerical order.
To the peasants a compromise was permitted.   Many
when compelled to shave yet kept their beards to be
buried with them, fearing lest without them they should
not be recognized at the gates of heaven ; and finally a
tax was substituted, of which the token of receipt was a
coin stamped with a nose, mouth, moustaches,[2] and a
bushy beard, and now throughout the ranks of nonconformity a shaven chin is nowhere to be seen.

We smile as we read these struggles of a great mon-
arch with his people for such trivial objects, Represent-
and as we read these reasons for the separation old Russia.
of a vast community from the Church of their fathers.
Yet it is but an extreme instance of the principle so
dear to the natural ecclesiastical man ; the doctrine of
keeping things exactly as they are.   In themselves too
the Rascolniks are historically interesting, as the likeness of the ancient Russian Church and society as seen
before Peter and before Nicon.   They are truly the
" fossilized relics " of an earlier state.   They are conservatives within conservatives ; orthodox with a super-

---

1 " They are continually dressing and combing it, and are very diligent in
looking at themselves in their mirrors, of which one, if not two, is in every
church." — *Macarius*, i. 325.

2 Life of Peter, 108.

lative orthodoxy. Whatever memorials they can retain
or win of their former heritage are to them beyond all
price. If a sacred picture is missing from an ancient
church, the suspicion always is that the Dissenters have
stolen it. A Russian Prince being at Rome a few years
ago, at the time when the city was agitated by the
theft of the head of S. Andrew from St. Peter's, his
Russian servant observed to him, with characteristic
gravity, that no doubt it must have been carried off
by a Rascolnik. The Czar is still to them an object
of reverence, but it is the Czar as he appears in ancient
pictures, not the modern Emperor. "I cannot take the
"oath of allegiance as you require," replied a Rascolnik
soldier to his commanding officer; "if you will allow
"me to take it to the real Czar, the White Czar, I will
"do it in a moment; but not to him whom you call
"Imperator. In our sacred pictures and holy books we
"have the portrait of the true White Czar. He wears
"on his head a crown, on his shoulders a large gold-
"embroidered mantle, in his hands a sceptre and a globe.
"But your Emperor wears a uniform, a three-cornered
"hat, a sword by his side, like other soldiers. You see,
"I know what I am about." [1]

For a like reason the Patriarchal cathedral at Moscow, already so often mentioned,[2] is to them (though
rarely entering its walls) a centre of devotion and reverence, even more than to the members of the Church
itself. There all is old. No saint, no noted tomb is
within those walls later than the fatal reforms of Nicon.
Demetrius of Rostoff and Metrophanes of Voronege, the
latest saints of the Established Church, whose pictures
have found a place in the adjacent cathedral of the
Archangel, have not penetrated into the old Patriarchal
cathedral itself. No false imitations of Raphael and

---

[1] Haxthausen, i. 328.   [2] Lectures X. and XI.

Rubens, no fancies of Catharine II. or Alexander I., break the antique uniformity of the paintings which cover the walls of that venerable sanctuary. Therefore it still unites the affections both of the Establishment and of the Dissenters. Once a year, on the festival of Easter, they come to gaze upon it; and then, in the open square in front of it, hold amicable discussions with their brethren of the Established Church. The controversy usually begins by remarks on the large fresco of the Apocalypse outside the Cathedral. They are, as may be inferred from the comparisons before mentioned, careful students of the Revelation, and the picture naturally opens the whole question of the schism from Babylon, much as it might in Ireland between Orangemen and Roman Catholics. They argue, we are told, calmly but with much earnestness, and often with a remarkable knowledge of the words of Scripture, and of the decrees of the Seven Councils. A wilder portion of the sect, who specially revere the memory of Peter III., as a martyr for the customs of their forefathers,[1] believe that the day will come when the great bell of the Kremlin shall sound long and loud to the uttermost ends of Siberia, where, according to their belief, that Prince still survives, and whence he will come back to his own, and set up the true Church on the ruins of the reformed Establishment.[2]

The greater part of the Starovers are settled along the banks of the Volga, and amongst the Cos- Their settlement sacks of the Don. But there are some hundreds at Moscow. at Moscow, who, since the reign of Catharine II., have intrenched themselves in two or three large settlements on the outskirts of the city. Let us follow them thither. A visit to one such community will give us an adequate impression of all. Beyond the uttermost barrier

<hr>

[1] Tooke's Catharine II., c. 8.   [2] Haxthausen, i. 302.

of Moscow we find ourselves on the edge of the primeval forest, which here comes up almost to the town
itself. An intricate road through lanes or gullies worthy of the days before the deluge of Peter's changes,
brings us to a wild scattered village, the village of
Preobajensk, or the "Transfiguration." It is celebrated
as the spot to which Peter in his youth withdrew from
Moscow, and formed out of his companions the nucleus
of what has since become the Imperial Guard, who from
this origin are called the Preobajensky regiment. But
there is no vestige of Peter or the Imperial Guards in
what now remains. A straggling lake extends itself
right and left into the village, in which the Rascolniks
baptize those who come over to them from the Established Church. On each side of it rise, out of the humble wooden cottages,[1] two large silk factories, the property of the chief among the Dissenters; for they number
amongst their members many merchants and manufac-
turers, and (as amongst the Quakers) there is a strong
community of commercial interests in the sect, which
contributes much to its vitality, and maintains the general respectability of the whole body. Hard by, within
the walls as of a fortress, two vast inclosures appear.
These are their two main establishments — one for men,
the other for women. For in this respect also they
exhibit a type of the ancient Russian life, in which, as
we have before seen, the seclusion of the women was
almost Oriental in its character. Within the establishment for men stand two buildings apart. The first is
The moder-
ate Star-
overs. a church belonging to the moderate section of
the Starovers; those namely who retain still
so much regard to the Established Church as to be willing to receive from them ordained priests. The clergy

---

[1] The settlement has been there since the great pestilence of 1771. Strahl,
322.

who seceded in the original movement of course soon
died out, and henceforth the only way of supplying the
want was by availing themselves of priests expelled
from the Established Church for misconduct, and of
late years they have been fortunate enough to secure
from the Metropolitan of the Orthodox Greeks in Hungary [1] the loan of a Bishop, who has continued to them
a succession of new priests. But there has been also
an attempt on the part of the Government and the
clergy, to incorporate them to a certain extent, by
allowing them a regular priest of the Establishment,
who is permitted to conform to their usages; and not
long ago a considerable step was taken by the Metropolitan, who agreed to consecrate a part of the church
never consecrated before, himself in some particulars,
as in the order of the procession, adopting their peculiar
customs. Even to this church of Occasional Conformists, as they may be called, the studious exclusion of
all novelty gives an antique appearance, the more remarkable from its being in fact so new. Built in the
reign of Catharine II., it yet has not a single feature
that is not either old, or an exact copy of what was
old. The long meagre figures of the saints, the ancient
form of benediction, the elaborately minute representations of the Sacred History, most of them collected by
the richer Dissenters from family treasures or dissolved
convents, are highly characteristic of the *plus quam* restoration of mediæval times. The chant, too, at once
carries one back two hundred years. The Church re-
sounds, not with the melodious notes of modern Russian music, but with the nasal, almost Puritanical, screech
which prevailed before the time of Nicon, which is by
them believed to be the " sole orthodox, harmonious,
and angelical chant." [2] But the principle of the Old

---

[1] Christian Remembrancer, xxxv. 85.   [2] Haxthausen, iii. 118.

Believers admits of a more significant development.
The Within a stone's-throw of the church which I
extreme
Starovers. have just described is a second building, nom-
inally an almshouse or hospital for aged Dissenters, but,
in fact, a refuge for the more extreme members of the
sect, who, in their excessive wrath against the Reformed
Establishment, have declined to receive even runaway
priests from its altars, and yet, in their excessive adherence to traditional usage, have not ventured to consecrate any for themselves. As the moderate Rascolniks are called " Popofchins," [1] or " those with clergy,"
so these are called " Bezpopofchins," or " those without
clergy." It is a division analogous to that of the
Lutherans and Calvinists in Germany, of the Presbyterians and Independents in England. Accordingly, the
service of these extreme Dissenters is conducted by
laymen, just so far as, and no farther than, could be
performed without an altar and without a priest. Their
only link with the National Church consists in their
retention of a few particles of consecrated oil, and of
consecrated elements,[2] preserved by constant dilution.
The approaches of their milder brethren to the Establishment they regard, naturally, as a base compromise
with Babylon. In many respects, the ritual of the two
sects is the same. In both buildings alike we see the
same gigantic faces, the same antique forms. But, un-

[1] See Palmer's Orthodox Communion, pp. 296–302.
[2] The rite of Confirmation in the Eastern Church, of which mention has
already been made in Lecture I. p. 118, is administered, not as in the Roman
Catholic and Anglican communions by Bishops, but as in the Lutheran by
Presbyters. But, inasmuch as the essential part of this rite in the East consists, not in the imposition of hands, but in the chrism or anointing with the
sacred oil, the derivation of the rite from the episcopal order is still maintained
in the circumstance that the oil, afterwards distributed through the parishes of
the diocese, is in the first instance consecrated by the Bishop. It is of this
consecrated oil that the Rascolniks retain the portion described in the narrative.

like the chapel of the Popofchins, or any church of the Establishment, the screen on which these pictures hang, the *iconostasis*, is not a partition opening into a sanctuary beyond, but is the abrupt and undisguised termination of the church itself. You advance, thinking to pass, as in the ordinary churches, through the painted screen to the altar, and you find that you are stopped by a dead wall. In front of this wall — this screen which is not a screen (so let me describe the service which I there witnessed, on the eve of the anniversary of the Coronation) — an aged layman, with a long sectarian beard, chanted in a cracked voice such fragments of the service as are usually performed by the deacon; and from the body of the church a few scattered worshippers (their scantiness probably occasioned by the refusal of the sect to recognize the great State festival) screamed out the responses, bowing the head and signing the cross in their peculiar way as distinctly as so slight a difference will permit. That scanty congregation, venerable from their very eccentricity, that worship in the dim light of the truncated church, before the vacant wall which must constantly remind them of the loss of the very part of the ceremonial which they consider most essential, is the most signal triumph ever achieved by the letter that kills over the spirit that quickens; a truly Judaic faith, united with a truly Judaic narrowness, such as no Western nation could hope to produce. It shows us the legitimate conclusion of those who insist on turning either forms, or the rejection of forms, into principles, and on carrying out principles so engendered to their full length.

That the Russian Church, containing elements such as these, should have survived at all the shock of Peter's revolution, is a proof of no slight The struggle with Peter.

vitality. But, after the first convulsion was over, it became apparent that (taking them as a whole) the religious feelings and the religious institutions of the country had embraced the change, and moved along with it. Many of the clergy did for a time make a stiff resistance; the unfortunate Alexis fell a victim to his intimacy with some of the disaffected Bishops; the Old Be-
A. D. 1719. lievers broke out into open rebellion; one of them attempted Peter's life; some thousands of them, in the reign of the Empress Anne, intrenched them-
A. D. 1730. selves in the convent fortress of Solovetsky, and died, fighting to the last gasp, like the remnant of the Jewish people in the war of independence. But they were, after all, only a section of the nation, only a small minority of the Church, condemned by the great mass of the national hierarchy. Like as they were in many respects to our Nonjurors, in this respect they were precisely opposite: the Nonjurors failed because they were a schism of clergy without laity; the Old Believers failed because they were a schism of laity without clergy. Gradually the wild superstitions which even Nicon had not dared to touch gave way before the searching thrust of the Emperor. Pictures that wept on arriving at the inclement climate of St. Petersburg he resolutely detected and destroyed. His last public act was to order the removal of many of the chapels and pictures in the streets of Petersburg, and the order was carried out in the presence of the Holy Synod by the formal destruction of a sacred picture of S. Nicholas, Theophanes of Novgorod striking the first blow with his hatchet.[1] In the oath still taken by the Russian Bishops at their consecration occur these remarkable provisions introduced by him, and pledging the hierarchy forever against both the pious frauds and the corrupt

---

[1] Hermann, iv. 444.

lassitude to which all ecclesiastical dignitaries are naturally tempted;[1] —

" I promise and vow that I will not suffer the monks to run from convent to convent. I will not, for the sake of gain, build, or suffer to be built, superfluous churches, or ordain superfluous clergy. I promise yearly, or at least once in three years, to require on my visitations that there may be erected no tombs of spurious saints. Impostors who go about as possessed, with bare feet and in their shirts, I will give up to the civil authorities, that they may drive out the evil spirits from them with the knout. I will diligently endeavor to search out and put down all impostures, whether lay or clerical, practised under show of devotion. I will provide that honor be paid to God only, not to the holy pictures, and that no false miracles be ascribed to them."

Promises such as these, introduced into the most sacred offices of the Church, must turn the face of its rulers, despite of themselves, in the direction which an ancient Establishment is slow to follow. Even Protestant Churches might have gained much had their Bishops and ministers been bound by a like solemn pledge not to support spurious readings or false aids of the truth, not to honor popular impostors, not to give way to prejudice or clamor when raised under the name of religion.

How far Peter succeeded in his reforms without impairing the national faith, is a question which it would be presumptuous to attempt to answer, unless with a greater knowledge than any foreigner can attain. But a few characteristic names emerge from the obscurity of the Russian hierarchy, which seem to justify the

1 Das Ausland, 1857, pp. 689–691. See Spiritual Regulations (Consett, 29), which give instances both of Christian and Pagan superstitions which are to be put down; amongst others, the deification of Friday, under the name of Petnitza. " They are like snow-drifts stopping the passage of men in the right road to truth." (p. 30.)

hope that the problem is not incapable of solution. Theophanes of Plescow, Metrophanes of Voronege, Demetrius of Rostoff, were the Cranmer, the Ridley, and the Latimer who assisted the Russian Henry in his arduous work, and who, whilst they earned the hatred of the Old Believers, have yet, at least in the two latter instances, won a reverent admiration from the hearts of the nation at large.[1] To Metrophanes is dedicated the chapel of the Russian monastery in Mount Athos. The tomb of Demetrius in the venerable church of Rostoff is contemned by the Dissenters, who cannot forgive the man that, when the Rascolniks said they would rather part with their heads than their beards, answered: "You had better not. God will make your beards grow "again; will he ever make your heads grow again?" But by many a pilgrim the grave is visited as of a canonized saint, and no work is more popular in Russian cottages than his "Lives of the Russian Saints."

Advancing to the next generation we arrive at
Ambrose. Ambrose, Archbishop of Moscow. He was known for his learning, especially in Hebrew, of which he gave proof in a translation of the Psalter from the original. It is, however, in his death that we catch the clearest glimpse of the feeling of his time. Long before his appointment to the see of Moscow, he had been archimandrite of Nicon's beloved convent of the New Jerusalem. Amongst the many traces which there remain of his munificence is a suite of rooms threaded by a secret corridor which was constructed by him as a means of escape, in consequence of a presentiment that he should meet with a sudden and violent end. It remains as a singular monument of an anticipation
A. D. 1770. strangely fulfilled. After his translation to

---

[1] For Theophanes, see Consett, p. 449. For Metrophanes, see Mouravieff, 402.

Moscow, the city was ravaged by a frightful pestilence.[1]
The people crowded to a sacred picture in such numbers
as to endanger the public health.   At the advice of the
civic authorities, Ambrose ventured to remove it.[2]   At
once the religious feeling of the Russian populace, so
terrible when really roused, was touched to the quick;
they rose in the same state of wild excitement as, within
our time, was seen at St. Petersburg in the panic of the
cholera.   There was at Moscow no Nicholas to overawe
them by his terrible presence.   They rang a tocsin with
the great bell of the ancient Novgorod, as it hung in
its belfry by the Sacred Gate.   The Archbishop fled to
the suburbs, and took refuge in the Donskoi Monastery.
He was dragged out, and stabbed to the heart, it is said,
by one of the Old Dissenters.   "I send you the inci-
"dent," writes the Empress Catharine in one of her letters to Voltaire, "that you may record it among your
"instances of the effects of fanaticism." We may repeat it here as a story characteristic, in all its points, of
the Church and people of Russia.

We pass on yet again a few years, and come to the
name which alone perhaps in the Russian hie- Plato.
rarchy has obtained a European celebrity, Plato, Archbishop, and afterwards Metropolitan, of Moscow. "What
"is the thing the best worth seeing in Russia?"   "The
"Metropolitan Plato," answered the Emperor Joseph II.,
on his return from Petersburg to Vienna.   Englishmen
know him through his interviews with Dr. Clarke[3] and
with Reginald Heber; and the gay Italian-like retreat
which he built for himself under the social name of
Bethany, in the pleasant woods of the Troitza Convent,
is at once a memorial and a type of the easy graceful
character which in him appeared at the head of the
once barbarian clergy of Moscow.   We see him, as he

---

[1] Strahl, 246.   [2] Clarke's Travels, i. 100.   [3] Ibid. i. 193–202.

sits on his garden bank, in his country dress and large straw hat, laughing heartily at the mistakes of Englishmen about the Russian ceremonies, and at their eagerness to see a worship which they could not understand. He was the favorite both of the civilized Catharine and, for a time, of her savage son. A portrait of him in the Bethany Convent represents him in his start of surprise when, by a device of the Empress Catharine, he heard suddenly in the service his name read as Metropolitan instead of Archbishop. Diderot came at her request to converse with him, and began his argument with "Non "est Deus." Plato was ready with the instant retort, "Dixit stultus in corde suo, 'Non est Deus.'" Of him too is told a story, sometimes given to a divine of our own. The Empress wished to put to the test his powers of extemporaneous preaching, and having told him that she wished to hear him read a sermon written by one of her chaplains, sent to him, as he mounted the platform for preaching, a blank sheet. He looked at it for an instant, and then began "God created the world "out of nothing," and preached on that theme a splendid sermon. He rebuked the madness of his pupil, the Emperor Paul, by refusing to receive at his hands a military decoration, and by opposing his intention of officiating at divine service. In his last decline he sustained the spirit of the Emperor Alexander by his letter of encouragement in the terrible year of the French invasion. Approaching nearly to the character of a European prelate, he was yet a Russian in heart and faith, and as such is still honored by the mass of his countrymen.

And if now we arrive at our own time, and ask how the Russian Church has fared in the nineteenth century, let me name three instances which show that the most modern of our Western movements are not altogether without parallels there.   Innocent, Archbishop of Kamt- schatka, is to the Russian Church as the Bishop Innocent of Kamt- schatka. of New Zealand to our own, an example of the revived missionary spirit in their vast colonial empire. Not in canoes or steamers, but in reindeer sledges, he traverses to and fro the long chain of Pagan islands, which unite the northern portions of the Asiatic and American continents, and has, it is said, brought many to the Christian faith.

Philaret, the venerable Metropolitan of Moscow,[1] rep- resents, in some measure at least, the effect of Philaret of Moscow. that vast wave of reactionary feeling which we sometimes associate exclusively with England, even with Oxford, and a few well-known names in Oxford, but which really has passed over the whole of Europe. As the gay retreat of "Bethany" brings before us the lively career of Plato, so the austere revival of mediæval hermitages in those same woods of Troitza, under the name of "Gethsemane," brings before us the attenuated frame and serene countenance of the aged Philaret, the gentle and saint-like representative in Russia of opinions and practices which in England are too near ourselves to be described more closely.

One third instance in conclusion.   The celebrated German philosopher Schelling, conversing with Professor in the Troitza Monastery. a young Russian Prince who had come to Berlin to profit by his instructions, asked him whether he knew a famous professor in Russia whose name he mentioned, but of whom the Prince had never heard

---

[1] To Philaret was intrusted the important State secret of the will of Alex- ander I. He crowned both Nicholas and Alexander II. He is one of the first preachers of the present Church of Russia, and his striking manner ren- ders his sermons impressive even to those who cannot follow the language. A volume of these has been translated into French. I am glad to have this op- portunity of acknowledging his dignified courtesy and affability when I had the pleasure of seeing him in Moscow in 1857.

before. "Young man," said the old philosopher, "you "ought to be ashamed of yourself for coming to seek "instruction in other countries, and not knowing what "is to be found in your own. Of all men now living, "there is no one else who has so well understood and "expounded the philosophy which you have come here "to study." The Prince returned, and lost no time in seeking the unknown prophet. He was found in the person of the parish priest of the village of Troitza, also discharging the duties of Professor of Philosophy in the adjacent monastery. In that monastery, the Oxford of Russia, Theodore Golobensky lived and died, a master of all the recent forms of German thought and speculation, yet esteemed and revered by all as an illustrious ornament of the Orthodox Church.[1] Reserved in manner and speech, never leaving his retirement, he yet has left behind him a circle of enthusiastic disciples,

[1] I speak partly from Haxthausen, i. 63, partly from what I heard myself. I cannot leave this part of the subject without a word on those remarkable essays to which, under the name of "Quelques Mots par un Chrétien Orthodoxe," I have so often referred, and to which the Letters of "Ignotus" in the Union Chrétienne, 1860, Nos. 30, 33, 36, 37, 41, 42, may be added. It is with much regret that I have learned, since writing the above, that their author's premature death in the course of last year has cut off all hope of confirming, by personal acquaintance, the impression left by his writings, and by the description of all who had ever conversed with him. M. Chamiakoff was a poet of an ardent temperament, and devoted to the ancient Orthodox traditions, which he regarded as the inestimable treasure of the Russian Church and nation. But, of all the peculiarities of his writings, none is more striking than the manner in which he united this devotion to his ancestral belief with a fearless spirit of inquiry both into ecclesiastical and sacred records. He was fully versed in German theology. His admiration of the character and learning of the late lamented Baron Bunsen was profound. He himself entered freely into the difficulties raised of late by Biblical criticism. Yet he never wavered in his faith and practice as an "Orthodox Christian." "Are you not afraid of these German speculations?" was the question put by an English traveller to another Russian layman, equally devout and sincere. "Not for a moment," was the reply. "We have a singular gift of comprehending the ideas of others, and of amalgamating them with our own firm belief. I fear nothing, so long as we are true to ourselves."

whose eyes flash and whose cheeks glow when they speak of him, and who still in their own way communicate his methods of instruction. " Cicero," he used to say, " maintains that there is no system of philosophy " which is not based on some fundamental absurdity. I " maintain, on the other hand, that there is no widely " propagated error which is not based on some funda- " mental truth. See the point of view from which any " error has arisen. Then, and then only, will you un- " derstand it."

I have thus glanced at some of the leading characters of the modern Church of Russia, and of its ex- Conclu-isting tendencies. They will be enough to show sion. that its inherent life has neither been choked by its own tenacity of ancient forms, nor strangled by the violence of Peter's changes. But what its future will be, who shall venture to conjecture? Will it be able now, in these its latter days, to cease from foreign imitations, Eastern or Western, and develop an original genius and spirit of its own? Will it venture, still retaining its elaborate forms of ritual, to use them as vehicles of true spiritual and moral edification for its people? Will it aspire, preserving the religious energy of its national faith, to turn that energy into the channel of practical social life, so as to cleanse, with overwhelming force, the corruption and vice of its higher ranks, the deceit and rude intemperance of its middle and lower classes? The Russian clergy, as they recite the Nicene Creed in the Communion, embrace each other with a fraternal kiss, in order to remind themselves and the congregation that the Orthodox Faith is never to be disjoined from Apostolical Charity. Is there a hope that this noble thought may be more adequately represented in their ecclesiastical development than it has been in ours? Will Russia exhibit to the world the sight of a Church and people understanding, receiving, fostering, the progress of new ideas, foreign learning, free inquiry, not as the destruction, but as the fulfilment, of religious belief and devotion? Will the Churches of the West find that, in the greatest National Church now existing in the world, there is still a principle of life at work, at once more steadfast, more liberal, and more pacific, than has hitherto been produced either by the uniformity of Rome, or the sects of Protestantism?

On the answer to these questions will depend the future history, not only of the Russian Church and Empire, but of Eastern Christendom, and, in a considerable measure, of Western Christendom also. The last word of Peter, struggling between life and death, was, as has been already described, *Hereafter*. What more awful sense the word may have expressed to him, we know not. Yet it is not beneath the solemnity of that hour to imagine that even then his thoughts leaped forward into the unknown future of his beloved Russia; and to us, however curious its past history, a far deeper interest is bound up in that one word, which we may, without fear, transfer from the expiring Emperor to the Empire and the Church which he had renewed, — " HEREAFTER."

THE ROMANOFF DYNASTY.

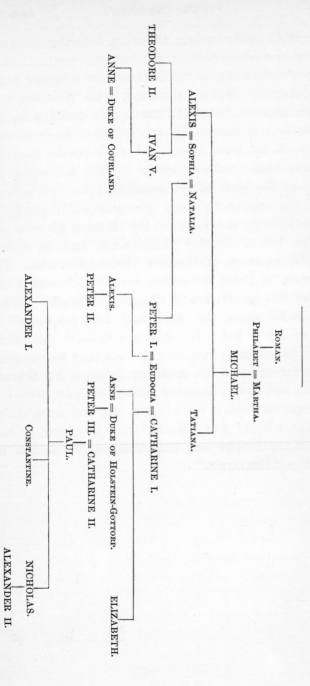

LIFE OF PETER

AND HISTORY OF THE MODERN RUSSIAN CHURCH.

1672. Peter born, May 30.
1673. JOACHIM, Patriarch.
1682. IVAN V., and PETER, Czars.
Peter's first flight to the Troitza.
Simeon Polotsky, first extempore preacher.
1683. Separation of the Rascolniks.
1690. ADRIAN, Patriarch.
1696. PETER, sole Czar.
1698. Peter in Holland and England.
1699. Disuse of the triumphal entry of the Patriarch.
1700. New Calendar.
1702. End of the Patriarchate; STEPHEN YAVORSKY, Guardian.
1703. Rascolniks wear a badge, and pay a tax.
1705. Foundation of St. Petersburg.
Toleration of foreign religions.
1709. Death of Demetrius of Rostoff.

1715. Peter's masquerade of the mock Pope.
1717. Peter at Paris; proposals of union from the Sorbonne.
1719. Death of Alexis, the Czarovitch. Expulsion of the Jesuits. Mixed marriages allowed, on condition of the children being brought up in the Orthodox faith.
1720. ESTABLISHMENT OF THE HOLY SYNOD.
1721. Peter, Emperor of all the Russias.
1722. Death of Stephen Yavorsky.
1724. Reform of the monasteries. Foundation of the monastery of Alexander Nevsky.
1725. Death of Peter, Jan. 28. CATHARINE I.
1727. PETER II.
1730. ANNE.

1738. Death of Theophanes Procopovitch.
1742. ELIZABETH. Foundation of the Troitza seminary.
1761. PETER III.
1762. CATHARINE II.
1768. Relief of Dissenters from civil disabilities.
1770. Plague at Moscow. Death of Ambrose.
1783. Gabriel Petroff, Metropolitan of St. Petersburg.
1796. PAUL.
1801. ALEXANDER I.
1812. French Invasion. (Death of Plato.)
1825. NICHOLAS.
1832. Metrophanes of Voronege (the last canonization).

CHRONOLOGICAL TABLE

In the following Table I have given the chief events in the history of the Eastern Church. The references, where necessary, have been made to such works as, in each case, contained the most precise and copious statement of the original authorities.

CHRONOLOGICAL TABLE.

Early Period.

33 ⎫ All the early Churches, except those of North Africa, belong, in
to ⎬ the first instance, to the Eastern Church: Jerusalem, Antioch,
100. ⎭ Alexandria, Ephesus, and even those of Rome and Gaul. The
 only Apostles, whose missions, by legend or history, extend to
 the West, are S. Peter and S. Paul.
 Legends of the foundation of the more remote Eastern Churches,
 — of Edessa by S. Thaddeus, and of India by S. Thomas.

135. Change of the see of Jerusalem into the see of Ælia Capitolina.

180 ⎫ Catechetical school of Alexandria. Pantænus, † 180. Clemens,
to ⎬ † 213. Origen, † 254.
254. ⎭

260. Sabellius in Egypt.

269. Council of Antioch condemns the Homöousion and the doctrines
 of Paul of Samosata.

302. Foundation of the Church of Armenia.

306. Melitian schism in Egypt.

309. Antony in Egypt (founder of Monachism).

312. *Conversion of Constantine.*

Foundation of Eastern Empire. Period of the Councils.

315. Eusebius of Cæsarea. † cir. 342.

318. Arius in Egypt.
 Foundation of the Church of Georgia, or Iberia, by Nina.
 (Wiltzch's Geography of the Church, 244.)

325. *Council of Nicæa* [First General].

325. Condemnation of Arians and Melitians; settlement of the Paschal controversy.
 Jacob of Nisibis. † 350 [according to others 338 at the former
 siege of Nisibis].
 Athanasius. † 373.

326. Foundation of the Church of Abyssinia. Pilgrimage of Helena
 to Palestine.

A. D.

330. *Foundation of Constantinople.*

336. Dedication of the Church of the Holy Sepulchre.

338 ⎱ Death of Constantine. Athanasian controversy; the West Or-
to ⎰ thodox under Constans, the East Arian or Semi-Arian under
360. ⎰ Constantius.

341. Consecration of Ulfilas, Apostle of the Goths. † 388.

362. Council of Alexandria avoids the division of Hypostasis and
      Ousia.

355. Basil (of Cæsarea). † 378.

      Ephrem Syrus (of Edessa). † 378.

351. Cyril (of Jerusalem). † 386.

360. Gregory (Nazianzen). † 389.

370. Gregory (of Nyssa). † 395.

379. Theodosius, Emperor. † 395.

      Suppression of Paganism in the East.

381. *Council of Constantinople* [Second General]. Close of Arian
      controversy in the Eastern Church. Condemnation of Mace-
      donius and Apollinarius. Elevation of the Bishop of Con-
      stantinople to the second rank, after next Bishop of Rome.
      Additions to the Nicene Creed (?).

385. Controversy on the opinions of Origen, raised by Theophilus of
      Alexandria.

367. Epiphanius. † 403.

390. Chrysostom. † 407.

391. Destruction of the Temple of Serapis at Alexandria.

410. Theodore (of Mopsuestia). † 429.

431. *Council of Ephesus* [Third General]. Condemnation of Nesto-
      rians, and of Cœlestius and Pelagius [but as followers of Nes-
      torius]. Prohibition of any new Creed.

432. Separation of Nestorian Churches (in Chaldæa and India).

415. Cassian (the semi-Pelagian) of Bethlehem and Marseilles. † 435.

412. Cyril (of Alexandria). † 444.

447. Legend of the Seven Sleepers. (Gibbon, c. 33.)

449. Second Council of Ephesus (Latrocinium) supports Eutyches.

451. *Council of Chalcedon* [Fourth General]. Condemnation of
      Eutyches. Promulgation of Nicene Creed in its present form.
      Recognition of the five Patriarchs : of Rome, Constantinople,
      Alexandria, Antioch, and Jerusalem.

440. Theodoret. † 456.

cir. ⎱ First collection of Greek ecclesiastical law under the name of
460. ⎰ "Apostolic Canons."

      Foundation of the Monastery of Studius at Constantinople.
      (Evagrius, ii. 11.)

461. *Simeon Stylites* (the Elder). † 461.

Separation of the Monophysite Churches of Egypt, Syria, and Armenia from the Church of Constantinople. (Gieseler, 2d per. § ii. c. 2.)

cir. } Dionysius the Areopagite (spurious writings of). (Gieseler,
460. } ibid.)

482. *Henoticon* of the Emperor *Zeno* [an attempt to reconcile the Orthodox and the Monophysites]. (Gieseler, ibid.; Gibbon, c. 47.)

Timotheus (" the Cat ") at Alexandria. (Gieseler, ibid.)

Peter (the Fuller), at Antioch (Gieseler, ibid.), introduced the formula " God was crucified."

491. Act of toleration for the Monophysites by the Emperor Anastasius.

518. Repeal of the *Henoticon* by the Emperor *Justin I.* (Gieseler, 2d per. § ii. c. 2.)

527. *Justinian*, Emperor. (Gibbon, c. 45.) † 565.

Foundation of the Convent and Archbishopric of Mount Sinai. (Robinson's Biblical Researches, i. 184.)

529. Close of the schools of Athens, and extinction of the Platonic theology. (Gibbon, c. 40.)

532. Building of the Church of S. Sophia.

544. Edict of Justinian condemning Origen and the " Three Chapters " (i. e. the writings of Theodore of Mopsuestia, Ibas of Edessa, and Theodoret). (Gieseler, ibid.)

545. Organization of the Monophysite Churches of Syria and Mesopotamia by Jacobus Zanzalus or Baraddus of Edessa († 578), hence the name of Jacobites. (Gieseler, ibid.)

Monophysites in Arabia. (Ibid.)

Nubians converted by the Coptic Church. (Ibid. c. 6.)

553. *Second Council of Constantinople* [Fifth General]. Confirmation of the Edict of Justinian.

570. Birth of *Mahomet.*

587. John (the Faster), Patriarch of Constantinople, assumes the title of Œcumenical Patriarch against the remonstrances of Gregory the Great. (Gieseler, ii. 2, 3; Gibbon, c. 45.)

589. Third Council of Toledo. Extinction of Arianism in Spain. Adoption of the Nicene or Constantinopolitan Creed into the Western Liturgy. Insertion of the words " Filioque." Beginning of the rupture between the Eastern and Western Churches, on the Procession of the Holy Ghost. (Robertson, vol. ii. 1, 7.)

Formal separation of the Armenian Church from Constantinople, at the Council of Dwin.

565. The collection of Canons of the Councils, by *John Scholasticus* († 578), combined with the ecclesiastical laws of Justinian, and formed into the ecclesiastical code of the Greek Church under the name of Nomo-Canon.

616. Rise of *Monothelite Heresy* in Syria; supported by Sergius, Patriarch of Constantinople, and Pope Honorius. (Gieseler, ii. 3, 2; Robertson, vol. ii. 1, 2.)

Struggle with Mahometanism.

622. *Flight of Mahomet to Medina.* (*Hegira.*)

628. Reconquest of Jerusalem from the Persians by the Emperor Heraclius. Institution of the Festival of the Cross, Sept. 14. (Gieseler, ii. 3, 1.)

632. Death of Mahomet.

634. Conquest of Syria by Omar.

636. ⎫ Nestorian Missions as far as India and China. (Gieseler, ii. 2,
to   ⎬   6; Robertson, vol. ii. 1, 8.)
781. ⎭ Theological College at Nisibis. (Ibid.)

638. " *Ecthesis* " of Heraclius. (Gieseler, ii. 3, 2.) ⎫
640. Conquest of Egypt by Amrou.   ⎬ On Monothelite controversy.
648. " *Type* " of Constans II. (Gieseler, ii. 3, 2.) ⎭

651. Conquest of Persia by Othman.

660. Death of Ali, and schism of the Shiahs.

Foundation of the Paulician sect in Armenia by Constantine († 684). (Robertson, vol. ii. 1, 8.)

668. Theodore of Tarsus (the Greek), Archbishop of Canterbury, first organizer of the English Church. (Robertson, vol. ii. 1, 3; Gieseler, ii. 3, 3.)

676. Foundation of the *Maronites* by Maro († 707). (Gieseler, ii. 3, 2; Robertson, vol. ii. 1, 2.)

680. *Third Council of Constantinople* [Sixth General]. Condemnation of the Monothelites and of Pope Honorius. (Robertson, vol. ii. 1, 2.)

690. Persecution of the Paulicians. (Robertson, vol. ii. 1, 8.)

692. Council " *in Trullo* " (in the vaulted chamber at Constantinople), called *Quinisextum*, or πεντέκτη; as completing the Fifth and Sixth General Councils on ecclesiastical regulations. The present restrictions on the marriage of the Eastern clergy established; i. e. no marriage to take place after ordination,

A. D.

and no Bishop to be married. This is the first Eastern Council repudiated by the West. (Gieseler, ii. 3, 2; Robertson, vol. ii. 1, 2. 1, 9.)

707. Conquest of North Africa by the Arabs.

712. Conquest of Spain.

Iconoclastic Controversy.

726. Beginning of the *Iconoclastic* controversy by the Edict of Leo Isauricus.
John of Damascus (Chrysorrhoas, Mansur), the last Greek Father, chief theologian of the East and supporter of the sacred pictures. † 760. (Gieseler, iii. 1, 1 ; Robertson, vol. ii. 1, 4.)

730. Annexation (by Leo Isauricus) of Calabria, Sicily, and Illyricum to the Patriarchate of Constantinople.

732. Final repulse of the Mussulmans from the West by Charles Martel.

754. Fourth Council of Constantinople. Condemnation of sacred pictures. (Gieseler, iii. 1, 1.)

787. *Second Council of Nicæa* [Seventh General]. Sanction of the veneration of sacred pictures. Its decrees condemned by Charlemagne in the Council of Frankfort (790). (Robertson, vol. ii. 1, 7.) (Its œcumenical character is well discussed in Neale, Introd. ii. 132.)

790. Theodore Studita, defender of the sacred pictures. † 826.

791. The "*Filioque*" inserted in the Creed at the Council of Friuli. (Robertson, vol. ii. 1, 7.)

809. The "*Filioque*" inserted at the Council of Aix la Chapelle. (Gieseler, iii. 1, 2 ; Robertson, vol. ii. 1, 7.)
Athanasian Creed now first appears in France. (Ibid.)

815. Pictures again suppressed. (Robertson, vol. ii. 2, 1.)

835. Spread of the Paulicians into Asia Minor. Cruel persecution of them by Theodora. (Gibbon, cap. 54.)

842. Pictures again sanctioned. Orthodox Sunday instituted. (Robertson, vol. ii. 2, 1.)

848. Preaching of Constantine (Cyril) among the Khozars (Crimea). (Robertson, vol. ii. 2, 4 ; Gieseler, iii. 2, 2, note *c.*)

858. *Photius,* the chief theologian of the East († 891), appointed *Patriarch* of Constantinople [by Cæsar Bardas, regent during the minority of Michael III.] in the place of Ignatius († 878), who is supported by Pope Nicholas I. (Robertson, vol. ii. 2, 3 ; Gieseler, iii. 2, 2.)

A. D.

Conversion of Sclavonic Tribes, and Struggle with See of Rome.

858. Restoration of heathen literature by Cæsar Bardas. (Hallam, Mid. Ages, c. ix. pt. 2; Gibbon, cap. 53.)

860. Foundation of the Churches of *Bulgaria* and *Moravia* by Constantine (Cyril) († 868) and *Methodius* († 900), from Constantinople. (Robertson, vol. ii. 2, 3; Gieseler, iii. 2, 1.) Bogoris baptized. (Robertson, vol. ii. 2, 3.)

862. Invention or improvement of Sclavonic alphabet by Cyril and Methodius. (Robertson, vol. ii. 2, 4.) *Foundation of Russian Empire* by Ruric.

866. First Russian expedition to Constantinople. Baptism of Oskold and Dir. Photius endeavors to reunite the Armenian with the Orthodox Church.

867. *Photius*, in Council at Constantinople, deposes and excommunicates the Pope. The acts of this Council are annulled in a Council at Rome, and a Council at Constantinople, called by the Latin Church the Eighth General Council (but not acknowledged by the Eastern Church), by which *Photius is anathematized.* The controversy is embroiled by the rival claims of Constantinople (through both Photius and Ignatius) and of Rome to the newly converted kingdom of *Bulgaria.* (Robertson, vol. ii. 2, 3, &c.)

870. Conversion of heathen Sclavonians and Mainotes in Greece. (Gieseler, iii. 2, 2.)

871. Temporary conversion of *Bohemia* by *Methodius.* (Robertson, vol. ii. 2, 4; Gieseler, iii. 2, 1.)

878. Photius, on Ignatius's death, restored to the Patriarchate. (Robertson, vol. ii. 2, 3.)

879. A Council at Constantinople reverses that of 867. (Robertson, vol. ii. 2, 3.)

880. Use of Sclavonic in Church services. (Robertson, vol. ii. 2, 3; Gieseler, iii. 2, 1.)

883. Mission of Alfred to the Christians of S. Thomas. (Gibbon, c. 47.)

886. Photius is deposed by Leo (the Wise); † dies in exile, 891. (Robertson, vol. ii. 2, 3.)

867 to 886. The Macedonian Emperors, Basil, Leo, Alexander, Constantine (Porphyrogennetos), favor learning. Bibliotheca of Photius. (Gieseler, iii. 2, 2.) Lives of the Saints, by *Symeon Metaphrastes* of Constantinople († 975), Annals of Alexandria, by *Eutychius* of Alexandria († 940), commentary by *Œcumenius* (950), *Symeon Theologus* (of Constantinople) (990). (Gieseler, iii. 2, 2; Gibbon, c. 53.)

A. D.

Description of the Empire, by Constantine (Porphyrogennetos). (Gibbon, c. 53.)

955. Conversion of the Russian Princess Olga. (Robertson, vol. ii. 2, 7.)

963 to 975. } Annexation of Naples and Sicily to the Greek Empire by Nicephorus and John Zimisces. (Gibbon, c. 52.)

976. Settlement of the Paulicians in Bulgaria and at Philippopolis, whence they spread into Europe. (Gibbon, c. 54; and Gieseler, iii. 2, 3.)

988. *Conversion of Vladimir, and foundation of the Church of Russia.* (Robertson, vol. ii. 2, 7 ; Gieseler, iii. 2, 2.) Controversy respecting the use of leavened bread by the Eastern, and of unleavened by the Western, Church. (Robertson, vol. ii. 3, 1.)

1018. Bulgaria finally annexed to the Byzantine Empire. (Robertson, vol. ii. 3, *ad fin.*)

1020. Michael Psellus (the younger), "the Prince of Philosophers." † 1101. (Gieseler, iii. 3, Append. I.)

1050. Invasion of the Greek Empire by the Seljukian Turks. (Robertson, vol. ii. 2, 4.)

1054. The Greek provinces of Apulia, on their annexation by the Normans to the see of Rome, are warned in a pastoral letter of Michael Cerularius (Patriarch of Constantinople) against the practices of the Latin Church. Excommunication by the Pope laid on the altar of S. Sophia (16th July), and answered by Michael. *Final Rupture between Eastern and Western Churches.* (Robertson, vol. ii. 3, 1.)

Crusades.

1065. Conquest of Armenia and Georgia by the Turks. (Gibbon, c. 57.)

1074. Conquest of Asia Minor.

1076. Conquest of Jerusalem. (Ibid.)

1089. S. David III., King of Georgia. — Flourishing period of the Georgian Church. (Neale, i. 63.)

1096. 1147. 1189. } Passage of the Latins in the first, second, and third Crusades through the Greek Empire. (Gibbon, cc. 58, 59.)

1096. Occupation of the Holy Places of Palestine by the Latins.

1070. *Theophylact*, Archbishop of Bulgaria, commentator. † 1112. *Euthymius* (Zigabenus), of Constantinople. † 1118.

A. D.

Nicetus (Acominatus), historian and theologian. † 1216.
(Gieseler, iii. 3, Appendix I.)

1182. *Maronites* join the Latin Church. (Robertson, vol. ii. 3, 2 ;
Gieseler, iii. 3, Appendix I. and note.)

Council of *Bari :* called to consider the relations of the Latin
Church to the Greeks of Apulia. Anselm present, hence his
treatise " *De Processione S. Spiritus. Contra Græcos.*"

1180. *Theodore Balsamon.* † 1204. (Gieseler, iii. 3, Appendix I.)

1190. Eustathius of Thessalonica. † 1198. Commentary on the
Iliad. Favorite of the *Comneni.*

1204. *Fourth Crusade. Occupation of Constantinople by the Latins.*
(Gibbon, c. 60.) Decline of the Greek language and literature. (See Hallam, "Middle Ages," c. ix. part 2.)

Greek Emperors retire to Nicæa.

1240. Invasion of Russia by the Tartars.

1261. Constantinople recovered by the Greeks under Michael Palæologus. (Gibbon, cc. 61, 62 ; Gieseler, iii. 3, Appendix I.)

1240. Rise of the Ottoman Turks. (Gibbon, c. 64.)

1270. Last Crusade.

Final Struggle with Rome, and with Mahometanism.

1260. Thomas Aquinas. *Opusc. contra Græcos.* (Gieseler, ibid.)

1274. Temporary reconciliation between the Emperor Michael and
Pope Martin IV. (Gibbon, c. 62 ; Gieseler, iii. 3, Appendix I.)

1260. *Abulpharagius,* historian, Jacobite Patriarch of the East.
† 1286.

1291. Expulsion of Latins from Constantinople.

1292. Armenians reconciled for a time to the Latin Church. (Gieseler, iii. 4, Appendix II.)

1300. S. Stephen Dushan, King of Servia. Patriarchate of Servia.
(Neale, i. 70.)

Ebed-Jesus, Nestorian Theologian of Nisibis. † 1318.

1320. Conquest of Asia Minor by the Ottoman Turks.

1339. Attempt of the Greek Emperors to effect a reconciliation with
the Popes. (Gibbon, c. 66.)

1341. Passage of the Ottomans into Europe. (Ibid. c. 64.)

1341 ⎱ Controversy on the uncreated light of Tabor. (Ibid.)
to ⎰ *Barlaam* condemned, joins the Latin Church. (Gieseler, iii.
1351. ⎰ 4, Appendix I.)

Barlaam, friend of Petrarch, and first restorer of Homer to the
West. (Gibbon, c. 66.)

A. D.

1363. Leo Pilatus friend of Boccaccio. (Gibbon, c. 66.)

1396. Battle of Nicopolis. Defeat of Christians by Bajazet. (Gibbon, c. 64.)

The Emperor Manuel visits France and England. (Gibbon, c. 66.)

1415. Manuel Chrysoloras. († at Constance.) (Gibbon, ibid.)

Theodore Gaza. (Ibid.)

Demetrius Chalcondyles. (Ibid.)

1450. George of Trebizond. † 1486. (Ibid.)

John Argyropulus. (Ibid.)

1420. Nicephorus, author of Ecclesiastical History. † 1450.

1438. The Emperor John Palæologus visits Italy to effect a reunion. *Council of Ferrara, Florence.* (Gibbon, 66.)

1440. Isidore of Moscow. Bessarion of Nice. Mark of Ephesus. Reunion (July 6th) dissolved at Constantinople and Moscow. (Gibbon, cc. 66, 67.)

1444. Nov. 10. Victory of the Turks over the Hungarians and the Greeks at Varna. (Gibbon, c. 67.)

1453. May 29. *Capture of Constantinople, and fall of the Greek Empire.* (Gibbon, c. 68.)

Gennadius, last independent Patriarch. Abdicated 1459.

1477. Expulsion of Tartars from Russia.

Modern Condition of the Eastern Church.

1525–1550. Portuguese mission to Abyssinia. (Gibbon, c. 47.)

1559–1632. Jesuit mission to Abyssinia. (Ibid.)

1599–1663. Portuguese mission to Christians of S. Thomas. (Gibbon, c. 47.)

1582. Patriarchate of Moscow established by Jeremiah, Patriarch of Constantinople. (Mouravieff, c. 6.)

1590. "Uniats," or Catholic Greeks of Poland. (Neale, i. 56.)

1600. *Cyril Lucar,* Greek Patriarch of Alexandria (1602). Adopts Protestant views (1612). Corresponds with Archbishop Abbot (1616). Patriarch of Constantinople (1621). Corresponds with Archbishop Laud (1627). Presents the Alexandrian MS. to Charles I. (1628). Murdered (1638). (Neale, Alex. Church, ii. 356–456.)

1613. Expulsion of Poles from Russia.

1642. Council of Jassy (or Constantinople). Condemnation of Cyril Lucar. "Orthodox confession of Peter Mogila."

1672. Council of Bethlehem. Condemnation of Calvinism.

A. D.

1679. Migration of the Greeks of Servia under Arsenius Tcherno-vitch, Metropolitan of Servia, into Hungary, and establish-ment at Carlovitz. (Christian Remembrancer, xxxv. 35.)

1764. Patriarchate of Moscow suppressed.

1765. Patriarchate of Servia suppressed. (Neale, i. 71.)

1801. Annexation of Georgia to Russia. (Neale, i. 65.)

1821. War of Greek independence against Turkey.

1839. Reunion of Polish Uniats to the Russian Church. (Mouravieff, 431.)

1850. The independence of the Church of Greece, recognized by Constantinople.

———

The dates specially belonging to Russian History will be found at the end of Lectures IX. X. XI. XII.

PLAN

OF

THE PATRIARCHAL CATHEDRAL OF MOSCOW

PLAN OF THE PATRIARCHAL CATHEDRAL OF MOSCOW

(THE USPENSKY CHURCH, OR CHURCH OF THE REPOSE OF
THE BLESSED VIRGIN)

IN WHICH THE METROPOLITANS AND PATRIARCHS ARE BURIED, AND
IN WHICH THE CZARS ARE CROWNED

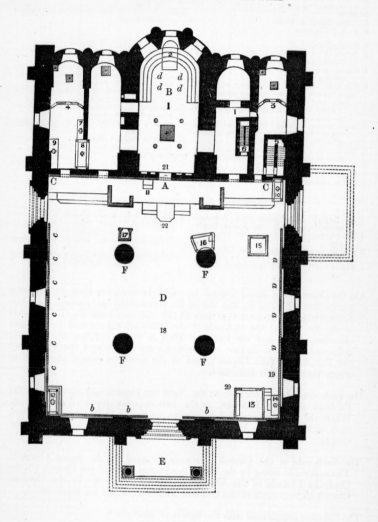

This Cathedral was built A. D. 1475–1479, by Aristotle of Bologna, under Ivan III., on the site of the original Church founded by Peter, the first Metropolitan, under Ivan I., A. D. 1325. For the general arrangements of Eastern Churches, see Neale, Introd. i. 175–216.

EXPLANATION OF REFERENCES.

A. "Iconostasis," or Screen for the Sacred Pictures.
B. "Bema," or Sanctuary.
C. C. "Soleas," or Choir.
D. Nave.
E. "Proaulion," or Porch.
F. F. F. F. Columns.

a. a. a. a. Pictures of the Seven Councils.
b. b. b. Pictures of the Last Judgment.
c. c. c. c. c. c. Pictures of the Life and Death of the Virgin.
d. d. d. d. Pictures of the Patriarch and Fathers of the Church.

1. Principal altar.
2. Throne of the Archbishop, Metropolitan, or Patriarch of Moscow.
3. Side altar, dedicated to S. Demetrius of Thessalonica.
4. Side altar, dedicated to SS. Peter and Paul. These two side altars are separate pieces of the one chief altar; but placed here to allow of access to them without passing through the Sanctuary.
5. Stairs leading to "the Chapel of the Blessed Virgin" in the cupola, where the election of the Patriarchs took place.
6. Stairs leading to the Sacristy, containing the relics and curiosities of the Church.
7. Tomb of S. Theognostus, } Metropolitans.
8. Tomb of S. Peter, }
9. Shrine, containing sacred relics.

10. Tomb of S. Philip, Metropolitan.
11. Sacred Picture of our Lady of Vladimir.
12. Tomb of S. Jonah, Metropolitan.
13. Tabernacle over "the Holy Tunic," presented to the Church by Philaret, Patriarch.
14. Tombs of SS. Photius and Cyprian.
15. The ancient throne of the Czar (called "of Vladimir Monomachus").
16. Throne of the Patriarch.
17. Throne of the Empress.
18. Place of the platform on which the Emperor is crowned.
19. Tomb of Philaret, Patriarch.
20. Tomb of Hermogenes, Patriarch.
21. Royal doors.
22. Platform in front of the Choir. (See Lecture XI. p. 477.)

The Pictures on the Altar Screen (A) *are thus arranged.*

1. The highest compartment, the Patriarchs ranged on each side of the Eternal Father.
2. The Prophets leaning towards the Virgin and Son.
3. Minute representations of the Life of the Saviour.
4. Angels and Apostles on each side of the Saviour.

5. The Sacred Pictures or Icons :
   a) "The Blessed Virgin," brought by Vladimir from Kherson.
   b) "The Saviour," sent by the Emperor Manuel.
   c) "Repose of the Blessed Virgin," painted by Peter, the Metropolitan.

On the Doors ("the Royal Doors," so called because the Czar or Emperor passes through them on the day of his coronation) are painted the Four Evangelists, to represent that through this entrance come the Glad Tidings of the Eucharist. On each side of the Doors are represented (in ancient churches) Adam and the Penitent Thief, as the first fallen and the first redeemed. On the farther compartments are represented the Virgin and the Forerunner (the Baptist), and at the northern corner the Saint to whom the Church is dedicated.

On each side of the entrance to the Nave are (sometimes) represented the Publican and the Pharisee, as the two opposite types of worshippers. Where the porch is extended, it contains the Pagan Philosophers and Poets, each with a scroll in his hand containing a sentence anticipatory of the Gospel.

The south side of the Church is always occupied by the Seven Councils. The north side either by the life of the Patron Saint of the Church (in the Uspensky Church, of the Virgin) or by the Parables. In the Donskoi Church all the events of the Old and New Testaments are represented.

The Columns are painted with the figures of Martyrs.

This Plan is inserted both as a general specimen of a Russian Church, and specially for the illustration of Lectures IX. X. XI.

INDEX.

THE END.

PRINTED BY H. O. HOUGHTON.